© James Hamilton

About the Authors

SUSAN JONAS (right), the editor of many books, has been a picture editor for *Discover* and *Time* magazines. MARILYN NISSENSON has been a writer and producer for CBS, NBC, and PBS. Both have two adult daughters and live in New York City.

Friends for Life

Enriching the Bond Between Mothers and Their Adult Daughters

Susan Jonas and Marilyn Nissenson

HARPER

NEW YORK · LONDON · TORONTO · SYDNEY

HARPER

A hardcover edition of this book was published in 1997 by William Morrow and Company, Inc.

FRIENDS FOR LIFE. Copyright © 1997 by Susan Jonas and Marilyn Nissenson. All rights reserved. Printed in the United States of America. No part of this book may be used or reproduced in any manner whatsoever without written permission except in the case of brief quotations embodied in critical articles and reviews. For information address HarperCollins Publishers, 10 East 53rd Street, New York, NY 10022.

HarperCollins books may be purchased for educational, business, or sales promotional use. For information please write: Special Markets Department, HarperCollins Publishers, 10 East 53rd Street, New York, NY 10022.

First Harper paperback published 2007.

Designed by Chris Welch

Library of Congress Cataloging-in-Publication Data is available upon request.

ISBN: 978-0-06-113819-5 (pbk.)
ISBN-10: 0-06-113819-3 (pbk.)

07 08 09 10 11 RRD 10 9 8 7 6 5 4 3 2 1

For
Sarah and Phoebe
Kate and Kore

Acknowledgments

This book owes its validity to the one hundred and thirteen mothers who shared with us their honest and heartfelt reflections about their relationships with their daughters. We hope that we have repaid them in the seriousness with which we have treated their confidences. For some, we have no doubt, aspects of their stories were painful to recount. We are grateful to every mother for her candor and goodwill, and we would like to be able to acknowledge each one individually. However, we are unable to do so because many of them requested anonymity.

We also wish to thank old friends and new—Beth Curry, Eileen Dever, Betty Hartog, Bettyann Kevles, Zane Kotker, Sally McMillen, Barbara Richert, Nellie Lou Slagle, Susan Tully, and Mary Willis— who helped us find women across the country who were willing to be interviewed.

From the start of this project, we turned to professionals for assistance in analyzing the material we were collecting in our interviews. We are particularly grateful to Dr. Stefan Stein, professor of clinical psychiatry, New York Hospital–Cornell Medical Center, whose early encouragement helped convince us to press forward; to Dr. Margarita Alvarez and Raquel Limonic, MA, clinical psychologists at the Latino Mental Health Program of the Department of Psychiatry at Cambridge Hospital and the Harvard Medical School, who shed light on the special concerns that face mothers from nonmainstream cultures within our society; and to Meryl Siegel, a financial consultant with training as a psychotherapist, whom we met as one of our mother/interviewees and to whom we subsequently turned for advice on the subject of how mothers and daughters can resolve their differences about money.

We would like to single out for special thanks two people who were of immeasurable overall help to us. Soon after we got under way we met with a college classmate, Dr. Phoebe Kazdin Schnitzer, a clinical therapist who holds a Ph.D. in psychology from Harvard and is the director of training at the Judge Baker Children's Center–Manville School in Boston. Dr. Schnitzer helped us understand some of the psychological and philosophical dimensions of the quest we had undertaken. She also demonstrated a wonderful capacity to frame hypothetical conversations in clear, commonsense language. Time and again we asked her to propose new, more fruitful ways in which a mother might address topics that had previously been hard to talk about with her daughter. Dr. Schnitzer also suggested that we consult a colleague of hers, whose theoretical work she valued.

The woman she recommended, Dr. Kathy Weingarten, had already come to our attention because we admired her recent book, *The Mother's Voice*. Dr. Weingarten also earned a Ph.D. in psychology from Harvard. She is an assistant professor of psychology in the Department of Psychiatry at the Harvard Medical School and has a private practice as well. Among Dr. Weingarten's professional interests are the role of mothers, mothers' stories, women's roles in families, and the use of narrative in therapy—interests that dovetail naturally with our own. In her clinical and theoretical work of recent years, she has specialized in the application of postmodern thinking to the study of mothers' lives. She is interested in the ways in which mothers are listened to well and poorly, and she has worked to identify and rectify the instances in which social acts that silence mothers' voices reduce individual women to voicelessness.

We consulted Dr. Weingarten repeatedly during our interview phase, checking out our perceptions and refining the kinds of questions we raised with women. We met with her several times; we spoke often on the phone. She sent us audiotapes of her considered response to our work in progress. We presented her with our initial interpretation of most of the interviews, our first complete draft of the book, and the penultimate draft as well. At every step of the way, she challenged our perceptions, forced us to think about our material in new ways, and goaded us toward what we believe is a much more profound understanding of the subject than we would have arrived at on our own. To Dr. Weingarten we owe our deepest gratitude.

We would like to thank Linda Gottlieb, Zane Kotker, Hugh Nissenson, Natalie Robins, and above all, Carole Kismaric, whose comments on early versions of our manuscript helped us to clarify our thinking and to make our own voices a more substantial part of the book.

Our agent, Pam Bernstein, and her assistant, Donna Dever, offered encouragement and thoughtful suggestions as our project grew from an idea into a reality. Pam, a near contemporary of ours who has a complex relationship with her own mother, was particularly insistent that we examine how emotional patterns get repeated or transformed from one generation to the next. Donna, a woman in her mid-twenties, helped us believe that daughters would be interested in hearing their mothers' voices revealed.

Since the first day we met with the team from William Morrow, we have been buoyed by their enthusiasm for our project. We are extremely grateful for the sensitive editorial guidance we have received from our editor, Claire Wachtel, and for the informed support of her colleagues: editor-in-chief William Schwalbe, assistant editor Tracy Quinn, copy editor Ann Cahn, director of subsidiary rights Lisa Queen, vice-president of marketing Jacqueline Deval, publicist Karen Auerbach, and book designer Chris Welch.

Most of all, we want to thank our daughters, Sarah and Phoebe Jonas, Kate and Kore Nissenson, for tolerating our foibles, for allowing us to tell the world about some of our contretemps with them, for making the role of mother a continuing and evolving joy, and for meeting us halfway as friends.

Throughout this book we have used full names when relating the stories of women who gave us permission to do so. The use of a last initial rather than a full name signals that a woman we interviewed asked us to protect her privacy. We have provided such women and their daughters with pseudonymous first names as well, and in some cases we have also changed those details that might compromise their anonymity.

Contents

Introduction

This book has very personal roots. Each of us is the mother of two daughters who range in age from twenty to twenty-eight. We're proud of them. During the six years that we've been writing books together, the three oldest have graduated from college, moved away from home, fallen in and out of love, and begun to establish themselves in the world. Two of them teach in urban public schools, and the third is an actress. The youngest, still in college, is thinking about a job in journalism.

When the two of us break for lunch every day, we often compare notes about how our girls are doing. We share our worries about the physical dangers of teaching in inner-city schools and the low pay scale of the profession in general, although we recognize that compared to acting, teaching provides steady pay and stability. We wonder if we should be flattered when a daughter consults us about buying a new sofa or concerned that she isn't making the decision on her own. Our older daughters are currently in the most serious relationships of their lives so far; how much can we probe about whether or not this may be a permanent commitment? On the whole, the conversations we have about our daughters are meditative, not agitated. From time to time we remind ourselves how lucky we are that our daughters seem to be handling the strains and pleasures of their lives quite well, that they let us in on much of what's going on, and that they seem genuinely happy to spend time with us. And yet two incidents that occurred while we were finishing our last book made us think twice about our complacency.

Susan: The summer before last, my older daughter, Sarah, and I drove cross-country. Sarah had just finished teaching for four years in Los Angeles and was bringing her car and her belongings back East to begin graduate school. I was really thrilled that Sarah planned the whole trip. We'd take the southern route through the Grand Canyon, Santa Fe, where we had friends, swing up through the Smokies and stop to see my brother in Maryland, then head for New York.

We were together every minute. We shared the driving, the hotel rooms, and sat opposite each other for three meals a day. It was basically a wonderful trip. But I couldn't help noticing that Sarah was continually picking and chewing at her cuticles.

Several times when she was driving, against all my better instincts, I reached over and guided her hand away from her mouth. A couple of times at dinner, I gave her what both of my kids call "the look."

Finally one day, just outside of Memphis, I couldn't stand it any longer. I said, "You're twenty-six. You're too old to have your fingers in your mouth." She turned red and screamed at me, "All you do is criticize. What I do with my hands is my concern."

I yelled back, "But it looks awful. You're a very pretty girl, and I can't stand it when you do something so unattractive."

She said, "Nobody minds but you. My friends don't think there's anything wrong with me."

And I said, "Your friends aren't going to tell you. That's what a mother's for."

We didn't speak for two states.

It's not that I thought she'd say, "Oh thanks, Mom, you're right" and stop chewing her fingers forever. But I felt that as her mother I had a right to speak my piece.

Marilyn: My older daughter, Kate, who also went to Los Angeles after college, called home one night to report that a hit-and-run driver had smacked into the side of her brand-new car.

She was in tears. She didn't know how to begin to handle it. Should she have the car towed? How would she get to work tomorrow? Should she rent a replacement? Should she have the insurance pay for it? Would that affect her premiums? Many of the questions were about things we couldn't answer—and she knew that. She just didn't want to cope, and she needed her father and me to comfort her.

We finally calmed her down. She began to figure out what to do. We praised her for handling the crisis so well, and she thanked us for listening. Everything was going along nicely, and then I made my fatal mistake.

I thought that since we were so chummy, it was a good time to remind her that she hadn't responded to a formal dinner invitation from an old family friend.

I could feel the ice forming across three thousand miles of telephone wire.

"I'll get to it when I can, Mom."

And the phone call was over.

We'd been in a similar place before—I'd remind her of something she needed to do and she'd pull away real fast. And what I wanted to know was—why was it all right for Kate to expect us to be there for her, yet not reciprocate when I asked her to do something that was important to me?

Mulling over these two experiences side-by-side, we realized that we were unsure what the relationship between mothers and adult daughters should be. Maybe our conversations with our daughters revealed more unresolved tensions than we had been willing to admit to ourselves. What was going on? We had expected our daughters' adolescent years to be turbulent, and they often were. In addition to the somewhat expectable fights over curfews, clothing, or household chores, what we remember most is the unpredictable responses to our attempts at communication. When a simple comment on our part elicited openness one time and withdrawal the next, and the rage that frequently accompanied the withdrawal seemed so disproportionate to the event. But we'd been led to believe that once they got past adolescence everything else would be smooth sailing. Now that our daughters were adults, it should be easier to talk to them. Why then were our conversations so strained?

Susan: Sometimes I walk around having a discussion inside my head. This morning, for example, it was clear to me that Phoebe "needs her space," as they say. So should I wait for her to call me and be cheery and supportive when she does? But then I think that's not natural. There's a give and take after all. Why wouldn't I call my daughter if I want to call my daughter? I'd call a friend. And I guess part of me thinks I'm not here just to be reactive. I'm a person, too, and I might want to talk to her. Do I have to squelch an instinct to call my own daughter because she needs her own space?

I sense she's keeping me at a distance the way I kept my mother at a distance, and it's more than I can bear. I think that's the most painful thing of all, because I tried so hard to be different and yet I wonder—am I ending up in the same place?

When we turned to other mothers of our generation, we found many were struggling with similar issues and yearning for a better relationship with their daughters. One woman said, "Emotionally I still want us—my daughter and me—connected the way we used to be. We enjoyed each other's company, and we liked to do the same things, whether we were just hanging out and talking or reading books back and forth. And now we only have these three-day bits of time. I'm always left wanting a little bit more. I don't want a lot, but I feel I never quite get enough."

Another mother said, "My daughter just doesn't want to hear anything from me, she doesn't want to hear any advice, she doesn't want to have any information, she doesn't want to know. She wants to live her own life, row her own boat. Except when she needs assistance." Underlying the wistfulness and anger in these comments is the feeling shared by so many mothers of newly adult daughters of being cut off, of being largely irrelevant to their daughters' lives.

Mothers and daughters share genes, they share the biological rhythms of a woman's body, they have a history of shared life experiences. Just as a mother nurtures and cares for those she loves, she assumes that her daughter will nurture and care for her loved ones in turn. Because of such strong biological and social ties, a mother feels she truly knows her daughter. And, for all of these reasons, she is deeply pained when the relationship reveals that in some important way she does not know her.

When we set out to learn what had been written on the subject, we found very little that offered mothers of young adult daughters a compelling framework within which to examine their roles and their relationships. A great deal is known about how mothers relate to their children when the children are young. And there has been quite a bit of recent research on the period when mothers are old, frail, and dependent on their daughters for care. But comparatively little attention has been paid to the relationship during the rich middle years when both mothers and daughters are leading full lives. In addition, we soon realized that what coverage the subject has elicited is usually framed in terms of dysfunctional families or advice to daughters about how to tolerate an impossible mother. Not one book focused solely on the needs, hopes, and wishes of *mothers* in this unique relationship, whether their personal stories were about rewarding experiences or troubling ones. In our culture, the voices of older women are seldom heard.

We undertook to write this book because we believe it is vital to take seriously the concerns of mothers like ourselves and to find ways in which our relationships with our daughters can be enriched.

Perhaps, on reflection, mothers should not be bewildered by a mismatch between their needs and those of their daughters. This is a period of major transitions in the lives of both generations. Young adult daughters are choosing partners, choosing careers, making their way in the world. Although some of their choices bring their mothers great joy, others are hard to swallow. How should a mother react to the news that her daughter wants to move far away from home? Or, for that matter, wants to move back in? What can a mother say if her daughter marries a man from a different religion or class, has difficulty in finding a partner, or settles down with someone of the same sex? What if a daughter decides on a career that's beyond her mother's dreams or beneath her mother's contempt? How can a mother who has always recoiled against ostentation reconcile herself to a daughter whose chief passion in life is shopping for expensive clothes?

Mothers of young adult daughters have their own issues: changing careers or planning to retire; coping with chronic or life-threatening disease; coming to terms with their own parents' aging and death; getting divorced; becoming widowed; making new lives with new partners or facing the prospect of living alone for the rest of their lives. Sometimes they find themselves also having to soothe daughters who are threatened by any change in the status quo between them. Often they are asking themselves how much of their experience they should share with daughters, especially if it involves revealing fears about their current and future well-being.

These are far from hypothetical situations. Time and again, mothers' eyes filled with tears or their voices took on a poignant intensity as they talked to us of crises caused by changes in their lives or those of their daughters.

Maris J. and her husband were devastated when twenty-one-year-old Gina got seriously involved with a young man who had no steady job and no education. "We've always tried to tell our children, you make friends and relationships with people who are your kind. When you think about having a child or a long-term relationship, try to choose someone who has some aspirations, some values in life. The person that Gina chose, it's not to say that his family aren't wonderful people, but this particular son is moving on the wrong track. And our daughter, for whatever reason, chose this person." When we asked Maris how she was dealing with Gina, she said, "I keep saying to myself, 'Well it's her life,' but I know in my heart that sooner or later we're going to have to pick up the pieces."

Liz P.'s twenty-eight-year-old daughter Tracy announced three years ago that she was gay. Liz says, "She is beautiful, accomplished, a transcendent person, a magnificent person." Liz had always looked forward to seeing Tracy as a radiant bride. "So it was a little bit like saying *shiva* for a dream that you have. We all have fantasies for our kids. This meant getting rid of the fantasy and dealing with a completely different reality."

Most women can see connections between their mothers' lives and their own, and they anticipate consciously or unconsciously that there will be a continuity between their lives and their daughters'. Judith R. has always lived in Marin County, California, surrounded by a large extended family. She has worked for one social welfare agency for over twenty years. Her twenty-seven-year-old daughter Kim is "kind of a wanderer, she never has a permanent address. Right now she's working as a waitress in Moscow to be with some Russian guy she picked up in Paris. I'm big on my kids having jobs that contribute to society in some way. She doesn't do that. She smokes. I'm disapproving of that. I guess I've always wanted to be a role model for her, and I'm definitely not." Judith sees all of Kim's decisions as a personal rebuke.

"She came home recently for a visit, and I assumed she'd stay with us. I cleaned out the closet and the drawers in her room. But she moved in with friends. It felt like a rejection. When I asked her what she missed most while she was away—hoping she'd say 'my family' even though I knew she wouldn't—she couldn't come up with anything better than 'Chinese food.'

"I try to train myself to expect nothing, but I constantly set myself up for disappointment. I'm not a person who expects nothing—I expect a lot, and I believe that people can often be more and do more than they think they can. So it's painful for me to say I expect nothing from her. But I do that to protect myself."

Judith is trying to come to terms with a relationship that is very different from what she expected or hoped for. Many other women we spoke to, perhaps not so acutely alienated from their daughters, nonetheless reported a sense of unease. Gay Block, who felt disconnected from her daughter, Alison, for several years and has only recently reestablished a closer bond, told us, "There's still this leftover feeling of guilt that I always had around my mother, whom I could never please. I feel guilty that I'm not doing enough for Alison, that I'm not a good enough mother, that I have to give more." Arlen M. contrasted her relationship with her two daughters: "With Martha, I'm close. I'm honest with her and I think she's probably honest with me. But I'm not as relaxed as I am with Harper. With Martha there's always the feeling that I need to prove something. I feel the need to stroke her, and that doesn't leave me as free and open as I am with Harper. I don't feel the need to stroke Harper at all; she's this person, and I'm this person, and we just get on great." Sandy J. also has two daughters, and like Arlen, she feels that though she loves them equally, she misses a true emotional connection with her older girl. "I would use the word rewarding and nurturing to describe my relationship with both Bonnie and Jeanne. But there's not the same closeness with Jeanne. I try to reach out to her in any way I can, but she keeps her distance. There's an anger there that goes back to when she was young. I can't put my finger on where it went wrong, and I don't think there's a Band-Aid for the pain."

"Stuck in the past" was a frequent refrain. Megan C.'s older daughter is now twenty-eight, but, as Megan told us, "If we're fighting, often she'll say that she's still mad at me for things I said to her when she was fourteen that I have no memory of. Like 'you insulted me when I was going out one night when you criticized the outfit I was wearing.' It wasn't significant to me, but obviously it was to her. And I say to her, 'I can't change what used to happen. I can tell you I'm sorry I said something rude, but there's nothing I can do to change that.' But can she accept that? No way. Kids just never forget!"

We met Megan C. because she is a neighbor of a woman we know. Megan volunteered to talk to us when she heard our friend mention our project. That contact was typical of the way we found the one hundred and thirteen women we interviewed for this book. We reached out in ever-widening circles from friends, to acquaintances of friends, to strangers that other interviewees were chatting with on a bank line or at a local farmers' market. One woman to whom we were introduced by another interviewee was so interested in what we were doing that she in turn enlisted five women from her church. Two women called us out of the blue because they had heard about our project through someone in their adult education class.

We wanted our book to reflect the experience of mothers from varied ethnic, racial, and religious backgrounds, and so we made sure to include the voices of African-American, Hispanic, Asian-American, Catholic, Protestant, and Jewish women. We recognize, however, that our sample is not statistically valid for scholarly purposes. We talked to women from small towns, suburbs, and big cities across the country; women who were divorced, either when their children were young or when they were in their teens; women who had one daughter or six; women with sons as well as daughters; women who were in the best financial shape of their lives, and women who were barely keeping their heads above water. We did not include women from our nation's most isolated or impoverished communities because we thought it would be insensitive to restrict the interview to our agenda, which focuses on the personal relationships between mothers and daughters, while ignoring the multiplicity of social problems—violence, racism, lack of access to meaningful work, among others—that such women so often face.

We also made a decision not to interview women whose daughters were struggling with alcohol or drug addition, anorexia, acute mental disease, or a physically abusive partner. We believed it likely that all other aspects of their relationships with their daughters would be overwhelmed by such problems, and that there are other books available that address these subjects and their attendant ramifications.

Only seven women turned us down. They said they were too embroiled in a crisis with their daughters to talk about it cogently, and there may have been some residual feeling that if they spoke to us they would be betraying their daughters' trust. All of our interviewees were sensitive to the privacy issue, but they were reassured by our promise to preserve their anonymity if they requested it. Since the authenticity of the mothers' voices is of paramount importance to us, we have neither combined nor created stories, and we've tried wherever possible to preserve the flow of the mothers' narratives.

The women we interviewed range in age from their early forties to their mid-sixties. Most of their daughters range in age from twenty-one to thirty-five. But our criteria were defined not so much by the daughter's chronological age as by her life experience—her progress in making those first important commitments to work, partner, and lifestyle. Thus, we included two mothers of girls in their late teens who were already parents. And we also included the mother of a thirty-eight-year-old who, according to the mother, doesn't have a stable relationship with a man at the moment and is still trying to settle on a career. Several women with daughters in the middle of our range also had older or more settled daughters, and we discovered, as they had, that there was wisdom to be gained from the totality of their experience.

We believe that one reason women were so eager to participate was that we invited them to talk for an hour, or as long as they wanted, about this most intense relationship. There were certain topics we expected to cover: How a mother feels about her daughter's choice of partner, her lifestyle, her choice of job or career, changes in the mother's life that are pertinent to their relationship, and the quality of the discourse between them. Obviously not every subject had equal weight in each interview, and sometimes, when a mother wanted or needed to talk at length about one subject, we thought it was more valuable to let her express all her thoughts and feelings than to interrupt her with our agenda. Whenever possible, we interviewed women with no other family members present. With their permission, we taped the interviews, which we transcribed ourselves.

We gave women the opportunity to express in their own voices—often for the first time—how close or distant they felt to their own mothers, and how much—to their despair or joy—their relationship with their daughters followed that pattern. They reflected on their dreams and expectations for their daughters, and on what they thought the role of a mother of an adult daughter could or should be. Zane Kotker, a novelist with a twenty-eight-year-old son and a twenty-five-year-old daughter, put a common dilemma most succinctly: "As a feminist I believe that society has placed too much of a burden on mothers. They're expected to make everything right for everybody else and take care of everything before they attend to their own needs. And, in theory, I say that has to end. Men should do more nurturing and women should also assert themselves more. They should be able to say, 'I can't do that today, I need some time for myself.' And yet, I also know—and feel good about knowing—that I've raised my daughter to believe that until the day I die, I will drop everything and run to her in the middle of the night if she needs help."

We take a mother's voice to be an accurate reflection of what she thought and felt about the events she recounted—at the time of our interview. She might have had quite a different point of view about the same incidents a day or a week or a month later. We also recognize that her daughter may have another story to tell. In the early stages of our work, we thought we wanted to talk with daughters, too. But then we realized that we weren't interested in adjudicating between two versions of "the truth." We believe that proving that a mother is "right" or "wrong" is ultimately less valuable than discovering why she feels what she feels and helping her to find the means to change the relationship if she wants to.

It is certainly true that daughters play their own roles in the conflicts that mothers told us about. Relationships are always about interaction. A daughter probably has as much need to trigger her mother's response as the mother has to react to her and vice versa. Poor communication can occur for a variety of reasons. Mothers and daughters may simply have fallen into habitual ways of talking about certain things—or the level of conflict may be deeper. A problem may be a reflection of a daughter's uncertainty about the appropriate boundaries between herself and her mother. For example, a mother may be too intrusive in expressing her opinions about some aspect of her daughter's life. In response, the daughter may be irritated by this behavior, but on some level she may also accept her mother's intrusiveness as an expression of concern. For both mother and daughter, bad communication is better than no communication at all because it keeps them connected. Although this book approaches these mother-daughter issues from the mother's point of view, we believe, in fact, that either person can begin to break old patterns, that it is possible to achieve a newer and better connection, and that both mother and daughter will ultimately welcome and profit from change.

We're also aware that some of the developmental issues, the crisis points, and the ways to improve the relationships that we discuss solely in the context of the mother-daughter pair are equally true for the relationship between mothers and sons; other subjects and insights apply equally to fathers and daughters, and so on in different permutations. Because the subject of this book is mothers and adult daughters, we have imputed everything we discuss to that relationship, whether or not that is uniquely the case.

Soon after we began this project, each of us decided to keep a journal. We wanted independently to examine our evolving relationships with our own daughters and our perceptions about the mother-daughter dyad in general. Soon we realized that the journals were a vital part of our entire enterprise, allowing us to keep separate accounts of our individual responses to what other mothers told us. Because different stories reverberated differently in each of our lives, it seemed important to preserve and think through our divergent responses before resolving them together. We also found that problems that either of us was musing about in a journal entry often became the subject matter of subsequent interviews. From the outset we believed that our personal insights and experiences had a place within the book; however, we were stymied by the technical problem of how to keep separate the "I" of Susan or the "I" of Marilyn from the "we" of us as joint authors. Midway through the project we realized that we could preserve our individual voices by incorporating excerpts from our journals in this book. With the permission of our daughters, we have done so.

Mothers of newly adult daughters frequently find themselves on unsteady ground. Sometimes their daughters seem to want nurturing, supportive mothers; sometimes they seem to want nonjudgmental friends. Sometimes a mother reaches out and her daughter draws back, other times it's the reverse. Many mothers have not figured out how to maintain what one woman described as that delicate edge between being intrusive and letting a daughter be on her own. "That's the problem," she said. "How do you stay at that edge without crossing over, but not stay too far back so that you don't have the relationship?" There are too many opportunities for misunderstanding and, all too often, frustration and anger.

The nagging and criticism that are the stuff of comedy routines about overbearing mothers and that were usually counterproductive when daughters were adolescents are even less effective when they are young adults. Although mothers may say that the trouble between them and their daughters is due to their inability to bite their tongues—the "Oh my God, why did I say that to her last night, I should have kept my mouth shut. If I want things to get better between us, I really have to keep quiet" syndrome—they do not want to stop their voices altogether. Nor should they. In fact, we believe that the harping, nagging voice is ineffective not because a mother is speaking at all but because she is expressing herself ineffectively. Instead of stifling her thoughts or blurting them out in anger, she can learn to phrase her beliefs—first to herself and then to her daughter— in different ways. She can develop a style of thinking and saying, "This is who I am, this is how I feel, this is what I want to communicate." She can move the dialogue with her daughter forward to the point where it is mutually respectful rather than mutually rancorous.

The way you communicate with your daughter involves more than just words. As Shirley Abbott, who has written two memoirs about her parents and is herself the mother of two daughters, said to us, "She knows what you think from the way you conduct yourself and the choices you make, your tone of voice, the conversations she hears and overhears. It's in the stories you tell, the family parties you give or don't give, the drinks you drink or abstain from, the candidates you vote for, and the way you blow your stack, or don't blow it, over some little thing." But examples from daily life are few and far between when mother and daughter no longer live under the same roof or even in the same town. And all too often it turns out that our daughters know very little about some important aspects of our lives. If we can learn to communicate more openly with our adult daughters about our own history, our interests, our needs and concerns, we are enriching our relationships with them.

When we hear about conflict between a mother and daughter, all of us are tempted, depending on our vantage point, to identify with one person and blame the other for her insensitivity and intractability.

But that is not a helpful point of view. This book is not judgmental. We believe mothers *and* daughters need to get away from blame and guilt, to break the cycle of recrimination and apology. Our culture frequently perpetuates the categorization of mothers as "good" or "bad," and many women torment themselves by trying to live up to an impossible ideal. We have been impressed by experts who propose a different paradigm—mothers are neither to blame for everything that happens in their daughters' lives nor can they fix everything that goes wrong. What a mother *can* do is listen to a daughter's reproaches or complaints, acknowledge the validity of her feelings, explain clearly how the issue appears from a mother's perspective, and encourage the young woman to take responsibility for her own life.

The span of time during which a daughter is a mature adult and a mother has not yet become vulnerable to the vicissitudes of age has increased dramatically in recent years. Today, mothers of newly adult daughters can look ahead to three or four decades of getting along with their daughters or to years of phone calls that end with a slammed receiver and family get-togethers that are wrecked beyond repair. If mothers can make the transition—if they can establish the tone and the substance of a respectful and loving dialogue—they can be friends with their adult daughters for life.

When we decided on the title for this book, we chose the word *friends* advisedly. For every woman who spontaneously described her daughter as "my best friend," another said the word didn't begin to cover the deep feelings she felt for her child. Some doubted whether mothers and daughters really could be reciprocally supportive; they felt that the mother would and maybe should always retain the primary caretaking role. But there's no other word in the language that simultaneously evokes the mixture of trust, mutual respect, and tolerance for each other's idiosyncrasies that characterizes the best of mother-daughter relationships.

We discovered along the way that there *are* practical steps to improve the relationship, and we've begun to use them. We've stopped nagging our daughters about their hairstyles and their cuticles. We no longer check to see if they've RSVP'd an invitation or paid their bills on time. When we have something we want to tell them, we try to say clearly what we mean and why it matters to us. We encourage them to speak to us with equal candor about what they're feeling and why. Our actions reinforce the fact that we acknowledge them as independent young women.

But the most rewarding moments in our quest have been when we have been led to think more deeply about the implications of the mother-daughter relationship, about the role of women in general, and about how the values we cherish are transmitted through generations. It is our hope that the results of our journey will provide a legacy for our daughters and for our readers and their daughters as well.

Part One

A Critical
Juncture

Chapter 1

The Developmental Paths
of Mothers and
Daughters

We met Maria R. one hot July evening in Northampton, Massachusetts. Maria is a forty-eight-year-old potter, who takes care of an elderly widow in exchange for rent. Her mother, with whom she always had a difficult relationship, died three years ago, and ever since, Maria and her brother have been squabbling over a small inheritance. A few days before our interview, her twenty-five-year-old daughter, Erin, had come home for a brief visit before starting a new job as a waitress in Provincetown. Maria told us that it had been a particularly stormy visit for both mother and daughter. "Erin's been having a really rough time," said Maria. "She just broke up with her boyfriend, she's tense about the new job, and she's facing one of those 'what do I do with my life' moments. And so am I. The day after she got here I had a rotten opening of a ceramics show. So I came home exhausted, and she said, 'Let's go out now, I'm starving.' And I said, 'Okay, just give me five minutes to cool off.' And she said, 'No. I have to eat right now.' And she ate something, so she wasn't hungry anymore. And I really got upset. I was looking forward to a few minutes' rest and then having a nice dinner with her. And then she throws me this curve. She said she was really depressed—she didn't understand the purpose of her life anymore. And here I'd taken a bad blow myself, and I just wanted us to go out to dinner together and enjoy ourselves. So my initial reaction is, I have my issues, too. So I am really angry and she is saying, 'Mom, why can't you just listen to me, I need you to just listen.' A moment of silence. And then I stormed out to the porch and she went to her room.

"I had just had a really lousy weekend—no sleep, terrible show, hot day, a nasty phone call from my brother. So I'm sitting out there thinking, Why do I always have to take care of everybody? Why can't someone take care of me? And then I begin to collect myself and I go back upstairs and I say, 'Let's talk. What's going on?' I said, 'I'm going through a lot, you're going through a lot, I want to hear what's going on.' Finally, she started talking to me. I said, 'What can I do?' I started to rub her back. I started to talk calmly to her, 'What do you need?' We spent an hour and a half talking, and it was a really close connection. I felt like I was helping her pull out of her funk. And then we went into town, got a cool drink for her and some junk food for me, and then we came home, watched TV, and we both calmed down."

Maria's story encompasses many of the issues that mothers and their young adult daughters typically confront as they continue their lifelong task of redefining their relationship. Erin is figuring out where and how she wants to live, making decisions about her choice of partner and career, and trying to establish a coherent pattern for her life. Maria is worrying about her career and how she will support herself in the future, while adjusting to the emotional impact and practical implications of her mother's death. Maria, having defined herself in the past primarily in relation to the people around her, senses that she must now concentrate on realizing her own potential. In the incident that Maria described to us, each woman wanted the other to be nurturing and supportive, yet each was reluctant to offer reciprocal support. The tension between them was resolved when Maria reverted to her role of primary nurturer and dropped her expectation of reciprocity. This solution got them through the immediate crisis. In the long run, however, their relationship will be enriched if they can find a way to resolve crises that is more responsive to both their needs.

Adult daughters must learn to rely on their ability to solve their own problems and to be sensitive to the fact that their mothers have issues of their own. Mothers must try to express their needs clearly, and, if and when they revert to the caretaker role, they should offer love and concern while fostering their daughters' ability to manage their own affairs. Together and separately, mothers and daughters at this stage in their lives have important developmental tasks to master as they move closer to the kind of *mutually* supportive relationships that are appropriate for two adults..

For the past fifty years or so, psychologists have been refining their description of the developmental tasks appropriate to the various stages of human personality growth. Popular manuals have accustomed parents to deal with the developmental steps reflected in the behavior of infants, toddlers, young children, and adolescents. More recently, psychological theory has begun to incorporate the notion that development continues into and through young adulthood and—even more revelatory—that men and women in the middle and older years have psychological growth spurts as well. Even now, little attention has been focused on the relationship between the developmental paths of young women and their mothers, especially at the crucial points where they intersect or diverge.

When our daughters were very young, our role was to nurture and protect them, and at the same time to support their first tentative steps toward self-assertion. Young children need to think that their mother intuitively understands their inner reality and will always be there to help when they can't do something by themselves. In retrospect, when the memories of the burden of such awesome responsibility have dimmed, this aspect of our daughters' childhood often takes on a golden glow. One mother told us, "I saw the other day a mother walking along the street with an eight-year-old girl who was just looking up at her mother adoringly, all wrapped around her, and you look at her and you think . . . yes! And that's the way your little girls are. But then they have to change and go through all these things. I never thought about what lay ahead, I really didn't think about it when they were small."

Helping a Daughter Master the Developmental Tasks of Adolescence

"All these things" that disrupt the idyllic scene frequently emerge in adolescence. Teenage girls are learning to deal with ambivalence and ambiguity, solidifying their sexual identity, and struggling to get a handle on their emotions. They are practicing the skills that will eventually permit independent living. They are often obsessed with their faces and bodies, which they believe reveal their inner selves. Teenage girls crave the approval of their peer group more than that of their mothers. It's the time of cliques, of "best friends," when girls define themselves by whom they ally with and whom they exclude.

"They have to have their secrets, no matter what they are. I think teenage girls have to think there's something that we don't know," Anne Navasky told us, remembering the time when her twenty-seven-year-old daughter Miri was sixteen. "With Miri, everything was a secret. She had her dates—every evening she was going to meet her friend Margaret for tea at a restaurant, and I would say, 'We have every kind of tea here,' and she would say, 'No, it can't be here.' And Victor would joke, 'Tea is the code word, they're doing drugs.' And she would say, 'No, we like to sit in the restaurant and talk. We know the waiter, we talk . . .' She would never meet people at home. So that was one set of secrets. She was very private."

Many of the women we spoke to look back on their daughters' teenage years with a combination of rueful humor and relief that much of the tempestuous acting out of that period has subsided. Ellen Sweets remembers chaperoning a dance at her daughter's staid private school, at which fifteen-year-old Hannah showed up nearly two hours late. With orange hair. "I went from wondering where she was, to worrying about where she was, to being incredibly angry." On the other hand, Ellen told us, "I always tried to keep a middle ground with her. After all, when I was her age, I tormented my mother by going drag racing and hitching rides on freight trains with the boys."

That kind of tug of war is characteristic of adolescence—when a girl's developmental task is to form a firm sense of self without severing her powerful connection to the woman who nurtured and helped shape her. The parallel task for her mother is to support her daughter's bid for autonomy and not to interpret it as a rejection of herself. This is often made more difficult by the fact that she is reevaluating her own life choices and frequently finding them wanting.

Developmental issues for mothers at midlife

Many developmental psychologists have commented on the fact that women frequently experience a profound crisis of self-confidence in their late thirties and early forties. Their marriages suffer inevitable rifts or ruptures. The excitement of a potential career has often settled into the everyday drudgery of a job. The reality that they could make things right, that they could control their experience, was proving to be false.

Psychologist Terri Apter has studied the development of adult women in Great Britain and the United States. In her book *Secret Paths*, she characterizes the tone of her interviews with women entering midlife: "Questions crept in at every turn; about what an effort was worth, what compromise could be accepted, where she had gone wrong, what she had done right, what she wanted to be, how she had to change either herself or her circumstances. Anxieties, anger, regret, fear, despair dwelt in lively concert beneath their composure. Voices broke with tears . . . points of impasse became magnified as they swung from self reproach to anger or despair. There was a *sense* of catastrophe." Not incidentally, these women were often in the midst of travail with their adolescent daughters. Just at the moment when a mother is questioning her own direction and her ability to solve problems posed by her own life, she is asked to be more directive with her own daughter. A mother's level of distress can rise if she internalizes her daughter's challenge to her authority as a further assault on her already shaky self-esteem.

Family therapist Marianne Walters suggests that one reason a mother feels so vulnerable during a daughter's adolescence is that, with society's concurrence, she tends to label the daughter's behavior as rebellious, oppositional, and critical of her. Walters proposes a different framework, one in which mothers are encouraged to see their daughters "as not so much struggling to free themselves from the maternal bonds that constrict them, but rather (as) moving toward a self-determined, powerful, autonomous position of their own." Within this framework an adolescent girl is understood to be learning to trust in "her own judgment and capacity to make choices; she is not simply being angry and oppositional." Thus, the conflict between mother and daughter can be viewed not as leading to a necessary rupture but as the product of two people seeking a different way to bond than they did in the past.

A daughter cannot find a comfortable level of autonomy all at once. She takes two steps away from her mother and one step back, and a mother who can tolerate the wild swings of attitude and emotion that characterize this dance helps make her daughter's transition toward adulthood easier for both of them. Says Carol Rusoff, the mother of Rebecca, twenty-five, and Annie, twenty-one, "I remember before my older daughter went to college, she came to me almost every night for quite awhile with nightmares about me like, 'Last night I dreamt you were a witch' or 'Last night I dreamt you were chasing me.' And my mother, a very wise lady, said, 'Ah, these are separation dreams. She's trying to make distance between you. She loves you so much she must make distance in her subconscious.' So while she was looking forward to leaving for college, my daughter was also scared of going. How was she going to leave her mommy? I felt lucky that she thought of me as being the dependable, always there, rock. I took it as an honor. So it was important for her to make this separation."

"Separation" was traditionally the word used to describe the primary task of adolescence, but in the last two decades that word has come under attack. A number of feminist theorists argue that because our culture places a great emphasis on the need for male children to separate themselves emotionally from their mothers, it was also assumed that the same kind of separation was necessary for young women. In fact, as psychologist Carol Gilligan has written, for girls to detach themselves completely from their mothers is neither "necessary or inevitable, natural or good." She argues, along with Nancy Chodorow and other feminist scholars, that adolescent girls achieve maturity by staying in connection with their mothers even as they establish their own personalities. Women's development properly reflects "the importance of attachment in the human life cycle." We acknowledge the usefulness of these perceptions and when we use the word *separation* in this book, it is with the understanding that it does not preclude staying connected.

In her book, *The Mother's Voice*, Dr. Kathy Weingarten, a family therapist and clinical psychologist, spells out what staying connected can mean. She calls it "mutual knowing." Rather than being reactive while their children negotiate the crises of adolescence, Dr. Weingarten argues, parents must learn to share honestly with their children more of their own experiences and feelings. At the same time they must develop the habit of listening attentively and respectfully. By giving voice to their own concerns and by listening well, they can encourage children to be equally open with them.

Helping a Daughter Master the Developmental Tasks of Young Adulthood

A young adult who has come through her adolescence with a consolidated sense of her own strength can more easily accept her mother as a multidimensional nuanced person with valuable experience in the adult world that she is beginning to enter. A mother who has listened respectfully to her adolescent daughter's expression of her needs, wishes, and feelings is preparing to accept the fact that her daughter is an independent person whose choices she may or may not agree with and may or may not have expected.

Continuing to negotiate a balance between separation and connection is as crucial for mothers and newly adult daughters as at any other stage in their lives. Our daughters are making major decisions about who they are and how they will live. They are shifting their primary loyalty from their family of origin to intimate friends and partners. They are assessing and making commitments to potential mates. They are developing an occupational identity. They are determined to rely on their own judgment as much as possible. However, because the autonomous self they have striven so hard to establish is still somewhat fragile and vulnerable to self-doubt, they often turn to us to validate their decisions. If they get in over their heads, they may still retain the vestiges of a belief that we can step in and make things right. But turning to us often feels to them less like a normal transaction between peers and more like a regression to an earlier period of deference and dependency.

As in adolescence, daughters in their early twenties often take two steps forward and one back on their path toward adulthood. Marta Guerrero says of her twenty-five-year-old daughter Yvette, "She's still like a little girl in some ways. She still wants Mommy to take care of her, Mommy to pay the bills, she still wants to be babied. And yet she's grown up in other ways. I know that she's gotten stronger. And she's more responsible."

Mothers, too, have not completely acknowledged the transition. "Most of the time I think of her as an adult," Mica Winterble says of twenty-five-year-old Sara. "But I still call her the ridiculous things I used to call her when she was little. I call her 'Booba,' or 'little one.' And she'll say, 'Oh, mother!' It's kind of a natural thing. I think any mother regrets not having that child anymore. But I can really be sincere in saying that I don't want that child, it's just the leftover of a time when we were very affectionate toward each other."

From Susan's journal, July 7, 1995

With Sarah at the Hawkins house in the country over the July 4 weekend. In the kitchen: Sarah, me, three or four of my friends, all of us helping to get a meal ready for the holiday. I was cooking shrimp to serve with a cocktail sauce one of the guests had brought. As I sieved the water from the cooked shrimp, Sarah asked, "What are they for?" I thought it was self-evident, so I answered, "For dinner." She said, "But how are we going to eat them?" I thought that she was talking simply to talk (a nervous tic that often exasperates me), so I said, impatiently, "Sarah! As hors d'oeuvres! With our fingers!" She said, "I didn't understand what you meant, for godsakes!" turned on her heel, and marched out of the room. I was mortified. I couldn't believe how angry she sounded.

Later, when I had a chance to talk to her alone, I said, still upset by the exchange, "What was that all about? Don't you think you overreacted to what I said?" She said, "But do you know how you were talking to me in front of your friends? Like I was a baby or something."

I realized that her hold on adulthood is sometimes tenuous. She was trying to be part of the adults preparing the meal, and she was asking silly questions, not for the answers exactly, but just to participate. So when I snapped at her, she felt humiliated.

Later, Sarah came up to me and hugged me, and said that she was sorry she'd stomped off, and I hugged her back and said I was sorry that I had hurt her feelings. We both felt better.

Sometimes a daughter's declaration of independence is crystallized in an instant. Diane Asselin, the mother of Michele, twenty-three, told us about such an epiphany. "There was a moment just after college when Michele took over the driver's seat. Her stepfather and I met up with her in Europe, and she was presumably leaving Israel, where she had been working for four months as an intern for the Associated Press. And it was a time when Israel was in such disarray—there were bus bombings and other stuff—and it was a great relief to know she was now coming home, that it was a great adventure, that it had been successful but now it was over. So she came to meet us in Vienna, and not only did she want to go back for another couple of months but the AP offered to pay her. And the big thing was not 'Mom, can I go back?' but 'I *am* going back,' and she had this fuck-you money.

"She was very nice about the danger—she was always good about calling the moment a bomb exploded, so her family would hear from her first. But she was in complete control of that decision, and that was a big, separating moment. I took her down at five in the morning to put her in a cab to go back, and you know, you think, well, I hope there's no bomb. But there was this separation. And if she keeps doing this line of work, she'll be flying in all these crummy small planes and other stuff. But that's what it is—it has nothing to do with me. And what would I want her to do?"

Clinical psychologist Dr. Evelyn Bassoff writes that, for the mother of an adult daughter, the art of motherhood requires "finding that delicate balance between involvement and disengagement from one's children, between holding and letting go." Diane is mastering the art. She worries about her daughter, she is connected to her daughter, she can comment on her daughter's decisions, but she doesn't expect to exert control over her daughter's life.

Developmental issues for mothers emerging from the crises of midlife

Over thirty years ago, clinical psychologist Bernice Neugarten, one of the pioneering scholars in the psychology of adulthood, isolated these key attitudes for adults aged forty-five to fifty-five: You look to yourself to make your world better; you become aware of physical vulnerability; you change perspective from time-lived-since-birth to how-much-time-do-I-have-left; you begin accepting the reality of your own death and that of your loved ones; you see yourself as having a particularly acute vantage point between younger and older generations; you expect to accomplish results; and taking stock, reflecting, structuring and restructuring experiences become increasingly important in your life.

Terri Apter takes Dr. Neugarten's work one important step further by differentiating between men and women in this age group. A middle-aged man often reacts to a setback at work or an intimation of failing physical powers with panic or depression, whereas a woman often reacts to a crisis in her life with a new confidence in her own knowledge and vision. "Sometimes, from deep within her, she makes the surprise discovery that her potential must be realized now or never. Ripe for significant change, she retrieves neglected needs and wishes, and finally wages battle against the dragons that have stood in her way. Proud of their battle, women emerge with a stronger sense of themselves and their own powers."

This sense of potency was characteristic of most of the women we interviewed. Again and again women told us they thought they were more confident than they had ever been about their abilities to get things done and to accomplish change. Those who spoke of excellent relationships with their adult daughters expected them to continue; those who felt there were still areas of tension between them believed improvement was possible. Almost everyone, without necessarily lacerating herself, tried to look at the relationship with a candid eye, critiquing her own behavior and indicating a willingness to change if change seemed warranted. On the whole, the women we spoke to did not perceive their daughters' bids for autonomy as threatening. In fact, mothers were generally most troubled by situations in which they believed that their daughters were more entangled with them than was appropriate.

Stuck in the Past

For mothers and daughters who have successfully arrived at a comfortable balance between connection and separation, occasional moments of regression are tolerable. But if mother and daughter have not completed the developmental tasks that they faced in the past, their relationship in the present is often characterized by rage, tension, and heartache.

A number of mothers described their relationships with their daughters as being "stuck in the past." For these women a seemingly innocuous incident often triggers unexpected anger from the daughter. Says Liz P., the mother of twenty-eight-year-old Tracy and twenty-six-year-old Louisa, "Louisa will take the most tenuous statement and say I'm manipulating her, and I look at her and think, What the hell is she talking about? I don't feel that if I see something when we're traveling, a poster or whatever, and I say, 'Are you interested in getting this framed?' that I'm being manipulative and telling her how to decorate her bedroom. What do I care what she has in her bedroom? Tracy can just say, 'Nah, that's not my taste, Mom.'

"I dance around a lot with Louisa. I'm so careful about what I say that I almost stutter. I think about what I'm saying—is she going to be angry? I'm much more wary with her than I am with my other daughter, and when you're cautious with someone, it interferes with the flow of the relationship. If you're with someone who you know if you say the wrong thing they'll be forgiving and it's okay, like an old friend, that's nice. But I know at any time that Louisa could kill me.

"I hope that one day if I ask Louisa something that she feels I shouldn't ask her, that she can tell me so without going through a vilification of me as a human being. If she sees me as ridiculous, she can laugh at it. Just be more accepting."

Liz says their problems began when Louisa was an adolescent and Liz and her husband got a divorce. "She was very close to her father, and she never forgave me for breaking up the family. And I was furious with my ex because he had two houses, and my kids couldn't have pizza, they couldn't go on school trips. I had to go to court to get him to pay child support. So I didn't speak kindly of him, and I know I did the wrong thing. But I couldn't forgive him. I think adult children should reach a point where you can say, 'I did the best I could at the time because that's who I was,' and they can forgive you for that. Maybe it's a copout but that's how I see life. So I think Louisa has to grow up and one day she has to forgive me for leaving her father and saying things about him that she didn't want to hear."

Judith R.'s twenty-seven-year-old daughter Kim doesn't berate her mother as actively as Louisa does Liz, but Judith told us that Kim has kept herself at an emotional distance from Judith and her husband for years. Kim, who now lives in Moscow, recently came home for her brother's wedding. Says Judith, "She was around the night before the wedding and the night of the wedding, and now she's gone again. I had hoped we'd have some time alone together, but she made sure that wouldn't happen. And it's more than just avoidance; it's remarks, irritation on her part. So I have felt during the little bit of time I have been with her that she is out to make sure she's on a different path, whether it's my presence or my values or my ideas that set her off."

Judith says this distancing has been Kim's style since she was an adolescent. "She wasn't rebellious. She wasn't doing anything that I necessarily disapproved of. She just pulled away." Before that Judith remembers them as being very close. "Her favorite thing was to be with me and spend time with me. I remember when she was a little girl she used to love to go to the supermarket with me. So we enjoyed each other's company, and now we don't. There's tension."

Getting unstuck

Like Liz P. and Judith R., several other women with tense relationships told us of similar, and seemingly irrevocable, deterioration from adolescence on, implying that they believe the relationship was smooth until then. Dr. Kathy Weingarten cautions against this interpretation. "In most situations where mothers look backward and trace the problem to adolescence—I don't think that any of these issues are ones that had their point of origin then," Dr. Weingarten told us. "Adolescents have culturally sanctioned latitude to act out in certain kinds of ways. They have enough independence skills and some degree of freedom, and they have a peer culture that will support them. So I think a lot of these disturbed relationships that manifest themselves in adolescence do not in fact grow out of the developmental tasks of adolescence but have their origins even earlier." Perhaps the mother had difficulty in seeing her daughter for who she was from the time the child was very young; perhaps she depended on the child to supply too many of her own emotional needs. Both mother and daughter will benefit if they can identify the actual dislocation in the family dynamic, and can place the alleged origins of their quarrel within a deeper context.

Jocelyn B., the forty-eight-year-old mother of Courtney, a twenty-one-year-old college senior, is beginning to understand the connection between the troubles that seemingly arose during Courtney's adolescence and an earlier history of skewed mother-daughter communication. Until recently every time mother and daughter have quarreled, they've ended up rehashing Courtney's list of teenage complaints:

"You made me go to that camp I hated, because you and your sisters had gone there. You and Daddy made me switch to private school when I was in eighth grade. You never came to my softball games." Jocelyn has been in therapy for the past four years; exploring her relationship with her own mother has given her some valuable insight with which to reassess her dealings with her daughter. When Courtney says, "You talked me into doing things I didn't want to do," Jocelyn knows in her heart that the underlying charge rings true—that until recently it was more important for her to please her own highly demanding mother than to pay attention to Courtney's needs.

"I now see that things began to go sour very early. We'd get into trouble over things like her wanting to wear this beanie with moose horns and these ratty corduroy pants she adored even when we were going downtown to have lunch with my mother. And rather than me saying, 'Fine, wear them'—after all, what difference does it make?—I forced the issue because I didn't want my mother to think that I didn't know how to dress my kid, and I *certainly* didn't want her to think I had no control over the situation. So it became a struggle, and I would get furious. Like, 'You're wearing a dress—or you're not going!' There were periods when it was just terrible. And Courtney was so angry so much of the time. And I wasn't really ready to stand up for myself with my own family, so rather than be Courtney's advocate, I was still trying to make her conform to things that I had conformed to in my relationship with both my parents.

"My mother is an amazing woman. She was a successful businesswoman at a time when most of her friends were staying home playing cards. And she's feisty to this day. But she's incredibly judgmental. She is a total control freak. Until about two years ago, she insisted that my sisters and I all come home for Christmas, and we all have to dress up in these red Santa suits. I mean the children and the grown-ups. She tries to be helpful, to fix everything. When my kids were little and got sick, she'd be on my doorstep in a minute, as if I couldn't take care of them myself. It was a way of infantilizing.

"And Courtney. I guess the real breakthrough event was last spring when she came home from college, and she was very angry. She's a very angry person anyhow, and she'd hurt her ankle skiing and had to come back from Colorado early. So she was lying in bed, and I'm trying to act like the mother—my mother—which is to take care of everyone. And I'm on the phone calling half of Westchester to make sure they were coming to this charity gala I was running. And finally I went upstairs to Courtney with some magazines I thought she'd enjoy, and she didn't even look up, and I just burst into tears. I said, 'I just can't do it anymore, I just . . . I feel like everything I do, you're always angry. I understand how hard this is for you, your leg hurts, and you've missed out on your vacation. And you've come home when I'm smack in the middle of something that I just can't drop. So I feel like I'm being torn ten different ways at once.'

"And I really wept. And that's when it came out that she felt that I *always* worried more about getting approval from other people, and didn't pay enough attention to her needs. And I said, 'You're upset that I'm trying to do too many things at once, and I'm upset that I'm trying to please everybody at once.' And for the first time we actually listened to each other."

Since that cathartic episode, mother and daughter are trying to be respectful of each other's feelings. Jocelyn has begun to let Courtney know more about herself, now and in the past. As Jocelyn completes, however belatedly, the developmental task of differentiating herself from her own mother, she is able to encourage her daughter's sense of autonomy as well. "Just last summer we were talking about the guy she'd recently broken up with. She had never confided much to me before, so it was very reaffirming to me that she would do this. Then she said something that was sort of devastating but also quite true. She said, 'You were never emotionally honest with me in the past.' And we talked about wanting to trust each other. And also accepting that it was going to take time. And because we both wanted it to, it was going to happen."

Jocelyn believes that she is capable of change just as firmly as she believes that her own mother is not. We were fascinated by the fact that almost every woman we spoke to felt that she was more capable of change than her own mother was. Most of the women—including many who described warm relationships with their own mothers—felt that the distinction is of vital importance. Says Jewelle Bickford, mother of Laura, thirty-two, and Emily, twenty-nine, "My husband and I were so young when we had our children—we were so unformed—and it was impossible for that not to have left some serious imprints. And so I think it's very, very important now that we redo some of those things. And that's the point I keep making to my daughters—that you never stop growing, never stop learning, never stop getting better. The legacy I got from my mom was different—she stopped growing a long time ago. And I am determined that that's not going to be me."

The Life We Were Supposed to Live

Most of the mothers of the women we interviewed were raised with expectations not dissimilar from those that governed *their* mothers' lives and those of generations of women before them. A woman's life was measured by her marital status and, by extension, her maternal role. Society assumed that raising children to adulthood was the culmination of a woman's life. Although individual women found their way to a definition of self based on their own needs and desires, theirs was not a common developmental path.

Beth Curry's mother embraced all the traditional values of the era in which she lived. To this day her mother fusses over her daughter's appearance. "She says, 'Go comb your hair, go put on your lipstick.' It used to rile me, but in the last few years I can sort of look at it and realize that it's important to her. She took a bath at 3:30 every afternoon to get ready for my dad to get home. When my sisters and I get together in July we joke about the fact that one of us is out mowing the lawn. We laugh and say, 'Mother wouldn't be out mowing the lawn, she'd be taking a bath!' "

Helen Rucker grew up in the same small town in northern Minnesota where her mother was raised. "My mother was educated, while a lot of her generation wasn't. But still her choices were not that different from her own mother's. You could have taught, or been a nurse, or a nun. And if you were *really, really* radical, you could go work for a company. Or if you needed the income. And usually, as soon as you got married, you had to quit. It wasn't a choice."

Women of that generation may have dreamed of more venturesome lives, but most were hemmed in by constraints of law, education, and custom. Alice Trillin says of her mother and her mother's friends, "They were in a role that they completely accepted, but was really inappropriate. They thought it was what they wanted, but it was really destructive. The women shopped and played cards. The men were very smart and did all the interesting things. They accepted the role, so it's hard to see that they were discontented. That whole suburban generation just didn't have enough to do. They lived very limited lives and didn't know it." And we—their daughters—inherited their expectations for our lives.

The two of us graduated from Wellesley College in 1960. Many of our classmates got married within weeks of graduation. The college offered not-for-credit seminars in how to make a household budget, how to shop in a supermarket, how to be a helpmate to your husband as he finished grad school or started his professional life. Those of us who were not headed straight to the altar were haunted by the specter of being "old maids" or "spinsters." We also assumed that if we married it would be forever. "Divorcée" described a moral as well as a legal failure.

While we were being taught to define ourselves by our marital status, the young men we knew were encouraged to think about who they were in terms of a career. Clarissa C. recalls, "Of course, there were different expectations for sons and for daughters when we were growing up. There was much anguish over my brother's choice of career. There were some anxious moments when it looked like he might possibly be a university professor or even stay in the army. Although in retrospect it seems fairly obvious that he was going to be a lawyer like my father. And I remember my sister saying to me, 'Thank goodness I'm not a boy, and I don't have to go through this career business.' "

Like our mothers, most of us who came of age in the 1950s and 1960s assumed that we would work until we had children, at which point our husbands would take over as breadwinners. Circumstances may have been different for minority and working-class women, but for the rest of us the notion of continuing to work outside the home *and* being a mother was unconventional. We knew a few women who went to law school or medical school because they had a passion for the profession. We also knew women who worked because they wanted or needed to be financially independent. But few of us were so focused. At best we might prepare for a job that would provide insurance in case things went wrong.

We were raised to be deferential. The needs of our men and children were supposed to come first. Says Lorelle Phillips, mother of three sons and a daughter, "My young married friends and I thought of ourselves as observers of the world, not players. When my kids entered school, I got active as a parent. That was acceptable. But at one point I wanted to run for the school board, and my husband said to me, 'How can you do that? You have four kids.' "

Lorelle ran anyhow, and—even though she lost—her decision was symptomatic of the immense change taking place in our lives. Betty Friedan published *The Feminine Mystique* in 1963. The NOW manifesto of 1966 declared: "We do not accept that a woman has to choose between marriage and motherhood on the one hand, and serious participation in industry and/or the professions on the other." As women's expectations rose amid other social turmoil, their role in marriage and the workplace was transformed within a decade. Social and cultural forces—the rise of feminist thinking, the rising divorce rate, together with the spreading awareness of Freudian and post-Freudian psychological insights—have been the catalysts for this astonishing transformation in the developmental psychology of mature women.

The Lives We've Led

About half of the women we interviewed did not stop working outside the home when their children were born. Others said that they were driven back into the workplace because they needed to support themselves, and frequently their children, after a divorce. Almost every mother who stayed home while her children were young eventually went to work, either for economic reasons or because she thought it was important to be out in the world in a paying job.

Within the last few decades, the role of paid work in a woman's life moved from tangential to central. And financial independence became a symbol of emotional self-sufficiency. When Verdine Jones was first married in the 1950s, it was very difficult for a woman to establish credit in her own name. "I have a Bullocks card which I've kept because it has Mr. Herbert Jones on it. Back then even if you were working you couldn't get your own. And in '78 I got my first credit card, from Broadway, and I always keep that one, too."

Verdine Jones has two daughters, Stacy, twenty-five, and Rhonda, twenty-eight. Rhonda and her three-year-old daughter live with Verdine and her husband. Verdine's mother was a homemaker with eight children who took in washing to help make ends meet. Verdine worked as a civil servant throughout her daughters' childhood, struggling to be the perfect mother and wife. She takes pride in having been able to juggle everything, although she thinks now that her dedication to housework was extreme. "I kind of feel that I did a lot of things that I didn't want to do, and I think my daughters kind of do what they want to do more than I did. If they don't want to cook, if they don't want to clean, they don't do it. When I was a young woman, I did what was required whether I liked it or not—I couldn't distinguish between the two. I used to get up at six o'clock in the morning, mop and wax, then fix breakfast, take the baby to the baby-sitter, go to work, leave work, pick up the baby, come home and cook, bathe the child. These girls are not going to do that."

Her daughters are not nearly so demanding of themselves, and Verdine has let up considerably herself. "They put more demands on other people to pick up their share of the load than I put, even on my husband. Rhonda can say some things to my husband that I've never said, that probably I've wanted to say. Men in my generation—regardless of race—dominated us, they ruled us, and they didn't truly appreciate it, the getting up, the setting the table, the dinners, the breakfasts, washing clothes, cleaning the house, and then going to work. They didn't appreciate that. But women now feel this is our time. I don't do anything anymore! I do not do anything! And my husband's having a difficult time with it. I don't think he knows how to wash his clothes, but I think it's my turn."

In her book about the continuing development of adult women, Terri Apter points out that although women of our generation initially modified our ideals and stifled our deepest needs in order to be better wives and mothers, we were actually far more self-aware and self-determined, and therefore more able to rethink our goals and reshape our identity, than any generation before us. We middle-aged mothers believe that ours is a watershed generation—our lives have turned out so differently from those our mothers envisaged for us and that we initially expected for ourselves. Perhaps every generation emphasizes its difference from those who went before, but we continue to believe that our experience has made us more flexible, less judgmental, and more respectful of our daughters' points of view than our mothers were of ours. And therefore we feel closer to our daughters than we think our mothers felt to us.

Separate but Connected

Barbara Weene is the forty-six-year-old owner of a beauty salon in Northampton, Massachusetts. After a brief early marriage, Barbara has been in several long-term relationships with men that have not worked out. Her most rewarding relationship has been with her daughter, Rebekah, twenty-six, who lives in California and works as a massage therapist. They are very close, as two women who have been the only permanent members of a family, can be. Barbara told us that she and her daughter are both in the process of making important decisions about life, love, and work. She recognizes that how they make those decisions, and how they support each other during the process of redefinition, will affect their lives separately and together for years to come.

In the process of reevaluating her life, Barbara has begun to think that she has deferred too many things that would bring her pleasure and has often subjugated her needs to those around her. From now on, she wants to be more aggressive in pursuing what will make her happy. "I feel like I've been in a waiting position for a long time— waiting to make the right amount of money, waiting to travel, waiting to meet the right partner—and I decided this year, I don't want to wait any longer. And that precipitated my saying to the man I was living with, 'I'm sorry that you're having a midlife crisis, but I can't sit by the wayside anymore till you decide what you feel about this relationship. It's been three and a half years; if you don't know now,

I'm sorry.' I've got to be more direct and more dramatic about what I want in my life."

Rebekah has been eager for Barbara to end the relationship, and her insights have helped her mother move toward a resolution. "She never liked him because she doesn't think he has taken care of me in the way she wants to see. She would like to see me with someone who appreciates me, and this guy doesn't nearly enough. She says, 'I see you acquiescing too much, and that bothers me, you shouldn't have to do that.' I think it bothers her as a woman and as it pertains to her own life. She'll say, 'This is the first time I haven't had a boyfriend and I'm trying to define myself without that, and what will I be if I don't have one? But she thinks that having a husband and a family—being a parent—is something she would love."

Barbara's reassessment of the patterns of her life in turn helps her see Rebekah clearly. "If I look back and think about myself at her age, I'd say that twenty-six is a tough age for a woman," Barbara said. "It's really transitional. You're not a child, you're not a grown-up; where do you find a partner?; trying to decide about children, yes or no; it's really a crossroads, it's really a tough struggle to figure out how you're going to make yourself into a person."

Rebekah has lived on her own since she was seventeen, although she once came home for almost two years. She'd like to be an artist or a musician but has not been able so far to get on a solid path professionally or financially. "Last night she called me," said Barbara. "She's strapped for money and wants me to help her once again with her rent. I've bailed her out many times when she's been in California. It's always a dilemma for me: Should I take care of her by making her feel like she's safe in the world and there's someone there that she can count on, or should I take care of her by stepping back so she can make her own way? Do I help her constantly with this or do I let her struggle with it herself? And it's always a mixed bag; it's always hard for me to define what those lines are. I vacillate—and I'm not sure how that affects her. At one point I'll be the adviser, and another time, the one who just listens, without judging, and lets her make her own choices.

"I talk to other mothers about this, about how much do we help them, how much of this is supportive and constructive. We say we love you, we care about you, and you have backing in the world, there's someone behind you, you're not alone. And how much is doing it for them and encouraging them to keep coming back to you, and not taking control of their own lives. Somehow both of these things need to happen, and you struggle over it."

Her daughter accuses her of not being enthusiastic about things she tells her. "I've had to think about that. And I suspect she's right, that out of my concern for her, I get into thinking, Is this going to be all right for her? And I just can't listen to a pipe dream and let it be a pipe dream. I have to think about the reality of it. So I'm trying to be an enthusiastic listener when she talks and not make any judgments, because ultimately it is her choice, and I want her to feel good about herself and that she's capable of handling anything. And that's what I would wish for myself, too."

The quandary for Barbara Weene as a mother, as it is for us and most of the other women we interviewed, is how to express love and concern without undermining our daughters' sense of their own competence. We're trying to encourage our daughters to make their own way while continuing to offer them support. We are searching for ways to stay connected while separate, separate while connected, so that our connection and separation will remain intertwined in the years that lie ahead.

Chapter 2

The Burden of
the Past

How Your Mother Mothered You

When Pamela J.'s daughter, Olivia, then twenty-six, was about to leave New York to take a job in Italy, Pamela suggested that the two of them schedule a session with a family therapist. "I said to her, 'You are going to Milan, and I don't know how long you'll be gone, and we have difficulty communicating, and I think it's important that we make some bold effort here to communicate because we're going to be so separated by distance.' And she didn't want to and didn't want to and finally she did.

"We went to this great therapist. And I sat there for two hours and listened to what a lousy mother I had been. And I kept trying to interrupt her, and the therapist kept saying, 'Hold it, hold it, let her finish.' And at the end of it, I must say I looked at her with immense respect to be able to say what she said and to be able to come to the conclusions she came to. She said to the therapist, 'When I'm in trouble my mother is there for me one hundred and fifty percent, but when I'm not in trouble I never hear from her. She doesn't care, she missed my sixteenth birthday when I was in boarding school.' And indeed I had. So the therapist said to me, 'What was it like for you? What was your relationship with your parents when you were away at college?' and I said, 'I never wanted to hear from them whether I was in trouble or not because they were always reading me the riot act.' So she said, 'It was kind of pleasurable for you to be off on your own and independent.' And I said, 'That's right.' And she said to Olivia, 'You have to listen to people's emotional experiences. And maybe what your mother did wasn't right, and it certainly wasn't right for you, but you have to understand where she's coming from as well.'

"My mother was one of ten children of a family that divorced in 1903," Pamela continued, "and of the ten, eight of them lived with my grandfather, including my mother. My mother had zero relationship with her mother. She always felt guilty and hated her; she had no parenting on this score except to assume that mothers and daughters didn't like each other and didn't trust each other. And indeed my mother and I didn't like each other and didn't trust each other. I came into my relationships with that baggage, and my way of coping with it was to distance myself, and it's that distancing that I have to reverse with Olivia."

Pamela and her daughter were fortunate to identify a behavior pattern that Pamela had unconsciously carried over from her past, a behavior that might have served her well in relationship with her own mother, but was causing trouble for her and her daughter.

Among the women we interviewed for this book it was almost commonplace to acknowledge the connection between their relationship with their mothers and their ways of interacting with their own daughters. Virtually every woman interrupted a discussion about her daughter to move seamlessly into a description of her mother. Each of us may embrace or reject the pattern our mother set, but none of us can avoid her influence. How she behaved when we were young played a decisive part in shaping our personality and affecting how we treated our daughters when they were young. Our mother's behavior when we were young adults—the age our daughters are now—influences us today.

The Legacy of a Loving Mother

A lucky few spoke glowingly of their mothers. She was "fun to be with," "someone I could always confide in," "totally accepting of everything I did." These women were not describing perfection; many of them knew there were subjects they couldn't mention to their mothers; many felt that their mothers were overshadowed by their fathers in making major decisions or in encouraging their daughters to set goals and go after them. But all of them believed that although their mothers were sometimes demanding or critical, they reinforced their daughters' sense of self-worth. The overall message their mothers transmitted was one of love and support.

Not surprisingly, almost all of these women reported happy stories about their relationships with their own daughters. Again, it wasn't perfect. There were stories of adolescent rebellion or of young adults making choices the parent might not have made, but the pervasive tone was of mothers accepting whatever the girls chose to do and resisting the impulse to see their daughters simply as extensions or reflections of themselves.

Maureen E., whose three daughters and two sons range in age from twenty-nine to thirty-eight, recalled with fondness a mother who could be supportive while speaking her mind. Maureen was an only child whose parents doted on her. She told us, "My mother was very bright. She wasn't educated, but she was a very smart woman. I remember one time having a fight with my husband and getting in the car—where do you go when you have a fight with your husband? Men go to a bar—where do women go? So I went to my mother's, and I sat in her kitchen, and I talked to her for awhile, and I could tell from the way she was yessing me—I never told her about the fight—that she was picking up something. And then suddenly she said, 'Now it's time for you to go home and make up with your husband.' And I said, 'What are you talking about?' And she said, 'You think I don't know why you're sitting here? You had a fight with your husband, and you think you're going to fix him by sitting here. Go home and straighten it out.' And I said, 'You're so mean!' She literally said, 'Get out!' She had very good instincts."

We asked Maureen if she speaks her mind with her three daughters. "Yes, and I do it because I know that when I overstep my boundary, they'll say 'Shut up, you've gone far enough, Mom.' "

Maureen is equally comfortable taking her daughters' advice or criticism. When her middle daughter, Margaret, was getting married, Maureen took all three girls with her while she shopped for a mother-of-the-bride dress. "I went into a dressing room and tried a dress on. I thought I looked kind of cute. I turned around and said, 'What do you think?' I could tell from the looks on their faces that they didn't like it, and Patricia said, 'Well, if you get a body cast and don't eat a stitch of food, you can wear it.' So they're very free in telling me what they think."

Maureen explains, "I mean, I come from a family like that. I have an aunt who called me two weeks ago—she's eighty-two—and she said to me, 'I think you ought to dye your hair,' and I said, 'Why?' She said, 'You're much too young to be gray,' and I said, 'Don't you know I'm sixty-two?' and I know she said this because she cares about me. So I asked my husband and the girls, 'Do you think I ought to dye my hair?' And then I thought, I'm not going to do this, no matter what they say." This legacy of concern coupled with straight talking that Maureen received from her mother and her aunt enables her to say what she means to her daughters and to accept what they have to say to her in the same spirit. For them, the candor that in another family might be interpreted as intrusive is an indication of loving care.

Belda Lindenbaum is the fifty-six-year-old mother of three sons and two daughters, Vicky, twenty-seven, and Abigail, twenty-one. Belda's stories about a loving relationship with her mother are made more poignant by the fact that her mother is eighty-three, has had open-heart surgery, and is more and more dependent on her. "My mother was always there for us. When my husband and I took a vacation alone, she baby-sat. Every time I had a baby, my mother either came to stay with me or she took my other kids to her house. She's just there for you in many ways.

"It's also true that she demands a lot. She will tell you to this day, you know, she likes what you're wearing or she doesn't. She's very definitive, much much more than I am, but that's the way she is, and I accept it. I try and remember the good things, the fact that she taught us how to work on relationships, that it was important. I try to take the good stuff and discard what I think is not productive. She's a very forgiving person also. So I try to remember that, and I work on that, because I am not a forgiving person. My mother used to say that she learned to be a mother by doing everything the opposite of her mother, and I say that I do some things the opposite of my mother, but not everything. I don't throw the baby out with the bath water. For example, I speak to my mother every day, but I don't speak to my daughter every day. I mean, I can speak to Vicky three times a day sometimes, but I don't expect her to call, and I don't call her every day.

"My mother and I are having a difficult time now. She's getting older, she's getting difficult, she has a Queen Elizabeth complex—'do for me, call for me, get for me.' But I think you have to have a good memory. I had a scare with cancer, and my sister was trying to find me just before I had to go in for surgery, and she said, 'Where were you?' And I said, 'Don't laugh, I went to have coffee with Mom.' I never told my mother I was sick, I just wanted to sit there and have coffee. And my mother did that for me—she made me feel loved and safe—and I remember that."

Carolyn Smith, mother of William, twenty-four, and Carrie, twenty-six, described her mother as "very kind, very loving, very giving," and Carolyn has emulated her mother's generosity with her own children. "I hope that I have been as unselfish as she was to me," she told us. "My mother always did things without asking for things back. I try to do the same with my children. If I give them some money or a car or a piece of furniture, they should feel free to do with it what they want. Once you give someone something, you need to trust that person to do the best thing with it for themselves. Many mothers forget to look and see what their child really wants. And it's hard to do." Caroline's mother did not assume that her wishes and her children's wishes were identical, and Carolyn carries on the tradition of giving the best gift of all—respect for a child's autonomy.

Evelyn Tang is a fifty-seven-year-old Chinese-born professor of neurology who now lives in Pasadena, California. Her mother, who became a prominent educator in Taiwan, tried not to let her own professional status and her high standards feel like burdens for Evelyn, and Evelyn exercised similar restraint as she raised her daughter, Frances, who is now an obstetrician-gynecologist. Evelyn says, "I reflect on my relationship with my mother to carry out my relationship with my daughter. My mother was a fully occupied professional until age eighty, and when she died one of my colleagues tried to comfort me and said, 'Your mother must be very proud of your achievement,' and I said, 'Oh, you don't know my mother. I'm not even in her league!' But to my mother's credit, she never pushed me in my study or my work. In fact, when we were taking college entrance examinations, she said, 'It's fine if you get in this year, but if you don't, you can do something else and try again next year.' And I picked it up and said the same thing to Frances, 'There's nothing to be nervous about when you're applying to a school. If you don't get in, perhaps you don't belong there.' "

One definition of a good mother is that she "does not inflict on the child [her] own needs at the expense of the child's." In practice that means that she can tolerate and even celebrate the ways her daughter is different from her; that she may have dreams for her daughter but doesn't feel rejected if she makes different choices; that she can stand by and let her daughter make mistakes because she knows she will learn from them; that she can admit when she's wrong; that she can be honest without being hurtful and accords her daughter the same right; and that she can express her opinions without requiring that her daughter abide by them. She knows when to tell her daughter the truth as she sees it and when to tell her what she needs to hear. In sum, she loves and values her child, and her love fosters rather than stifles her daughter's sense of self-worth.

Motherless Daughters

What happens when your mother is not around for as long as you need her? Letty Cottin Pogrebin, the mother of thirty-year-old twin daughters and a twenty-eight-year-old son, told us that she has only happy memories of her mother. "Whatever I did, whatever I said, I was just great the way I was, and I think it's marvelous having someone like that in your life. It gave me a sense of what family is. Family is the place where you're marvelous, where you're welcomed. More than welcomed—you're the best thing to come through the door, and I really have felt that way toward my kids. And I truly don't think I would know how to love a child if I hadn't been loved that way."

But Ceil Cottin died when Letty was fifteen. "So after my girls were fifteen, I was flying without a map. I've never been an adult daughter, so I don't know how it feels to be mothered by someone when you're in your twenties, which is probably why I made mistakes." Letty thinks that she was too opinionated, too quick to tell her daughters what they should do, when that was no longer the best approach. "I didn't have anything to measure myself against. I have this mythology that my mother would have remained perfect. And that I wouldn't have felt negative toward her, but who knows? I don't know if my mother could have survived feeling as positive toward me if I was as much an iconoclast in her presence as I've been in her absence all these years of my adult life. After all, I have lived as a feminist and a bit of a political troublemaker."

Lacking the experience of how her mother might have reacted to her late adolescence and adulthood, Letty has, by her own admission, put her mother on a pedestal. In her capacity as mother of adult daughters, she has measured herself against this ideal of perfection and found herself wanting. She is probably too hard on herself. But hers is one of the pitfalls that lurk for a woman whose mother died prematurely.

Six of the women we interviewed told us that the early loss of their mothers had drastically affected the entire course of their lives. Lib O'Brien, fifty-one, is a part-time professor of English at a university in New Jersey. "My mother died in childbirth," Lib told us. "I know very little about her, because people didn't talk about her to me, and I wasn't smart enough to ask about her until it was almost too late. And my father was in the war. So I went to live with his mother. My grandmother reared me, and when my dad came back, she lived with us. So she was the mother I knew. Then when I was eight, my father married my stepmother, and she and I had an up-and-down relationship. I spent summers with my grandmother until I was fourteen. She died when I was sixteen. So loss is a major part of my life. You may not be surprised to learn that I wrote my Ph.D. thesis on the topic of loss in the work of Toni Morrison."

Lib says that the birth of her own daughter, Keri, twenty-two years ago, triggered intense feelings of grief and anxiety. "I wanted my daughter to have a mother that she could relate to. I remember the day she was born, I cried. I'm assuming that it reminded me of my own feelings of loss and pain. I was really afraid I couldn't give her what she needed. The fear is still there. I know that I'm fearful in general. I know that I have passed that on. And she's worked hard to overcome that. She is really gutsy and brave. I'm a little mouse. And I tell her this. I have talked openly about my fears when she was born, or even now, that I won't be good enough. She knows my background, and I've certainly talked about that. When I've caught myself being really ridiculous and overprotective, I would say, you know this is where it's coming from."

In her book *Motherless Daughters*, Hope Edelman addresses the subject of women whose mothers did not live long enough to raise them. Many of her subjects lost their mothers in early childhood, others when they were in their teens. Still others had mothers who abandoned them. Whatever the circumstances, they all reported that when confronted by their own daughters, they felt hampered by the loss of a mother-model. They had to learn to parent on their own.

Not the Mother You Wish You'd Had

Most of the women we spoke to described their mothers in less than adulatory terms. It wasn't that their mothers were dreadful, or unloving, but they were unable consistently to provide the kind of love their daughters hoped for. Their mothers seemed to the daughters to be "intrusive," "distant," "controlling," "judgmental," "withdrawn," "insensitive about what I wanted or needed." As mothers themselves, they were determined to be different.

Peggy R.'s mother is almost eighty-seven. She is widowed and lives in a retirement community. "She drives all of her friends around," Peggy told us. "She's one of the few people her age left who *can* drive. She's very active and quite mobile. This summer she came to visit us at the beach. But we're not close, not the way Leigh and I are." Leigh is Peggy's twenty-eight-year-old daughter. "I think one reason why my relationship with Leigh is so important to me is because I was never close to my mother. She took very good care of us, but there was no emotion. And Leigh is also not close to my mother. Leigh always felt that her brothers were the favorites, and that she was unappreciated because she was overweight as a child. So while she'll be dutiful, I can't say that she's overly fond of her grandmother.

"It's hard to have a conversation with my mother that gets too far underneath. First of all she's not of that generation, second, she's British. You didn't talk about things a lot. You certainly didn't discuss your feelings. You pushed it underneath, or you took it out in work, or you did something else. I think the idea of psychiatry would have been shocking to both my parents. You may go to your minister, but basically you didn't talk about personal things.

"I was much more my father's daughter always. And it wasn't until after he died that I was able to see some of the characteristics that mother had and really get to know her a little better. So I made a conscious effort to get closer. But she's not the kind of person that I can go and do what I can do to Leigh or Leigh does to me, which is hug or tease. My brother's children are easier with her. But for me there's still a lot of the past there."

From Marilyn's journal, October 27, 1995

The anniversary of my mother's birthday. Or was it yesterday? An embarrassing admission that I can't ever remember a date that she put so much stress on. She was a big celebrator of events, and I breathe a sigh of relief every Mother's Day, because I don't have to send her a present.

What's my gripe? I believe it's that she sentimentalized rather than felt. She liked to call my girls "her little angels," even though she didn't have all that much to do with them on this earth. She demanded filial devotion. She made giving presents such a big deal, and botched it so often, that every event that required one took something out of me.

I've been thinking about her a lot because of this book. Trying to clarify what she did well and what wasn't so great. I've decided that she was a "good" mom when I was little. You knew where you stood with her—or did if you were a precociously smart little girl. I think I figured out very early that she came first—maybe I figured it out when I was an infant and she was depressed. Anyhow, she came first, her self-esteem had to be satisfied by any human transaction. Then came the people she cared about: in no particular order, her mother, her sisters, my father, and me. Since my needs seldom conflicted with any of theirs, I came out okay in most transactions. And, as it was very important to her that the world view her as a good mother, so she was.

She and I were also very lucky that I was the kind of kid she could show off.

Where we ran into trouble was in my adolescence. First of all, I could have used a little less competition. Who needed the shopping trips where she preened in front of mirrors and, after being coaxed and approved by me, bought herself whatever she wanted. While I, age twelve, five feet four inches and weighing a hefty eighty-five pounds, had trouble finding anything that didn't hang on me like a sack. And second of all we got into trouble as I shaped my inchoate dreams to move out into the world. She had no ability to recognize that my aspirations for myself might not be those she had for me. In fact I doubt that she ever got to the stage of thinking of me as anything but an adornment to herself. For that matter, she and her siblings never got past thinking of themselves as adjuncts to their mother. So—we could be pals, we could spend time together, she was spunky in her limited way, nice to my friends, fun to be with, but I could hardly say, and she would never tolerate hearing, "I want a life on a wider stage. I want to marry someone whose idea of achievement is not being on the board of the local savings bank.".

It isn't that we fought, though we certainly had quarrels. It's that I pulled away, physically, and emotionally, and certainly intellectually. I didn't confide in her. I didn't engage. And we never reconciled this. I wonder if we would have in time. I rather doubt it. Because, and this I only see now, disengagement had been her mode from the start. From her depression, through her self-involvement in mourning the death of her parents and her oldest sister, and her absorption with all her ailments during my childhood, to her suffering in silence in the later years.

But I have to give her this—because she was so consistent, and because she was certainly attentive and available when I was young, I grew up with a considerable sense of self-confidence. So that by the time I was ready to pull away, I could do it with a minimum of backward glances.

Says Harriet B., mother of Jane, twenty-five, "My mother doesn't get real close to people. She *thinks* she does but she doesn't. I was really much closer to my dad. Mother is one of these people . . . she's a Pollyanna-type person." Several years ago, Harriet had a major family crisis. Jane had dropped out of college and announced she was moving to the West Coast. She wanted no contact with her family. "At some of the really bad times, I would try to share something with Mother, and she'd cut it off. I'll never forget, the day after Jane left, Mother came by, and she said, 'How are you?' or something inconsequential. And I tried to let her know that this was really serious. We sat down in the kitchen, and I could hardly talk. And she said, 'Tell me about it.' I know that deep down she probably wanted to help. I started talking, and then she looked at her watch. I said, 'Have you got a meeting or something?' And she said, 'Well, yes. I've got a beauty parlor appointment in ten minutes.' And you know, she's out the door! I know it would hurt her to hear me say this about her. Because she doesn't think of herself that way."

Jewelle Bickford, a fifty-two-year-old investment banker with two daughters, says, "My mother is a cold woman. She loves me, I know, but she's not good about showing it. My relationship with her is a theme in my life forever, because she was too upset by her life circumstances to concentrate on us. Sometimes she had money, and sometimes she didn't, and she didn't have the confidence, or the education, or the background to deal with the reverses. She was always a kind of absentee landlord, either depressed or distracted.

"My mother used to react as if to say, 'I'm perfect, why are you picking on me?' And I'm willing to show my kids that I'm not perfect. They've seen me struggle with my mother and in my marriage. They've seen that life is a process. My kids have an image of me striving to get it right.

"Now I've worked things out with my mother. I accept her. I don't expect her to be someone she can't be. Now my dialogues with her go pretty well. Because I've changed—she can't."

It struck us that when these women described their relationships with their mothers the tone they used was one of resigned sadness. They were sorry rather than angry that their mothers had remained somewhat removed or impersonal. Many factors probably played into their relative equanimity: Although they complained about their mothers' relative lack of warmth, they all reported feeling that they were loved; their mothers may have had the virtue of consistency—a mother who always reacts the same way in a given situation makes it easier for a child to know what to expect; their mothers may not have been so invasive as to leave irreparable deficits in the daughters' sense of their own self-worth. Several of them stressed how important their fathers had been in imbuing them with a sense of competence. Whatever the particular constellation of events, although these women criticized their mothers for being too cool or distant, somehow they had developed enough ego strength to react differently with their own daughters.

From Susan's journal, July 31, 1995

I wonder if other mothers feel the way I sometimes do, that I need a mother myself, that I don't possibly know enough to be a mother, that I'm still a kid, still finding my way, how can I mother two other human beings. Sometimes I feel that I don't know how to really love, that I am so critical, so judgmental of everyone else's behavior that I am incapable of loving. On the other hand, I am a very giving person. I am very sensitive to others, very empathetic. And I'm sure that, in some way that I don't understand, both aspects of my personality have their origin in my relationship with my mother. I never felt that my mother loved me for who I was. I am not blaming her, it's just a sad fact of my upbringing.

As I interview women, I also feel sad for my mother. I am sure she felt cut off from me, perplexed by my behavior. I don't think she wanted me to be a friend—I was always to be the child and she the parent, but I'm sure she would have liked me to be more open with her, to have shared more of my life.

Last night Phoebe and I had dinner together at home; it was somewhat festive since this morning she was driving with her father in a rented van to Boston, where she's going to live for the next two years. And I'm leaving tomorrow for Pittsburgh, where I grew up, to interview some mothers for our book. And with our book on my mind, I asked her if she had a good sense of what my childhood had been like, because I thought my upbringing informed how I raised Sarah and her. She said she knew a little, maybe not enough, so I told her a bit about my mother and me, about my stormy adolescence, about my distance from my mother, about the triangle with my father, who always took my side. She wanted to know where my brother fit in— did he fight with my parents? Many questions.

I told her how sad I felt these last years, and especially since working on this book, that my mother and I were so estranged, that I so deliberately cut her out of my life. I said that I was sure my mother was pained that I was such a mystery to her—all she wanted was a sweet, obedient daughter who would agree with her on many things, and what she got was a sullen, withdrawn girl who frequently screamed and yelled at her. I told Phoebe that my mother was very critical, and that as a defense against being uneducated, she derided education and extolled good common sense—which she felt she had in abundance. I said that I think that's where my supercritical nature comes from—that although I try to do things differently with her and her sister, sometimes I can't help myself. I told her that when I was pregnant I used to worry I would not be a good mother, because I felt that I had been mothered so inadequately. Phoebe remembered I had told her about the dreams I had when I was pregnant about how I would inadvertently crush the baby or sit on the baby. So what I was telling her wasn't brand new, but she certainly seemed to listen in a new way. I told her I felt terrible that I knew so little about my mother's childhood and adolescence.

I ended up saying that I hoped she would ask me questions about my life, because once I was dead she would never know—and I didn't want her to feel as much in the dark as I do about my parents' and grandparents' lives. It was a wonderful exchange, and it would not have taken place without the impetus from this book.

It is possible that we as a generation are particularly critical of our mothers. The dissemination of psychological insights has led to a changed ideal of the family unit; we now believe that our primary mode as parents should be nurturing rather than authoritarian. Whereas our mothers were raised to believe that any challenge to parental authority, any criticism of parental personalities, was a sign of disrespect, we have been encouraged to examine all our familial relationships with greater honesty. As Peggy R. suggests, this division between our mothers and us has often made serious, intimate conversation impossible. In addition, whether or not we have been active in the feminist movement, all of us have been affected by its challenge to the social status quo that governed our mothers' lives. We have attempted, with varying degrees of success, to throw off the notion of ourselves as adjuncts to the men in our lives. We have taken paying jobs, not just because we needed the money. We have gotten divorced and discovered the pleasure of making our own decisions. We may have been dismissive of our mothers because they did not provide us with a model of the women we wanted to be. And we may have felt estranged from them because they were unable to be supportive of the decisions we made.

Mothers Who Left Psychic Scars

Some women told us that bad mothering has blighted their entire lives. They feel that their mothers not only disapproved of them but that they actually were unloved. "My life with my mother was a constant fight," said Judy Tasanos. "In my eyes, I could never do enough or be enough for her. Every time I looked for her acceptance, the door was closed. I kept going back. Once I was sitting at the kitchen table, crying, and I said to my husband, 'When does it end? I'm thirty-two years old and look what she's doing to me,' and he said, 'When she dies.' And it was true." It *is* true that after death an unloving mother no longer has the power to inflict fresh wounds. Unfortunately, death does not erase a daughter's feeling that there must have been something wrong with her that caused her mother to withhold love.

Parentification

Women like Judy, who admit to themselves that their mother didn't love them, or loved them but expressed that love in very destructive ways, or shifted erratically between loving them and rejecting them, have taken a very difficult and liberating step. They recognize that the mother to whom they turned for love, care, and protection was in fact the person who made impossible emotional demands on *them*. In her influential book, *Prisoners of Childhood*, Alice Miller argues that children who have been forced by a parent to accept the parent's version of emotional reality learn to suppress the validity of their own feelings and consequently suffer a serious injury to their sense of self-worth. And they will repeat the cycle with their own children, looking to the next generation to supply the validation of their self-worth that was denied to them by their parents. Psychiatrist Ivan Boszormenyi-Nagy, an early theorist in the family therapy movement, describes this phenomenon as "parentification," which he defines as "an effort at re-creating one's past relationship with one's parent in a current relationship with one's children."

Parentification need not be pathological. The occasional reversal of roles, enabling a child to practice taking on emotional responsibility, is healthy. It helps a child prepare for maturity. But, in Boszormenyi-Nagy's view, it becomes pathological when parents constantly misuse small children to satisfy their "possessive, dependent, destructive, or sexual needs." If parentification is couched "in an exceedingly guilt-laden atmosphere of obligation, [it] may constitute a bind which traps the child." Eventually, parentified children will look to balance accounts elsewhere, often with a sibling, more commonly with their own child.

The pattern of mothering that is passed on from generation to generation is never exactly the same. It can be modified by factors such as the respective temperaments of individual mothers and daughters, a supportive spouse, and whether or not a mother's mother is still alive and making demands. Some of the women we spoke to who said their mothers were difficult also told us that they were fortunate to have found a substitute for her—a father, an aunt, a teacher, a grandparent—who loved them and provided a role model for how they could love their daughters. Other women gained insight into their situation through psychotherapy. Nonetheless, as Dr. Kathy Weingarten told us, mothers who have had the misfortune of a bad relationship with their own mothers have a challenging task. "There are some injuries that are much harder to put aside than others. Some injuries really do create deficits—a harsh word—that despite all of a mother's good intentions, she may not be able to move beyond." Mothers who have suffered from a mother who did not love them or loved them erratically may or may not inflict an identical injury on their children. But the deficit will likely take its toll. They may well turn to their own children to repair their sense of neediness and, in doing so, parentify them.

"My mother never thought anything I did was good"

Miriam H. is a fifty-seven-year-old high school teacher who lives alone in a condo apartment in Hallandale, Florida. She seemed dubious about meeting us and changed our appointment several times. Given her wariness on the phone, we weren't sure how willing she would be to discuss her relationship with her daughters. In fact, when we finally did meet, Miriam was eager to talk, and she recognized that her story properly began with her own mother.

"My mother was deranged. Unrelenting. Right from the beginning she didn't care about me. When I was born she had abscessed breasts and they didn't know what to do—she was hospitalized several weeks with a great deal of pain—so she always recounted to me the story of the association of my birth with unnecessary pain. Right from the very beginning to the very end of her life, no variation. I think she was so thwarted, twisted, and tormented that she would swear at people on the street, she would do crazy things that for a shy frightened kid were terribly embarrassing. She would fight and swear at me in front of my friends.

"She was an unhappy woman. She came from a divorced family at a time when Jewish women weren't divorced—her father just walked out of the house one day and abandoned her mother—so maybe something just clicked in her. She was always difficult. And maybe no one really wanted her. I don't know what it was, what I represented. Who knows?"

At a very early age, Miriam tried to protect herself by withdrawing from her mother's rage. "I was a reader when I was a kid—she was always shouting, shouting, shouting, and I had to get refuge. So I would read. There were no books in our house so she would take me to the library, which was very good, and I would take out maybe ten books and start to read them. And then she would say, 'You've got to go out! All you do is read!' So I don't regret that I never got close to her. She did terrible things to me, and I didn't deserve it. I wasn't a bad kid. I was shy, kind of nervous, and as an adult I didn't deserve it either."

When Miriam finished college, she announced that she was planning to travel in Europe and then go to graduate school. Her mother was furious, refusing to support her emotionally or economically, and her father didn't rise to her defense. Her parents didn't speak to Miriam for twenty years. They did not come to her wedding and never saw their grandchildren. Five years ago, when her father was dying of cancer, Miriam called him. "I said to my father, 'I'm coming to see you in the hospital,' and he called me back and said, 'It will really make your mother angry.' And I said, 'So what!' And he said, 'Because I have to live with her. She doesn't want you here!' I went anyhow. I finally saw my father once in the hospital, once at home, and once at his funeral."

Miriam has not shaken off the burden of her mother's abuse. She has few friends and has hardly dated since her divorce over a decade ago. She hates her job as a teacher in a big urban high school and has little to do with her colleagues. She told us that she hears frequently from former students who want to keep in touch, but she denied feeling gratification from what seemed to us to be a tribute to her importance in their lives. She's still a reader and, although she lives frugally, she travels every summer. Most of her energy seems focused on her relationship with her children and her determination not to do to them what her mother did to her. "I know what it is like not to have family support. I couldn't do that to my children, because I had that experience, and I would never, never repeat it for them."

Miriam's older daughter, Rachel, is twenty-four. She lives in Denver and works as a paralegal. Her younger daughter, Leah, twenty, lives in northern Florida, working as a waitress and struggling to get through college. Miriam sees each of them two or three times a year. Miriam sympathizes with the fact that her mother must have felt rejected when Miriam insisted on travel, on study, on leaving her mother behind. "I left, but in some way now that I have daughters far away, I see it's really hard; you really have to keep yourself decent and not begrudge them their life and movement. You have to find out, with care, what matters to them. I'm very careful about not prying or probing, and encouraging them: 'That sounds interesting. What else are you doing?' because otherwise—I can catch glimmers of how drastic it must have seemed to my mother that I left."

Because she has no model of how a mother should behave with an adult daughter, Miriam struggles to maintain an appropriate balance between being sensitive to her daughters' needs for independence and her own desire to stay connected. At times, she cannot resist her need to be too involved in her daughters' lives. She and Rachel speak regularly four or five times a week, but sometimes she finds herself calling twice a day. Hesitant about offering advice in her own words, she bombards both girls with clippings from magazines and newspapers about career choices, money management, and other things she wishes she could discuss with them. She seeks from them a degree of validation—a reassurance that what she has to offer is valuable—that she did not get from her mother.

The situation is particularly volatile with her younger daughter, Leah. Against her better judgment, Miriam gets drawn into a style of confrontation with Leah that terrifies her because it reminds her of the battles she had with her own mother. She and Leah fight over Leah's course load, her friends, or her finances, and then don't speak for days. "Sometimes I think the way Leah feels about me . . . obviously not quite the same because she keeps calling me . . . but she must be angry at me and feel that I'm always criticizing the way my mother did. But my mother never said she loved me, and I tell Leah that a lot. And my mother never said to me that she thought I was attractive—she would say the opposite—and I always tell Leah that she's pretty. And my mother never thought anything I did was good, and I praise Leah when she does well in school. Of course, then I go and tell her that twelve hours a semester isn't enough, and she takes that as criticism." When Miriam catches herself acting too much like her mother, she employs a strategy she has developed to salvage such situations. "Whenever I reach a point with either of them when I think I can't take it anymore," she said, "I'll always do something to make certain they know I'm in their life. With Leah, when she says, 'Well I think it's better if we don't speak anymore,' I'll send her a letter saying, 'I know this is a tough time and I really love you.' I never heard that from my mother, she only said it in a perfunctory fashion."

Miriam recognizes that her girls think that her periodic bursts of anxious phone calls and letters are intrusive, even bizarre. "They'll tease me and say I'm crazy, and that really sets me off. My mother used to say that. They'll say, 'You're crazy, you're crazy.' Maybe that's contemporary slang, but my mother would say it to me because I was shy and wanted to stay home and read or write. So when my kids say it to me, it drives me wild. So when they say it, I'll say, 'Really, I'm not. I'm frustrated, I'm upset.' I hate being teased period.

"With Rachel, things are basically all right," Miriam said when we asked her to sum up her current relationship with her daughters. "We can travel together. We can argue and then make up. Maybe it's because we recognize that we're both women, that we both have difficulties, that we both get tense. With Leah right now the relationship is not so easy. She's still apt to withdraw when she's angry with me. And I hope she gets to know me better in the next little while because I have a lot to offer. I don't think my mother had a hell of a lot to offer. I never had a mother. I had this woman who never liked me, and she should have when I was a little kid—maybe not later on—so I never had a role model. How am I supposed to know these things? So I don't know what I should or should not do or be as a mother. The M word gives me trouble."

"I felt I couldn't depend on her"

Erica R. also told us about growing up without feeling secure in her mother's love and being determined to be a different kind of mother to her daughter. Erica is fifty-three, an executive with a design firm in New York. She is handsome and has a European reserve and a stately presence which suggests self-confidence, but which Erica says is somewhat misleading. "I'm very fragile in some ways. If something goes wrong, to me that's horrendous. I think I'm still a very anxious person, there's part of me that's still anxious. I want to do so much, and then I set myself impossible tasks, so that I haven't been able to accomplish what I've wanted to. Not only in terms of work but managing my personal life: doing some good work, doing cultural things, reading more. I always have the sense that I can't do it."

Erica attributes her self-doubt to the fact that she had a troubled childhood and an absent, disapproving mother. Erica was born in Romania to a wealthy family that fled to England when she was four because of the war. "I did not like my childhood. It was a series of very unstable situations, and my parents were very young and spoiled, and there were many aspects of their life that they weren't prepared to cope with very well." Erica cannot remember a time when she and her mother were close. "When I look at old photographs I see that she's often holding my brother, and I'm always pulling away. I think I found her to be mercurial and self-centered, and I probably resented the fact that she couldn't make my world stable and normal. But she was a very nervous woman, too. She made scenes all the time, and I found it very upsetting. I felt I couldn't depend on her. And my mother was very judgmental and somehow always seemed very disappointed. She didn't approve of me: I wasn't beautiful enough, bright enough, all those things. And I remember thinking, Oh, I don't really think it's true. So somewhere along the line somebody must have told me I was okay, and I've tried to figure that out."

Her parents separated soon after they reached England. "My mother went to Paris and kind of stayed there. And I was in London with my poor father."

"You mean she abandoned you?" we asked.

"Well, I think she kept meaning to come back," Erica told us. "Eventually we did go and live with her. But I think she had no intention of coming back to England and leading a life that she felt was incredibly horrendous and burdensome. So I think she left with the idea that we would eventually join her."

Because her father was in financial difficulty and her mother had some money, Erica and her brother did join their mother in Switzerland after the war. "And my grandfather was also around, and he really became my father. He was wonderful and paid a lot of attention. He would take us on trips and helped stabilize things. My brother was two years younger, and he was very unhappy. He was so upset by what was going on and my mother's scenes, and I would say, 'Look, we just have to survive this. Our lives are a jumble but we just have to work our way through this.'" In effect, Erica tried to be a mother to her younger brother, while she had no one to turn to who could play that role in her own life. Because her mother essentially abdicated her parental responsibility, Erica was forced to become an adult too soon.

Erica went to boarding school in England and subsequently moved to New York. Her mother died in 1985. Erica worked in advertising and married a writer. Her daughter Katya was born in 1970. "I really wanted her to have a good childhood. And I knew that the danger is that one repeats at least some of the same things one's mother has done—or has some of the same neuroses—but I was determined not to do that." Her marriage ended when Katya was ten, and she went back to work full time. She was very worried about her financial and professional future, but despite her anxieties, she never lost sight of Katya's need to feel secure even though the world around her was in disarray. It was essential to her that her child be more protected than she had been.

"After all, a child has her own problems at school, her own life, her own society. That's enough to worry about. And I don't think she felt insecure. She didn't feel that I was not going to be able to cope or sustain some sense of home and togetherness. It was more that she was worried about me, wished I weren't in such pain. She saw me being extremely nervous, overwrought, overwhelmed, but she's always said she never felt for a minute that that touched the affection I had for her. So we kind of struggled together.

"I would *not* repeat what had been done to me. I was determined to look at my child for who she is. What so often happens is either you want the child to be like you or you want her to accomplish the things you haven't accomplished, or to take on talents and a different kind of persona, so they can make up for what it is you are lacking. Well I was lucky! I always liked her! I don't know what I would have done if I had had some bratty horror! I've always loved who she is, I was always really proud of her. There were times when she didn't study hard enough, but it was never oh, you must excel in every possible way. I mean I realized that she excelled in some things and not in others."

After college, Katya returned to New York. She now works for a television production company. She has a serious boyfriend. She and Erica sometimes go for weeks without seeing each other, but they talk almost every day. "Actually we're very good friends. We discuss everything—her personal life, her feelings, her trials and tribulations, her anxieties. And what we're discovering more and more is we're so alike.

She says, 'Mom, that's good but also bad,' because she knows I'm a very hyper, worried, nervous sort of person."

The roots of Katya's anxiety surely lie in her childhood responses to her mother's overwhelming anxiety in the face of financial and emotional stress. In addition to worrying about her mother, Katya may have felt that she should be able to ease her mother's fears. A child can neither ignore nor fulfill such a responsibility, and the tension is apt to create a pattern of anxiety that a daughter will carry with her throughout her life.

We asked how Katya seems to be dealing with her anxiety. Erica said, "I think she has it much more under control. She has a much better sense of who she is and what she wants. She very much wants to be good at what she does, to be interested and involved. And that's coming from ambition and also just being a responsible person. What she doesn't have that I have is the fear. A lot of my energy comes from, oh my God, am I going to be able to do this? She has much more self-confidence than I."

"There was never any encouragement to do something to have my own life"

Gay Block is a well-known photographer and coauthor with Malka Drucker of *Rescuers: Portraits of Moral Courage in the Holocaust*. She is now working on a book about her mother who died four years ago in order "to have some closure on a relationship that was so awful." This work has sharpened her insights into the complex ways that her relationship with her mother shaped her behavior toward her two children, Barry, now thirty-two, and Alison, twenty-nine.

"In the context of working on my book about my mother," Gay told us, "I've realized that sometimes things that I was writing about her—my feelings about her or my relationship with her—I realize that Alison did the same thing, or there were the same issues, or I did the same thing to Alison that my mother did to me. I didn't see it that way before, but now that my mother's dead I see it that way. I also realized that having such a terrible relationship with my mother—I mean I really hated her and wanted her dead—consumed too much of my life.

"I grew up with a terrible self-image because of the things she would say. Always she was competitive with me for my father's attention or anyone's attention. She'd say I was fat all the time and that clothes didn't look nice on me. She was always telling me which men danced with her when she would go to a party and how many men told her she was beautiful. Or if they liked her dress or her hair or whatever. She was not an understanding, giving mother in any way for me.

"She was very directive, very dictatorial, and so you never did anything without her telling you how to do it unless she wasn't around. The thing I think was missing more than anything else from my house was that there was never any encouragement to do something, to have my own life. I guess the benchmark story for my childhood was when I was in the fifth grade. I went to school in an outfit that I thought looked really great, and I had the best day I'd ever had in my life, and I came home and I was so happy and my mother said, 'Don't you know that plaids and checks don't go together?' So then I thought what a fool I had been. And now I think I get it—and I've learned this from my own experience with my children. Their laughter sometimes made me angry. I now realize that my happiness as a child had the same effect on my mother. I don't completely understand why, but I know that's what it was about."

Gay believes that her mother lavished all her love on Gay's older brother and undervalued everything that Gay had to offer. What love she got came mostly from her father, and when he died, she felt bereft. Unable to handle her grief, she started psychoanalysis. Therapy helped her focus on her anger toward her mother and helped prevent her from reproducing exactly the kind of mothering she had had.

"I tried to be more present. I was more present, there's no doubt about it. I wanted not to have the favoritism toward the son, and it didn't come naturally, so I had to really talk about it and work on it in analysis. Then I remember doing some wonderful close things with Alison when she was young—maybe seven or eight. And at times feeling the sadness that Alison can do this with me and I never did this with my mother. And, of course, when Alison was angry at me at times, I thought she should only know what it's like to have a mother who wasn't there. I may not have been there as often as she wanted or as often as I should have been when she was in high school, but I know I was there the way my mother wasn't there."

Alison's high school years coincided with major events in Gay's life. In addition to suffering from her father's death, Gay separated from her husband and came out as a lesbian. Alison was so upset that she moved in with her father for several months, and even when she came back to live with Gay, she was too embarrassed to tell her friends that the other woman living there was her mother's lover. Gay also took some time to adjust to the reality of her new life. "It was hard for both of us. To tell the truth, this was not what I expected for myself either."

At the same time Gay also began studying photography and thinking about a professional career. All these changes absorbed most of her energy just when her daughter needed more of her attention. "Alison is quite aware of the things about me that she dislikes," said Gay. "She's gotten over being upset by my love life, but she complains that I never spent time alone with her, that's how she would say it— never—and that I didn't pay enough attention to her during her high school years. And there was some truth to that." Despite her best intentions, Gay was imposing on her daughter some of the self-involved behavior that she suffered from with her own mother.

Understanding the roots of her conduct, and recognizing that Alison's complaints were true, didn't make it any easier for Gay to break the pattern. "It was extremely painful for me when my daughter was having trouble with me. And a lot of that came out in my being angry at her—not on the surface but behind her back. And I thought, how could this happen to me? And I wondered, is it happening because she saw the difficult relationship I had with my mother. You know, what goes around comes around. But I thought this just doesn't make sense. She just can't do this, because I put in too much and I care too much about her. How could she? My capacity for love is greater than my mother's was."

Gay's insights enabled her to turn her capacity for love into a tolerance for her daughter's need to express her anger and to work through her own complex feelings toward Gay.

Gay says, "I know that part of what interfered in Alison's and my relationship for a long time was this understandable guilt I would feel—that I was a failure as a mother. That I wasn't doing enough for her. Just not being real enough. And that sprang from insecurities, but also it was a legacy of the way my mother made me feel—that I wasn't a good enough daughter for her—so it was hard not to see my daughter as my mother. Which I think is a real thing with mothers and daughters." When a mother feels that she is failing her daughter, it can revive old fears of failing her mother. She unconsciously fuses her mother and her daughter in the role of the person whose love she wants but feels unworthy of receiving. Her response is either to blame herself for not loving enough or properly, or to become quite angry because she feels unwarranted rejection.

It took eight years for Gay and Alison to work through their difficulties. At one point, both of them were in therapy. Sometimes it was easier for the two of them to keep their distance rather than get into painful arguments, but Gay also made it clear to Alison that she loved her and would never turn her back on her. Recently Alison has made great strides in her career and has married a man who Gay thinks is a wonderful choice. Perhaps not coincidentally, the tension between mother and daughter has eased, and they have had moments of great honesty and intimacy. "I like seeing what I call the progress of her going off from her life at home and becoming her own person," Gay says. "That's where I feel a pride that I helped her to be that, and that's where I feel sadness about my own life, because I had to work very hard to become independent, and it happened much much later. And I even feel envious of her at times."

Before her mother died, Gay was able to see her in a more forgiving light. But she is aware that nothing will ever heal all her wounds. As our interview was winding down, Gay said, "I think Alison and I are very loving and very open with one another now. And for me, there's a lot of poignancy. I don't know if today I'm just feeling extremely poignant. The poignancy is in my identification with her and the blurring of the boundaries between mother, me, and her—seeing me as a daughter and me as a mother."

The stories we heard from Miriam, Erica, and Gay about destructive relationships with their own mothers are dramatic examples of the pain that parentification inflicts on a child and, very possibly, on her children as well.

> *From Marilyn's journal, January 26, 1996*
>
> I've been dreaming a lot about my mother—or about generic mothers—since we started this project. My mother appears from time to time, usually at about age forty to forty-five, and the encounter seems meaningful during the dream. But I can't get to the root of what the dreams are telling me. I can't recapture the essence afterward.
>
> I've been reading Alice Miller, *The Drama of the Gifted Child*. And I see how her thesis played out with me and Kate when she was very young. Because I so needed to protect myself from being hurt by my mother's self-involvement when I was very young, I must have pulled back myself. I became this feisty, cool kid who could take care of herself emotionally. It suited my mom to have that kind of child. And I got praised for it by my dad and my aunts—everybody who colluded in the notion that we shouldn't make demands on her. In turn, when Kate needed to cling to me, when she was around two or so, and she was having a terrible time being left at a play group, I pulled back. And we had some of the same problems a year later when she started nursery school. I ignored her very real fear of abandonment because of my own need to do what my mother did— show me off as this wonderful, independent little thing. I denied the authenticity of Kate's own emotions. That example is quite stark in retrospect. I wonder what others I don't see.

We were moved by the wisdom these women had struggled to achieve and the progress they had made in breaking pathological cycles. All three had done some of this work with the help of psychotherapy. Therapy allows women to express the hurt they felt at their mothers' hands. It enables them to shuck off permanently the false belief that some flaw in them caused their mothers to withhold love. As Dr. Evelyn Bassoff writes of similar women whom she has seen in treatment, "Feeling and talking through the pain—the humiliation of being an unloved child, the anger toward the cold mother, the anxiety of turning into her, the fear of maternal retribution for hating her— became the healing salve. . . . [They] came to understand that their mothers, who were unfortunate, inadequate, insecure people, *did not have the power* to hurt them anymore. . . . As important, they learned that by virtue of their growing self-awareness, they *did have the power* to behave differently with their own daughters than their mothers had behaved with them."

But Gay Block cautions that progress does not come without cost. As if she were speaking for all the women who have fought hard not to repeat with their daughters the pattern of bad mothering their mothers transmitted to them, Gay concluded, "So whereas the relationship with my daughter is so good and makes me so happy, there's still inside me, at least at this minute, real poignancy. Not exactly a mourning for my mother as for my life."

"Too connected"

Women who feel that they were rejected and unloved by their mothers labor all their lives to overcome psychic scars that rejection left behind; they also labor to avoid inflicting similar wounds on their daughters. Another group of women we spoke with—women who feel that their mothers bound them too close in the name of love— have a related but different problem: How to show their daughters how much they love them, yet let them go free.

Paula S. is a writer who lives in Providence, Rhode Island. She has been married since she was eighteen to a successful local businessman. She had four children by the time she was thirty. Her daughters Maud and Jessie are now thirty-four and twenty-eight respectively. They have each settled in other New England cities and are well launched in their careers. Maud is married. But for Paula, it's a constant fight not to intrude in their lives. "Too connected," Paula explains. "That's the problem, I'm too connected to them. I'm one of these mothers who has more trouble letting go of my kids than they have leaving me. I'm one of those old-fashioned mothers like my own who never let go of me, so I don't really have a model for how to do it easily.

"I really think that the happiest and most wonderful part of my life was raising my children, that was the pinnacle for me, and I miss them all the time," Paula told us. "I long for them, I really do. And when Maud went off to college, when the boys left, when Jessie left, I was a basket case. I'm not proud of that, and I don't know that my friends were ever as bad as that, but I was. I absolutely adored being a mother and having babies and all that stuff.

"Separating from the girls was always hard for me, even harder than from the boys. I think with the boys there was a built-in understanding that they would eventually move on. With the girls, it was the kind of thing I had with my mother, that one never had to give up one's daughters, they were there forever, and that's a terrible thing to do to one's daughters, it's awful. They should be treated like the boys. And that for me was a horror because I felt so close to them, and I know that that wasn't in their best interests."

Paula's father was never a part of her life. Her brother was eight years older, so she felt like an only child. Her mother was hardly the classic stay-at-home smotherer. She married several times and had an active social life. "She was always off gallivanting and having a blast," Paula remembers. Nonetheless, when she focused on Paula, she wanted her full attention. "She held me close. She didn't cook, she went out at night to parties, but still she was deeply connected to me. Somehow I knew I could never go away to college, I knew I could never leave. I *could never* leave. It was never an issue. I knew that from day one, my job, my whole being, was connected to my mother." Somehow Paula's mother communicated to her daughter that her well-being depended on her daughter's never leaving her. Paula was, in Dr. Boszormenyi-Nagy's terms, "parentified" by her needy mother. As he explains, "Children are unceasingly loyal and will assign themselves as physical and psychological guardians to one or both parents if they sense insatiable, unmet needs for comforting."

Paula married right after high school, but this marriage hardly represented an escape from her mother's control. "I married a man she approved of, a family she approved of, a city she approved of. She had no argument. There was nothing she could say, which was part of my compliance." Paula says her husband connived in her continued submission to her mother. "He was taken in by her—she's enormously charming and seductive—he always tells me to be nice to her, he's supported the relationship."

Paula suddenly interrupted her narrative to admit to us that she had not told us the truth about her age. At the beginning of our talk she had said she was fifty-six. "Actually I'm fifty-nine," she said laughing. "My mother made us lie about our age so she could lie about hers. It's not a good thing to lie about your age. It doesn't help, it doesn't help anything, it makes you feel rotten, something snags inside. All my life, my brother and I both had to downscale three years—which meant me getting married at fifteen! When my mother turned eighty, she finally came clean, and it was much easier to be with her."

Paula's brother was allowed more leeway, while she was expected to be the ever-dutiful daughter. "There came a point—when I was married—when even I had had it with my mother. We went to a delicatessen, and we were screaming at each other behind our menus, and the waitress came and said, 'Ladies! Ladies!' The issue was favoritism—that she favored my brother. And I had resented her for this my whole life."

After their fight in the deli, Paula and her mother didn't speak to each other for three months. "As my mother put it, 'We had a little vacation from each other.'" And then they talked some of the issues through. Paula says she has come to realize that her mother didn't favor her brother at all. "It was just a different relationship," says Paula, "because he was a boy and she was more on guard with him, she was much more careful, which you tend to be with sons, which I tend to be, too. You just sort of respect their boundaries a little bit more, almost as if you don't have the same privileges with them. Of course, that's wrong, and it's unfair to a daughter as well."

Like many of the women we spoke to who felt something their mother did to them was very painful, Paula reacted by trying to do the exact opposite. Since she felt too tied to her mother, Paula forcefully encouraged her girls' separation. "I pushed them out. When Maud went off to college—and Maud is particularly close to us, for a number of reasons, she has been diabetic since she was six, and as a result the normal worry is multiplied by a zillion—anyhow, when she went off to college she called home a lot, so we changed her bedroom into a guest room to kind of signal to her that she was out of the nest. We went up to see Maud often, but we did change her room around, and she resented it. But I also think she understood why. Later on she said to us, 'Now I understand why you changed my room, you wanted to discourage me from feeling so connected to everything.' Her blanket, her teddy bear, her dolls—it was like pulling the rug from under her, but I felt in the long run it was best."

Paula may have overcompensated in her fight against being too connected. She resists the urge to pick up the phone and call her daughters as frequently as she speaks to her mother. "I remember having the burden of my mother on my head, and I don't want to burden my children." She lets them call her. Jessie calls frequently just to chat. Maud may call once every two weeks. Paula reports, "If I call her, she sounds thrilled." Paula thinks Maud perceives her as distant, busy. "I think they resent me for the fact that I pulled back. True it's been hard for me to let go. I know that's contradictory, but I have pulled back. So I'll tell them that I'd love them to come for Christmas, and Maud will say, 'Wow, it's nice that you want us to come!' But I know what I'm doing and why. I don't even want to tell them why because I think that's a little burdensome. I sometimes think the kids think I was maybe a little too disinterested. But it really wasn't disinterest—because it was the fear that I would do to them what my mother did to me." Paula would rather live with the knowledge that her children think she's too distant than reproduce what she calls "my sense of imprisonment by my mother."

"I was her whole family"

"I don't want to be a burden to my children" reverberates in the story of Cynthia G., another woman whose mother has frequently been just that. Cynthia is a sixty-year-old public relations executive in Los Angeles; she has two daughters, Leslie, thirty, and Nicole, twenty-eight. She has been divorced from their father for twenty years and happily remarried for the last nine. Last year she was operated on for the removal of a malignant lump in her right breast, and her prognosis is favorable. Her friends and her daughters have often listened to Cynthia's account of her unusually complex attachment to her mother.

Says Cynthia, "I feel a physical bond with my mother, with her life, with her body. It occurred to me that she divorced at the same time as I did, and we got cancer, not at the same time, but the same kind, and I've inherited her constitution. So I've always suspected that cancer would be a part of my history, my destiny. But I don't think I feel that her life choices are mine in any way. Having said that, I don't know how I feel my life choices are going to influence my children. Are they destined to be divorced? There is a long line of divorced women in my family, including my grandmother. I've stressed the importance of not smoking because of the cancer in the family. We have a family myth about the Jackson girls—my mother and my aunt—and there's me and my cousin Willa, and of the grandchildren, there are four daughters, so there's been a matriarchy. The Jackson girls have conveyed both a sense of continuity and history and humor, so there is an unconscious flow of the repetition of your mother's life, of the women in the family having an interconnected fabric."

Cynthia's parents separated soon after World War II. "I spent four years thinking my father would come home from the war," says Cynthia, "but he didn't." She and her mother went back to live in Kansas City, her mother's hometown. Soon thereafter her maternal grandmother died. Her mother fell into a serious depression characterized by terrible migraine headaches, and Cynthia took care of her. They moved frequently during her early teens. Money was tight. "My mother and I were very close at that point. She depended on me. I was her whole family, but I got used to it." What Cynthia had more trouble getting used to was that her mother was so often bitter, convinced that things happened to her that weren't her choice—that she was not living the life she expected to live. In her bitterness, she was judgmental and nasty. Cynthia tried to protect herself by not sharing most of her feelings and even the facts about her life.

"So I have this awful dichotomy with my mother," says Cynthia, "where I do love her, but don't like her; I do have respect for her strength, but I don't have much respect for the way she views the world. I think she has isolated herself, and I disagree with that approach. She's terribly angry and has never tried to understand what that has done to those around her, and those are bad marks in my book."

Despite these insights, Cynthia reports that she has always had separation problems with her mother. Even in her thirties and forties, as a wife and mother, her wish to assert herself withered before her need for her mother's approval. When her mother came to visit Cynthia and her children several times a year, her style of commentary was always the same: The new sofa didn't go with the corner armchair; the chicken was overcooked; the girls were noisy and disrespectful; they shouldn't wear black all the time. Cynthia told us, "The girls and I have handled some of this with humor. We have the 'Grandma Helen Clean Closet Award.' And we have other shorthand ways to discuss her behavior—her wish to control and to make constant judgments. But it never completely takes the sting away."

Cynthia has not been able to tell her mother how she feels about the moments when her mother is too intrusive; she has been unable to establish the appropriate balance between separation and connection. Instead she keeps her mother at bay with humor, or with a kind of superficial deference that is actually distancing. The "yes-Mother-I'll-do-it-when-you-know-you-won't" response.

In an effort not to make the same mistakes her mother did, Cynthia has tried to convey to her daughters that she doesn't think of them as her only means of emotional support. "I've had to do that more with Leslie than Nicole, because Nicole lives in New Orleans and Leslie lives close by. When I was ill I tried to make Leslie feel that she was incredibly supportive but that she wasn't the whole support system. She had an automatic response that 'I am the daughter, these are things I need to do,' which is partly the family response, what I do with my mother. I wanted Leslie to know there were other people around helping me. It's my task to help my daughters, help them understand that they're not at my beck and call. That would be the burden part that I want to avoid with them. I think the thing I've done is to show them that I am happily integrated into a life of my own, with a husband that I love and friends who are vital to my existence. To me that is an enormous step toward separation that I never got from my mother. She was always unhappy in her situation and isolated from people, and I was the only person around so I could never get away."

Cynthia stays involved in her daughters' lives and likes them to be involved in hers, seeking an equilibrium she never found with her own mother. She gives herself good marks for not meddling in her daughters' love lives or their careers. She and Leslie shop together, have dinner together "at a frequency that is comfortable for us both." She is conscious with both girls of letting them decide how much time they spend with her and what they do together. When Cynthia emulates her mother by overstepping her limits, she can tolerate being chastised, as her mother could not. Cynthia told us, "Leslie is always willing to say—maybe not the first time but the second time—'Mom, you can't call me three times. It kills me to come home and think I have five messages, wow, a single woman in L.A., and find that three of them are from my mother!' "

Nonetheless when Cynthia senses that one of her daughters is treating her in a way that is reminiscent of the way she has treated her mother, she feels very threatened. "When Leslie puts up a wall," says Cynthia, "I see it as a reminder that probably has to do with what I experienced growing up with my own mother and a lack of total separation there. It's come up recently with her condo, and I can't actually figure out how much of this is for her sake and how much is for mine. I imagine that if her apartment were neat—a word I pull out of my own mother's lexicon—that she would feel happy there. She has no nest. That's my own definition of safe and happy—a nest. I'm trying to convince myself that it's not Leslie's definition, but I don't get very far. I'll call and give her the name of a cleaning service, or I'll volunteer to take her vacuum cleaner—which hasn't worked in months—to the repairman. And Leslie will say, 'Mother, I'll do it myself.' And then she does nothing."

Even though Cynthia knows she ought to be less intrusive, she can't stop herself. "I just don't feel that I have the personality to totally say, 'I have done what I can do, your life is your life now. There is absolutely nothing more that my worrying can do for you.' I always think that if I worry a little, it will be okay."

Cynthia has some awareness that what she sees as helpful, Leslie sees as controlling and critical. And the mere suggestion that her behavior is perceived by her daughter with as much hostility as she viewed her mother's activates her greatest fears. Cynthia says, "I worry that at some point Leslie and Nicole may decide that I am either unlikable or burdensome—not burdensome in the way that they are going to have to take care of me, but 'oh, why do I have to go to dinner?' " She is still seeking the middle ground. "I think that's a very important goal for me—staying a vital participant in the friendship and defining what that will be, and how often, whether it's just talking on the phone or being together, I don't know yet, but my fear is that I will become a burden or an irrelevant part of their lives."

The Compulsion to Criticize

Cynthia described her mother as critical and controlling. And, with the exception of the handful of women who thought their mothers were unwaveringly supportive, almost everybody we interviewed said the same: "My mother was too critical."

We heard this from women like Miriam H. and Gay Block, whose mothers' criticisms were unrelenting. We heard it from women who tried to put it in a good light. "My mom was always my best critic." Or "My mom set high standards; she assumed I could do anything she thought I ought to do." And from women who were able to laugh it off. "She says perfectly awful things to me, but that's just the way she is!"

Everybody had a story. Said Nellie Lou Slagle, "I never wanted a close relationship with my mom. We never talked about anything beyond the weather and the niceties of life, because if we did, I would have had to accept the criticism that would go along with it. So I kept everything really important out of our relationship."

Megan C. told us, "I was not the daughter my mother wanted. She would have had a daughter who stayed Catholic, stayed in Ohio, certainly didn't marry a Jew, didn't move to New York, wasn't in theater, wasn't a writer, wasn't a freelancer, wasn't divorced. So my mother and I have always had major, major problems." One of her mother's favorite weapons was to retreat into punishing silence. "If she got really mad at me she would just stop talking to me entirely, and I would practically have to grovel before she'd start talking to me again. I moved to New York when I was twenty—I had to get away."

Time and distance have helped Megan understand what was behind her mother's relentless criticism. "I think my mother always resented me. On the one hand she was proud of me, on the other she was jealous of whatever I achieved. She was jealous because she thought my father loved me more than her, and I think he did." She's also learned that while she can't change her mother, she can protect herself by limiting her exposure. "There's no point in baiting her, there's no point in talking about being pro-choice to an Irish Catholic, there's no point in antagonizing her. And as long as we can limit our talks to nice little things, it's fine."

Ellen Sweets said, "In her way, my mother was a loving person. But she was not particularly nurturing. She always did the right things—I was given piano lessons, a perfect wardrobe, elocution lessons, I was taken to art galleries and concerts. However, she was not the nicest person for a child to grow up with. She was often unkind in ways that, looking back on, I don't think she realized. She was very, very critical. And preoccupied, it seemed to me then, and it seems now, to a ridiculous degree with other people's perceptions. So, of course, I was a rebel. I was one of three black hippies in the Midwest."

Ellen was holding down a responsible job on the St. Louis *Post-Dispatch* when, at age thirty, she discovered, to her amazement and joy, that she was pregnant. Ellen was divorced, she'd had two miscarriages, and had been told she could not have children. The father was someone she had no interest in marrying, but she made up her mind to have the child. Her mother was horrified. "It was bad. Real bad. Mother said, 'What are our friends going to say?' And for the first time ever, I summoned the courage to answer, 'You know, I don't really give a damn; they're your friends. You handle them. I have a different kind of friend.' "

Carol Rusoff told us, "My sister and I consider our mother a real stumbling block in our lives. Of course, the things that come easily to us, we have forgotten to thank her for, and the stuff that's really fucked up about us we completely put on her—our feelings of not completely being enough, of not quite measuring up, and always being the unrealized potential of ourselves. The message I got was, 'Oh, you have such a pretty face, do something with it. Why aren't you elegant, why aren't you striking, with such a face! Why aren't you more? With talent as a theater person, why aren't you famous?' Even in her compliments to both my sister and me, there's a false sense of grandiosity that is outrageous—'I admire you so much, you are so beautiful, you are so wonderful, you are so so so' to the point that for little girls or big girls you don't accept it; it's not in the bounds of reality."

Carol has two daughters, Becky, twenty-five, and Annie, twenty-one. "With them I've tried to make the love more unconditional, to teach them that my opinion is not so fucking important. I try to give my opinion once and try not to give it unsolicited. My sister argues, and so does my mother, that so-called unconditional love isn't meaningful, because it's uncritical; it's too simple, and it means less to your kids. Whereas I believe the opposite. They think it's part of the job to be diagnostic about what children are doing and help them with their wisdom, but I don't think I have such hotshit wisdom. If my kids want help, they ask for help, and God knows I give it." Even Carol has to fight the impulse to say just the kind of thing she swore she wouldn't. "I have to put the brakes on, to stop myself from saying, 'God, you're taking three classes with the same professor? Do you think you're getting a bang for your buck in your senior year of college, Annie?' "

Why we repeat the behavior we most deplore

Why did virtually all the women we interviewed who said their mothers were critical confess that sometimes when they speak to their daughters, they hear their mothers' words coming out of their own mouths? Or why, if they say nothing, do they still convey their critical attitude?

Earlier we discussed the fact that when a parent, out of neediness, persistently assails a child's sense of self-esteem, that child will often repeat the pattern with his or her own children. It is just in that way that a lifetime of maternal criticism makes its mark. If your mother's criticism has damaged your self-esteem, you are endlessly self-critical, and any imperfection on your children's part is further proof of your inadequacies. So you criticize them in a fruitless effort to make them, and you, appear better. Another explanation for the propensity to incorporate some of your mother's behavior, even though it offended you, is that if you didn't separate from her appropriately, you may hold on to a familiar pattern as a way to remain connected. It somehow feels better to reproduce the kind of mothering your mother offered you, even if it was imperfect, than to sever all emotional connection to her.

We believe that there are ways to break these patterns. We believe you can relate to an adult daughter in ways that do not "parentify" her, that you can come to respect her as someone who is very definitely not you and whose life choices do not reflect on you, and that you can minimize the unconscious repetition of behavior that stands in the way of the greater intimacy you wish the two of you could achieve. You can find ways in which the relationship with your daughters can be enriched no matter what has gone on in the past. The first step is to come to terms with the image of your mother that you carry within you, which frees you to choose the ways in which you want to be like and unlike her in relation to your own daughters.

Coming to Terms with Your Mother

At this stage of life, no matter what your relationship to your mother has been, you probably are able to be more accepting of her than you were in the past. Megan C., who fled from Ohio, now laughs at her mother's foibles. She can also acknowledge her mother's strengths. Megan even gets a kick out of how her mother responds to Megan's somewhat outrageous daughter, Amber. Says Megan, "Amber's really out there. She's dyed her hair green, she has three tattoos. She's a club kid, goes out in a parade of costumes. And my mother? If I had done what Amber does, she would have killed me, but with Amber she says, 'Oh, that Amber!' "

Psychologist Terri Apter believes that by the time each of us reaches middle age, and much of our impatience or anger with our mother has abated, we often regret how little we really knew of her life. "We hear her silence at the same point we recognize the sound of her voice in our own. This is the strange, reverberating resolution we come to at midlife. We do not win an adolescent battle, but accept the blurred boundaries, which are less threatening now, as the self becomes more layered and flexible. We acknowledge the connection and its implacable permanence, but no longer feel bound and constrained by it. We may also feel a new need for a different closeness, as we try to hear her story anew."

Alice Trillin has tried to hear her mother's story anew. Alice was an only child who was doted on by both parents. "I was very close to my mother as a child; she was very warm and loving. Of course, she was incredibly overprotective, which I think came from the fact that it took her five years to get pregnant, and she almost died having me and then couldn't have any more children." Her mother's anxieties were compounded by money problems. Alice's father had made and lost a considerable fortune by the time Alice was born, and thereafter, while her parents dreamed of recouping their wealth, the reality was that they could scarcely pay their bills.

"It was in my early teens," recalls Alice, "that my mother began to behave strangely. At the time it was happening I understood it a little. My grandmother had just died, and my mother loved her a lot, but had also fought with her a lot, and that probably contributed to it. And then, of course, she was always worried by my dad's financial ups and downs. Also she went through an early, very difficult menopause at about that time. And as a teenager I was wanting some independence. She was probably a bit scared of me. I was really smart, and she was proud of this, but also knew that my accomplishments would ultimately take me away from her. We began to have these awful fights about the most insignificant things, and her irrational anger really scared me." Alice chose to avoid these confrontations.

"Since so much of what my mother did and said wasn't rational, I made a conscious decision to do what I thought I should do and not tell my parents. I did this as a way to survive."

In the years after her mother's death from Alzheimer's disease in 1976, Alice has thought and written about their relationship and tried to tell her daughters, Abigail, twenty-seven, and Sarah, twenty-four, what went wrong and how she wishes it had gone differently.

Alice told us, "When my mother got sick, I thought at first that it was just an exaggeration of her former craziness and not really the serious illness it was. I was mad at her for being crazy and for making my dad's life so difficult, but most of all I was scared watching this person I loved turn into someone I didn't recognize. About the time her illness got really serious, my father also had a stroke. And for a long time I devoted a lot of my energy to taking care of the two of them—negotiating with doctors, with various social agencies, and nursing homes for their care. Toward the end I realized that there was very little I could do, beyond the practical things like getting them good care.

"After my dad died, and she was in a nursing home, I went to see her pretty regularly, although I sometimes skipped a week or two. Everyone said she didn't know whether or not I was there, and I convinced myself of that. But I don't think it was true. I was drawing this curtain between myself and my mother. I just withdrew emotionally from the pain of seeing her that way.

"It's important for my kids to know the good legacy I got from my mother," Alice says. "Because we don't do it all by ourselves, it isn't an accident. Her good qualities. How you treat your friends, would you be there for someone who's sick? And I think these things come more from your mother than your father. Honesty—what are your priorities? The private things not the public things. I see my mother as this person whom I wish I had known. My father's business failure caused terrible problems for the family, but he and my mother loved each other. So no matter what on the surface is going wrong, if you sense that there's really a great love, that's sustaining for a kid. My mother and father knew how to do that. They always stood up for each other. That gave me strength. That's what I looked for in my life.

"I really understand now what was going on with my mother. She had a life that caused her to behave in a hurtful way, but she was also a good lady. I have tried to balance those two things. Because I believe that Abigail and Sarah need to see that all these things matter. And I've tried to counteract with them what I took to be the saddest thing, which is that my mother and I couldn't be honest with each other. Which is something that I really try to be.

"Sometimes when I talk about my mom, I've actually been in tears. Abigail will pat me on the arm. It's about how sad I am that someone I cared about so much wasn't so successful at communicating and getting the joy that I get out of my kids."

In the years since her mother's death, Alice has learned that her mother was probably addicted to pills. "She was dependent on various uppers and downers prescribed by the local doctor for her 'nerves.' My aunt told me. I had no idea. Her behavior was very erratic at times. And I thought there was something the matter with me, because we couldn't talk to each other. And only later did I realize that she was ill.

"I have dreams that she gets better, that she becomes the person she was until I was twelve. I have this fantasy that she's well again. My dad has made money again, and she's just sitting in the garden, and I bring my children to see her. And it makes me sad that it didn't happen."

As we age, it becomes easier for us to understand our mother's strengths and weaknesses in the context of her life, her options. Among the things we recognize—as we try to "hear her story anew"— is that she was subject to *her* mother's strengths and weaknesses. The more we can see her objectively, the more we can understand who we are and why, as mothers, we make the choices we do. When we share with our daughters our knowledge of the forces that shaped *us*, we can help them begin the task of seeing us with similar objectivity. If we can be clear about what we say and do, why we say and do it, and what really matters to us, we take great strides in helping our daughters see us in all our complexity, not just as their mothers.

Part Two

Unresolved
Tensions

Chapter 3

Your Daughter's Personal
Style and Habits

It was our responses to our daughters' personal habits that started us on this project. We were each dismayed to discover that we were still bothered by our respective daughter's cuticle-biting and procrastination. We believed that the girls were too old to be doing what they were doing, and we were somehow ashamed that we cared. We knew they resented our behavior, but we felt powerless to stop. Perhaps if we said it just one more time, perhaps if we could find a better way to say what we meant, we could get the results we wished for.

Over and over in our interviews, we heard women apologize for similar failings: "I know I shouldn't care, but. . .," "I try not to notice, but. . .," "I try to keep my mouth shut, but . . ." Some problems seemed trivial: She wears too much makeup; her hair's in her face; she wears safety pins to hold up her hems; she doesn't write thank-you notes; her apartment's a mess. Others had more troublesome implications: She's too fat; she and her friends all smoke; she doesn't stick with her medical regimen. These complaints have a certain familiarity. It's unlikely that your daughter just began doing the things that drive you to distraction. She knows you disapprove of what she's doing—you've probably been telling her so for years. What you say and how she responds are part of a drama you've been enacting since her adolescence, when she began to assert her right to make decisions for herself.

Purple hair, black lipstick, green nails—these are typical expressions of adolescent self-assertion. And, although deep down parents know that it may not be productive, few feel guilty when they chastise an adolescent who shows up for dinner with a nose ring or when they comment as she leaves for a dance wearing combat boots. Then suddenly she's no longer an adolescent—although her behavior may be the same—and your old response feels even more futile. Mothers sense that something different is required of them, but they're not quite sure what.

Missy L., whose oldest daughter, Marcia, is a twenty-year-old college junior, finds herself in the middle of the transition. "I feel uncomfortable talking about the things that still bother me, with her hair being one of the little things that makes me crazy. It's down to here, and in her face, and she's so pretty, and you can't find her in there. I've almost come to the point where I don't say anything, or if I do, I tease about it. But she's so defensive about it, probably because I've said so much."

"Like what?" we asked.

"Like 'I'll pay for you to get your hair cut.' Her dad says, 'Five dollars an inch,' I mean he'll go further than I will. But she won't do it. She'll put up a wall with us very fast. In high school, where there were things like hair, or boyfriends, or drinking—the little things that lots of people go through—we got a lot of door slamming and more anger than I was comfortable with, but this is something new." Missy sees that Marcia is changing—the wall is an attempt to distance herself rather than react as she did as an adolescent. But Missy hasn't figured out yet how she should act in response. "Adult relationships—

I'm just learning about them, and they're hard. Of course, she's not quite an adult yet. It's tricky."

Virginia M.'s daughter, Ginny, is three years older than Marcia L., and Virginia has had a few more years to get used to Ginny's emerging adulthood. "We have certainly had fights, I mean, mothers and daughters do. I could say to her, 'Your bangs are too long—I think your bangs are too long.' And we could have a morning or a daylong tension about that sort of thing. But I think when a child becomes a certain age, you don't say those things anymore." Virginia remembers what it feels like to be nagged. "My mother was still telling me that I needed to tend to my eyebrows when I was thirty years old. I remember my mother peeking behind my canisters and cleaning up, and I had just done it two days before. You really cannot do that." Does Virginia practice what she preaches? "I try to," she says with a laugh.

Even when the consequences aren't serious, mothers of adult daughters know that nagging is fruitless. Diane Asselin produces educational television programs. She's an attractive, straightforward midwesterner. She characterizes the relationship with her daughter Michele, twenty-three, as rich and open. Diane is proud of the purposeful way Michele is pursuing a career as a still photographer. "I see she has the ability to get things done, and if you discover that about your kid, it's a big relief," Diane says. "I have a lot of confidence in her, but I still do those things. I still say, 'Have you thought about this? Does your bra show when you do the job? Do you wear that crummy T-shirt?' She has this way of leveling it out. The other day she had on a white bra and a stripy black T-shirt, and she was just going to the airport, and I said, 'God, why are your straps showing like that? Would you ever wear anything like that when you went to work?' And she said, 'Well, I guess if you have to ask that, then I'm a total loss, and there's not very much you can do about it anyway.' So she's cool enough about me that she doesn't have to make an issue of it. I bet she does wear terrible things to work!"

Nine out of ten mothers we spoke to would not have reported this story with Diane's good humor. We asked why she thinks she can be critical of Michele without making her angry. She said, "It's because of her self-esteem in terms of her father and me. She's gotten so much praise in her life that you've got permission to say something about her dumb T-shirt." She laughed. "So it isn't a big deal, but does she love hearing it? Of course not."

Some mothers think that if they don't actually say anything, they can't be accused of nagging. One mother confessed to having perfected an "icy look that can penetrate steel." Another said, "I cringe, but I don't say a word." Judith R. told us she does not permit her twenty-seven-year-old daughter, Kim, to smoke when she comes home for a visit. "I'm very disapproving of the fact that she smokes, and I don't have to say anything for that to come out. When she disappears every twenty minutes because she has to have a cigarette, I know why she's going, and it's annoying to me. I can barely look at her when she comes back into the room." One woman told us she never criticizes her daughter's smoking directly but does occasionally reach into her daughter's pocketbook to throw away her cigarettes.

Other mothers think they can take the sting out of criticism by camouflaging it. Theirs is the cheery "Let's both pretend that nothing's wrong" mode. Lois A.'s thirty-four-year-old daughter, Karen, lives halfway across the continent from her parents. She is an only child whom they worry about constantly. Will she get married? Will she lose fifteen pounds? Why doesn't she talk more about what's going on in her life? Lois says, "I try not to be critical of her anymore, I try not to ask her about her weight, I try not to ask her about her social life. I'm very broad about it, I'll say, 'Oh, what did you do last weekend?' not 'Who were you with? Where did you go?' I'm just very careful about those things, because I really don't want to alienate her, and I can feel her being very defensive if I start to talk about certain things."

Weight is one of the things that makes Karen defensive. "The last time we were in Boston, she saw a rowing machine that she liked, and we offered to buy it for her for her birthday. She said, 'No, I'll buy it myself,' but we sent her a check anyway. Or like last night when we were talking and I said, 'Oh, have you been bicycling?' That's the way I will ask. I'm not going to say to her, 'Are you working on the weight?' I will say, 'Have you gone bicycling this summer?' " Lois's intentions are good, but since these issues have caused strain for years, her evasions are probably quite transparent in Karen's eyes. Daughters are quite capable of filling in the blanks and hearing the nagging even if it isn't overt.

Most mothers nag. Most hate the fact that they nag, but are unable to stop. Three women we spoke to were particularly articulate about the circumstances that provoke their impulse to nag, their daughter's negative response to their criticism, and their inability to overlook the behavior that they find so troublesome. All three said that there are days when they forget about the problem and days when they can think of nothing else. All three would like to find a different way to communicate their concerns.

Rationalizing the Impulse to Nag

From the moment her thirty-year-old daughter, Leslie, bought herself a one-bedroom condo half a mile from where Cynthia G. lives, Cynthia has been helping Leslie fix it up. They've shopped for furniture together and sorted through family china and silverware to equip her kitchen. Leslie has been delighted to take Cynthia up on her offer to buy a new kitchen table and chairs. Nonetheless, over a year after Leslie moved in, the apartment looks to Cynthia as if Leslie is still "camping out." Cynthia has been frustrated because although she believes Leslie isn't happy about the way the apartment looks, she hasn't done anything about it either. From time to time Cynthia has commented on the books piled on the floor, the lack of blinds, and the absence of towel racks. In desperation, Cynthia bought bookshelves, window shades, and hired someone to fix up the bathroom and kitchen. "These were things I felt compelled to do," says Cynthia. "Partly for reasons of aesthetics, partly for safety. But all of it adds up to safety and order and a place you call home and a nest. I guess I wanted her to feel she had a place that was comfortable, where she could get her thoughts together."

Cynthia says that this sense of a nest has been passed down from her own mother. "My mother's chief involvement in life is her nest, yes, I would say so. I don't emulate her style except in the concept of having things somewhat orderly. Things put away, drawers not jammed, give me a sense of calm as opposed to anxiety. If I open up a drawer and it's very full, I get a vague wave of anxiety which translates into a concept of losing control, not knowing where things are.

"The concept of nest became integrated with my own sense of my life so I decided it must also have a place central to Leslie's sense of who she is. But I don't know that that is so. It may be that Leslie will never dwell on her apartment, and it's only my urgency that feels that if her apartment is in order it will help the rest of her life seem more managed. And I do believe she understands that these are efforts to help that I need to make.

"I assume she has thoughts about this apartment that we have not discussed. Maybe it's difficult for her to fix it up because maybe she wants to think about getting married and not living there—maybe living there means something isolated and singular. Those are issues we have not talked about."

Cynthia told us the apartment issue has come to a head in what she characterized as "the great vacuum cleaner war." "I couldn't stand the fact," she explained, "that when I came to visit her, there were puffs of dust all over the place. The vacuum cleaner had been broken for six months, and we began the dance about the vacuum cleaner. Me: 'You should get it fixed.' Leslie: 'Yes, Mom.' Me: 'You'll feel so much better when it works again and you can clean up these floors.' Leslie: 'Yes, Mom.' At one point I gave her the name of a company that would pick it up and fix it, and she still didn't do anything about it. Months later, after much joking, and not so subtle nagging, she finally admitted that the vacuum cleaner needed to be fixed, and we agreed that I would get it fixed."

Cynthia has vowed that the vacuum cleaner war will be her last, even though she knows it will be hard to keep her word. "On the one hand, it is her life, and she gets to organize it; on the other hand, when I see her apartment in chaos, I get so anxious that I have to jump in." We mentioned that several women we interviewed said they believed that by the time their daughters were thirty, it was no longer appropriate to tell them what they should do or say. Cynthia disagreed. "Maybe it's because she lives so near to me, and our daily interaction brings up issues that make me think I'm not done yet. I keep thinking in terms of teaching her more about how to run her life." Aware that she is being intrusive, aware that her need to be so comes from her own anxiety, aware that her daughter should be in control of her own life, Cynthia nonetheless repeats her intrusive behavior and falls back on the rationalization that she's doing it for her daughter's own good.

Biting Your Tongue

Brenda W. never tells twenty-eight-year-old Jennifer what bothers her, but she knows that her daughter senses her disapproval. Brenda told us that Jennifer has been "enormously overweight" since she was an adolescent. Brenda tried to help her develop a strategy for sticking to a diet, and it made Jennifer "bananas." Brenda's therapist said, "Let it rest. You're her mother, you can help her fifteen other ways, but you cannot do this one head on." That may have been good advice as far as it goes, but in the experience of Brenda and other women we spoke to, it doesn't go far enough. The problem persists—not saying anything adds to Brenda's frustration without resolving any of her anguish. Much of the time Brenda says she's able to "be totally neutral" about Jennifer's obesity; at other times she's tormented. "I took her and her cousin out to dinner the other night, and she orders a hot turkey sandwich with mashed potatoes and gravy, and then she had apple pie with ice cream. It just made my heart sink."

Brenda had a weight problem herself as an adolescent, so she has some understanding of her daughter's situation. She says, "When I was in high school I was the biggest girl in the class, I looked like the teacher. By the time I was a sophomore in college I weighed over a hundred and fifty pounds. But at the beginning of my junior year I stopped eating and the weight fell away."

Because there's a history of high blood pressure and diabetes in her family, Brenda worries about the long-term effect on Jennifer's health. She's also troubled about the social stigma attached to being overweight. Jennifer is between jobs right now, and Brenda thinks her appearance is a disadvantage in the job market. "You get rejected time and time again. People can't see past it, particularly in our society.

"I think it would change her life in terms of her own self-confidence if she could deal with it. What I know about myself, when I dropped all that weight," Brenda says, "was that I couldn't do it until I felt good about myself. I had to have some confidence—it's such a chicken and egg game, but I had to feel worthy to deal with it, and that is a concept that I might be able to share with Jennifer at some point, but that's as close as I can get to the subject."

Brenda would feel better if she could talk more frankly to Jennifer, if only to acknowledge the subject that hovers like a black cloud over their entire relationship. It does not lessen tension to refrain from mentioning the thing that matters so much.

Vacillating Between Speaking Out and Remaining Silent

Roberta S. is also tormented by the fact that she has a daughter with a serious weight problem. Over the years Roberta has alternated between nagging Lucy, who is now twenty-seven, and saying nothing. From time to time she has made attempts to talk dispassionately about the social ramifications of obesity. Currently she's back to the silent mode, which, she ruefully admits, does nothing to alleviate the distress she feels.

We met with Roberta in the Boston boardroom of the large government agency she heads. She exuded an air of cheerful no-nonsense competence. She had cleared exactly one hour for our interview, and she ticked off the considerable accomplishments of her entire family almost matter-of-factly. However, as she told us of her inability to resolve her anxiety about her youngest daughter Lucy, her voice softened, and her eyes filmed over. Roberta described Lucy as a "dark-haired, fair-skinned, classic Irish beauty. Just a beauty. And I think that was very important to me, because I saw the payoff for that in our world. I saw the homage paid to that, how much easier so many things were if you had that. I thought, she's been given this blessing. And I didn't focus on how much of a burden it could be. And it was an enormous burden for her. Being so pretty. She got unwelcome attention from sleazy men on the street. Perpetually. She thought that's why people liked her, and that's not how she wanted to be liked. And she had so much personality and intelligence, and she was afraid that was being shortchanged by how she looked. So she began to abuse how she looked, and she gained a lot of weight.

"And to this day she's overweight. Ferociously. And I think she holds on to it as an insulation between herself and being perceived for her exterior self rather than who she really is. She's very overweight. We're talking like about seventy or eighty pounds and she's tall to begin with, so she looks large, lumpy, and ungainly. She is what anyone would call 'fat.' And it's very hard for me to use that word. It was very painful for me that she did that to herself. And refuses to fix it, although I think she could. And obviously, it's become an issue between us. I tried to do all the intelligent things to not make it an issue, and probably made every mistake in the book, while trying not to."

In retrospect, Roberta thinks that nagging was particularly ineffective. "Half the time I think the mistake was in raising the issue at all with her. It is something a person needs to do for herself. You live in your own body, you control your own body, nobody else can control it for you. So by raising the issue, it became an obstacle. Would I not love her if she were fat? That gave her all the excuses to back away from the issue because I was pressing it. I mean, as soon as my mother wanted me to do something, I didn't want to do it. It was an automatic, visceral response. Sometimes when I wanted to do something, I would pray that my mother wouldn't say 'do it,' so that I wouldn't lose the desire. And so obviously, sometimes I think the mistake was on that side. On alternate days, I think I should have *insisted* that she do something. Been much more forceful and directive."

After Lucy graduated from college with honors, she moved to Houston, where she knew no one. She got a job at NASA, at a time when the agency was cutting back, and is now getting her Ph.D. in geology. Roberta said that when she has suggested to Lucy that, since things are going well for her, maybe she would like to tackle her weight problem, Lucy says, "It's not a problem to me. I'm a happy person. I have a good life. I am the right person in the right place doing the right things." And Roberta thinks, "How can I possibly say, 'Hey, you'd be a whole lot happier if you weren't as fat'?"

To Roberta's knowledge, Lucy has not had any serious relationships with men. "She's very sociable, she has lots of friends. But I don't think she's had the kind of love life that I would have wished her to have. And it's difficult to bring up the subject because it touches on the issue between us of how she treats her body, and all the implications of that. But in my own direct way, I have said, 'Lucy, you're limiting the people with whom you can have close relationships, because people can't help having impressions about your body. And instead of being a beautiful woman, you've chosen to be a not-beautiful woman. And people are gonna respond to that.' "

Lucy's weight affects the whole family. Roberta told us that her husband also has trouble talking about it. "If the issue is raised," she said, "he gets mildly defensive about her. You know, 'That's just how she is. That's her body. Society is wrong. They shouldn't be valuing skinniness. My mother wasn't skinny. She's that kind of woman, and why can't the world accept it? She shouldn't have to change.' " For both of them, Roberta believes, "that leads to the underlying issue, which is the extent to which your children achieve the perfection that you desire for them. And the issues are naturally going to arise over the gap between one's standards and their performance. And I think as I get older it gets easier to deal with the gaps and the disappointments."

Roberta says her current mode is "to back off. Most days, I don't worry about it. Most days I can enjoy her presence and enjoy her in spite of it. And some days I am deeply troubled by it. Usually, since we see each other irregularly and don't spend day after day together, the hardest time is when we're first together again, and it hits me. And she sees it hit me. I don't say anything, but we don't have to say anything. I've always known what my children were thinking, and I'd be very surprised if they didn't know what I was thinking most of the time. Conversation can be deeply rich even when unspoken, and no matter how hard one works at keeping things hidden, they don't stay hidden."

Roberta tries not to criticize her daughter; she wants to accept the fact that the problem is Lucy's, not hers. "She always leads me to believe that when she's ready, she will take care of this problem. She's so happy now, and doing so well in grad school, that I have this hope that she's finally ready, she's gonna take care of it. And, in any case, I've decided that she's twenty-seven, and I have to be out of this issue.

"Now that she feels comfortable," Roberta counsels herself, "it would be a particularly cruel time to remind her to lose weight. I'm trying to concentrate on the joy that she's feeling. However, I want her to be as happy as she can conceivably be. So anything that I think mitigates against that is painful. I can't accept it."

Why—if *not* nagging seems like a step in the right direction—does tension over these issues persist? Dr. Phoebe Kazdin Schnitzer, a clinical psychologist at the Judge Baker Children's Center in Boston, practices, supervises, and teaches family therapy. She is also the mother of a son and a daughter in their twenties. Dr. Schnitzer believes that nagging and stifling the urge to nag are two sides of the same coin. A mother gains little when she suppresses her impulse to speak. "The attitude that a woman should just keep her mouth shut, that she should 'stop nagging already,' needs to be scrutinized. It's a commonly held view that mothers cause trouble by being too critical, so that the solution becomes—just avoid criticizing and things will get better. A mother says to herself, 'My daughter's behavior infuriates me, but if I want our relationship to improve, I really have to keep quiet.'"

But what is nagging? And what makes us do it? Dr. Schnitzer argues that nagging is "a symptom of a stifled voice, of a woman who says too little. It's a symptom of a mother who has never sat down with her daughter and said, straightforwardly, 'Look, once and for all I want you to know how I feel about these things, because I don't think I've adequately expressed what it means to me to see the hair, the clothes, the weight, et cetera.' Instead of giving less voice to these issues, *more* voice has to be given, but *in a different way*." That's why biting your tongue and all those other half measures that mothers adopt to keep themselves in check—the staccato, the stutter of criticisms—don't help.

"Silence isn't enough," says Dr. Schnitzer. "I don't believe in biting your tongue. I believe in just the opposite. If you can find a time when the two of you can agree to talk, you can say to your daughter, 'I feel an obligation to tell you exactly what I think about this. I don't expect you to act on what I have to say, or even like it, but I hope you can listen to me. And I also hope that you can help me understand what this means to *you*.' Then if you have fears, you express them; if you're uneasy about her behavior reflecting on you in some way, you acknowledge it; if you're concerned about how the rest of the world sees her—whatever the issues—you try to be honest about them.

"It's a kind of honesty that's hard to muster. But the only thing that will clear the air is more communication rather than less. Learning to express your opinions and to share your experiences in a different way, being able to say 'This is who I am, this is how I feel, this is what I want to communicate' gives your daughter a different model to follow. When you speak to her candidly and with respect, she may be more inclined to respond in the same fashion. You move closer to the possibility of having a mutually respectful dialogue."

From Susan's journal, August 17, 1995

Sarah and I have a new issue brewing—what to do about furniture for her yet-to-be-found New York apartment. First off, she said she wants to keep the two chairs I gave her for Boston—the two with the stuffing hanging out that her cats have clawed to death. I remarked to her that the cats had ruined those pieces, and she said, "Well, you said you didn't want them back." I said, "Yes, but I didn't realize they'd be ruined." I said, "Well, maybe you want to drape some sheets over them to make them more presentable." She got huffy. "Well, Mom, that's what happens when you have cats." The presumption being that she'll always live with wrecked furniture.

I told her that I would pay for the new stuff she needs, and that we should try to find sofas and chairs that her cats can't destroy, but that it would help if she would keep their nails clipped. By this time she was quite short with me—we should buy cheap furniture so she doesn't have to worry about them hurting expensive stuff. I said I had no intention of buying expensive items, just durable but nice pieces. I said, "Let's not have a fight, let's compromise. I'll buy you inexpensive rattan that they won't be tempted to destroy, but you keep their nails short, okay?"

I realized that with her coming back to New York—to my backyard as it were—it does matter to me that she keep a nice apartment. Why? In case my friends happen to visit? Perhaps. I also think anything less than a fairly well-kept place will offend my aesthetic. And yet I know she's not an extension of me. So I will try to submerge my feelings and remember the mantra, it's her life.

August 30, 1995

Tonight Sarah called from Boston in the middle of cleaning out her apartment. She asked me again if I thought she should cart the two chairs to New York. I said, "The chairs are a mess. I would chuck them, I wouldn't want to live with them. But that's me, not you. If you don't care, then bring them." I was conscious of not feeling guilty about what I was saying. In fact, I was conscious of saying what I actually meant rather than a version of what I meant, and her tone of her response suggested that my clarity helped. She said, "So maybe I won't bring them." I felt it was a good conversation, not because she agreed with me, but because it didn't escalate emotionally.

Overcoming the Need to Nag

You can take the first step toward a mutually respectful dialogue no matter how big or small the area of contention has been and no matter how volatile your discourse with your daughter has been in the past. Leah P., a fifty-five-year-old film editor, confesses to a history of nagging and tongue biting that she hopes is now behind her. For years Leah and her twenty-eight-year-old daughter, Joan, have clashed over issues of taste. Leah is a tall, well-dressed woman with a striking mane of perfectly groomed white hair. "Joan knows that style matters a lot to me, and she shares that interest," Leah told us. "She's certainly not indifferent to the way she looks. But she's had some trouble finding a style that's right for her and not a copy of mine. And I haven't helped. I've probably been all too free with advice about what she should wear, how she should fix up her apartment. And she's been all too dependent on my advice. Then there are times that she'll ask me what I think and get mad if I offer an opinion. I've come to see that she's trying to find her own look. She needs to do it, and I need to let her.

"Now her hair has always been an issue," Leah says. "For years she wore it hanging down to her waist, usually in her face, and I would suggest how great she'd look with short hair. About two years ago I stopped carrying on about it, and last summer she had it all cut off. Do I see a cause and effect? Of course. I also think she's matured a lot and getting more confidence in her own sense of style.

"So it was with some trepidation," says Leah, "that I broached the subject of hair recently. She got a terrific haircut—even shorter than before—and it looks fabulous. She's got a great face, great bones, and it really shows her off. But, in my opinion, she vitiated the effect by taking her bangs and plastering them down on her forehead. And it's a subtle thing, but by doing that she accentuates the narrowness of her features. Whereas when the bangs are swept back, it lifts her whole face.

"Is this the end of the world? No. But I hoped I could mention it to her and maybe, just maybe, she could hear me out. So we were having dinner together, and I said, 'Joan, I'd like to say something about your hair.' She cut me off. 'I'm not interested in what you think. I love my new hairstyle.' I felt myself getting frustrated and angry, and then I stopped and thought, I don't want this conversation to play out the way these conversations have played out in the past. So I said, 'How come it's all right for you to tell me that my lipstick is too dark, and I think about it and decide that maybe you're right, but it's not all right for me to say something to you, which you don't have to accept? You can accept or reject what I have to say. I would just like you to hear me.' And she said, not exactly cheerfully, but I sensed really trying to remain open, 'Okay, what *do* you think about my hair?' I believe neither of us wanted this to turn into something unpleasant. So I said my thing about your beautiful face, bangs off the beautiful forehead, and so on. She listened and she said, 'Thank you, mom. I hear you. I'm wearing my hair exactly the way the stylist did it. And I really like it the way it is.' And I said, 'Okay,' and that was that."

This is a small matter but a huge step for both mother and daughter. "I feel that something important and different happened," says Leah. "This was a dialogue. We never used to have dialogues, we had shouting matches. To be able to talk about different viewpoints without either of us feeling violated or trashed was something very new. I'm sure she still felt threatened, at least at first. But both of us were working to try and understand each other.

"We both talked rationally, clearly, and respectfully to each other. There was a tacit acceptance of the fact that we disagree," says Leah. "And there was a kind of closure. I think I'll never bring up the matter of her hair again."

From Marilyn's journal, August 30, 1995

Why is procrastination my issue with Kate? Is it because I know I'm vulnerable to it myself, and it's particularly exasperating to see something you don't like about yourself mirrored in your child? By any standard except my probably impossible ones, Kate's a total success. She did well in college. She's done a terrific job teaching, with little training or resources behind her. She takes care of her own life. She gets most of her daily decisions done with maybe a little more sturm and drang than necessary, but she's not paralyzed by them. She's put together a wonderful circle of friends.

So she procrastinates. So what? She never quite finishes the list of things she sets out to accomplish. She waits until the last possible minute to do things, so she sometimes doesn't do them the way she would like to. Why do I still care about that? Of course, I know that she cares too, so it isn't just my problem. And maybe I do play some part in perpetuating her behavior—it's one of the ways we stay connected. She'll mention in a conversation that she hasn't done something, or that she needs to do something or whatever. And I pick up on it. I get anxious. She picks up on my anxiety and we're off and running. There are better ways of being connected!

For example, last night on the phone, she announced that she'd finally finished writing a bunch of letters to her students from last year. Something she's been meaning to do since the beginning of the summer. Rather than indicate any of my investment in her overcoming procrastination, I simply said, "That must make you feel good."

September 19, 1995

Kate mentioned to her father and me last week that she was concerned about her boyfriend. He dropped out of college four years ago, and now after three years in the navy and another year working, he was returning to school. He was having trouble getting down to work, he was afraid of recapitulating his previous underachievement, and Kate was worried for him.

"You know, Mom, I feel just like you used to be with me. Wanting to tell someone to get down to work, not to procrastinate, to get started on a paper ahead of time, and all that stuff. It's really tricky." She laughed. So did I. And then I said, "Well, the only thing I have to offer is that it usually doesn't do much good." And we laughed again.

So she called today and mentioned that over the weekend he had taken hold of himself, rewritten a paper, and done some reading ahead for another course.

What a breakthrough! That she would tell us something so intimate, and that she could empathize with and laugh at my earlier behavior. I've been elated all day.

What if the matter is more substantial than hair? Or time management? What can you say if, for example, your daughter has an eating disorder, a weight problem, or a history of failing to take her medication for a chronic illness? "If I were a woman who's still in torment about something she thinks is a serious concern, I would feel as a parent an obligation to revisit the subject from time to time," says Dr. Schnitzer. "I would say to my daughter something like this, 'Look you're going to do what you want, but we haven't talked about this in a long time, and I want you to know that it still concerns me.' Maybe you can have a dialogue about it and maybe not, but at least you've fulfilled your obligation as a parent to let her know your concerns. I would hope that a thoughtful message like this would eliminate some tension and also eliminate your need to give or withhold the nonverbal communication that has undoubtedly filled the air.

However, you have to remember that while you may improve the nature of your relationship with her and the quality of the dialogue between you, *her behavior may or may not change.*"

Dr. Kathy Weingarten makes an important observation. "Often it is not the superficial manifestation of a problem—the daughter's weight, her messy apartment, her hair—that really 'nags' at the mother. It's the significant and profound issues beneath the surface. She may pick up cues about them from her daughter, or she may very well have very good ideas herself. So the mother may want to find a way to engage in a dialogue about those underlying issues." Cynthia G. mentioned in passing that she and her daughter have not discussed Leslie's apartment in the context of her daughter's possible anxiety about being nearly thirty years old and unmarried. Cynthia suspects that Leslie may fear that the apartment is a powerful symbol of her single status and all that means in our society. Does Leslie have any thoughts about that? Is there an underlying issue *she's* avoided talking about that would help her mother understand her reluctance to take full responsibility for her apartment? If Cynthia can pitch their conversation at this more consequential level, perhaps these women can move from a pattern of nagging and resistance toward a true dialogue.

Such conversations are not undertaken lightly. The fact that certain issues have been avoided is testimony to their potency. Very often they touch on the core of a daughter's sense of who she is. Roberta S. has approached some of the underlying issues that concern her about her daughter's weight by talking about the social implications of obesity for women in our culture. But she has not really elicited Lucy's explanation of what value being overweight has in her life. She might say, "Help me to understand. You've said you're happy now. But I have trouble understanding that. Our culture puts such a premium on being an attractive woman, and you have chosen to be a not-beautiful woman, when in fact you know you could be a beautiful woman. Can you talk to me about that?" Or she might approach the subject by revisiting what she thinks were the origins of Lucy's problem. "I imagine this is a very complicated issue for you. But I have some thoughts about how it all got started. I wonder if you used weight initially to fend off unwanted attention from men. Because when you were younger you may not have had many other resources to protect yourself. Maybe being fat is no longer an appropriate way to deal with that. Is this something we can talk about?" If you undertake such a conversation, you must keep in mind that you are speaking not to get a result—her behavior may very well not change—but to strengthen the nature of the dialogue between you. You replace nagging with a discourse based on honesty, clarity, and the willingness to hear each other out.

Addressing Cultural Assumptions About Women

When we reexamined all the stories of women who told us—with deep shame or almost offhand—that they caught themselves nagging their daughters, it turned out that almost all the cases had to do with their dissatisfaction with some aspect of their daughters' self-presentation to the world. One woman said, "About physical appearance—weight, eating, biting nails, what you wear on a date or to the office—I don't think I'm any different from other mothers, I rag them because physical appearance is so important in our culture for women that we all are critical of our daughters in ways we don't even understand. Not of our sons. Because of our culture."

If that is so, then the explanation that nagging stems from not saying enough rather than saying too little has even more resonance. We may not be clear in our own minds about whether we should tell our daughters that they should be whoever they want to be or whether we should encourage them to conform to what society wants of a woman. In 1995 Americans spent more than $6 billion on skin care products and another $8 billion on cosmetics. Women between the ages of twenty-five and fifty-four were the biggest spenders. What are the implications of that?

Women in our culture have been conditioned to believe that they must aspire to a certain kind of beauty in order to attract men. The image relentlessly peddled by the fashion, cosmetics, and diet industries is that of a tall, thin, and eternally youthful female, an ideal that most women torment themselves trying to emulate.

There is nothing wrong with wanting to look attractive. If a woman wants to wear cosmetics, if she cares about fashion, if she watches her weight, and she's doing those things for herself, that's fine. But if she needs to beautify herself in order to shore up a beleaguered identity, if she needs to beautify herself in order to get ahead in the world, then her pursuit of beauty is destructive.

It is true that as a woman's intelligence and competitive spirit are allowed more free reign, as the concept of natural beauty is given more credence, as non-European fashion models present challenges to the fantasy that there is only one kind of female beauty, the notion that a woman should aspire to a single ideal of what is attractive is breaking down. But how we look still matters. And in our society it matters more for women. That's where the problem lies. Mothers may have trouble speaking clearly about the subject because, while they may resent the tyranny of beauty as an ideal, they don't want their daughters to be penalized if they choose not to comply with it.

Maria W.'s daughter, Shannon, has been quite resolute in rejecting a standard of appearance that our mainstream culture has endorsed. Shannon, twenty-three, is an aspiring filmmaker. She and her friends have adopted a definition of beauty that is far different from that of her mother or the community in which they live. Maria has moved through successive stages of "giving advice, nagging, biting my tongue, and then finally realizing that I truly no longer cared. I mean, we went through the 'Don't shave your hair within a quarter of an inch of your scalp and dye it blonde.' 'Don't get a tattoo, you will want it off.' 'Don't draw pictures on your forehead. Because the police will pick you up at night.' And they picked her up at night, and I said, 'See, I told you.' And of course she replied, 'Oh the oppressive brute police in our society . . .'

"Now her hair is dyed black," Maria told us. "It looks great. I've said my piece, and I don't comment on that stuff anymore. I mean my kid is not a middle-class kid, she's a middle-class manqué kid. And that makes her a member of the Generation X culture. So the things I'm working on now are like—How do you get them to go to the dentist or get car insurance? These are kids who don't want a Social Security card because they don't want to belong to the system.

"Last summer we went to my family reunion, and she showed up in the little frilly too-tight, too-short dress with the big clunky boots. And everyone else looked as if they'd stepped out of the J. Crew catalogue. So, of course, they all laughed at her. And she knows that they're going to do that. But she does it anyway. And you've got to stop talking to her about it.

"So I said to myself, 'If she's gotta do this, then just let it go. Just let it go. You don't really care what they think of you. And if they think less of you because of what she's like, then, too bad.'

"Of course this is the Republican side of my family. If I take her to the other side of the family, they say, 'Oh, has she always been stylish like that?' "

It's taken more than a decade of painful confrontations for Maria to see her daughter's style with detachment and humor. Along the way, she has rejected nagging as useless. She has explained clearly to Shannon what she perceives the consequences of Shannon's behavior are and why she has been concerned about them. She has sustained a dialogue rather than give in to the impulse to rage at the girl and drive her away forever. She has learned that it means much more to her to maintain their relationship than try to impose on her daughter an ideal of attractiveness that is contrary to Shannon's sense of who she is.

"This has gone on so long," says Maria, "that when I look at her and see these strange clothes, these tattoos, this dyed hair, I have trained myself to really not see it. I see this person who is very beautiful, with a beautiful smile, who is very wise and kindly and a thoughtful human being. So I have to say, 'I'm going to love you no matter what.' "

Your Daughter's Love Life

When our daughters were adolescents, our primary concern about their love life was that they not be led into sexual experiences that they were not ready for. Of course, if a daughter was dating a nice young man, we felt good about her judgment; if he was less than ideal from our perspective, we could charitably assume that she would tire of him soon enough. We were quite comfortable looking at all her romances as experimental relationships that she would enter into and then probably drop. But when a daughter becomes a young adult, we tend to evaluate every boyfriend as her potential lifelong partner.

It is true that today society no longer defines a woman solely in terms of her relationship to a man. Women are increasingly identified as much by what they do as by whether or not they're married. The rising divorce rate suggests that their work may be more of a constant in their lives than their husbands are. Many of the moral imperatives to get married have weakened: Premarital sex is often taken for granted; out of wedlock birth has lost much of its stigma; more men and women are living openly as homosexuals.

Our expectations for our daughters reflect these changes. Most of us think it's good for young women to postpone marriage until they have formed a strong sense of self. We recognize the inevitability—and many of us see the desirability—of premarital sexual experience. We want our daughters to be able to support themselves. We're sensitive to the fact that they may not marry, and we try not to burden them with pejorative comments about single women. If they're gay, we acknowledge it.

Nonetheless, one of our most fervent wishes is that, in good time, our daughters find loving, supportive, permanent partners. We recognize that a single woman still has a tougher time in life; women still take on social status from being married and from the men they marry. We also don't want our daughters to be lonely, and we believe that life is enriched by sharing it with a partner.

Of all the choices our daughters make, their choice of partner is the one we mothers anguish most about. When we see our daughters happily married or in a serious relationship with someone we like, we feel that we can relax a bit, that our major job is done.

Reflections on Marriage

Nancy Washington, a college administrator and mother of Linda, a thirty-two-year-old pulmonary specialist, and Laura, a twenty-eight-year-old financial adviser, is very proud of her daughters' achievements. She also says, "I very much wanted them to get married. More than some of my friends. Some of my friends are much more relaxed about it. But I told just about everyone, 'I want my daughters to get married.' I've enjoyed my marriage most of the time, and I wanted them to have that experience. It was almost a fixation with me.

"My husband and I were at a party one time in Pittsburgh, and we met a woman who worked in New York as a nurse. And my husband was talking to her about Linda—I think Linda was still doing her residency—and so on. And when this woman saw me, she said, 'Oh, you must be so proud of your daughter.' And I said, 'Yes, but I'd like her to get married.' So it turns out, it was just a coincidence, my daughter was in the operating room the next week, and this woman came in, she was the nurse and she realized who Linda was. And she said, 'Oh, I met your mother in Pittsburgh last week, and she wants you to get married!' "

Nancy laughed while telling us this story as if to underline her embarrassment that as a contemporary professional woman she was so focused on her daughter's marrying. Belda Lindenbaum, mother of five including Vicki, who works for a management consulting firm, was more forceful in expressing her relief when Vicki got married at twenty-six. Of all the women we interviewed, Belda has preserved the purest, almost Jane Austen-like perception of the cruelties of the marriage market. "The dating scene is so awful, it's like fruit, you're ripe one day and overripe the next, and I hate it." Belda says she's been sensitized to this by her sons. "They date girls for months and then leave them. It's miserable out there. The boys say it's not easy to find the right girl. But they have a longer shelf life and girls don't!"

In our travels around the country, the only place where women consistently reported a strong emphasis on marriage at a fairly early age was in the South. Arlen M. is an attractive fifty-year-old who teaches in a dropout prevention program in a public high school in Charleston, South Carolina. Her older daughter, Martha, twenty-six, is in a serious relationship, and her younger girl, Harper, twenty-three, is engaged. We asked Arlen to talk about the pressure young southern women feel to marry. "I think southerners have a more traditional idea of what they think the normal life of a woman should be, and that is being married, being a mother. In addition to that, it's what they see all around them. Our friends are pretty stable. They are active in their church. They are married, they have children, and their family life is important to them. So even without the pressure of the culture they would be missing something if they weren't part of a family."

But even in the South things are changing. "Girls around here are not getting married as young as we did," Arlen told us. "Harper is one of the first in her group." Like most of her friends, Arlen married within weeks of her college graduation. "In hindsight I wish very much

I hadn't done it. And I always told them that I wanted them to work at least a year before they got married. I thought I went from being somebody's daughter to somebody's wife to somebody's mother so fast my head was spinning. I didn't have a clue who I really was and I don't want that for my girls."

The Kind of Man We'd Like Her to Marry

When our mothers said, "I want you to find a man who can make you happy," they meant someone who would earn a good living and take care of us. We're more concerned that our daughters find a man who is supportive emotionally as well as financially. One woman told us, "If I were choosing a partner for my daughters, I would find someone who comes from a happy home." Another said, "I have told her to marry someone who, as best as she could tell, was well loved, especially by his mother." Yet another has said to her daughters, "Make sure the guy is interesting. You're in it for the long haul."

From Marilyn's journal, March 10, 1996

Hugh's 63rd birthday. He's sick again with a stomach virus. I'm putting together our tax information, feeling self-righteous, and at the same time, slightly resentful, because he's lying in bed, reading and watching television. In the best of times the division of labor here is only slightly different—he concentrates on his work, while I work *and* juggle the household responsibilities. I grant that mine is not the have-it-all problem we're wrestling with in this book because, with household help and a flexible work schedule, I've never really been up against it the way yuppie mothers and single mothers are.

When we were starting out, Hugh expected a deference to his wants and needs that I concurred with. I would never do that now. Over the years I've learned to be more assertive, and he's learned to respect that and do more around the house than he used to. In that I don't think we are so different from lots of other households.

But the fact is that our family is somewhat atypical. Because what traditional dads do in traditional families, Mom does in ours.

And I wonder what effect this model has on our girls. They value Hugh's intelligence, his talent, and his commitment to work, and I think they know how important that is in our marriage. But they've grown up in a household where Mother makes the money decisions, does the driving, answers the practical questions. Clearly I love handling so much responsibility, being in charge. Under my laissez-faire demeanor I'm as much of a controller as the best of them. I like to be right. I like to make the lists and the decisions.

I worry about the effect my behavior has on the girls. Both Kate and Kore are confident in their own ability to do those things—well maybe not confident, but they expect to do them. I presume that the men of their generation are less primeval than the boys were when we were young. Nonetheless, will the girls have clashes with men I never had? Will they presume too much? I want, Hugh wants, they want, for them to be assertive, independent, and yet capable of building a relationship. Have we given them mixed messages about how to do it?

Beth Curry, mother of two sons and a daughter, Caroline, twenty-six, told us she was once at a dinner party when the talk turned to the qualities one should look for in a partner. She jotted down on a cocktail napkin some ideas from the group to share with her children, and she has kept the napkin to this day. Beth's list:

sense of adventure (or appreciation of)
kindness
sense of family
patience
sense of humor
generous spirit
likes you the way you are
good to make decisions with
how much do you smile together?
appreciates the sanctity of marriage

Evelyn Tang talked about marriage over the years with her only daughter, Frances. Frances is now thirty, married, and herself the mother of an infant boy. "One wisdom I shared with my daughter since she was a little girl, and I like to share it with other girls. My mother always said to me, 'Don't consider how he is treating you, but consider how he is treating everybody else. Because when he is in love with you or wants you to be his wife, he'll act to please you but that is not a true color. Only when you observe how he treats other people is that the true color.' "

Barbara Weene stressed finding someone with similar values and interests. She told us about an incident ten years ago, when her sixteen-year-old daughter was torn between two boys. "One was handsome with a fast car, and he wanted sex, et cetera. The other guy was the son of a writer, and he was creative—wrote songs and poetry—and she said, 'I feel I can say anything to him, he cares about what I think, he has a lot of respect for me, but he can't kiss.' And I said, 'Well, how important is that? Let me put it to you this way, there are two choices. You can teach the guy who doesn't know how to kiss, how to kiss, if he's your soulmate, or you can go for the other guy who certainly knows how to kiss but doesn't have the soul connection for you. Which one would feel better?' And she said, 'Well, I want to think about that,' and a couple of days later she came in and said, 'I decided I'm going to teach Adam how to kiss.' And then she was in a significant four-year relationship with him."

From Marilyn's journal, April 24, 1996

Kate and I spent a wonderful weekend together at a spa. In the middle of a conversation that she initiated about several of her friends who are getting married, we got to talking about how you know that the man you're dating, are in love with, is in fact the man you want to marry. I pick up from her tone that we're to keep this conversation somewhat general and philosophical, rather than about her specifically, but that's okay. And I also remember that I liked the gist of such a conversation that one of the mothers (Angela A.) reported to us the other day, so I shamelessly copy her. "The most important thing is not the choice of the guy. It's whether or not you're really ready to get married. Where you are in your own head. How sure you are of who you are and what you need from another person. When you've arrived at that place for yourself, then you will make the right choice." Kate said, "Um," but she didn't seem uncomfortable, so I went on. "It seems to me that when you're in a relationship that seems pretty good, you want to ask yourself if it's just pleasant or if it really brings something extra to your life. Are you mutually supportive, or is the work mostly being done by one person? Can you imagine that you'll continue to grow separately and together?" Things like that. Interspersed by more "ums."

I'm really on a roll here. So I push on. "And let's not forget sex. Are you getting what you like? Can you talk about it openly with your partner?" That seemed to be more than she could tolerate, and I must confess it was close to my limit, too. The subject moved on. But I think there was a hint of a new level of intimacy between us.

Says Jewelle Bickford, "The most important thing I have to say about this subject is that even a good marriage can't give you everything in life. I have a close business friend, and my husband has no idea how close I am to him. Nat can't fulfill my needs to talk about trading financial instruments, which is such a large part of my life. So I want my daughters to understand that marriage can't be everything. Your husband can't fill all the roles. When you're young and you think about a good marriage, you think that you'll be everything to each other. You can't be. You need good women friends, other friends. I rely on my women friends enormously, and I want my girls to understand that you have all these relationships, and it doesn't weaken your marriage. It makes it stronger."

Arlen M. told us, "I don't want my girls going into any kind of relationship with their blinders on. Because Martha has had so many boyfriends all along and because she thought each one was the big one, I have said to her several times, ' There is more than one person out there that you could marry and be happy with. I am convinced that I could have married other people than your father and had a good solid marriage,' but she doesn't want to hear that, because she wants this romanticized idea of who her parents are. And the other thing that bothered me about her was that she thought she needed a boyfriend all the time. That bothered me very much. In our society you can't count on having a male hanging around all the time. I wanted her self-sufficient. I didn't want her to need to have a male to complete her identity, so I've really worked on that with her."

Kathy Weingarten's mother gave up a promising career in journalism to raise her two daughters. She urged Kathy to find a man who would think it was important for a woman to be serious about her career, but she assumed it would be Kathy's responsibility to manage family and household. Dr. Weingarten thinks that was good advice for its day, but would frame a different message for women in the future. In her book, *The Mother's Voice,* she rehearses what she could imagine saying to her daughter, who was then in her early teens: "If you are going to be with a man, be with one who will think that your work is as important as his; who will think that family is as important to him as it is to you, and who will work at a job in which his bosses and his peers believe that fathering is as important as mothering and support that belief."

Evelyn Tang, the Pasadena scientist, always assumed that her daughter Frances would marry, but she instilled from the start a sense that women should be able to take care of themselves. "When she was younger I told her, 'Getting married is great, and being single can also be very satisfying. As you pursue more education, your choices of men will be shrinking, not because you don't want them but because they may not want you. However, it's important to develop one's potential instead of thinking you'll settle down here and wait for someone to pick you up.' I said the only thing you can count on is yourself, not your parents, not your spouse, not your children, but standing on your own two feet. So I think I prepared her for singlehood if that turned out to be the case. And then she got married perfectly."

Marrying Across Ethnic or Cultural Lines

Evelyn, who was born in mainland China, married a man she had known since elementary school in Taiwan. Her daughter Frances chose an American of English descent who grew up in Sacramento.

Evelyn and her husband were not troubled by Frances's decision. "There are Chinese fathers of our generation who would make the statement, 'You can never marry a non-Chinese,' and I always felt very puzzled. If you don't like non-Chinese, why don't you go back to China? If you are making your life in this country, you should integrate."

We asked women how important it was to them that their daughter choose someone of the same faith, race, or ethnic group. Most thought that, all things being equal, it's easier to marry within your group. As Marianne Collins, a devout Catholic who works for her archdiocese, said, "It's important to me that they marry someone with a lot of commonality. The more things you have in common, the more compatible you're gonna be."

A small but vocal minority felt that racial and religious differences were too powerful to ignore. Nancy Washington, who, with her husband, is a leader of Pittsburgh's black community, was unprepared for the intensity of conflicting emotions she experienced when her daughter Linda came home from medical school with a white fellow student. "When the girls were growing up, we always said we wanted them to be exposed to everyone and everything. And some of her best friends were not African American, and we said, 'Oh, isn't that wonderful.' And we celebrated different holidays and made quite a to-do about how wonderful it was to live in this diverse world. And then when she brought someone home who was diverse, it was, I suppose, more something that I hadn't thought of than someone I was objecting to. It hadn't occurred to me that this would be the natural outgrowth of the exposure that she had.

"She knew that there were problems. She's a very Afrocentric person, more so than my husband and I are. And she's been at least intellectually very aware of her heritage and had thought a lot about it. And he was very aware of *his* heritage. So it wasn't a matter of here we are both just people coming together; they were both aware of who they were and how different they were. And it wasn't even a matter of liking each other for the difference but of liking each other for the similarities in education and the goals in life, and their differences weren't going to go away." Nancy is very relieved that the relationship broke up, and that Linda is now married to an African American.

Miriam H. hopes she has left nothing to chance. She keeps a kosher home and has given her daughters a strong religious education. It is important to her that they marry Jewish men. "Not only important but essential," she says. Miriam has also told Rachel, twenty-four, and Leah, twenty, that there are additional things to look for: "How is the boy in relation to his family—not who is his family—but how does he see his parents? The moral issue—is he an honest boy? What's his education? What does he want to do? Is he hard working? Does he stay away from drugs?" But she is sometimes worried that they haven't understood her complete message. "If I were to bring up the matter, and I'm very careful and seldom bring it up, they'll say, 'As long as you love someone, that's all that matters.' And that's not all that matters! If they don't marry Jews, I'm not sure it will be the end of the world, but it may be!"

It was striking to us, however, that when faced with the reality of a marriage that crossed ethnic, racial, or religious lines, most of the women focused more on the character of the man their daughter had chosen than on his background. Paula S. told us she is delighted with the man her daughter married last year. "Sure it would have been nice if he were Jewish, but I've learned that the secret is whether this person brings out what's good in your kid and really isn't going to hurt your child." Caitlin C. and her husband raised their children with a strong consciousness of their Irish-American heritage and were brought up short when three of their daughters married men who, though Catholic, are from different ethnic backgrounds. "Peg married a guy whose family is from Cuba; Bobby's family is from Colombia; Nick's mother is Italian and his father is Basque. We have a lot of the Iberian Peninsula in our family now, and this was very foreign to me," says Caitlin. "But I see that family is as important to them as it is to us, and they've brought us other wonderful traditions, different music for holidays, different foods. Nick's family has introduced us to opera, and to a wonderful fish feast on Christmas Eve, and this year we went to Peg's in-laws for a wonderful pig roast on Labor Day."

When a Mother Objects to Her Daughter's Choice

When the women we interviewed told us about their objections to a daughter's choice of partner, their worries centered around the fact that the daughter had found someone who would not allow her to fulfill herself within the relationship. "He's a taker, not a giver," said one mother. "He seemed like a star, and I didn't raise this child to walk two steps behind anybody," said another. "This guy is too needy." "I was afraid she would be an accessory." "He's an angry man, verbally abusive." "He's not as smart as she is." "She lets him dominate her." "When she says, 'But Mom, he's changing,' that just sends up a red flag."

Did they voice their objections to their daughters? And how did the dramas play out? Some women chose not to speak up because they didn't want to seem interfering; others spoke their minds and now berate themselves because they fear their daughters have never completely forgiven them for it. A handful found a formula that worked for them—they said what they believed, and whether or not their daughter acted on their advice, the mother-daughter relationship was strengthened in the process.

"She's an adult, she doesn't want to hear it from me"

Many women suppress their trepidation about their daughter's partner because they cannot put their finger on what bothers them or because, as one woman said, "You don't really want to believe that terrible things can happen to your children." Often they feel uneasy about challenging their daughter's ability to make important decisions for herself. Two women told us painful stories about their internal conflict as they watched a daughter make what they feared would be a destructive choice.

Elana B. is a fifty-six-year-old mother of four. She grew up in the Midwest and moved to Philadelphia after her divorce. She feels close to all her children, particularly her eldest, Myra, thirty-five. But Elana always believed that adult children should be allowed their distance, a philosophy that was tested when Myra announced her engagement almost four years ago to a man whom Elana didn't warm to. After the marriage, Myra and her husband were planning to move across the continent to Portland, Oregon, which only added to Elana's concern.

Elana told us, "I never found him very charming, but I suppose he could be. I just didn't like him, but I didn't know him well enough. Myra introduced me to him very nervously. She said to me, 'What do you think of him?' And when you've just met someone once, you're very loathe to say, 'Well, I found him a strange person.' I think Myra's delaying moving to Portland had very little to do with her reluctance to give up her job and very much to do with her knowing in her heart of hearts that she was making a gigantic mistake.

"The guy's father was a recovered alcoholic. And her fiancé hated his mother, which I took to be a very bad sign, and I think I said this to Myra. Myra kept talking about him in a very defensive way, how bright he was, how he was this and that. Which I found very strange. I think it was important for her to think she had my approval."

After the wedding, things deteriorated very fast. "When she got out there he kept her a near prisoner," said Elana. "Then he was verbally abusive to her—this was after they were married a couple of months—he would tell her he didn't love her anymore. I went out to see her because I was very disturbed by her calls. I couldn't bear what was going on. He would be darling and nice to me, and then he would turn to her and talk to her like he was an abusive parent talking to a child. And I could see her personality deteriorating. I could see her losing ego, losing her ego, it was horrible. I wanted her out of that marriage. And then he began accusing her of making me turn on him, which somehow made him the injured party. It was ludicrous."

By this time, Elana was able to say very forcefully what she thought. "I told her to get out. She said, 'I'm not a quitter.' And I said, 'Myra, I don't know that this should last. Either you have to go into therapy and him too, or if you're unhappy you've got to get out.' She said, 'I don't have any money, what can I do?' And I said, 'I'll give you the money.' But she couldn't bring herself to go. Then two months later when I was in Seattle on business, she called me and said, 'He wants me to leave.' And I said, 'Well, you ought to want to get out!

Just get out! Get out! Take whatever it is that you can't live without and abandon the rest and meet me here! He's dangerous, get the hell out of there.'

"So she came to Seattle, and I arranged to meet her in my hotel. I told the desk to let me know when my daughter arrived, but they didn't. An hour later I went downstairs and there she was sitting just passively—I mean you can imagine, just sitting there passively for one hour—just waiting for me to come, not knowing what to do. She was in shock. She looked like a beaten animal. It was unbelievable. So I took her up to the room. She looked horrible. She wanted a haircut so we went out and got a haircut. And she didn't have a coat and it was cold, so I bought her a coat. I think that was the low point of my life."

Myra moved back East and got a divorce. She's recently begun dating again. She and Elana see a lot of each other. Elana says, "I think she's beginning to understand that this could have happened to anyone, that it doesn't necessarily have to mean that her judgment was poor. He tapped into some insecurities that probably all of us have, and it's only human to behave like that. We still don't necessarily talk things out—it's my northern temperament, my Germanic side, though I'm very emotional. I told her I didn't like Joel, but I didn't tell her until after the disaster—I figured she's an adult, she doesn't want to hear it from me.

"After that incident I decided I would always say my piece. I would always say 'I don't like this' and 'I don't like that.' I'm not going to make a big deal of it. I'm going to say it in a somewhat dispassionate way, go on record that I'm very concerned about whatever it is. It was a growth experience for me, too."

Like Elana, Louise D. picked up signals that her twenty-seven-year-old daughter Julie might be making a disastrous marriage, and she, too, felt strongly that she should not say anything. Within six months of the wedding, Julie revealed to her parents that her husband Scott was a cocaine addict. By the time she finally moved out—a year and a half later—he had been arrested several times and was serving a six-month jail sentence for possession of drugs.

Louise is a dedicated and gifted teacher; she has thought a lot about how to foster independence and a sense of competence in children. Since Julie and her two brothers were adolescents, Louise and her husband Andrew had tried to maintain a policy of laissez-faire. "I recognized especially when they were teenagers that the best thing we could do was to just be there. To recognize that they were not going to live my life for me, they were not too interested in my standards, my interests. We would love each other, we would be there for each other, we wouldn't be afraid to disagree, but the understanding was that we were just sharing information, sharing points of view. Because each of us had our own life to lead."

Louise also told us that she was very conscious of bringing up her children differently from the way she herself had been raised. "My two older sisters and my mother are the kind of women who jump in and take control and make things happen either by spending lots of money or talking people to death. They're skilled in the art of the putdown. And I wanted my kids to feel that I respected them—their right to make their decisions about their life. I didn't want them to be afraid to make a mistake."

Julie had finished college and was working as an accountant in Atlanta, when she first told her parents about Scott. They worried that he seemed unfocused. He had been going to college off and on for several years but still didn't have his degree. "His parents were willing to pay for his car, but not his education, which sent a very strange message to us," said Louise. "I saw my daughter growing in her confidence and ready to take on the world, and I was afraid he was going to drag her down."

Louise also noticed that when Julie came home to make arrangements for the wedding, she seemed tense and angry. "And I later found out it was because she was having mixed feelings about what she was getting into, but at the time I thought, well, maybe she just doesn't like being around my mother and my sister. Or she's pressured because she has to take off from work.

"In any case, I don't feel that I had the right to say to her, this is a mistake. And I honestly felt, if it is a mistake, she'll get out of it. There was also the fact that whatever we said probably wasn't going to mean anything, and that if we harped on it too much it might push her toward him. But when we heard about the drug problem, we said, 'Get out.' At first she wouldn't. She wanted to treat it like an illness and get him help. And it got worse and worse. We made it clear that if she wanted to leave we would support her—pay her moving expenses, give her security for a new apartment, and so on. We said we thought she was in a dangerous situation, not only from his druggy friends but from AIDS, too: So we approached it from that point of view."

We asked Louise if, in light of the outcome, she wished she had spoken out earlier. "No," she said. "Again, I felt it's her life. And now my attitude is, it's done, it's over with. And Julie's grown tremendously. I think she wants to remarry eventually and have a family." Louise believes that the crisis has brought mother and daughter closer together. "As Julie becomes more experienced, she's more willing to see my point of view. We can talk about things and consider them. I guess I've proved myself enough times that I'm not going to come down on her and say, 'I told you so,' or 'That was stupid. What did you do that for?' So I think she trusts me more."

Louise is not second-guessing her role in Julie's drama. Elana is not so sure: Her words convey a belief, or at least a wish, that if she'd spoken out, her daughter might have acted differently. Mothers tend to blame themselves for things that go wrong in the lives of their children, and the higher the stakes the more responsible they feel. They tend to assume that if their words had been different, or more forcefully stated, they could have brought about a more positive outcome for their daughters. Hindsight makes us all even more vulnerable to self-laceration. But neither Louise nor Elana knew that the man her daughter was marrying would turn out to be such a disaster. They had only an intimation of potential trouble. By the time the evidence was clear that these marriages were destructive, neither mother had any trouble speaking out or being directive, and their daughters accepted their advice. The daughters do not hold their mothers responsible in any way for their bad marriages. And in both cases, the mother-daughter bond is, if anything, tighter after the traumatic experience than it was before.

Our children will make mistakes throughout their lives. We cannot prevent that, and we should not hold ourselves responsible. Blaming ourselves when an adult daughter makes a bad choice is inappropriate, unnecessary, and counterproductive. We need to remember that she is living her own life. She made the choice she did because she needed to, for reasons she needs to discover. The most helpful thing we can do is to encourage her to examine the dynamic that compelled her into an inappropriate relationship in the first place.

However, this doesn't mean that we can't say anything if we see what looks like a bad situation in the making. Saying what you believe clearly and respectfully is always the best policy. Elana might have responded more actively to Myra's defensiveness. Louise might have asked Julie why she was so skittish during the weeks before the wedding rather than assuming that she knew the reasons. As Dr. Phoebe Kazdin Schnitzer emphasizes, "A major goal of speaking out is to be true to yourself. Not necessarily to get a result. Nor to convince. Speaking out has to be separated from the success or failure of the daughter's action. You're doing it in order to live up to your definition of responsible parental behavior."

"Once you say it, you can't take it back"

Letty Cottin Pogrebin's thirty-year-old twins, Robin and Abigail, are both happily married to men who Letty and her husband think are terrific. Letty told us that she and her daughters (and her son) live near each other in New York City and are very close. The girls have followed their mother into journalism, and they share her commitment to Jewish family values and to feminism. Letty says there are no tensions between them. But before Abigail met the man who is now her husband, Letty told us, "I had a big falling-out with her over a man in her life." Although they have seemingly put the incident behind them, Letty still believes that her speaking up was hurtful.

"We had a very strained, very painful period," said Letty. "And I blame myself. I think I could have kept my feelings to myself and just let the thing play itself out. Had I done that, it probably would have ended anyway." In 1990 Abigail moved to California to live with a man that Letty had trouble accepting. "I had problems because of the kind of person he was, and because he wasn't Jewish, which meant a lot to me. And also I had a lot of disagreements with him politically, which means a great deal in this house. Our differences were deep and serious. And again, I think I said it much too flagrantly and forcefully. It was an ongoing point of contention. He wasn't a bad person, but where our family was concerned, I found him devious and conspiratorial. He tried to present us as people I didn't think we were. He recast us, so that we seemed to be negative. We were a very close family, and all of a sudden he was pulling Abigail out and turning her against us, and it was changing the whole dynamic of our lives. So we said something. I think I said it all, I said it right out."

Letty's husband also disliked the young man, but the question of Jewish identity was particularly important to Letty. "I have a really strong historical sense, in that I really feel connected to my ancestors, and I didn't want that heritage to come to a dead end with my daughter. I feel linked up with the generations. I value everything that's come down to us from the ancients, and I honor their memory and their struggles, and it just loomed as such a betrayal of all those people and all that suffering that I might have a grandchild who genuflected in front of a crucifix and was baptized. Abigail said they planned to raise their children with both religions, but I couldn't really imagine that."

What, we wondered, was the problem with having stated her view? Letty said, "Once you say it, you can't take it back. You can't not keep after it. It's there, like an elephant in the living room. And every time we talked to each other she knew how I felt about him. And I think it was a kind of reproach to her because it was implicitly a criticism of her choice. I never said, 'How could you love a person like this?' but that's basically what was underlying my words."

Letty and Abigail have talked about this period. "She has forgiven me, but I think I was very hurtful to her. I made it hard for her. Eventually she reached a decision to break up this relationship, but I may have prolonged it because of a kind of rebellion that was built into the situation: How could she be sure she was leaving him because of her feelings rather than because of me?"

From Susan's journal, February 1, 1996

Last night Sarah and I had dinner at Ollie's, near her apartment. I want her to feel that she doesn't always come to me—she has said that Gerry and I still expect her to come to our houses, as if our houses were still more home than hers—so I took the bus to 116th Street and met her after her workout at the gym. We had a lovely dinner together. We talked about her work and my work. We talked about cooking, about recipes.

She had some questions to ask me. What was the guy I almost married before her father like? How did my parents respond to him? Why did I break the engagement? I told her about the first time my parents met him. He had driven in from Boston and was dead tired but put himself out to have dinner with them at some fancy restaurant, then on to a nightclub to hear jazz. Next morning I remember standing in the kitchen of my Yorkville apartment and hearing my mother say over the phone, "He's too short and his hair is too long." And while I was still reeling from that salvo, she added, "And he yawned throughout the entire evening." Later when I decided that I probably wanted to get married more than I wanted to marry him, I almost married him anyway to spite her.

The discussion about my broken engagement led to a talk about marriage and how you know when it's the right guy. And that led to Sarah's admission that she is afraid about marriage, can't imagine herself married, because Gerry and I divorced when she was ten, and she doesn't have a model for a lasting relationship.

Certainly the divorce was very traumatic for Sarah—it's bound to be. Her fear of being abandoned has played into her difficulty in ending some of her past relationships. She'd be the first to admit that she hangs on longer than she feels she should. But that doesn't explain everything. Her father has remained very much in her life. One of the reasons I married him was that I somehow knew he'd be a good father, and he has been. I also know that she picks the kind of person she does because she likes to take care of people who are in pain. And when we were divorced that was certainly the role she fell into, she was the strong one, she took care of her sister. She appointed herself to that role, even though she was too young for it, and it has remained part of her self-definition. I hope that in time she won't be so wrapped up in meeting someone else's needs that she ignores her own.

We asked Dr. Schnitzer what she thought about the possibility that a mother speaking her mind might actually drive her daughter to do the very thing the mother fears. "I don't think that is a useful question," she said. "It doesn't help to second-guess yourself that way. You can't see around corners. You can't predict the future. Your obligation is to maintain your own integrity.

As long as you make it clear that what you're saying reflects what *you* think, and that you realize your comments may or may not be important to her, it's appropriate to speak out."

And what happens if you convey to your daughter the fact that you have reservations about the man in her life, and she marries him anyhow? Must it affect your relationship with her? Once having made critical remarks about her choice, can you ever become friends with him? "If she marries someone you disapprove of," says Dr. Schnitzer, "you are not required to ingratiate yourself with him. It may eventually develop that you come to see his good side, but all that is really required is that you treat him courteously and speak courteously to your daughter about him. It's your relationship with your daughter that really matters. If, despite having heard your views, she has gone ahead and made this marriage, you need to accept it and be open to her perspective. That *doesn't* mean that you diminish your concern. In fact, you should do everything possible to stay in a dialogue with her, to stay connected to her. So that she can talk to you in case, over time, she develops concern about the marriage herself."

Staying connected despite your reservations about him

Anne S. is a straight-talking, almost brusque executive, part of a management consultant team in Boston that specializes in turning around troubled businesses. She says of herself, "I'm good at running things. I'm the oldest of five, what more do you want?" Her second child and only daughter, Wendy, twenty-eight, has been raised with every advantage and shows every sign of being on the same fast professional track as her mother. Wendy fell in love with a man she met through work and married him last summer. Anne was appalled at her choice and told her so. "I can't remember the actual words," Anne told us. "But I must have said words to the effect of 'he's a jerk.' " She spoke her mind to Wendy soon after the couple first met, and again when Wendy announced that they were going to get married. And when we interviewed her, six months after the wedding, she was still exercised. Her voice rose, "He's basically an office manager, he's just totally boring! He doesn't have much background. He's had no experiences, and here's Wendy who was brought up so the world was her oyster. It seems like a screwy match. And this isn't just my opinion. Her friends have said the same thing. They were all calling me before the wedding. 'Can't you do something, Anne?' " When Anne and her daughter quarreled about the young man, Wendy defended him. " 'It's just that he's never had any advantages, Mom. As soon as he's had them, then . . . ' And I said, 'Why do *you* have to give them to him? I don't get this.' "

When Wendy announced her engagement, Anne couldn't sleep. I thought, Why is this upsetting me? It's not my life! You want the best for your daughter, but it's *your* perception of the best. And we have these narrow ways of looking at things that aren't true for somebody twenty-eight years old in the 1990s. I'm looking from the perspective of someone who was twenty-eight years old in the sixties. In many ways, it's my problem. That doesn't make it go away, though.

Wendy and her husband are renovating their house, and Wendy has asked Anne to help out with the contract. Wendy calls several times a day with business gossip she thinks will interest Anne. Anne tries to be gracious to her son-in-law, but Wendy, perhaps sensitive to her mother's true feelings, does not include her husband when she invites her mother to go out to dinner or a movie.

Anne's priorities are very clear. She may still think that her son-in-law is "dull as dishwater," but her daughter is more important to her than any other person in her life. "I don't want to lose my daughter. If Wendy is happy, that means a great deal to me. As for the guy—you don't have to like it, but you have to accept it. And when you accept it, you have to stop bitching about it and get on with life. It's no longer discussible. Because otherwise, you're putting your daughter in the position of choosing, or trying to make peace. Everything would just be uncomfortable all the time. It would be awful. I couldn't live that way. I assume that if I did that, Wendy would have to say, 'Mom, I'll see you at Christmas,' and I wouldn't blame her. I wouldn't blame her at all."

June H., fifty-one, works with her second husband, the owner of a small manufacturing company outside of New Haven. June's daughter, Ally, twenty-six, is a successful actress. Ally has earned more than enough to support herself since she was a child, modeling and performing in television and movies. "She's always kept a level head about how to manage her career and her finances, and she's been terrific about handling the good and bad sides of a certain amount of fame." However, June's confidence that her daughter knows what's best for herself was a bit shaken when Ally introduced her parents to her fiancé.

"As all parents, I think that the choice of a husband or spouse is never as good as you think it should be, right?" said June. "I don't think Stan is as good for her as she could have chosen, but I'm not the one who makes the choice. He's also an actor, but I'm not sure he's very ambitious. I've never said it directly to her. I would ask questions leading to that so that she could think about it." What kind of questions? " 'If you had to quit your career, and you wanted to have a family, how would he support you?' And her answer was, 'I'm not marrying him to support me. I never want a man to support me, so I don't intend to ever put myself in that situation.' So she'd thought it out carefully. She loved him for really good reasons. He has a very close family relationship. The whole family lives in the Los Angeles area, and she felt good around his family, they were very nice loving people. And they loved her! And he knew about her business. She could ask his advice, and I think there aren't a whole lot of people in that business that she could communicate with, whom she felt she could really trust."

Ally is a very competent businesswoman. She manages the family finances. She pays the bills. June says, "I would like him to be able to give more to my daughter to make it a little easier for her. But of course that's what I want, not what she wants."

June's ability to differentiate her daughter's wishes from her own reminded us of Anne S.'s comment, "You want the best for your daughter, but it's *your* perception of the best." Neither woman interpreted her daughter's choice as a personal rebuke, which enabled mother and daughter to stay connected.

"We've come to see that he's really right for Johanna"

Having assumed the worst about their daughters' choices, two women we spoke to told us that they have found themselves not only accepting but in some sense even embracing their new sons-in-law.

Brenda W. and her husband Robert, had grave doubts about their older daughter's fiancé. Three years ago, when she was twenty-seven, Johanna told her parents that she wanted to marry Steven, who was seventeen years older than she, divorced, with two teenaged children; he was also Jewish, and Brenda and her family were Presbyterians. Their relationship with Johanna had never been smooth. Moody, introverted, stubborn, and opinionated, with few friends through school, she was, Brenda told us, "just not easy to live with."

When Brenda saw that Johanna was getting serious about Steven, she and Robert voiced their objections. "We said, 'Johanna, we would prefer you be with someone who is more your age. And we would prefer you marry someone of our religion. And there's emotional baggage here—you'll have stepchildren.' And Johanna said, 'Well, I'm not going to be the children's mother. And Steven is going to become a member of our church because he wants to.' And when they talked to us about getting married and it was really on the table, she said, 'I know you have these objections, and there's nothing I can do about them.' 'And they won't interfere with our marriage' is how Steven put it."

Once she saw that Johanna was determined to marry Steven, Brenda said, "I entered into it very wholeheartedly and gave her the wedding of her dreams. And we've come to see that he's really right for her. We were having dinner with them one night, and she was going on and on about something, and her husband put his hand on hers and said, 'Johanna, now let somebody else speak.' And she did, quite graciously. He could control her. And Robert and I looked at each other and thought, Wow, we never could control her."

Brenda believes that Johanna has found herself in this relationship. And that Steven probably has, too. "They give each other a kind of security and confidence so they each do better at their jobs and in their social life when they're together." Brenda and Robert welcome Steven at every family occasion. Says Brenda, "Actually I think he feels that he's fine with me. He is into holistic medicine, massage. Things that I care about, too. So he and I can relate on that level. In fact, he's introduced me to his massage therapist. And Robert . . . well, he and Steven haven't quite gotten where they should. Robert still tells people, 'He's not exactly the son-in-law I would have imagined.' He is unwilling to let go of his preconception. But then he'll say, 'It's really okay, and I'm getting to appreciate him.' "

Mandy, now a twenty-seven-year-old aspiring violinist, was also a difficult child to live with. Her mother, Priscilla D., told us that Mandy, unlike her brother and sister, had a somewhat turbulent adolescence. "She was just hard to please," recalls Priscilla, who also remembers nights when she "cried a lot or stayed awake" in reaction to her daughter's behavior. Things came to a head during Mandy's junior year in college, when she announced she was going to marry Darryl, a classmate she'd met in the evangelical Methodist congregation of which she had become a member. Priscilla and her husband were appalled.

"It wasn't the religion per se. We're Episcopalians, but not very active. And our older daughter has married a wonderful Lutheran boy whom we're crazy about. We just thought Mandy and her boyfriend were very young and very immature. They were very susceptible to these evangelical ministers who were really far out. I was horrified, just sick about it. We trotted out all the usual arguments, 'You're too young, you should wait until you finish school,' anything to put it off and maybe she would grow beyond it.

"Well, she didn't listen to more than three words, so it didn't matter what I said. She was into her Jesus phase, and they were married by this narrow-minded little born-again evangelist, and that's the only place we put our foot down. We said 'You're not going to have this man saying grace in our home.' But other than that, I thought—and I really felt—It's *your* life. So we planned the wedding together and we held the reception at our home—without the minister."

It wasn't easy for Priscilla. "Mandy was still an adolescent at that stage, so there was no pleasing her. She says now she doesn't like to look at the wedding pictures and see my unhappy face in them. But I think she's also projecting her own feelings, now that she's got some distance, I think she deeply regrets the way she approached it."

To Priscilla's amazement, the marriage is turning out well. "This young man has matured and astonished us with his progress. He's rather insecure, and she is also, and their needs seem to mesh. In keeping with their characters, it's somewhat tumultuous. There's a lot of fighting and making up." The couple are no longer active evangelicals. "It's all past for Mandy," says Priscilla. "And he still believes, but he doesn't go to church."

Priscilla says, "I never expected to like him, but I really do. He's become a member of the family. He's become very successful in his career—he's a percussionist—and it's wonderful to see how much he supports her in her work. My other son-in-law is like that, too. Young men today are a different breed!

"If you want to know what I think about mothers giving advice to daughters," Priscilla concluded, "I think humility is the key. I would never have bet a dollar on this marriage surviving, and it's now six years into it, and it's very healthy."

Priscilla and Brenda did not come to their change of heart overnight, but with time they moved from grudging acceptance to mild tolerance to the discovery that the son-in-law they resisted was a better choice for their daughter than they could have known. "Humility" is indeed the key. It's important for a mother to remind herself that her daughter may know more about what's best for her than her mother does.

Not every story has such a happy ending. But no matter what the outcome, our advice for a mother who has serious reservations about her daughter's choice is the same: Find a way to tell her what bothers you and try to draw out her feelings about it. You may discover that it is an issue for you but not for her, and be consoled by that. If, despite what you say, she goes ahead with a marriage that turns out to be a catastrophe, at least you will know that you did what you could to guide her. And if your tone has consistently been one of loving concern, you will have conveyed to her the fact that, if necessary, she can turn to you to help her rebuild her life.

What If She Doesn't Marry?

Many of us remember, and our daughters probably do, too, a widely publicized study in 1986 that reported on dismal matrimonial odds facing a woman who failed to get married by the time she was thirty. The study stated that a thirty-year-old unmarried college graduate had a 20 percent chance of finding a husband. By the time she reached thirty-five, her chances dropped to 5 percent, and by forty, she had a one-in-a-hundred chance of tying the knot. In fact, the report was wildly off the mark. A follow-up study by demographers at the United States Census Bureau produced much more reassuring—but not widely disseminated—statistics: At age thirty, a college graduate's chances of finding a husband are about 50 percent, at age thirty-five about 35 percent, and at age forty, 20 to 25 percent. So things aren't as bad as we were first led to believe. Nonetheless, the women we interviewed whose single daughters are approaching the upper edge of our age group told us of their rising anxiety that their girls may not marry.

Martha R.'s daughter Emily, thirty, is an emergency room nurse. Emily has never had a serious relationship, "no one even temporarily permanent," according to her mother. Martha knows that she's lonely because they often talk about it. "Emily says most of the men she meets seem infantile." She's willing to go to singles bars, she's not averse to a blind date. But nothing has panned out. "I think she's so hungry for a relationship," Martha goes on, "she's so intense—if she meets someone she's attracted to she wants to embrace them—and I think this scares people. If someone has the inclination to pull away a little, probably that person would pull away a lot. And then she feels rejected."

We asked Martha how she and her husband will deal with it if Emily doesn't find a man. "How we've always handled things—if it's good for her, it's good for us." And if it's not what she wants? "Then my heart will break. What will I do? I won't do anything. I'll tell her that she's strong enough to be alone. And that she has many good friends and a loving family. That's what I'll say. I don't know how I'll feel."

Cynthia G.s' older daughter, Leslie, has just turned thirty. And Cynthia reports, "There's been a change in Leslie's universe. About half of her friends have gotten married. And she and the other ones who haven't are very worried. Demonstrably worried. We sort of joke about it. I don't think I have ever said that I expect that they should be married by now, by this age. Or that I expect a grandchild. My own mother says, 'Where are the grandchildren?' I would never say that. But when her friend Gwen comes here with her baby—who's my goddaughter—and I say to Leslie, 'Oh, Sophie is so adorable,' I wonder how does that make Leslie feel. Or if I shouldn't say it. But that's ridiculous.

"There are a lot of people in my family who never got married. I had four maiden great-aunts. One was a pediatric nurse, one was a lawyer, the other two had important jobs with the Brotherhood of Railway Workers. They had independent lives, and they did not feel sorry for themselves. They were all amazing women, and I think they had rich lives. My kids knew them and liked them. They called them 'the grandmas.'

"I don't know that I've said that it doesn't matter if they marry or not. I would like them to get married and have children. But I think I'm open for anything that made me feel that they were satisfied with their lives. And I don't feel that I have to be a grandmother," said Cynthia. "I could always have my goddaughter."

And What If She's Gay?

Eight of the one hundred and thirteen mothers we interviewed said they had a daughter who was a lesbian; another three reported daughters who had had a homosexual relationship but were now involved with men. (Only one of the hundred and thirteen mothers is gay, having come out when her daughter was in her early teens. Her daughter is now married.) Gay literature is filled with anguished stories about homosexual men and women who cannot speak of their sexual preferences with their families, of parents, tormented by shame, who deny in the face of clear evidence that their children are gay. None of the women we talked to fit this pattern. They were all sad that their daughters faced social opprobrium, however diminished, and that their daughters were probably going to miss out on the kind of family life that the mothers would have wished for them. All of them were compassionate and respectful of their daughters' sexual preference, even if it took a struggle to get to that point. More than one confessed that she had not quite relinquished the fantasy that her daughter might yet find happiness with a man.

Sondra L.'s daughter, Alexis, now thirty-two, came out when she was twenty-six. "At first I was devastated," says Sondra. "I felt it would have a very negative effect on her ability to have a happy life—now whether that's a stupid fifties way of looking at things I don't know—but I just felt this girl is not going to have children, she is not going to be able to live in the mainstream of life. Whatever she chooses, whatever she wants to be, she's going to be different. And no matter how open we are today, there are still worldwide big problems. I just died.

"Alexis could probably tell from the pale white face that I was floored, and I think in the beginning I said stupid things like, 'I don't think this is a good thing for you to do'—well I mean, ridiculous. She and I had these back and forth things over several years. In the beginning she'd get very upset, and I'd get very upset, but gradually I think I've come to terms with it. I really just want her to be happy. I'm still not sure that this is the best thing for her, but there's nothing we can do about it. I have fantasies that one day she'll meet this gorgeous guy. I know I'm pathetic, but I'll never totally want this for my daughter."

Sondra told us that Alexis is in a nice relationship now. "I like . . . Patty," Sondra admitted with some chagrin that she has trouble remembering the woman's name. She believes that Alexis has benefited from their relationship. "Patty's family is maybe not as sophisticated as ours, but they have some basic good strengths that Alexis has learned from. My family were not the most other-oriented people in the world. And Patty has pointed out to Alexis that she can be very selfish. So Alexis has profited from that very much, and Patty has benefited from Alexis's sophistication. So she's madly in love with this girl, but who knows what will happen in five years? I don't know, though I seriously doubt that she's going to reverse her sexual orientation."

Adrian P.'s twenty-five-year-old daughter Camilla had an affair with another woman during her last year of college. And according to Adrian, "although she is sexually unclear about herself, she thinks she is more likely to be gay than straight." Mother and daughter have discussed Camilla's sexuality at length. We asked Adrian how she feels about Camilla's being gay. "Well, there are a couple of levels of that," she told us. "It was very in-your-face when she was at school. She felt the world was ready for any kind of sexual behavior, and I felt in a lot of ways it wasn't. I think sex is something private, so I certainly would be uncomfortable if she were aggressively, defiantly being gay. I would feel that is dangerous. I'm not tremendously comfortable with discussions about gay bars. I mean, do you know for example there's something here in New York called the Clit Club? I found it interesting, but I'm not sure I need to know this, but she was very comfortable describing it to me.

"And the second issue is how she feels about her body. And if she is gay, she still has to sort out this issue. She defiantly says that women are more accepting about your body, and in her mind a perfect body is someone who is six inches taller than she is and is both strong and slender. So that's another thing."

Like Sondra L., Adrian is not denying her daughter's sexual preference even though she remains ambivalent about it. "I think I've
gotten to the point that what will be will be, I'm just concerned that
she find somebody who will treat her properly. If she's really able to
make a relationship with anybody that's a good one, that will be okay.
At one point about two years ago she told me that a friend said, 'Do
you think your mom would be more comfortable if you were with a
white woman or a black man?' and she and I both said, at the same
time, 'a black man!' So I'm obviously having trouble with this. I mean,
I can think about it rationally, but it's something that I'm so far away
from in my own mind in terms of something I could imagine for
myself, that I can't really understand the impulse."

Scottie W. and her husband live in a suburb of Hartford, Connecticut; they have three daughters and a son. Twenty-two-year-old
Nina hasn't yet had a significant affair with another woman, but she
is quite clear that she is a lesbian. Nina came out to her parents in a
long letter she wrote from Madrid during her junior year abroad.
Scottie now believes that there were signs of Nina's homosexuality in
high school, so she wasn't shocked by the announcement. And when
Nina came home, Scottie was quite forthright. "I told her, 'I don't
think a person can change, so if that's what you are, work with it,
and make a life for yourself. I have certain rules that are still going
to apply. If you're going to come home with somebody and you're a
lesbian, and you haven't made a strong commitment to each other,
you're still going to sleep in separate bedrooms. But I would much
rather know that you have found someone important to spend your
life with. If it's a woman, okay, it's still better than being alone.' "

Once a mother accepts the fact that her daughter is gay, even though
she may continue to worry about the social discrimination her daughter faces, her everyday concerns are very much like those of any other
mother. Will my daughter find a loving partner? Will she be good
enough for her? Will we be able to get along? If I'm not happy with
the woman, what can I say to my daughter, and how can I say it?

Ann Gottlieb talked to us about her daughter, Mara, a twenty-five-
year-old graduate student in social work. Mara told her parents she

was gay when she was a senior in high school. "So since she was eighteen, I've known it in my mind," Ann says. "But in my heart, I didn't really accept it until two and a half or three years ago. It is certainly something that I am accepting of now, but there are issues that go along with that that have been difficult, and we talk about them." Which issues? "She was involved—and still may be—with a woman that I'm not thrilled about. And it's not the fact that she's a woman. If it were a man I wouldn't be any happier. This is one of those fire things between the two of us; this is something we do not see eye to eye on at all."

Mara's lover is ten years older than Mara. She is a police officer. Ann says, "Jan is uneducated and has no curiosity. But Mara sees in her a goodness that she's not ever seen in other people, and also this woman is a protector—she takes care of Mara—and Mara likes the security of the relationship. Also, for her, Mara can do no wrong, and maybe since Mara grew up in a home where I saw a lot that I picked on, it's a very comforting feeling for her to have this person who is so incredibly accepting. But Jan offers her no intellectual stimulation. Here is Mara who is just starting to see the world, she's just starting graduate school, she's smart. So I would like her to find a partner who has the same kind of curiosity and passion for what she's doing as Mara does, and I hope that she will make Mara happy."

When the Subject Is Sex

Women of our generation recall few candid conversations with our mothers about sex. Most of us certainly absorbed the message that nice girls didn't "do it" before marriage. Some of us had mothers who went so far as to imply that sex in marriage could be a wonderful experience. But mostly, as Meryl Siegel says, "There was never a discussion with my mother about sex in any form. In fact, one might wonder how I came to be."

In retrospect, we were shockingly innocent. Jewelle Bickford told us, "I took a course in human sexuality at Sarah Lawrence when my daughters were in high school. You have to understand about me. I dropped out of college to marry the only man I have ever slept with.

I was so uptight. I was raised a Southern Baptist. I was like a vestal virgin. In the course we were supposed to say the most shocking or painful word for us. I couldn't say it. Someone in the class said, 'I bet it rhymes with duck.' I said, 'No, the closest I can get is Fussy.' "

Says Nancy Hernandez, "I was brought up in a very strict environment, I was not allowed to go outside. When I got married—it's a funny story—I used to hear people talk about rubbers, and I thought they were rubber bands. So when I got married, we went on our honeymoon and I took along two boxes of rubber bands! I didn't know there were condoms. So my husband . . . I said, 'I don't want to get pregnant right away, at least put on these,' and he looked at me and said, 'No, no, no! What is that?' 'These are rubber bands, they keep talking about rubbers,' I said. So he went to the phone, and he ordered some condoms—and that's how naive I was brought up."

These days sex is much more openly discussed in our culture. Most of us are more comfortable than we assume our mothers were in acknowledging the existence of sex in our lives. And we are committed, as we believe they were not, to letting our daughters know that we know that it exists and that it is important.

From Marilyn's journal, July 20, 1996

For years Kore and I have had fun spotting hunky-looking guys on the street or discussing which young movie stud of the moment we think is attractive. But she has obviously bracketed those conversations and kept them at a considerable remove from an acknowledgment that they indicate that I have actual sexual tastes, and therefore, practices.

And although she seems so much more of an adult every day, she continues to get squeamish when the subject of adult sexuality is broached. She hates any hint that her father and I (*still,* I would think, in her terms) have a sex life together. She doesn't like us to reminisce about our travels together before we were married, which I believe Kate, on the other hand, thinks is quite romantic. I'm reminded of all this because tonight at dinner Hugh and I were talking and joking about friends our age who have just come back from their honeymoon. She covered her ears and said in a little girl voice, "I don't want to hear about this."

I guess this is the last vestige of adolescence. As she has more sexual experience of her own, she will be able to tolerate the acknowledgment that her parents (and parental figures) do also. But I suppose it never gets easy.

Both my parents were uncomfortable revealing anything about their own sexual appetites. And, although I know that children have a vested interest in denying that their parents are sexual, the evidence suggests that my parents were barely so. My father was as puritanical as my mother and perhaps even quicker to speak disparagingly of a peer who exhibited a forthright sexual appetite. In my enlightened, and somewhat contemptuous view, they were both severely repressed. I'm light years better, but still probably reticent compared to many. I'm happy to indicate to my kids that I have appetites and activity. For what it's worth, I'm also quite immodest about my own body. (Why does immodest sound like it has negative connotations?) I've always been comfortable revealing myself in the nude around them and talking about gynecological matters. I've never had any trouble letting them know that I expect them to have full sexual lives, starting well before they get married. But I only talk about sex in the most general way, and never with a hint of details. Do they in turn see me as repressed? Is this a situation specific to mothers and daughters? Mothers and children?

One of Nancy Hernandez's daughters had her first sexual experience at age sixteen—before she was ready in Nancy's view. "She was very open and she told me, and it hurt me a lot. But I recognized that they want to explore. She went into pot, she drank, she had a few glasses of wine according to what she said, and she had her first sexual encounter. I went through hell. But I thought, I have to be there for her, I just can't say good-bye or whatever. So what I did every day was to be sure I spoke to her, have her sit with me, tell me what she feels. I might not agree, but at least talk to me. And she did, and this year she's like a new person. She says, 'I know I did wrong last year.

Every adolescent goes through a phase, and that was my phase, and something now that I wish I hadn't done.' She's very close to my older girl, and she spoke to her, and her sister told her, 'Well, if you're going to do it, here's what you have to use. Here's what type of condom you have to use, and you have to be careful because you never know. Just because you use a condom doesn't mean that it's one hundred percent.' "

Nancy believes, "You have to be down to earth with your kids, you have to sit with them, speak to them," to keep in touch with what's going on in their lives—a conscious departure from the way she was raised. "My mother was very cold-hearted, in the sense that you don't talk about sex in front of her, you don't walk in underclothes in front of her, you have to be dressed all the time. So I thought that when I have a child, I'm not going to be the way she was with me. She was so strict. I knew that what I went through, I didn't want my daughters to go through."

Jewelle Bickford, whose daughters are thirty-two and twenty-nine, told us, "Sex is important in my marriage. There's lots of physical affection in our household. The kids have walked in on us. They could hear us, too. We had a four-poster bed that made a lot of noise. Nat adored that bed, and it was hard to get rid of it. But we had to because of the fact that the kids could hear us making love. They saw us being affectionate, saw us fight and then make up. And I think I've always tried to convey to them how important sex is to us. But I do believe in being short on the details of my sex life and long on truth."

Verdine Jones would agree. Verdine's daughters, Rhonda and Stacy, are twenty-eight and twenty-five, respectively. Verdine says, "I feel that between girlfriends you can talk about sexual satisfactions, that type of thing, but I'm not going to discuss with my daughters my sexual satisfaction. How to talk about my sexual relationships and positions with my daughters about their father, I just can't do that. I can probably accept what they're saying about their boyfriend . . . they're both pretty free, the oldest one especially, the youngest one is still pretty close-lipped about sexual things. She's kind of secretive." Does that bother Verdine? "No. I kind of let each one go their own pace and let them know if you need anything I'm here. If you're uncomfortable and don't want to discuss it with me I can accept that. There's other people, I don't feel that I have to know everything. There are probably some things I don't want to know!"

We asked mothers how they handled a variety of sex-related issues: Do you stick with the traditional "don't ask, don't tell" policy even though you know she's probably sleeping with her boyfriend, or do you openly acknowledge that she's sexually active even if she's not married? Do you let her share a room with her boyfriend when she comes home for a visit? Do you discuss ways to achieve sexual pleasure? Has she had a premarital pregnancy? What about abortions?

In a world haunted by AIDS and other sexually transmitted diseases, almost every mother felt she could say, "I hope you're being careful," at the very least. Beyond that, the answers ranged all over the lot. Some women were admittedly quite circumspect and were comfortable with that. Others wished they could be more candid. Some were quite pleased and amazed at how free their conversations with their daughters have become.

"There's nothing we can't talk about"

A handful of women said that virtually no subject was taboo. Cynthia G.'s two daughters, Leslie and Nicole, are thirty and twenty-eight, respectively. "We talked a lot about the importance of physical attraction," Cynthia told us. "Because they were teenagers while I was divorced and dating, I think we talked more freely than we might have otherwise. I thought it was important to be open with them about the importance of physical attraction in my life and that I thought it was a very significant component of a relationship. So because we talked about it so early, we were always very comfortable revisiting it.

"Once I remember talking about what it's like to make love. We love to have backrubs in our family. And I talked about how it's important to find out what's pleasing to the other person. And I used the backrub as a metaphor. With one of my girls I have talked about very intimate details. She and I have had conversations that have sometimes been difficult for me to hear. About her experiments with bisexuality, her trouble having an orgasm."

Faith H. is the mother of Melissa, twenty-eight, and Deborah, twenty-three. She remembers talking easily about sex to the girls from the time they were small. "When they would ask me questions, I was just real up front. There's nothing we can't talk about, particularly with Melissa. Not too long ago we were sitting drinking coffee, and she said to me, 'I'm going to ask you something mom. How old were you when you had a climax?' And Deborah said, 'That does it!' And I said, 'I was pretty young, Melissa.' And she said, 'How young?' And I said, 'Maybe thirteen or fourteen.' Deborah said, 'I cannot believe you could ask her that question!' Well, it turns out neither one of them has had a climax, and my mouth dropped open when they said that. And I don't have any real advice to give them because I didn't really know what the problem was.

"Well, I do have a clue. I think Melissa is holding back because she hasn't gotten to the point in a relationship where she trusts a man well enough to have a climax. But I just said, 'You need to be with someone you trust and love a lot, and that will come.' I mean that's a pretty pat answer, but that's kind of how I feel about it.

"I even told Deborah that when she was little, she used to get in the tub, and she would put her legs up and let the water run over her, and she said, 'I can't believe I did that!' And I had thought at the time, well she's going to be really open about how she approaches sex, but I guess not. I never had a problem like that."

Says Roz S., whose daughter, Mary Ellen, is thirty, "We have no trouble talking about men and sex. There's nobody in Mary Ellen's life now. And she really misses sex, and how do you get it. 'You know,' I said to her, 'that's when you learn about masturbation.' I remember way back when, when I was first divorced, I was twenty-six years old, and I thought, Oh my God, what am I gonna do? and being this Catholic girl, I had no idea of anything. Because I wasn't gonna sleep around, it was masturbate or nothing. And Mary Ellen said, 'Oh my God, that's so awful!' And I'm, 'Well, yes, it's certainly not ideal. But I'll tell you, picking somebody up in a bar isn't ideal either.'

"And I told her I remember finally getting up the nerve to have one fling after my divorce, and my gynecologist telling me, 'Roz, you're young, you're attractive, I'm going to give you these birth control pills.' Well now, when I think of it, I'm so glad the guy wasn't diseased, because no one used condoms.

"I remember the bad old days when all of birth control was the woman's problem. And in talking with my daughter, I want her to demand responsibility from men. And I think she does. I tell her I want her to look out for herself, but I don't want her to take it all on herself. And I don't want my sons to think it's the girl's responsibility either."

"I don't want them sleeping with people"

What makes Cynthia, Faith, and Roz unusual is not their acknowledgment that their daughters are sexually active. It's their degree of comfort with that knowledge and the frankness with which they discuss the subject with their daughters. At the other end of the spectrum are women who know that their daughters are sexually active, the daughters know they know it, yet they continue to focus their discussion with their daughters on the value of abstinence until marriage.

Arlen M.'s younger daughter, Harper, twenty-three, is engaged, and Martha, twenty-six, sometimes spends the night at her boyfriend's house. "I can't be sure they're not sleeping with their young men. I haven't asked. When they go places with us, we take the girls' special friends, and they sleep in separate rooms. And that will always be the case, and they know where we stand on that. By the same token we try and be halfway realistic. No, I don't want them sleeping with people. It's medically risky, psychologically risky, all kind of risky. I think all that is still true—that a guy won't respect you and you won't respect yourself. I think you lose some of that. I do. We've told them that we don't think sex outside of marriage has the meaning it should have. And part of that is you're just too vulnerable. You don't have the closeness or the history. But I admit, when you've gone with somebody for seven years, some of that gets gray."

The wish that the stated morality of our girlhood still prevailed is not unique to Arlen. Several women, most of whom stressed their strong religious convictions, told us they hoped or believed that their daughters were virgins until they got married, or at least engaged. And for some the wish persists even when the facts are otherwise. Emma H. knows that her daughter Bobby Sue is sexually involved with her boyfriend, and Emma and Bobbie Sue can talk about it, but Emma can't shake her deepest belief that sex outside of marriage is a mistake. "I have made it clear that in today's world first of all, there should be no such thing as recreational sex, that time is over. So we've had these frank discussions.

"Bobbie Sue called me after she had been going out with George for several months, which wasn't long enough in my mind. And she said, 'I've got good news and bad news.' I said, 'What's the good news?' And she said, 'Well the good news is you're going to be proud that I'm doing what you told me. George is going to have an AIDS test, and I'm going on birth control pills.' I said, 'What's the bad news?' And she said, 'We're going away together the weekend after next.' And I went, 'Ohh.' You know, I wasn't so glad she told me. She knew I would have been more disapproving if it hadn't been a serious boyfriend. But she also knew I knew it was coming because she had been going out with him awhile. I could see how she was acting and how much in love she was. So I had immediately started saying, 'Now Bobbie Sue, you need to think about . . . before you get involved . . . you're awfully young. I can't make that decision for you, but I hope you'll be responsible.'

"Most of my friends don't have that kind of conversation with their daughters, and I think it's because I was single. They had an awareness that I was intimate with the guy I was going out with, and I wasn't married. So I laughingly say, and the truth of it is I believe this, maybe because I'm southern, that I really don't believe in sex outside of marriage. I honestly don't. I think it would be absolutely wonderful if that was a reality still. But it's not. It wasn't with me, and I don't expect it to be with my girls—but wasn't it wonderful then? When I married my first husband—I had gone out with him from the time I was thirteen until twenty-two, I had never had intercourse. I wouldn't say I was a virgin! But I wasn't going to get pregnant doing what I was doing, and I was having a great time. So I'm thinking, it can be done. But maybe that's not the healthiest. And I don't expect it. But wouldn't it be nice?"

The fact of their own unmarried status has forced a number of women to deal with their inconsistency about sexual mores. Clara T., the divorced mother of Willa, twenty-two, said, "It's something we went round and round about. Because I couldn't come to a logical solution that sat well with me. I'd say, 'Here's what I'm comfortable with. In the family home you don't sleep with your boyfriend, even though I know you're practically living with him.' And she accepted that I couldn't sort it out any better than that."

Things became more complicated last summer when Willa was living at home, her boyfriend was around a lot, but still not allowed to stay over, and Clara was getting more serious about a man she had started seeing during her frequent business trips to Germany. "He was coming to visit me, and it became humorous. Like, where's he going to sleep? If I want him to sleep in the room with me, then I better change what I say to her." Clara spoke separately to her lover and her daughter. With some relief that the subterfuge was ending, all agreed that they could tolerate the other couple sharing a bedroom under the same roof.

Clara made herself face up to what the other women who didn't let their young adult daughters sleep with boyfriends in their parents' home were avoiding. When a mother says, 'I know she's sleeping with him, but she can't do it here,' there's still some denial of the daughter's sexuality. And sexuality in general.

Allowing a daughter to sleep in the same bedroom with her boyfriend in our home forces us to confront all the things that sex means to us. The subject of sex reminds us of some of the deepest secrets of our own identity. We seldom feel comfortable acknowledging the full range of our sexual fantasies to ourselves; it can take years before we are willing to explore them with a therapist; we may never be able to express them to a partner, let alone a friend. Any conversation that involves sex can trigger these anxieties.

The subject of sexuality is especially potent for mothers and daughters. From the time daughters are adolescent, mothers are caught in what psychologist Marianne Walters describes as a double bind between presenting themselves as a mother and as a woman. In our culture, she writes, "Images of sexual woman have been divorced from those of mother. Seldom do we encounter in literature, film, or the popular media, mothers whose sexuality is explored and treated as part of the womanness they bring into motherhood. And when mothers do present themselves as sexual to their daughters, it is usually to advise them on how to protect themselves, rather than on how to be self-directed and achieve satisfaction in their sex lives . . . Small wonder that a mother's messages to her daughter about sex are mixed. Empowering her daughter sexually can be dangerous; cautioning her will be inhibiting. . . . Whichever way she goes, the message will be, must be, mixed."

When daughters move beyond adolescence and the prohibition against sexual experimentation becomes less necessary, few mothers feel comfortable readdressing the mixture of the message—diminishing the warning and stressing the empowerment. For one thing, the habit of not talking candidly about sex has been established. For another, because both mothers and daughters have internalized the idea that sexuality and motherhood exist on different planes, neither is comfortable when a mother reveals herself as sexual. Daughters may hold back from revealing their sexuality because they believe their mothers will not understand. And our culture does nothing to help this impasse because, as Marianne Walters points out, mother/woman is still not seen as an integrated whole.

When an Unmarried Daughter Gets Pregnant

Occasionally, despite constant admonition and the availability of birth control measures, an unmarried daughter gets pregnant, and her mother has to find a way to deal with this reality. Of our sample, fourteen women mentioned a daughter who became pregnant while she was not married. Four of the pregnancies had occurred when the daughter was in high school, and all of those ended in abortion. The mothers involved said that any misgivings they had about the procedure were completely outweighed by the fear that their daughter's life would be severely restricted if she bore a child at that age. Of the daughters who got pregnant when they were older, five had abortions, and four chose to have the child without getting married. Only one mother told us that her daughter married in order to make the baby legitimate. For all these mothers, the issues and the implications were extremely complex.

Georgia S.'s daughter Mallory got pregnant during her senior year at college after a very brief affair with a classmate. Georgia said, "I never would have thought I'd have a daughter who'd need an abortion. But in church we had examined the issue so if it ever happened we would have a better basis of how to react. Our minister said that when you are in that situation you don't need to make that decision then. You need to have already decided what you would do if it ever happened to you, because when you're in the situation there are so many things going on. And that is the gospel truth.

"I was so afraid that my husband was going to force us to have that child and raise it. I was terrified, both for Mallory and for me. And he seriously thought about it and I knew he would. Luckily, it was just like the minister said. I had examined what my church said about it, what society said about it, what I thought about it, and I knew the minute she told me about it exactly what we needed to do. Now if she had pushed to do otherwise, that would have been different, but she didn't.

"Our family OB-GYN, the first words out of his mouth were 'Mallory, I have to tell you that you are pregnant, and I assume you want to terminate this pregnancy,' which for him was a real big step. He was giving her that option, and she took it. She was not in a relationship with anyone, it was a rebellious thing, she was a senior in college. If she had been in a serious relationship with somebody, I think we would have reexamined that. But I have never regretted that decision."

Gail E.'s twenty-two-year-old daughter, Toby, *was* in a serious relationship—she was engaged—but Gail came to understand that there were still issues surrounding Toby's premarital pregnancy. "Toby was living with Charlie, but not married, and she got pregnant and had an abortion. And I just thought that was awful. I couldn't imagine why they needed an abortion when they were planning to get married anyhow. But I knew that it was none of my business. They had set the date for after Charlie finished business school, and they would know where they'd be settling, and what their circumstances would be and all the rest of it.

"And then this happened unexpectedly, and she came to me and said, 'What do I do?' And it was too complicated for me to have an opinion on. Although I was suffering terribly inside. It was inappropriate for me to say what I really wanted to, which was, 'Toby, this is what you must do. You can't possibly have an abortion, you know, abortions are not to be used this way.' I mean I can't live her life, even though it just killed me."

We asked Gail what she did say. "I didn't say those things. I said, 'Toby, I understand that you do not want to have this baby unless you're married, and that the problem for you is not, are you going to marry Charlie and do you love him—because Charlie is supportive, he's willing to get married—but you feel these are not the circumstances under which to get married.'

"And there was no backlash from Toby. There was gratitude and love. I kept my suffering to myself, which frankly I think is appropriate, but just from a religious point of view—we're practicing Catholics—it was just horrible for me. And having gotten married under those circumstances myself—even though I've never admitted it to them—I can certainly sympathize with what she was going through. That was another reason why I was able to be objective. But having made a different choice, which was to get married and have the baby, it was very hard for me."

Two years ago, when Rosie Smith's unmarried daughter, Tisha, then eighteen, told her parents she was pregnant by a young man she had no intention of marrying, Rosie assumed that Tisha would have an abortion. "She knew she had made a mistake, but she did not feel she could terminate the pregnancy. I have to admit I would have liked her to because I did not think it was right for Tisha to have a child at that time, and I told her so. She was entering her second year at college. I did not think it was the right thing to do."

Rosie argued with Tisha until her daughter was in her seventh month. "She understood that she'd made a mistake, but she wanted to have that child. I thought she had no idea, absolutely no idea, what she was getting into. I thought she needed to finish her education, and that is what I had always pushed. I had told her many years ago when I talked to her about birth control and life skills, ' Tisha, if you ever want to have a child, I am not opposed to you having a child as a single parent but first finish your education, get a foundation for yourself, get a profession, whatever it may be. I don't care if you're a manicurist, you get that, and then if you choose to have a child and you're not married, it's fine with me. Don't put walls in front of yourself, stumbling blocks in front of yourself.' And that's what it's turned out to be. Not that her baby is a stumbling block, but Tisha cannot get up and go out when she wants to, she's got a child to take care of, she's got responsibilities."

Verdine Jones's daughter Rhonda, who was twenty-five at the time, also decided neither to terminate a pregnancy nor get married. "She was teaching school, and she told me, 'Look, I'm pregnant, and I'm going to have the baby, and I'm not getting married.' I said, 'Well, I don't particularly appreciate that.' I said, 'Usually people get married and the baby comes after.' If she had married him I would have done my best to make things as smooth as possible for them. But I could see her reasons for not wanting to marry that young man—he was jealous, and he was kind of unstable toward employment. So she chose not to marry him, and believe it or not I kind of support that."

At first Verdine's daughter refused to have much contact with her baby's father. Verdine thought this was a mistake. "I would tell my daughter, 'Regardless of what you feel toward this man, you chose to have this baby. You were no child, you were no teenager, and even if you were, you should let your child know that side of the family and not impose your negative ideas or beliefs.' " Verdine suggested to Rhonda that she take a little gift to the child's grandparents at Christmas. She did, and that has actually eased the relationship somewhat between Rhonda and her former boyfriend. He has begun to spend more time with the child. And Verdine is very pleased about that for the child's sake, although she thinks the young man is still somewhat irresponsible. "He's not much for financial support, but he baby-sits, and he takes her places, and she dearly loves her daddy."

Verdine Jones and Rosie Smith have had to live with the consequences of a decision that they opposed but were not able to prevent. Rhonda and Tisha are living with their children in their parents' homes, and we will have more to say about the tension that can arise when three generations live together.

The outcome of any decision an adult daughter may make about how she expresses her sexuality, about making a permanent commitment to a man, or a woman, even her decision whether or not to terminate an unexpected pregnancy is not within a mother's control. Nor does a mother necessarily have as much insight into what's best for her daughter as she thinks she has. What a mother can do is state what she thinks about her daughter's decision—especially if she has grave concerns about it. As a mother you have an obligation to speak up as long as you can express yourself in a way that's respectful of your daughter, and as long as you can accept that she has the right to make up her own mind about what matters most to her.

Chapter 5

When Your Daughter Lives at Home

Nan Lyons is a sixty-year-old novelist and travel writer who lives in New York. Her daughter, Samantha, twenty-six, left New York at eighteen to attend UCLA and lived in Los Angeles for three years after college to work as a drug counselor in the public schools. Last year Ivan Lyons, Nan's husband and writing partner, died. Although Sam came back to New York frequently during her father's illness, neither mother nor daughter ever expected to live under the same roof again. In the wake of Ivan's death, Nan coveted her privacy. She wanted time to be alone with her grief, and she had taken on several stressful writing assignments to see if she could build a career on her own. Just as Nan was beginning to reconstruct her life, Sam announced that she had been accepted to graduate school in New York and, for financial reasons, would need to live at home. Nan thinks that because of Ivan's death, Sam probably felt she had to reconnect with Nan as well. Nan was sympathetic to Sam's plight but reluctant to take her in.

What used to be considered as a period of dislocation for mothers whose children had moved away from home—the so-called empty nest syndrome—is in fact for many women a time to tend to their own needs. At midlife, women are happy for the companionship of their children, but relieved that they no longer have to take care of them. It is a time when, as family therapist Monica McGoldrick writes, "Women are grateful and energized by recapturing free time and exploring new options for themselves. They are not nearly as sorry to see the child-rearing era end as has been assumed and are often passionately interested in developing themselves and their own personal lives. This phase gives them, for the first time, an opportunity to discover who they are and to develop their own creativity."

Megan C., a divorced mother of two daughters, told us, "It feels nice to be alone. If you consider that I got married at twenty-two, had my first child at twenty-three. I never lived on my own!" A year ago her older daughter, Amber, moved back home for six months because of a health emergency. "I could hardly turn her away, but I couldn't wait till she was well enough to leave. I'd gotten used to having the house the way I wanted it. I could cook what I like to eat—or not cook at all. I'm a night person. I work happily until two in the morning. All of a sudden I had to tiptoe around lest I wake her up."

Boomerang Kids

Sam and Amber's solution—Nan and Megan's problem—is widespread these days. Young people are beset by a precarious job market and the high cost of housing; they have college loans to pay off and mounting graduate school expenses; many of them are delaying marriage or, if they did marry, are getting divorced. Although the assumption of most middle-class Americans is that after their children have finished their schooling they will live independently from their parents, reality often dictates otherwise. According to the 1990 U.S.

Census, among adults twenty-five to thirty-four years old, 32 percent of single men and 8½ percent of single women were living at home with their parents. And most experts agree that these figures underestimate the total number of young people who will return home at some point. Young adults who move back in have acquired a rubric—boomerang children. They leave, they come back, they may even repeat the cycle.

Says Arlen M., mother of Martha, twenty-six, and Harper, twenty-three, "My husband and I were talking to some of our friends about this the other day. I don't know if it's our age or our children's age or what, but we're not in the least bit interested in having them around all the time. They're in and out all the time. We'd just as soon they not be in and out all the time. We've had 'em!"

Our daughters' lives are not yet settled. Their visits are intended to be temporary, or at least finite, "just until I get back on my feet," "till I save up money for grad school." Sometimes the visits are indeed short; sometimes they drag on. Pauline E., mother of four, told us, "I've had Jonathan live with me twice for a year at a time; I've had Gail for nearly two years when she came home from Europe; I've had Margot after her marriage broke up, and she came back to New York looking for a job; Annie's the only one who would rather die than ask me if she could move in." Arlen M.'s daughter Martha came home after college to look for a job. Arlen told us, "In no uncertain terms, my husband and I said she could have her old room and we'd feed her for half a year, and then she had to be out." The six months' rule seems to be commonplace—many mothers told us they have enforced it, or are ready to, at the drop of a returnee's suitcase.

Living with a young adult daughter is potentially a very difficult situation: Both of you are confronted every day with a time warp—your living arrangement is the same as it was when she was a child, but she is no longer a child. You may both slip back into old patterns of behavior. While Martha was home, Arlen told us, "The hardest thing was that the things I expected her to be an adult about were not necessarily the things she thought she ought to be an adult about, and the things that I still considered her a child in, those weren't the areas she wanted to be considered a child in. For example, she'd come home for lunch and leave her dishes in the sink. Well, there weren't any dishes in the sink until she left hers in there. She didn't think about it. By the same token if she comes in at three o'clock in the morning, I'm not excited about that, and she's thinking, well, I'm not a kid."

When a daughter comes home, whether for two weeks or two years, it's helpful to try to understand why she's there. Is it really because of her short-term practical needs or are there also more basic issues that can be identified and addressed? Nan Lyons recognized that, yes, Sam needed to keep her expenses as low as possible while she was in graduate school, but there were emotional reasons for her return as well. Says Nan, "Because her father had died, and I was her only living relative, she needed to be close, to watch me. I think subconsciously she feels that if I disappear, everything disappears. She knew she wanted to be back home. And home was the operative word."

Fortunately Nan had always been very open with Sam, so it felt natural to talk candidly to her about living together again. Nan initiated a conversation that set the tone for their new relationship. "I told her that having someone else in the house—even somebody that I loved enormously—would inhibit me, because I would feel guilty about being depressed, or guilty about crying when I wanted to cry. Because I would feel that she was there and I would have to be up for her, and not drag her into this. So I thought that that would be a difficult thing for me. And I had to say this right up front so she would understand my reluctance to have her move into the house. It wasn't my reluctance to have her in the city, or close, but to give up my privacy.

"And I don't think kids ever want to hear that. They may respect it, but they don't want to hear it. That's a very visceral kind of thing, that you don't want them to come home. But because we were open and honest, I could tell her up front that it was going to be bad, and why that was, and then we could go on from there. So we talked about it, because it was very important to me that she understand that there would be periods when I would just close my door because I would *have* to close the door. And that had never happened before in our relationship. There was never a time when I wasn't available."

From Susan's journal, Febrary 2, 1996

Our interview with Nan Lyons today reminded me of an incident that took place during that period two years ago when Sarah came back here to live between the end of her job and the beginning of graduate school. I went to the theater with friends and we had dinner afterward. When I got home at around one in the morning, I was amazed to find Sarah anxiously waiting up for me. "I thought you'd be home an hour ago," she blurted out. "Why didn't you call when you knew you would be late?"

At first I was mildly amused. I said, "I'm often late, and it didn't occur to me that you'd be upset." I've lived alone for a long time, I come and go pretty much as I please, and I haven't been in the habit of being accountable to anybody. But, of course, she was right. So I thought, I'm going to have to do things differently. I'm going to have to be as attentive to her legitimate concerns as I would expect her to be to mine. It was both touching and strange to have the shoe on the other foot.

Once they had addressed the closed door issue, Nan and Sam had to figure out together how they would divide their space. "She came up with a marvelous solution that would never have occurred to me. I assumed that she would want her old room back, and I'd been using it as an office since she left. So I was going to have to train myself to work someplace else, because I thought that was *her* room, and it never occurred to me not to think of her in it. And after she was home for two or three days, she came to me and said, 'I don't want to make you angry, or add to the problems of this whole situation, but I feel very depressed in my old room. It's bringing me back to when I was a child. And I don't want to be that. I want to go forward. So what I really want is a place that's new, that's my own. Would you mind if I took the maid's room?'

"Now, I would never have ordered my daughter to live in the maid's room. It's a bad, bad mother thing, like Cinderella. And she said, 'I'll paint it blue and put up stars, and make it my own.' Well that solved my problem, because I immediately moved my computer back into her room. And that was the transition."

Do you think she's regressing at all? we asked. "My first thought was, she's going to regress as soon as she crosses the threshold. How could she not? She was the person who had an office and a job and was Miss Lyons, who administered all these programs. And now she's the student, with homework and no one taking her seriously, and she's living with her mother. So it's a struggle. For example, she won't cook for herself. So if I'm cooking, great, if I'm shopping, great. She doesn't make demands, but on the other hand she doesn't do it for herself. Sometimes we eat together. Sometimes we eat separately. She doesn't eat the way I think of as eating. She nibbles or grazes. And after Ivan died, I stopped cooking. I don't like to be in the kitchen for a long time. I don't like to do the things that I used to do. I don't do it for myself, and I didn't want to have to be Mommy again in the kitchen."

So how do you handle that? "We talk about it. I tell her it makes me feel a little guilty that I'm not doing it. But I can't do it right now. I'm not able to do it. And she has accepted that."

When a daughter moves back home, some degree of regression by both mother and daughter is probably inevitable. But both women can successfully mitigate the strains of living together if they work out new ground rules for each person's responsibility in everyday life. A mother can ask that her daughter honor house rules that are important to her. But she's no longer responsible for shaping a child's good habits—she no longer has to be in what one mother called "the Mommy mode."

Pauline E. is a fifty-eight-year-old divorced woman living in a two-bedroom apartment in New York. At the moment her oldest daughter, Margot, thirty-four, has been in residence for four months. Margot returned to New York when her marriage broke up, and she's hunting for an apartment. Margot and Pauline had not lived together in nearly fifteen years, so they both had some adjusting to do. "The only thing I asked Margot to do was to clean up the kitchen," Pauline told us. "Margot is not a housekeeper. I'm immaculate, although living in New York, I've let up some, but I said to her, 'We have these wonderful little visitors, these roaches.' I said, 'You've got to do the dishes immediately after using them.' Initially she had a little trouble with that, but she's become neater. And her room is neater than I've ever seen it. She does dip into my closet which we giggle about. When I saw something down on the floor, I said, 'Would you mind? That's mine. Would you mind hanging it up?' She now hangs it up. Otherwise my expectations are fairly minimal."

Pauline has eased their living together by focusing on things that really matter to her and by telling Margot directly how she feels about them. And, as she is eager to admit, "I've let a lot of things go. As long as she keeps the kitchen neat, I don't even mind some things that used to bother me, like putting her socked feet up on a coffee table. Maybe I've loosened up. I think, It's innocuous—it's not worth arguing over."

Margot has changed, too. "Margot—who never used to set foot in the kitchen—is now a fabulous cook. She's taken over a lot of the cooking chores. So now I'll say to her, 'What should we have for supper?' She cooks this wonderful Indian- and Italian-style food. The kitchen looks unbelievable, though. When I cook, I do the dishes as I go along, but she'll probably never do that. I do the dishes now. It used to be that I cooked and the kids did the dishes. Now we have this big role reversal."

Pauline clearly enjoys having Margot living at home and is in no hurry to push her out. "We joke about her leaving. She says, 'I want out of here as soon as possible.' I say, 'Really?' 'Yeah.' 'Why? It's not a bad deal.' 'I want my own space,' she says. 'I want to get my things out of storage.' 'You can go visit them,' I say.

"I certainly understand it, but I'll miss her terribly when she goes because I know I won't see her all that much. I mean we sit and watch TV, we'll chat. It's freer, it's easier than it's ever been—not that it was ever that difficult. But when your children see you as an adult in a living environment that is also their living environment, even if it's only temporary, they have a very different perspective on you than if they didn't live with you."

However, the circumstances were not at all the same when Pauline's middle daughter, Gail, came home to live at the age of twenty-three. "It was nine years ago. Gail had just come back from Europe. She was completely at loose ends. And I said, 'Why don't you work for a few months at a temp job and save some money while you figure out what you want to do?' Well maybe after a year and a half, I had to say, 'Gail, you know I love you. I love having you around, but I'm going to do something that's semi-tough love. I'm going to throw you out. For your own good. Figure out what you want to do. You're too comfortable here. You're working as an office assistant, you're earning no money, you're going nowhere, you haven't graduated college, you're brilliant. This is ludicrous. I'm going to miss you a lot more than you'll ever miss me, but I'm going to throw you out.' "

Pauline's ultimatum had unexpected results. Gail began to take stock of her life. To Pauline's surprise, the plan Gail arrived at required that she stay home even longer. Which her mother accepted, but with much better defined terms. "The next thing I know she says, 'I'm going back to college again, and I'll need to live here to save money.' She had boomeranged in and out of college, I might add. She was never mature enough to stick. I said, 'You're *what?*' So I said, 'Okay, if you do, I'm not giving you anything other than room and board. Limited phone calls, too. I'm not giving you tuition—you'll have to manage that on your own.' She said okay. She went to Queens College, which was a real bargain at that time, and sure enough, two years later she graduates with honors, is accepted into Harvard, Yale, Penn, for her Ph.D. program with all kinds of scholarships behind her, so she's fine. So that's my big success story with Gail."

Brenda W., whose two daughters, Johanna, thirty, and Laura, twenty-five, have both lived at home for various periods after college, believes that the level of comfort between the generations "depends more on the personality of the kids than on the parents even—how secretive they are, how concerned about their own privacy, and whether they think they have to play a role for us." Brenda says that when Johanna was home for a short while, it was hard for Brenda and her husband. "Johanna is a very private person who has a very vivid inner life and probably a very vivid real life, too! And it just had us nonplused. But Laura being Laura, things go more smoothly. She takes it upon herself to call us and say I'm going to be late. When she is there she'll make an effort to talk with us and tell us what is happening in her day, what is happening with friends. And then she'll go into her room— she doesn't even shut the door although she could—and I know she watches television or is on the phone—whatever she wants to do in her room, and we don't think anything of it. We're incredibly lenient—whoever the current boyfriend is, he sleeps over. We never say a word. If she's around on a weekend, we'll all go out during the day, go to a museum, look at stores—and she's happy to be with us. And we all have fun. And if she has her boyfriend with her, then we include him as well."

Laura is living at home now because she's at her Wall Street job eighteen hours a day, seven days a week. "She says why pay for an apartment she'll never be in," according to Brenda, "and we have room. It's working out smoothly—it would not have worked out smoothly with Johanna. The girls are very different."

Johanna always seemed somewhat aloof from her parents and her peers. "She really did not have close friends growing up," says Brenda. "I have to say that. After college, she moved back in with us with a street dog she had adopted. And between the dog who was basically not housebroken—I've since replaced some of the couches—and Johanna, who was very unhappy—she wanted to be a writer and she was trying to find herself in work, and she would be unemployed for long stretches—we had a hard time. And she had strange people that she took up with; they weren't bad people, but they were not the type we expected from our background or hers. We opened our house to them, and they would come to Thanksgiving dinner. And then she got a permanent job. And from that point on it was, 'We'll help you move out as soon as you get an apartment.' And once she got a job and an apartment she started finding herself."

Laura will also move out a year from now. She plans either to go to business school or to get a job with more reasonable hours. She and her parents recognize that even a young woman in her present pleasant circumstances would rather have her own place. Brenda says, "From our point of view, we have no problem. But I think from her standpoint, she would like to invite people over to have dinners and cook, and if we're there, she somehow doesn't feel as comfortable. One weekend her boyfriend Rafael was here, and I said, 'We're going out early,' and she said, 'Oh good. That means Rafe and I can cook fondue.' And then I realized, yeah, she would cook more often if she had her own place."

When You Want Your Daughter to Remain at Home

Cultural assumptions

A generation or so ago it would have been unlikely, and probably traumatic, for unmarried children from Jewish, Irish, Italian or African-American families to live apart from their parents' households, but within these communities mores are significantly different today. Shelagh C. was raised in a tightly knit Irish enclave in Queens. She lived at home until she got married at twenty-one. Shelagh and her husband are the parents of six adult daughters and a twenty-year-old son. "When Colleen, my oldest girl, graduated from college, she got an apartment in the city, and I nearly died. She wanted to leave this beautiful suburban home with the canopy bed to live in this prerevolutionary building! And I couldn't understand it. But she wanted to do it, and I wasn't going to stop her. My mother was alive, and she said, 'But you have to stop her,' and I said, 'No, I'm not going to do that. She wants to do this, and she should.' And I'm sure she had some tight times. But she never came back, and she went on and was very successful. That was the toughest one. As each of the girls followed her footsteps, it became easier."

Among new immigrants, the preference of parents that their daughters stay home until marriage is as strong as ever. Farouz P, an Iranian woman living in Los Angeles, told us, "In our culture we prefer the children live with the parents rather than to live alone." While her two daughters were in college, they lived at home. Isabelle, twenty-five, continued to stay with her parents until she got married six months ago. Clemence, twenty-three, plans to go East next year for law school, but, Farouz explains, "For sure, she will come back again. If she didn't get married, when she finishes her law school she will come back home. Her home is here."

The expectation that a daughter will remain at home with her parents until marriage is especially strong in Latino communities. Mauricia A., born and raised in Havana, always assumed that her daughter Bianca, thirty-one, would follow that pattern. "I think it's, one, my background. In Cuba you lived at home, whether you were a son or a daughter, until you got married, because you lived in big sprawling homes, and it was another life. And second, when my children were growing up we always sat down to dinner every night, and we talked. And children were welcome. So my house was a place of a family and of family life. Why do you bring children into this world and then send them out in the world at eighteen like a lot of my friends? And then they wonder why the children don't love them."

Soon after Bianca returned from college, there was a family crisis. "My husband's economic situation took a turn for the worse. And we had to sell our apartment and move to a smaller apartment. And he had a middle-aged crisis and left me. And she became my sole emotional support. She became the mother and I became the daughter—I now realize it. Our roles were reversed. She was a nourisher and I was a nourishee. And I didn't see the danger of it, so I allowed it to go on. She was by this time twenty-five or twenty-six."

During that time Bianca had several romances, but none of them very serious. Things continued to deteriorate at home. Although Mauricia's husband had moved back in, there was financial and emotional friction between them, which Bianca often witnessed. Mauricia said, "She, as an erudite, articulate intelligent person, would stick in her two bits, and I realized that that was not good. But she was not making enough money. I didn't want her living in a walkup someplace alone, so I allowed her to stay on at home. I would never have told her she had to move out until she had a boyfriend and was going to marry him. And married him. But things changed. And, as a fortune-teller once told a friend of mine in China, 'There can't be two tigers on top of a mountain.' Two grown-up women cannot live together; it's not meant to be."

Mauricia took things one step at a time. "I didn't tell her right off, 'You have to move out.' I began by saying, 'You should start saving money and thinking about getting your own apartment. Because with your father's economic situation, I don't know what's going to happen in this house. And in any case, you shouldn't be in the middle of all this. You should have a healthy life.' The idea sort of grew on her.

She didn't argue. The problem was finding a nice apartment. After she had put some money aside, we started looking at apartments, and she got excited about living on her own."

Finally Bianca found an apartment twenty blocks from her parents, and coincidentally, landed a better paying job. "I said, 'Darling, you've just got to go. For your own mental health. I would love you to live with me for the rest of your life, but suppose I have a stroke—I'm fifty-eight—or cancer. And you would be stuck living here, and being my mother, my nurse, and that's not what I want for you.' So she moved. We still talk every day, we go out to lunch, we have coffee together, but our relationship is much healthier. I still talk to her about my life, but in a more general sense, not as a crutch. There is more of a healthy distance."

Although Mauricia's dreams for both her daughter and herself have not been fulfilled, she's quite resilient. A few years ago she started her own business, and she raced off after our interview to work out at her gym, despite having recently broken her wrist. Bianca has advanced to an important international marketing job; her recent serious relationship with a man, however, has just ended painfully. "I never thought I'd be my age and be in my financial situation," Mauricia says. "Or that I would have a daughter nearly thirty-two who isn't married and no grandchildren. But I've learned to deal with things as they come along."

The safety factor

In her ideal world, Mauricia would have had her daughter stay at home until she established her own home with a husband. Some women just want another year or so to make sure their daughters can cope on their own. Several mothers expressed concern about their sheltered twenty-two-year-olds living and working in the city. Lib O'Brien lives in suburban New Jersey. "I'm very fearful of the big bad world out there for a girl. And I recognize the double standard. It's very different with my son. He's in New York till eleven or twelve at night and comes home through the Port Authority, and I don't think a thing of it. But when I know that Keri's going to be in the city I'm just a basket case."

Last spring, Nellie Jenkins's twenty-one-year-old daughter Natalie was looking forward to June graduation from college. Natalie had already lined up a job on Wall Street, and it was Nellie's assumption that she would want to come home to live in their comfortable suburban home which is within easy commuting distance of New York City. "I wanted her to get a little more secure in knowing how to cope with the city, and I think I wanted her with us a little longer, too." During a visit home in March, Natalie discussed her plans for the fall. "One night we were sitting at the table having supper, and I almost choked when she said, 'Laurie and I are going to get an apartment in New York when we graduate.' I almost died. My husband said I did real well. All I said was 'Oh?' and I'm sitting there thinking of my baby living in New York City." Although she was very uneasy about Natalie's plans, Nellie tried not to interfere, and her husband even put the girls in touch with several real estate agents he knew.

After checking out a couple of apartments, Natalie realized that she could afford to live away from home only if she moved in with several roommates. "So one night she calls, and she says, 'You know ma, I've been thinking about two, three of us getting an apartment together, what kind of privacy is there? I could be home with my own room and not have to deal with that.' And I'm on the phone going 'Thank you Jesus . . . yes!' "

Nellie began to negotiate with her daughter about how she and Natalie would handle practical matters like money and household responsibilities. "By this time she had accepted the job at J. P. Morgan," Nellie said. "And she wanted to pitch in. 'You know I'm not expecting to come home and live on you and Dad,' she said. 'You know I'll contribute whatever you feel I should.' And at that time I wanted to say, 'You can come and live for free,' but I knew that wasn't a good thing to do." They agreed that Natalie would contribute fifty dollars a week to the household and pay for her phone. Nellie and her husband set to work getting Natalie's old room ready for her return. "We painted, we bought new blinds, we put down new carpeting because the room had been like a little girl's room, and we're making it into a room for an adult. And I'm saying, 'Okay fine, it will be a guest room when she leaves,' and we didn't discuss moving again." Now that Natalie is home, Nellie told us, "Saturday mornings she gets up, cleans the bathroom, whatever I'm doing, she'll help. She takes care of her own room, she's kind of a neatnik. It's not clean-clean, but things are where she wants them."

Figuring out how to acknowledge Natalie's status as an emerging adult was a bit trickier. According to Nellie, her daughter said, " 'Well you know, Mom, I'm not a child anymore. I'm grown, I'm a woman. And I feel that having been away from home for four years I've changed, and I'm not sure that you're ready to deal with whatever changes I've gone through.' And I said to her, 'Well you haven't given me the opportunity either, you know. I've never dealt with you as a woman who is making her own money, who can come into our home and contribute, whom I can trust to do the right thing because that's what you've shown to me. I've not seen that side of you either and you have not seen that of me.'

"I knew exactly what she meant," Nellie said. "Natalie has always lived under rules and regulations here. I am the granddaughter of a Baptist minister, and we were raised nine girls, very strict. As a result I have carried over some of my mother's ways with Natalie and her sister. I feel that it has made them, is making them, very strong. I think that Natalie meant that she was not used to keeping a time clock if she went out. If she chose to stay out, then she stayed. If she chose to come back at four or five in the morning, then she did that, when she was away. Here, we discourage that kind of behavior. So we worked it out. If she was going to be gone all night, she had to tell me when she left home. 'I'm going to the city. I'm going to spend the night with my friend,' whatever. She understands my fears about her safety. I would sit on the edge of the bed and wait up till she got home. And I think that she saw and understood."

Nellie's reasons for wanting her daughter to stay at home and Natalie's reasons for wanting to be there may have been different, but it suited both their purposes for Natalie to settle in. Nellie understands that this is a temporary solution. She expects that Natalie will move out in another year or two, "when she gets a little more seasoning, a little more of the being able to go into the city, and getting accustomed to the hustle and bustle."

Wanting your daughter to spend a sort of postgraduate year at home getting "a little more seasoning," as Nellie put it, is not an unreasonable wish. After all, even if your daughter seems to have good self-protective instincts, you can't help but worry about her. Violence against women is an unfortunate constant in our lives. A girl who has known only the protective environment of a quiet suburb and a sheltered college campus may well need to acquire some street smarts. But at some point your daughter needs to take responsibility for herself. A mother who holds on may be using her concerns about her daughter's safety, financial stability, or comfort to mask her own needs.

Holding on

A mother may want to keep her daughter at home because she fears loneliness; she might want a buffer against her husband; she might think she can impose constraints on her daughter's sexual behavior; she may be unwilling to give up the role of active caretaker. Audrey A. was devastated when her older daughter, Lynn, twenty-five, announced she wanted to leave home. Audrey is the superintendent of schools in a large midwestern city, and has recently received national recognition for innovative educational programs. When Lynn finished college, she moved back into her parents' house, back into her own room, which was exactly what her mother wanted. Audrey doesn't understand friends who are eager to have their grown children out of the house. "Some of them even subsidize rent for their kids! I clearly had a very very different picture. I'd like all of them—my girls, my nephews—to live with me. I really would."

But after three years during which—from Audrey's point of view—they lived together quite happily, Lynn started looking for her own apartment. "We had had a couple of heated discussions about her not coming home for the night. And that was unacceptable to my husband, and I told her she had to tell him if she was going to stay with friends. 'I can't wake up and have to explain to him that you're not here.' And while I don't think that's what precipitated her leaving, it played a part."

Lynn wanted her independence. "She said, 'I'm twenty-five, if I don't go now, I'm never going.' And I said, 'This is crazy. You have a room, you have a car. You have everything here. You can't afford anything like this anywhere else.' But she wants to be independent, so ultimately I have to respect that." Lynn moved out several months later. Recounting this part of her story, Audrey began to cry. "It was traumatic. I was sick for a month . . . I didn't feel sick. I *was* sick."

Audrey recognizes that a lot of her turmoil was because of her own needs, not Lynn's. "I do a lot of mothering out of guilt. My mother and I had—do have—a very difficult relationship. Consequently, a lot of my life I have tried to make things better for my girls, tried to befriend them. So I guess I was offended that she wanted to leave." Audrey described her own mother, who was also a very successful public official, as "unemotional. I can't remember any touching or kissing. Very task-oriented. Very domineering. A real pusher. And that's part of the reason why I got married at sixteen, why I left home right after I graduated from high school. Because I wanted to be free of her." When Lynn moved out, Audrey saw it as a replay of her own life. "Probably because of my relationship with my mother, I felt like her moving out was sort of a rejection. I worry a lot about my relationship with the girls. The guilt is about not being a good mother—if I had been a better mother she wouldn't have left."

Although her wound is still raw, Audrey is wise enough to know that her reasons for keeping Lynn at home were not respectful of her daughter's needs. Rather than jeopardize her relationship with Lynn, Audrey let go. And in fact, she and Lynn are probably more comfortable with each other now that Lynn is out of the house. "She always listened to me, but I think she listens more now. She calls more often, with 'Well what do you think?' I don't usually call her. She calls me. But if I don't hear, I'll call. We keep in close touch." Audrey's second daughter, Jane, who is still in college, has announced that she isn't going to live at home when she graduates. How will Audrey cope? "You know, you get a little more prepared . . . I can't say that I like it, but I know it's better for everybody if you can let go."

Three Generations Under One Roof

Difficult as it can be to accommodate everyone's needs if a mother and daughter are living in the same household, the problems are multiplied a hundredfold if the daughter moves back home with a child. Of the women we interviewed, eight have had daughters and grandchildren move in at some point. The young women have needed help either because they can't make it as single parents or because their marriages have broken up. In either instance, their needs—and the burdens on their parents—are both emotional and financial, which compounds the problem for a mother who wants to see her daughter function as an adult.

The impact on your life

When your daughter moves home with her child, your world turns upside down. Your living arrangements, your sense of order, your relationship with everyone else in the family, are all affected. Rosita J., a sixty-two-year-old homemaker, lives in a tract house south of Los Angeles with her husband, her twenty-year-old son, her twenty-five-year-old daughter, Gloria, and Gloria's six-year-old son, Billy. Gloria returned home with Billy when her brief marriage ended soon after Billy's birth. Rosita and her daughter try very hard not to get in each other's way, but she says, "I think any young woman after they become an adult would like to have their own things. If they want to put a bouquet of flowers here, they want to do it their way. And I don't forbid her from doing anything here, but there's nothing like having your own home."

For several months, Barbara K. picked up hints that her twenty-three-year-old daughter Penny's marriage was in trouble, and as much as Barbara disapproved of divorce, she knew that she had to do whatever she could to support Penny if she decided to leave her husband. "I always felt that once my kids were married, I could sit back and relax, and I was really not going to invite them back in my house.

But one morning in early June, a Sunday, she came over with the children and she was very upset. And Penny doesn't really complain a lot or lean on me a lot, so I knew just from her demeanor it was serious. And I don't know where it came from, from the depths somewhere of maternal instinct, I said, 'Would it make things any easier if you and the boys moved back in here for a while?' And she said it certainly would."

Within days Penny and her two young sons were ensconced in her parents' home. As much as Barbara was happy to help Penny out, she resented the disruption in her life. "Normally when I come home from work I can just sit and put my feet up. If I don't feel like cooking right away I don't have to do that. That wasn't so anymore. In the morning I was used to quietly having my grapefruit and coffee and quietly reading the paper before I left for work and all of a sudden I had Cheerios all over the table." Barbara went on, "The thing that really bothered me—which I didn't like about myself—was that I hated the lived-in look of my house. When I came in and found kids' toys all over the house, because kids are like that. That was such a shallow thing. And yet it bothered the hell out of me."

Dorothy O.'s thirty-four-year-old daughter Kathleen and her three-year-old granddaughter have been living with Dorothy and her husband since the baby was a newborn. "It may sound picayune," says Dorothy, "but at night the little girl will want to watch a tape and she's cranky. So even though my husband wants to watch the news, I'll say to him, 'Just let her watch it, it will calm her down.' Because our supper is kind of disturbed if she's cranky."

Every mother with a grandchild living under her roof found herself taking on some of the responsibility for child care, whether she welcomed it or not. Rosie Smith, an admissions officer at a private elementary school in Santa Monica, who is also active with her husband in community affairs, has had to fit one more responsibility into her busy schedule. Her nineteen-year-old daughter Tisha brought her baby home to live with her parents. "This term, Tisha has a late class on Monday night, so I pick the baby up from her child care—fortunately it's just around the corner—I bring her home, play with her, feed her, and put her to bed. She's a good baby, but it's exhausting."

Verdine Jones retired from her job as a federal parole officer to help her daughter Rhonda care for her little girl. Rhonda was living at home with her parents after finishing college when she got pregnant and decided not to marry her child's father. She cared for the baby herself for two years but was eager to get back to work. Verdine had looked forward to her retirement, because she had expected to relax and pursue a long-deferred interest in real estate management. Instead she was doing full-time child care.

Verdine, like Rosie Smith, is African-American. It is not uncommon for African-American grandmothers to play a significant part in raising their grandchildren or to live in multigenerational households. "My mom kept my kids while I worked," Verdine told us. "But she was much better than I am. I wish I had some of her patience. I stayed home one year with my grandbaby," she said, "and I didn't like it!" Verdine laughed. "I love my grandbaby, but your day is consumed; this child consumed my entire day. And I told my daughter, 'Baby care is a full-time job. I would prefer to go back to work and assist you financially. You could look for someone to come in, a young girl, and pay her to stay with the child, and let you have some space and time.'"

Dorothy O. says, "I watched my granddaughter the first year while my daughter continued to work full time in the city. And probably people think, Well what's wrong with that? Why can't you watch her? I did that for a year. My daughter left at eight in the morning, and she didn't get home till about seven in the evening, and by five o'clock I was practically in tears. This little girl was very active. One time I took her for a walk to town, and on the way back I had to carry her all the way home." What is a routine activity for a young mother in her twenties or thirties can be a physical burden for a sixty-one-year-old grandmother. When the arrangement became too much for Dorothy, her daughter stopped working and took over caring for the child herself.

Every morning at six o'clock, Barbara K.'s daughter left for work before her two young sons woke up. Barbara had to feed and dress the boys and get them ready for day care. "It made me reach back to when I had little children," Barbara says. "We sang the same songs that I sang when I had little kids, and told the same stories. The morning was the worst time because they missed her so badly. They usually woke up crying. And little Johnny has a blankie like all kids do, and one morning he had this thing in one hand, and he was clutching one of her shoes in the other, and he said, 'Where are you, Mommy?' And then every morning, 'Where are you, Mommy?' It got to be like a mantra. I realized quickly that I had to give these kids the tender loving care they really need, so I made it a game. Every morning we did a little game. Just going down the stairs was a game. Just having breakfast. Looking out the window at the squirrels. So I changed, I became kind of a different person for awhile. I think children do bring out a different part of you. And it was not a bad thing." Several of the women we spoke to had come to see that—if the burden of caretaking was not too onerous—they did enjoy the opportunity to get closer to their grandchildren.

Rosita J. says, "I always told my kids, 'If you have children, don't call and ask me to baby-sit, because I want to be free, fancy free, so don't count on me.'" Then Gloria came home with Billy. Rosita had been against her daughter's marriage; she knew that having a child would make it very hard for Gloria to finish her education. Nonetheless, Rosita pitched in. To her surprise, she loves being involved. "When I had a grandchild, my feelings changed. When I take care of him, I love him and I spoil him. So I think there's nothing you can gain by dealing in the past. This marriage happened for a reason, and I do believe all things happen for a reason. And when I look at my grandson, what can I say? Maybe if it weren't for that relationship, Billy wouldn't be here."

Different ideas about child rearing

How do a mother and a daughter who live together handle the inevitable differences between their styles of child rearing? The grandmothers all praised their daughters for being good parents in very trying circumstances. But they also told us that they disapproved of some of the things they saw their daughters doing. And, because the behavior was happening right before their eyes every day, it was hard not to offer their opinions. "I'm talking to you as the mother of seven," Dorothy O. finds herself saying to her daughter Kathleen when she thinks Kathleen is not firm enough with her own baby. "She gives the little girl choices, and the baby gets all fussy. And I say, 'Why are you asking her what she wants to do? Just pick her up and go. That's what I did with all of you.' I said, 'Just go.' And she took that very well. I mean it's totally different today the way they raise their kids. They'll say, 'Come here.' And the kid doesn't come. And they end up yelling and screaming. And my other daughter does that too. And I say, 'Just take them by the hand and lead them.' But I do see that it's harder for Kathleen because she's the single parent."

Barbara K. says, "I feel like Penny spends a lot on her children. It's her money—and it wasn't that I felt she should be giving it to me—it was just like a ritual though. Friday night they had to go to Toys 'R' Us and pick out something. And a couple of times I said to her, 'You know, this is really crazy. . . .' But I realized after a while that she has guilt about leaving these children all day and that's the way she tries to make it up to them. I didn't do that with my children. So what? We have different ideas."

It's not easy for a young woman, already shaky because of the collapse of her marriage, to mother her children in front of her mother, in her mother's house, after she's used to doing it without that kind of scrutiny. "Mealtime could be stressful for Penny in the beginning," Barbara told us, "because the boys could cut up at mealtime, and she would be uncomfortable. Until we said, 'Look, we've had children, don't let this bother you because you think it bothers us.' So I learned a lot about my daughter in the time she moved back in. I learned that she is really a more uptight person than I ever thought she was. Because I saw her in a different light. I also learned that she's a wonderful mother, and that's a great thing to know about your daughter. She really does love those children, she cares for them almost too much."

Verdine Jones and her daughter have come to a tacit understanding that although Verdine won't be a full-time baby-sitter, she will continue to play an active part in rearing her granddaughter. She sees her role as trying to shore up her daughter's maternal skills. "Rhonda's the ruler, the head, and I'm like the assistant. I'm there for financial and emotional help, but one reason I'm not rushing to move Rhonda out," Verdine told us, "is because she's got a lot to learn about taking care of her baby. For one thing her patience is so short with the baby. I know she's tired when she comes home from work. And she has this responsibility. So maybe it's good that she's here with me. Rhonda is good with kids, she's just not always good with her own. And she knows this. The baby is always underfoot, and she loses her temper. Something else I see is—before the baby was born Rhonda wanted a baby bed so she bought one, and that baby slept in that bed maybe twice. Other than that she slept with Rhonda. And I used to tell her, 'You better put that child in her bed. Why don't you do that?' And that's when she says, 'Ma, this is my kid.' So, of course, now the baby won't go to bed unless Rhonda is going to bed. And if Rhonda is not here, my husband or I have to sleep with the baby.

"The other thing we disagree about is that Rhonda is a freer person, I'm more of a disciplinarian. If the baby wants to eat something like a cookie before dinner, if it was my kid, I'd say 'no.' But I say to her, 'You go ask your mom if you can have that.' I constantly have to tell myself, that's Rhonda's child. I love the child to death, but that's Rhonda's baby. And I know that one day she's going to move. And she should leave. She needs to be head of her own thing."

Planning for the day when she can be on her own

From the moment Penny and her two boys moved in, Barbara K. and her husband began planning for her to reestablish her independence. "When she told us she was in trouble, we said, 'Penny, there's room upstairs, and it will be your house for awhile, as long as we both know that it's temporary until you get on your feet.' And she was very amenable. It was just as hard for her as it was for us." Penny had a good job, but her savings were depleted. She hoped that by staying with her parents for a few months she could put aside enough money for a security deposit on a rental in her parents' neighborhood. "So the three of us decided that it would probably take four to six months. I mean we didn't put a definite date on it. We just said, "Let's hope that by the fall you're able to do something.' As it was, it was November—about six months in all."

The dislocation that everyone felt because of Penny's return home with her boys was minimized because, from the start, Barbara, her husband, and Penny set a mutually agreed-upon goal for her leaving. In their case, things were undoubtedly made easier for several reasons: Penny already had a good job; she was used to being in her own household; she was clear about the fact that she wanted her stay to be as short as possible; and Barbara was able to offer total support without feeling that she was sacrificing her own needs for an unlimited length of time.

Verdine Jones, Rosita J., and Rosie Smith are as convinced as Barbara that their daughters should move on—even though attaining that goal may take them a longer time. Verdine is in the process of buying a small apartment building, partly as an investment, and partly so that her daughter and grandchild will have a place to live. Rosita's daughter, Gloria, has one more semester to go to earn her B.A., and, after five years at home, she's finally able to think ahead to a teaching job and the possibility of living in her own apartment. Rosie is helping her daughter apply for subsidized housing for single parents. Otherwise she and her husband are willing to have Tisha and her baby stay home for one more year until she finishes her degree, because, as Rosie says, "We know there's no way she can do everything all by herself. We want to make sure that she gets her education, that is first and foremost, so she can take care of herself, because she's going to have her daughter for a long time."

When you're ambivalent about having her leave

Neither Dorothy O. nor her daughter have such firm goals about Kathleen's moving on. Kathleen has been home for three years, and she is vague about her future. According to Dorothy, "Every once in a while she'll say, 'I think I'm going to get my own place' or 'Maybe after the first of the year, I'll look for something full time . . .'" Dorothy, too, is ambivalent. "At this time in our lives, I feel it should just be my husband and me." On the other hand, she's uncomfortable about saying that forcefully to Kathleen. Instead she rationalizes: "I'm not sure Kathleen is ready to make it on her own; maybe she needs another year to get herself together." "I think her little girl needs more stability in her life." "If she moves out she'll have to put the baby in day care, and I really don't like that. Maybe because I stayed home with my kids."

Dorothy admits she's avoided discussing any of this with Kathleen. "I'm not very good at confronting people. Sometimes I think, Maybe I should say something to her, and then I'll think, No maybe this isn't such a good time. And then I'll wait. I've always done that. I did it with my husband, maybe that's why we've been married forty-three years. And the same thing with my daughter, I'll think, Well maybe not now, I better wait. She's not in too good a mood. And then I wait, and then I never bother to say it." Unable to locate or express her real feelings, Dorothy has let the situation drift into a stasis which no one has the courage to disrupt.

Resolving your ambivalence

When a mother feels that a seemingly permanent live-in arrangement is wearing her down, how can she break the stalemate and enable her daughter to leave? Virginia S.'s younger daughter Nell, thirty-three, and her son Ben, now seven, have lived with Virginia and her husband, George, since Ben was six months old. Nell talks from time to time about moving out, but she shows a certain lassitude about getting on with life. "What I really resent is that she acts as if she were entitled to stay," says Virginia, who is conflicted about whether or not she wants Nell and Ben to leave. If there weren't subliminal issues of dependency and lack of trust binding this multigenerational family together, Nell would have moved out a long time ago. Virginia's story raises questions: How much can you do to help a daughter who is needy? What do you owe a grandchild you adore? What do you owe yourself?

Nell got pregnant intentionally; there was no man in her life, so she arranged for fertilization at a sperm bank in Atlanta, where she was living at the time. She worked for a large corporation that had excellent health benefits and a model day-care program. When the company unexpectedly closed the division where she worked, she spent a few months looking for another job before asking her parents if she could come home.

Virginia and George are both professionals. He is a partner in an accounting firm; she is a senior actuary at a large insurance company. They live in a comfortable suburban ranch house near Raleigh, North Carolina; there's a large backyard with a tree house and a wading pool for Ben. The family room is decorated with his artwork, his model planes, and his gymnastics trophies. When we met Virginia, she and Nell had just finished making plans for Ben's birthday party the following week. Nell, who works as a teacher's assistant in Ben's private school, was about to drive her son to a swimming lesson; her father would pick him up later. It seemed like a warm family, with everyone pitching in to provide a nurturing environment for Ben. But even though Virginia and George are doing their best to make this living arrangement seem natural, Virginia confided to us that underneath the surface there is strain and confusion for all three adults.

"You're supposed to have more time when your kids grow up and leave," she says. "But George and I are snatching time together as we did when our children were young. He walks in from work, and Ben is right there jumping on him. By the time Ben's in bed, George and I are both exhausted. Having a little one in the house takes its toll." We asked if Nell and Ben were a drain on her parents' finances as well. "Not in the short term," Virginia said, although Nell pays no rent. "We don't need rent money from her, but her being here complicates our plans for the future. In a couple of years it would probably be smart for us to sell the house, buy ourselves a smaller apartment or a house, and invest the rest of the money for our retirement. But Nell's presence—and especially the fact that this is Ben's home— makes that hard to contemplate."

Virginia also recognizes that their living arrangement in some ways enables Nell to regress. "I become very resentful when she acts like a child. And being here, she tends to do that. I would like her to be her adult self more with me. She has few responsibilities in the house. She is the ultimate slob. Her room is a mess. She has no fixed responsibilities. Episodically we talk about what I expect. I would like her at a minimum to pick up after herself and to help Ben learn to pick up after himself. And to keep her room and his room tidy. And to make meals a couple of times a week. But she couldn't care less. She says these things are my issues, not hers."

These periodic discussions sometimes lead to short-term resolutions. Nell cooks every Wednesday for a few weeks. She makes sure that Ben puts away his things when he comes home from school. But before long they're back to where they started. Virginia doesn't like to nag. "I'd rather eat out on the nights that I get home from work late than keep the pressure on her to cook when I can't. I'd rather have a cleaning service clean Ben's room than nag at her about that." Lately, Virginia admits, Nell has done a better job of keeping Ben's room neat, but her own is still a mess. "I still do more than my share," says Virginia, "and I tend to resent it." Does she say that to Nell? "No, mostly to George. I pick my battles with Nell."

Virginia's inability to demand more responsibility from Nell, her unwillingness to enforce her own desires, stems from an underlying fear. "There have been times when Nell has nearly used the threat of leaving, with Ben, as a kind of blackmail. She's never actually said it, but it's there. For Ben's sake we tolerate these things. And sometimes I really resent it, because it's a hold she has on us. It's a way she has of controlling us because of Ben."

We asked Virginia if, given this bind, she could imagine the situation changing. "Well, it could change at any time, I suppose," she said, somewhat doubtfully. "I don't see her moving out just because she wants to. She would like to, but on the other hand essentially she's got it good. A lot of things are done for her. She goes to work, she takes care of Ben, and basically that's it. Keeping house and cooking meals are not high on her list. Unless she has to, she prefers not to." It sounded to us as if Virginia was removing herself from a role in the drama. Before we could probe more about this seeming passivity, Virginia herself brought up her inability to take a firm stand. "We've never really tried to help her find an apartment she could afford. Not really. I've been criticized by some of my friends for this. They think there's something terribly wrong about this. But in most cultures around the world, extended families are the norm. In the past it was the norm in this country, and in many subcultures it still is. So

I don't see any reason why she should be forced out, why she and Ben should have to accept a lower standard of living, just because somebody thinks the American way is to be independent."

But in the culture in which Virginia and George are rooted, it is unusual for a daughter to be living at home. And Virginia's own ambivalence underlines this fact. Even as she reiterated her claim that extended families should be able to live together, she mentioned again her resentment at feeling taken advantage of. "There's a lot of ambivalence, both ways. I resent her control over me, via Ben." By now Virginia was in tears. "And her lack of participation. I really resent that." We asked again, was she saying that if Nell took seriously her responsibilities within the household, everything would be all right? "Well it would make life easier for me," she equivocated.

What are the underlying reasons that Virginia and George have tolerated these living arrangements for so many years? Says Dr. Kathy Weingarten: "When I see parents who are intractably muddled about whether or not to allow a daughter and her child to continue to live with them, it's often because the parents don't actually have confidence that their daughter can manage by herself. If they did, they could be clearer about their goal. When a family frames the problem as 'We're not ready to say to an adult child, "Sink or swim, get out there and make it on your own," ' you can be pretty sure they're afraid that child can't swim." The love and concern that Virginia and George have for Ben plays into that pattern—they probably don't think that Nell can be as good a mother without their help as she is with it. "What's usually required in these cases," says Dr. Weingarten, "is a lengthy preparation in which you deal with the issue of your confidence in her."

What are some steps Nell's parents might take to get the process of disentanglement moving purposefully? How can any family break such a logjam? First of all, the family members should probably begin by having a frank discussion about how they're going to carry out any conversations about their situation. Do they want to do work with a therapist or some other kind of facilitator? If they decide to go it alone, they should create a structure so that the conversations take place at a set time and place, rather than on the fly over dinner or on the way to a movie. And they should try to stick to the topic and complete a specific agenda at each meeting, making sure that anything unfinished is put on hold until the next meeting so that the process doesn't seep into every other aspect of their daily life. For this particular family, the agenda might well include Virginia's frustration and anger, Nell's passivity, and the inability of each family member to explain to the others exactly how he or she is feeling. The ground rules should encourage everybody to use words like "I feel . . ." "I don't like it . . ." "I would like . . ." Each person should express what he or she sees as the best outcome for the future, and what steps he or she believes need to be in place to reach that goal.

It is important for every member of the family to try to identify and build on the daughter's areas of competence. Virginia and her family might focus on how well Nell managed when she was living in Atlanta, and how she could reactivate those skills. "You can talk about what else a daughter might need to be able to cope alone," says Dr. Weingarten. "What you're really trying to do in this circumstance is build up the strength of the adult child so that the parents feel empowered to take a step because they believe that she will be able to manage."

If your goal is to have your adult daughter living on her own, and she is living at home for any but the most practical reasons, you probably have to go through some version of this exercise to help her leave successfully. Only after significant groundwork has been laid is it likely that you can move on to practical issues: When might she move out? Will you subsidize her? How can she find her own place? And so forth. This process can take a long time—months, perhaps a year. There will be clashes and hurt feelings. But ultimately you and your daughter should gain confidence that she will be able to make a successful life for herself in the years ahead.

Chapter 6

Can She Fend for
Herself?

The two of us have had surprisingly parallel lives. We both grew up in western Pennsylvania, our parents knew each other, and we were college classmates. We both came to New York in 1960. After a year or two of graduate school and some entry level jobs, we each went to work at a major communications corporation—Susan at Time Inc., Marilyn at CBS. Even though our fathers never thought of us as pursuing careers, they were thrilled that such important institutions took us seriously enough to hire us. Our mothers took an interest in the clothes we wore to work and any news they could glean of attractive young men working in the same offices.

It took several years for our parents to accept the fact that we would continue to work after we got married, and that we were as committed to our work as men were. Our mothers, who were proud that their husbands could support them, felt sorry that we had to continue working. That we enjoyed it never entered their minds. Our fathers took a different tack. When, after five years, we each contemplated moving elsewhere within the industry, they were aghast: Switching from job to job, even for a promotion, looked irresponsible. Where was our company loyalty? And besides, having entered the shelter of a benevolent large corporation, why would anyone ever want to leave?

Of course, some of our peers always assumed that they would work and in fact did so: Some women chose to be doctors or lawyers or business professionals, knowing that they would have to organize their lives according to the rules devised by the men who dominated those worlds; others, driven by financial necessities, supported themselves and their families with whatever jobs they could find. Most African-American women have always been raised with the expectation that they would have to work outside the home for most of their adult lives. But most of the women we talked to in the course of this project, who spoke of the important role that work had actually played in their lives, told us how unprepared they had been for that eventuality. Like us, they'd found that a job path chosen lightly in their early twenties had turned into a lifelong commitment, or they'd entered the work force in their thirties because of a divorce, the need for a second income, or a feeling of incompleteness.

Today about 70 percent of women aged twenty to forty-four, whether married or single, work for wages. Nearly 60 percent of married women with children under the age of six are employed outside the home, as are more than 70 percent of those with school-age kids. The numbers are even higher for mothers who are divorced. Women also manage their own money—and not just their checkbooks and household accounts. Recent studies estimate that between 80 and 90 percent of the women in this country will be solely responsible for their own finances at some time in their lives, and that they will eventually control the assets of four out of five American households. Women have learned to juggle mortgage payments and consumer credit, keep their own tax records, worry over retirement planning, and so forth. Reflecting the astonishing change that has taken place in one generation, almost all of the mothers we spoke to had raised their daughters with the expectation that they would take care of themselves, whether they were married or not. They would be cognizant of money matters. They should expect to work, they should think about work in terms of a career, and they should make their commitment to their job as important as it has always been for men. Mothers hoped that they had conveyed to their daughters the belief that a career offers the opportunity for self-definition and control over one's life.

The Changing Workplace

The women we spoke to were also aware that some classic assumptions about the availability of jobs are no longer relevant. Blue-collar jobs have been dwindling for over a decade. More recently, change has hit the middle class. Every day the news brings fresh stories of corporate downsizing, of former middle managers from IBM and AT&T opening their own consulting firms in spare bedrooms. Colleges are abolishing tenure track positions, doctors are looking for work. The largest private sector employer in America is Manpower Inc., a temp agency.

Clarissa C., sixty-one, who recently retired after twenty years as an employee of the federal government, told us about the effect of corporate cutbacks on her older daughter, Donna, thirty-three, who is now the director of advertising for a small chain of gourmet food stores in New England. Until a few years ago Donna worked in advertising sales at a magazine in New York. "She worked her way up there, and then she saw them go through this huge change. Her company was swallowed up by some corporate giant, and that giant in turn was swallowed up by another giant, and there was massive dislocation. And a lot of people were let go—a lot of her friends. She saw people who had worked there for twenty years and were very high in the company suddenly given twenty-four hours to clean out their desks. And it's left an indelible mark on her. I think she and her husband both suffer from this generation's insecurity, the fact that this job market has changed so much from when I was young."

Entire industries are virtually disappearing. Betsy R.'s husband was forced to retire at fifty-one after spending his entire career at a midwestern newspaper. Six years later he has still not landed another steady job. Betsy's daughter, Jill, twenty-four, chose to study journalism, despite her mother's objection. "I told her it was a dying field; jobs are being cut faster than they're being created. And the people who run papers today have no sense of obligation to good reporting, public service, any of the things she cares about." At first it looked as if Jill had beaten the odds. She was hired by a leading metropolitan paper and assigned to an investigative reporting team. Within six months, however, the paper was bought by new owners, who immediately cut the payroll by 10 percent. Jill was laid off. She has sent out more than fifty résumés and not gotten one response. "She's beginning to realize that the long-term prospects are terrible. Which her father and I tried to tell her, but of course she didn't want to hear. There's not much chance that Bill can turn his career around, but I sure hope Jill figures out a way to make a go of it in a world that doesn't seem to want what she has to offer."

How do women think their daughters can prepare themselves for the changed workplace? The mothers we spoke to recognized that education, while still a predictor of success, is no longer a guarantee. Clarissa C.'s younger daughter, Edith, twenty-eight, had trouble finding a job even after four years of college *and* a masters degree. "Edie was a typical liberal arts graduate—didn't know what she wanted to do and all that. So she went to graduate school for two years and got a degree in classical literature. That was probably a mistake from a practical point of view because it delayed her entry into the job market, and when she did enter it, the recession had started, and she really wasn't qualified. She had no skill other than a basic liberal arts education. And that didn't interest anyone—no one in Boston wanted someone who could read Latin. She worked for a temp agency; she tried all kinds of things. But she couldn't really support herself, and she had no health insurance. So we had to supply the health insurance. And we had to help her out during those lean years, so she naturally became more dependent on us than she had been since she went away to college. And that was not good for her. She hated it, she just hated it."

Clarissa and her husband believed that Edith needed to find a skill that was intellectually satisfying but practical as well. "We suggested that she go back to grad school and get another degree in something. She thought about it, investigated it, and decided to go for a degree that combined history and library science. She got herself a grant at Simmons which took care of tuition. And once she got into library science I could see that she was much happier because she was acquiring a definite skill. She got interested in archives and in preservation. You could just tell, she was getting what she needed. She probably should have done it right after college." Edie is now working in the historical division of a large public library and is mulling over an offer to move to a research library at a state university.

"You need to reinvent yourself on the job all the time," says Cynthia G., mother of Leslie, thirty. "Leslie is caught up in the entertainment industry; she was always interested in popular music. After college she wangled an entry-level job as assistant to a powerful agent. Then she moved with him to Polygram. And then she managed a rock band on the side. Her job at Polygram involved looking for musical theater properties that they could invest in and record—until they closed the division and she was out of work. Now she works freelance for a TV cable station in programming. She's developing new programs, and what she wants to do is produce. So on the side she got some money from them to produce a documentary about an up-and-coming rock group.

"She loves what she does. She's put together a great list of credits. She's always up to try something new. So I am very pleased for her, almost envious, that she is able to focus on getting into a career where she has found her métier. I was not able to do that. Leslie has a very sound, focused sense of what she wants to accomplish in her professional life, which I didn't have and still don't. I've been much more chaotic."

Leslie knows that her current assignment may last no longer than previous ones have. "She could be fired at any time—there's no job security," says Cynthia. "The woman who hired her got fired four months later. Then three other people around her got fired. The head of the whole company got fired. And because they call her a consultant, she has no benefits, no insurance. She's perfectly happy with that because she's earning enough to pay the premiums herself, and the company is giving her the chance to do a lot of things. They keep giving her new things to do because she's very capable and they don't have to pay her a full-time salary. But it is very stressful."

Cynthia is sympathetic because she too has moved from job to job. She thinks Leslie is honing valuable skills. "She has learned how to sell herself and to take nothing for granted. She has learned how to look for niches that are of interest to her and not just to take the first job. It isn't as though she is desperate and takes whatever is available. In this quick survey of the market she managed to get herself in a place where she thought she was going to succeed.

"Actually I am reassured that she has done so well. Because when she first started out she was quite timid. She kept saying, 'I can't do this, I can't do that.' She took a lot of risks. They threw her into adult competitive situations all along the way. And she's learned how not to play herself down. She told me that one day she was in a meeting and one of the big honchos at her station was ranting, 'and we've been without a development head for seven months!' and Leslie said in effect, 'What about me?' The next day when I called her voice mail, her message no longer said, 'This is Leslie.' It said, 'This is Leslie, development and programming.' So I think she lands on her feet. And I think my own experience has made me understand this is as good a way to live as any other."

Says Pauline E., mother of thirty-four-year-old Margot, "For years she would complain to me about her job. She was the executive director of a small museum, and she had to deal with difficult board members, and she was constantly having to get by with not enough funding. So I would say, 'Why don't you do something else? Contemporary arts is a horrible way to make a living.' And she would get infuriated with me, because I would be very candid with her—that's an area I know a great deal about. That's *my* business, too." Pauline has worked for nearly twenty years as a fund-raiser and financial management consultant for nonprofits and more recently as a personal financial planner.

Margot finally left her job, moved to New York, and is now helping to develop a financial information service, which is scheduled to go on-line next year. She's excited by the opportunity to exercise her management skills in the for-profit world. She's been asked to consult on several projects in the arts field and to help prepare a business plan for a small book packager. We asked Pauline, "What do you think of Margot's change of career?" "I think it's great," she said. "I believe in flexibility. Fund-raising will not be my last career. I have made immense changes in my life in terms of where I live and what I do and the kind of life I lead. I think everyone has to do this now. So I think this on-line project might suit Margot for awhile. But I think she has a lot of ideas, and I'd be willing to bet that this won't be the last thing she does in her life. I bet that she'll have a number of jobs, and I think this kind of flexibility is imperative if anyone wants to have a satisfying work life today."

Like Cynthia and Pauline, Diane Asselin has given considerable thought to the work world of the future. Because her daughter Michele, twenty-three, is just starting out, it's too soon for Diane to be able to see an upward trajectory in Michele's work experience. Diane recognizes how hard it is for some young people to get started today, and she believes that it's important for mothers to focus less on the particular jobs a daughter happens to land than on her ability to get things done. Diane sees in the tenacity with which Michele has tackled every assignment a good omen for her daughter's future progress.

For a year after Michele graduated from college, she worked for a company that produced CD-ROMs. She got some experience in writing and some in video production. She worked long hours and was praised by her bosses. When the project she was working on ended, they asked her to stay on in a better job with a higher salary. But Michele wants to be a still photographer, so she left the company to work free-lance as a photographer's assistant. Diane knows that this is a precarious career choice, but she's already observed that Michele has been "dogged and diligent about every job she's ever taken on, and that's a quality of work that's valued by employers."

From Susan's journal, April 19, 1996

Today I visited Sarah's school. We'd planned this day for months; I was coming as an author and she had set up an "Author's Corner," where all the books Marilyn and I have written were on display. From the moment I walked into the school, I felt so proud of my daughter, the teacher. She was in total charge of twenty-eight kids, kindergarten and first graders, all in the same class. The kids were ethnically, economically, and racially mixed. In the hall, one little boy stared hard at me and said, "You look just like Sarah. Sarah's older. But you're old!"

The day started with the children sitting on the carpet, me too, and Sarah sitting on a chair telling the kids this was a special day, because her mother was there. She asked me to show the children pages from my books—which were easy for them to like, because they had pictures in them—and to explain briefly how a book comes to be. Then we had a question period: Where do I find the pictures, how did I decide to be a writer, how old was I (!), and so forth. Then the class broke up into several sections and following Sarah's instructions, I took charge of one group and helped the kids do their math. Meanwhile Sarah moved around the room, helping individual kids solve a problem, speaking sometimes in English, sometimes in Spanish, always keeping control over the entire class. She was calm and collected. In charge. The kids seemed to adore her. The day went quickly by—art, lunch, playground, individual projects, recess. Sarah and I remained behind to clean up the room and get it ready for the next day. We took the subway home together. What a remarkable day.

Diane is a television producer. Over the years she has hired many young people to work on her projects, so she has had ample opportunity to judge their performance. "I think one of the biggest problems parents have today about young adult daughters is wondering how they're going to fit in as workers. Parents have that worry. And I feel a little bit luxurious at the moment because although Michele doesn't have a fixed thing locked down, I see she knows how to work, and if you discover that about your kid, it's a big relief.

"And some of my friends are not discovering that about their kids. It's this business I call 'process,' of not only dreaming your dream but seeing the steps to getting there. And how many kids do we know who can't do that? Who you wouldn't hire if they came to you, even though you love them because they're your friends' kids? When you're a parent and you suddenly realize that your kid *doesn't* know how to do these things, you think, How am I going to compensate for that particular lack of information? You may have done all these wonderful parenting things, but you didn't give them the ability to function in the outside world. And you can't give that to someone at this stage in the game. You can't send them to yet another school to learn those old practical list-making things."

Although she knows that Michele in fact has these skills, Diane confessed that sometimes she lets her worries undermine her confidence. When Michele told her she was going to turn down the CD-ROM company's offer in favor of striking out on her own, Diane told us, "I said to Michele—the old-fashioned me—'What I would like to see on your résumé is a promotion, and most people don't get a promotion on their résumé for at least two years.' I said, 'Why don't you just stay for that? Why don't you just do that?' I sounded just like a father! But she was very convincing. She had all the same worries that I did, and she made me see that taking a risk was part of her self-definition. So now she's working as a photographer's assistant— she makes $150 here, $150 there—she is entering this life of stress that we've all had—but I think she'll do just fine."

"She Lives with No Concern for the Future"

Diane's daughter is just starting out in her career, and her mother is happy to see that she has good work habits and a sense of purpose. Other parents are upset because they fear their children are avoiding testing themselves in the workplace, not making a mature commitment to work. "Slackers" is a word that's recently come to describe a group of twenty somethings who move from job to job, city to city, unwilling to compete in a capitalist economy that they think has no place for them anyhow. Their lives are an open rebuke to their parents' work ethic; the aimlessness they have embraced as a positive value can drive their parents wild.

The necessity for job security has been a major theme in Judith R.'s life since she was a child. Her father lost his job in the Depression, and the family moved in with her grandparents for two years. When Judith and her husband were in their mid-thirties, he left a secure teaching job to start his own business. Five years later he had to declare bankruptcy. "I've worried about money all my life," says Judith, "and I'm always planning for the future. My daughter Kim has never been concerned about money; she manages to live without any concerns for the future."

According to Judith, Kim started off purposefully. Her first job was as a trade show coordinator in San Francisco. Then she ran a small catering business. "I hired her for several parties," said Judith, "and I was very impressed with what she did. She's very good at making things happen." Two years ago Kim horrified her parents by leaving California to follow her boyfriend, an aspiring musician, to his native Russia. They live from hand to mouth, paying rent when they can, camping out in other people's living rooms when things are really tight. "At the moment Kim is managing a café-bookstore in Moscow, and it sounds like she's doing a bang-up job, but I don't see where that leads. I could see if she was living there because of something in her life that was drawing her there or if she was making a life for herself there. I didn't want my daughter trailing around after a rock musician. And my guess is that she will leave this job shortly anyway and do something else—maybe manage his tour.

"She doesn't want things. I said, 'I want you to have comforts. I want you to have a nice place to live and . . . things.' She's not interested at all, she travels very light. My husband has said to her, 'I really wish I could see you acquiring some sort of hardcore skills that you'll be able to do something with once you figure out what you want to do.' And she says, 'You know I'm not even thirty.' She doesn't see herself as old enough to be concerned with anything like that."

The prevailing tone of Judith's description of Kim was critical. Yet buried within her assessment of her daughter's shortcomings were implicit acknowledgments of Kim's coping skills. Kim has found jobs wherever she's lived and done well at them; she supports herself; she seems, as far as Judith knows, to be enjoying her life. Given Judith's own history and the reality of today's job market, it's not unnatural that she should be concerned about some of Kim's decisions. However, if Judith could learn to focus on Kim's resilience and her "ability to get things done," perhaps she would begin to be more sanguine about her daughter's future.

An Unconventional Route to Success

Carolyn Smith and her husband had confidence in their daughter's ability to do well the thing she loved doing. What they questioned was whether she could make a career at it and whether the steps she envisioned to move toward her goal were realistic. The Smiths were able to listen to what their daughter had to say in her own behalf, although her argument challenged conventional wisdom.

By the time she was eighteen, Carrie Smith had been riding horses competitively for years and was beginning to earn a reputation as a trainer of hunters. She proposed turning this talent into a full-time career. Carolyn told us, "Carrie had just graduated from Sewickley Academy. She's very bright, she'd been accepted to good schools. All her classmates were planning for their freshman year. She sat us down and said, 'I know you want me to do this, for you, to go to college, and I know it's a good thing for me to go to college, but I feel that I can always go to college. I can't pursue my career the way I want to if I go to college. I mean I'll lose everything I have—my momentum and my name.' And since we didn't have the finances to support what she needed, she needed to rely on her ability to work the market with her skills. So it was either go to college and find another career or stay with horses, and horses is what she wanted. So we looked at each other—we were talking about schools that cost $20,000 a year—and we thought, If she were willing to go to college, we'd have been willing to pay that. But she really wasn't. So why create problems for ourselves and for her, why create a lot of unhappiness?"

Carolyn and her husband had always said they wanted to raise their children to be happy, not to do what the Smiths wanted them

to do. "So as long as Carrie was happy, and as long as she was financially capable of supporting herself, we told her go ahead and do it.
But we would not give her a penny. If she ever felt that she wanted
to go to college and resume that other life, then we were here to give
it to her. But we would not finance her horses because we couldn't."

At the time Carrie was working with two well-known riders. She
trained horses for them and rode their horses in shows when they
couldn't. Gradually she added other clients, and her reputation grew.
Carolyn says, "It was a long, very patient couple of years for me. She
never asked us for a penny, and she hasn't relied on a man either to
give her things that she wanted. She's married now, but she's financially independent. I can see her being a top trainer in the United
States for the rest of her life."

What If She's Pursuing an Unrealistic Dream?

What if your daughter has all the right work habits, all the doggedness
in the world, but just can't get ahead? One mother told us of a daughter who keeps applying to medical school although she has been
rejected four times; another has watched her thirty-five-year-old support herself as an office temp while writing three novels which have
been rejected by every publisher she has submitted them to. A third
is upset because her daughter has been living in New York for the
last ten years trying to make a career as an actress. "She gets work
from time to time," the mother told us. "She's done some regional
theater. She's done a movie of the week. She had a small part in a
touring company of *Jesus Christ Superstar* for awhile. In between jobs,
she waitresses. She isn't happy, maybe because she sees as well as I
do that she's not going anywhere." Is there anything these mothers
can say that will help their daughters relinquish what the mothers
think of as an unrewarding, self-defeating pursuit?

Each of these mothers recognized that this was very touchy territory. Each said her daughter had devoted some years and a great
deal of hard work following a dream that was obviously very personal,
very central to her vision of who she is, very reflective of the core of
her identity. Each of the mothers told us that she had spent hours

practicing speeches she had not given, drafting letters she had not sent, trying to tell her daughter that her goal may be unrealistic, that she should think about doing something else. We asked Dr. Phoebe Kazdin Schnitzer what advice she would give women like this. Was there *anything* they could say about their fears that their daughters were not talented enough to make the grade? Says Dr. Schnitzer: "I feel that it's *always* possible to speak one's mind, but this situation, in particular, requires a great deal of sensitivity, because it is not helpful simply to tell someone she's not talented. You have probably been over this ground many times with your daughter, and there's been ample commentary in both directions. So I would say to the mother, 'If you're going to address the subject again, figure out what you're really worried about and articulate that very clearly to yourself. Then decide whether or not your worries are worth sharing, because some of them might be, and some of them might *not* be. If you worry that she's not ever going to be rich and famous, maybe that's not worth articulating. But if it is on the level of economic survival and personal satisfaction, those concerns are of a very different order. Perhaps you are picking up that she is worried about all the risks and difficulties in the work itself. Writing novels and acting are high risk jobs. Or perhaps the real issue is that you're worried that you're going to end up supporting her—and that will be frustrating for both of you."

Perhaps these worries betray a mother's fear that her daughter doesn't have enough talent to succeed. Dr. Schnitzer asks, "What does that mean? Not talented enough for what degree of success? Does her so-called lack of talent mean that she's not getting any satisfaction from her work? Does it mean that she won't get jobs, that she faces a life of rejection on a weekly basis? That she feels bad compared to her peers? You should ask yourself what you think will happen as a result of her alleged lack of talent. The important thing when you're talking to another human being is to be sure about what you're sharing. Is it good to be sharing the fact that you think she's not talented enough? I don't think so. But it may be worth sharing that you're concerned about what the future holds for her in the way of personal satisfaction or financial security."

Dr. Schnitzer believes that if an issue has been a source of tension between mother and daughter for some time, any reintroduction of the topic should be framed in a way that signals to the daughter that her mother is treating it with the utmost respect. "I would tend to formalize it. I would step back and say, 'I've been thinking about your work, and I have something I'd like to say.' Especially with someone who's more mature, I would *not* take for granted that she wants to hear my thoughts at all. I would ask very respectfully if it's okay to share my thoughts, and ask if there's a time that's convenient to do so. I would not assume that she's going to say yes. She may say no. And if she says no, then I would say that I hope that we can talk together about this at some point in the future.

"Remember, none of these daughters is a fool. There must be good reasons why she continues to do whatever it is that she is doing. So I would begin by indicating appreciation of her choices, the commitment she has shown in pursuing her goals, or whatever is involved in it that you can praise. Then I would present my own thoughts as clearly coming from my personal perspective. 'I'm worried about you because: I'm concerned about whether you can make a living at it; I'm very concerned about whether you're getting the satisfaction out of it that you deserve, that's warranted by the amount of effort you put into it.' Or, 'I'm worried because you may be overlooking what I think are your tremendous strengths in other areas. Please help me understand.' If your daughter can respond to your interest by talking about her reasons for pursuing her goals, you may learn something which will help you see why she's doing what she's doing. If she cannot share her views, you simply say what you have to say. And then you stop."

Can You Have It All?

Since the days when the two of us were young mothers, the work options for women have expanded, while personal demands on them have stayed the same. Our country does the poorest job of any industrialized nation in providing programs and support for working mothers. We wondered what kind of guidance mothers felt they could offer their newly adult daughters about the working woman's eternal dilemma: How to balance family and work without sacrificing either

of them, or herself, in the attempt? Not unexpectedly, women tended
to extrapolate from their own experience.

There was no overall consensus on the have-it-all question. The
women we talked to recognized variables like a young mother's financial situation and the flexibility of the career path on which she
might be embarked. But while they recognized that it might not be
possible, most women told us they hoped their daughters would be
able either to stop working altogether while their children were young
or to devise a part-time schedule. They felt that day care was generally
a poor substitute for a mother's care, even though they recognized
the inevitability of it.

Many, but not all, talked of how a daughter needed to get her husband to take his share of the responsibility for raising the children and
running the household. But only *one* woman out of one hundred and
thirteen said she was planning to be a full-time baby-sitter so her
daughter could continue to work. It did not seem to us that the women
were selfish. They spoke with delight about spending time with their
grandchildren and helping their daughters when they got into a jam.
But they were committed to other paths of fulfillment in their own
lives—working, going back to school, enjoying the newfound leisure of
retirement—or stressed by other family responsibilities. Whatever
their particular reasons, they did not want their daughters to take their
availability or their willingness to baby-sit for granted.

Straddling the fence

Susan Tully, a forty-nine-year-old interior designer, is the recently
divorced mother of Owen, nineteen, and Megan, twenty. Susan quit
her job as a management trainee for a major airline when her daughter
was born. After her kids started school, she worked part time. She
made sure to be home when they got back from school and has
discussed with Megan how lucky she was to be able to do that. "When
Megan was an adolescent, she wanted to be a doctor," says Susan.
"She wanted a town house in New York, and she wanted a place in
the country, and she wanted children and a nice husband. She wanted
to have it all. Then somewhere the conversations seemed to switch

to 'I want a man to take care of me.' And I said, 'That's the worst thing I've ever heard.' I said the career-motherhood dilemma is something we're all still trying to work out."

In her design business, Susan has many young couples for clients. "They're yuppie types. The husband and wife are both working, they have children, they have nannies. I talk to Megan about them—sometimes it's easier to paint a picture for her than say, 'Do this or do that.' Recently I was hired by a doctor. She was very late for our appointment. She had just delivered one baby and had another woman in labor. She has three young sons and was building a house. She fit me in between deliveries. My daughter was very interested in this client; she said, 'My God, Mom. She's got it all.' I told that to the doctor, and she said, 'I don't have it all. I'm doing it all, but I'm frustrated under the weight of it. You can't have it all.'

"And now I'm with this other couple, they're both corporate lawyers. They have a two-year-old, and the wife is pregnant again. The only time we could meet was at her office at lunchtime. The three of us were looking at some samples, and at about one-thirty the phone rings, and it's the nanny. The woman says, 'You're going to have to excuse us. We have a conference call every day with our daughter before she takes her nap. We ask her what she ate for breakfast, and how her day was, and what she had for lunch.' She explained that they keep the child up until nine-thirty so they can see her before she goes to bed. Part of me thought this was pathetic. And the other part thought, these people are really trying.

"And I told Megan about it. Because it's a problem she's going to face in the next few years, if she wants to have a profession. And we went on to talk not just about the woman's role in child rearing but what she can demand of her husband, and how much slack he's willing to pick up."

Like Susan Tully, Clarissa C. stayed home while her daughters were young. Her older daughter Donna, thirty-three, is thinking about starting a family, but is terrified about walking away from a solid job and the income it provides. "I would like her to be a full-time mother when the children are young," says Clarissa. "I really would. I don't think there's any substitute for it, those first three or four years of life. And they know I feel this way. But Donna keeps saying you know, they won't have any choice, she won't have any choice. But actually I think they would have a choice if they really wanted to make it. She could at least get a part-time job or do some kind of advertising or publicity work at home. But of course she would not earn as much money. They're buying a house and she's scared to death about mortgages and things like that. Her husband is calmer about all this, thank heavens, and after listening to her doom and gloom for a while, he did say to her in front of us, 'Well, you do have to take risks in life.' She's just totally hyper about it all. But I think once it happens to her she will calm down a bit. I'm counting on maternal emotion to enter into the picture."

Alice Trillin also stresses the importance of full-time mothering in a child's early years. Alice taught English at City College in New York during the years that her daughters were young, but she observes that her hours were flexible and she had a lot of support. Only after the girls were in their teens did she shift to her present career, producing educational television programs, which often involves long hours and travel. Alice's older daughter, Abigail, is planning to be a lawyer—a notoriously rigid profession—and Alice is not sure if Abigail will be able to put her career on hold to stay home for several years. Her own experience, Alice fears, offers an example that may be unrealistic. "I think the whole question of balancing work and motherhood is an area where I haven't been as helpful as I should be, because I don't know what the answer is. I was lucky. Because I was teaching, I was able to be home for my kids. I only regret time I *didn't* spend with my kids. Looking back, and I've talked to the kids about this, they had a bad role model. Our life wasn't very realistic. Bud worked at home, and if they needed him, the door was open. Of course, we had child care, but I worked in a way that there was freedom, too. I could be home at two or three o'clock or work two or three days a week. This won't be the case for Abigail.

"So what I've said to both my girls is 'You have to have a husband who will share responsibility. And you should maybe find a job where you can take off for a couple of years and then go back.' But I've also said, 'I don't know how it will play out. You shift your goals as life unfolds. Let's say you have to choose a mommy track at a law firm. And then maybe later you can be more ambitious.' I don't know. I've always said to them that you have to find a balance. You must work, because without it you won't be a happy person—I mean, look at all those frustrated women of my mother's generation. And that won't be good for your kids. But if you ever have to choose, you have to be there for your kids. The most important thing in your life is to help decent people grow up."

Angela A. told us that her two daughters, Gretchen, twenty-eight, and Betsy, twenty-six, are both rising executives at large corporations. Gretchen, who is married, helped her company set up a child-care program even before she got pregnant. Now she uses it for her six-month-old daughter. One day she was late picking up the baby, found the child feverish in her crib, and immediately berated herself for failing to meet her baby's needs. Gretchen is beginning to think about having a second child, and Angela suspects that she may step off the fast track for awhile. Says Angela, "What Gretchen has discovered is that she's missing part of what her baby is doing, and that's become a complex question for her to answer. She's worrying whether the intellectual challenge of a part-time career will be as satisfying as a full-time career. And I've told her I think that life is a series of struggles about balance. This is my child who is truly driven; anything she does she likes to do perfectly. The problem for her is, can I be excellent and still have some joy in my life and create this sense of balance."

In addition to her two daughters, Angela also has five sons. When her children were young, Angela worked as a counselor at a private school where the hours were compatible with motherhood. She also had a private psychotherapy practice in her home. After the children were grown, she moved to her present job as the chief executive at a small company that creates computer software for schools. "I told Gretchen I had once turned down a job that on the surface looked perfect, but at that point in my life, it didn't suit. She was interested in what it felt like to do that. She's asked me, for example, did I feel

I sacrificed a lot to have children. I never felt that way. I wanted a large family. I enjoyed each of them so much. And essentially I thought I had given a tenth of what I had gotten from the relationships with each of them."

Like Alice Trillin, Angela has conveyed to her daughters her ambivalence about whether or not a young mother should place her career on hold, or jeopardize it, when her children are young. As long as our culture places a low priority on support for working mothers, which includes but is not limited to systematically providing adequate day care, women will be haunted by this problem. As more women pursue high-level careers and establish a presence in corporate and public life, and as more women advocate for a working mother's agenda, perhaps new models of day care and a new respect for day care will emerge. And women who choose to, or need to, work full time when their children are young, will no longer have to justify themselves to the society around them.

Go for it

Only two women, both of whom had reached the top of their professions, stressed that despite the hardships of combining family and a career, there are also great rewards. And that a young woman should not hold herself back from going for it all.

Susan Cole argues that while it may be difficult at times to combine having a career and raising a family, it's a goal that can be pursued—and attained. Susan and her husband have two children, Simon, twenty-nine, and Alexis, twenty-five. Because her husband is an artist, Susan has always been the family breadwinner. When the children were young she was a college administrator. She has been the vice-president in charge of faculty and administration at Rutgers and is now the president of Metropolitan State University in St. Paul, Minnesota. Susan has been an innovator in the field of making higher education available to minorities and others for whom it was not a traditional option. "Let me put it this way—I think life is tough. No one ever gave me anything. I didn't inherit money or connections or any of the things that grease the passage through life for you. Everything I've ever done I've had to work hard to get. And I think that if you want things, you can work hard and get them. That's my failing. My characterological failing is that I believe that. And yet it's not always true. You can't always get things through hard work and effort, yet I continue to believe that you can. One of the contradictions of the human mind is that you *can* believe things that are not true.

"So one of the messages I've always given my kids is that if you want to do it, you can do it. And why would anyone want to settle for less than all the things that are important to you? There was no way I was going to give up having a family, and there was no way I was going to give up my role in that family, my time with my kids. I wasn't willing to give up any piece of it. I baked, I bought the kids' shoes, I went to the games and the concerts. And there was no way I was going to give up my work, and my time at work. So I think you just put all those pieces together. And you don't follow rules. You don't let anybody tell you the way things have to be done. You make your own rules, and that's how you get it done." Susan smiled, and added, "Yet all of this may or may not be true."

Shirley Strum Kenny, president of the State University of New York at Stony Brook, has four sons, and one daughter, Sarah, twenty-five. Dr. Kenny remembers being in a car pool when her children were young. She told us, "One day I was driving and a kid said to me, 'You put on your lipstick at the same traffic light my mom does.' And that showed me the world in which I was living—we were all mothers on the run. And when the children were young it was really frantic. I was an assistant professor at the time. My husband and I used to make seven breakfasts and seven lunches before we went to work. You had to learn to organize very well, but I did always work, and it was unusual in my time. My kids were born in the sixties. That's when you were supposed to make a very creative environment for your children, and here I was off doing my own thing. It was really frowned on—heavy duty guilt trips—but I thought my kids were better off, that I would have driven them crazy if I had been at home. Because I just had too much energy.

"I can remember one year when I did not teach. I had a two-year-old and my second was due, so I stayed home and worked on my dissertation and I became complacent. I would look at the grocery ads, at the coupons to see if the peas were two cents cheaper here, and I would clean up the house three times a day with that two-year-old following me around. I couldn't even see the dirt, but it was as if I had to have an outlet. So I came to see I was not a happy caretaker for my children unless I had something else to do."

Dr. Kenny's daughter Sarah is working in a bookstore. She plans to go to graduate school next year to earn an MFA in sculpture. "We're as different as two people could be," says Dr. Kenny. "She's very artistic. I have no artistic ability whatsoever. She stays busy, there's no loose time, she also sings with a band. So it's hard for me to say where this is going to take her. What I would say to Sarah and the other young women of her generation is 'You should do whatever makes you happy. If you're better off working—as I clearly was, and I think my children profited from it, too—then do it. If you want to be home, do that. They're both good choices.' "

In March 1996, Dr. Kenny was interviewed by *Newsday*, about working women and Having It All. Of her female students, she told the newspaper, "I find they have an assumption they'll have a career. When I was in school that was not true. When I started out my career, I would die rather than have anyone know I had children when I was doing university duty. At my first meeting of a graduate committee, (my son) Jonathan had fallen off a slide. . . . I told them I had to leave. There was an emergency. . . . I didn't tell them what it was. Now you sit in committees with men who say, 'I can't stay past four, because I have to pick up the children.' It's much healthier that way."

Financial Matters

When we asked women what subject they had the most trouble talking about with their daughters, we expected the most frequent answer would be sex. In fact, it was money. "It's the one subject we do *not* discuss," said one mother who has no trouble talking intimately with her daughter about subjects like what to look for in a lover and her own intermittent bouts of depression. "Well . . . I do bring it up from time to time, and she always cuts me off with, 'I don't want to talk about it, Mom.' " Another woman told us, "My husband and I are never in sync about money. It's a complicated issue for us, and we don't handle it well with our girls either. It's definitely the most difficult part of our relationship with them." A third woman, who runs a financial management firm with her husband, believes so strongly that money might rob their four young adult sons and daughters of ambition that she confessed, "We haven't even told our kids how much money they have. We've invested money in their names that they don't know about. We even fill out their income tax forms so they won't find out." These parents did not give graduation gifts when the children finished college, which the mother now thinks was "pitiable, pathetic."

One mother we interviewed, a financial counselor with therapeutic training, corroborated our discovery. "Sexuality is much less taboo these days than money," Meryl Siegel told us. "I see it all the time as an issue between partners and between parents and their grown-up children. I think money issues are a tangible measure of anxiety."

How and when do you help her out?

Too often we find ourselves enmeshed in an adult daughter's finances with no firm guidelines about how to help her fend for herself. She may have a job but not earn enough to live on. She may earn enough to get by but not live the way we would like her to. She may mismanage the money she has. Are we obliged to help her out with money while she gets started? Is it bad for her if we do? Most mothers we spoke to felt that if you have the money you should support your daughter until she finishes her education. Most were perfectly willing to pay for health insurance or car insurance if a daughter was not covered by her employer and not earning enough to pay for it herself. Mothers admitted that these payments were actually insuring their own peace of mind as much as anything.

But after that, there was no consensus. There were mothers who spoke forcefully in favor of helping whenever you can, and mothers who spoke with equal conviction that it was detrimental to a daughter's maturity to help her anymore.

Lyttleton Rich typifies the "You've got to do it on your own" school. Lyttleton is a corporate headhunter in Charlotte, North Carolina. She has always talked directly with her daughters, Mary, twenty-four, and Elizabeth, twenty-one, about how she expects them to handle financial responsibility. The girls had to get paying summer jobs from the time they were in high school. While they were in college, Lyttleton bought them cars and paid the insurance, but with one proviso: 'You can keep the car as long as you maintain a certain GPA.' When Elizabeth fell below the standard, her car was sequestered in Lyttleton's garage. And Elizabeth never challenged her mother's action. "I'm strict but I'm fair," Lyttleton says, "she knew I wasn't going to pay for her to have this privilege if she was going to abuse it."

This year Mary is studying for a graduate degree as a physician's assistant. Her father—Lyttleton's ex-husband—pays for her tuition and her health insurance. Lyttleton pays for the car. But Mary doesn't have enough money to cover all her living expenses, and her mother is not rushing to make good on the shortfall. "She just took out a loan to help her this year, and I think that was good for her to do."

Lyttleton has already told her younger daughter, Elizabeth, not to count on financial aid while Elizabeth tries to establish herself as an actress in New York after she graduates from college next spring. "I think I will say, 'It's up to you to support yourself. If you want to act, wonderful. And if you want to work in New York and try to get a foothold in whatever career path, fine. But you're going to need to wait on tables and get Saturday and Sunday jobs. I'm not going to support you.'" The issue is not that Lyttleton couldn't help out if she wished to, but that she believes she has fulfilled her responsibility by paying for their education. "They've had the benefit of going to any school they wanted, and they didn't have to work while they were in school . . . No, I don't think I'd support her."

We asked if Lyttleton would be willing to pay for acting classes if Elizabeth were covering all her other expenses. "She would have to present a pretty good plan of where that's going. I mean two acting classes in the morning—that's a pretty hard call. I really want her to pursue this and give it her best chance, but how supportive I'm going to be financially while she pursues it, I don't know.

"I've asked her, 'Don't you want to get your teaching certificate so you could at least teach drama down the road if in fact you can't make a living at acting?' But she doesn't want to do that. And that's okay. She can always go back and get the appropriate courses. I'm worried that she's not going to be able to make a living as an actress, but she needs to give it a chance."

Lyttleton Rich was in the minority. More women believed, as Lillian P. did, that you should give your children as much help as you are able. Lillian, who says very matter of factly that she received no help from her parents, told us, "I've seen some kids give up a dream because they have to support themselves, and I think that's unfair and sad." Lillian and her husband both have good jobs in advertising agencies. They supported one of their daughters for five years while she tried to break into screenwriting. In the past two years, the girl has sold two scripts to producers and is now self-supporting. "I'm glad we were able to help her," says Lillian. "I don't think she ever took advantage of the situation. She was always a hard worker."

Not everybody had the resources to be as generous over such a sustained period as Lillian, and not many had daughters who were so financially dependent. Most mothers addressed the issue in terms of a daughter who was working but not making quite enough money to get by or who needed periodic infusions of cash to get over an unexpected hurdle. Carol Connolly, a writer in St. Paul, Minnesota, has three sons and four daughters. Carol told us, "I think you should do everything you possibly can for your kids in terms of money. You should do it all. I don't think you spoil kids or ruin their lives by paying for their car or helping them buy their first house, and I wish I could have done that. But I couldn't. I didn't have the resources. I could only help out with little bits here and there. And my kids, with the exception of the oldest daughter, are like the X generation. They're not having an easy time financially. So I say to them from time to time, 'Do you need a little money? Are you doing okay? Do you need a loan?' And they usually say, 'No . . . no . . . no.' Unless they really need it. And then I do what I can."

Pauline E., the mother of three daughters and a son, has always tried to help. "I've always given them little handouts, probably too much. I've been criticized by my friends for that. A couple of years ago, when I was making the transition to my current job, my income dipped. I could have used the money I had given them over the years, but I don't begrudge it. They needed help. I don't regret it. One of my daughters always pays me back. Another would if she had the money. The other two kids never will. And I don't really care."

What we found most interesting was that we could not correlate giving or not giving with good or bad relationships between mothers and daughters. Women who reported not giving did not say that their daughters withdrew from them as a consequence. Women who chose to give did not report any increased dependency. We believe that the clarity with which they spoke was more important than the stance they took. Their daughters knew what kind of financial help they could count on and what they could not, and the issue was stripped of the emotional trappings that so often accompany it.

Brooke D., the mother of Alexandra, thirty-two, and Alicia, thirty, says, "I believe absolutely in giving money to your kids if you can afford it." And Brooke has learned a way of reducing tension even further. Brooke and her husband make it a point to give both their girls a gift of money each year. "I also believe absolutely that you must give each girl the same amount," she says. "Otherwise it's a nightmare. I didn't used to do that. We would give them something if they asked for it, and we would comment on what they wanted it for. When Alexandra wanted money to buy a BMW, I was horrified. I told her, 'We'll give you seven thousand dollars, and you have to raise the rest yourself.' I gave her hints about how to raise the rest— get an interest-free loan from her grandfather. I was bossing her around. I thought she should buy a cheaper American car. We argued about it. She said a status car was important in her job. She did get the rest of the money—she's good at putting together deals. Now I would do it differently. We just give each of them a round number each year. If Alexandra wants to blow all of hers on a fancy car, fine. I don't have to get involved with it."

Brooke came to a crucial realization. If you give money, whatever the amount, and dictate the terms under which it is to be used, you are in effect telling your daughter that she is not adult enough to make decisions for herself. On the other hand, a gift with no strings attached shows that you trust her to do what's right for her.

Money as metaphor

Giving or not giving a daughter money is tricky for so many women because very often a conflict that seems to be about money is not fundamentally about that at all. More often than not it's about love, or power, or control.

Scottie W. is a forty-seven-year-old mother of three daughters and a son. She lives just a few blocks from her parents in the same Connecticut suburb in which she grew up. She reported a very tangled relationship with her own mother, who to this day can't acknowledge that Scottie is an independent woman. Although Scottie resists most of her mother's suggestions, she is assaulted by a steady stream of directives on matters ranging from religion to child rearing, education, or sharing family holidays.

When we interviewed Scottie she was in the midst of a career change. She had just sold a thriving real estate management firm she had founded six years earlier and was contemplating opening a crafts store. Scottie told us that since her husband, Ned, is a successful businessman, she was more focused on finding work that interests her than maximizing her income. The topic of money led Scottie to talk of her middle daughter, Nina, twenty-two, just out of college, and living in Portland, Oregon. "Nina likes to live well. She has always earned a lot of money, more than any other kid I knew. One summer she earned four thousand dollars. And she had a dorm job in school, plus she got free food. But she spends every penny she has. One semester she ran up four hundred dollars in parking tickets. In her junior year, she went to Madrid and left me with all these bills that she had asked me to pay. And she had said, 'Oh this one will be fifteen dollars and that one will be . . .' And it turned out that they were triple the amount it was supposed to be. And I had to make it good for her. And I told her it was the last time I was going to do that.

"But all through her senior year there was an undercurrent. She came to us for money again. She and several friends wanted to go to Portland over Christmas to look for work. And so we thought, okay, this is legitimate. We'd said we'd never give her anything except school expenses, but it seemed wrong to turn this down. So she went. But she only partied. And never did anything about getting the job. And when she came back, we were like, 'You don't understand. You're going to have to support yourself after you graduate, and you're not doing anything about it.' And it was really bothering me. It became a big issue last spring before she left school. Nina kept asking for more money to get started. 'Aren't you going to give me anything?' and I'm saying, 'We told you. We explained this to you.' But it took a while to sink in. And she kept saying that we were horrible because we weren't doing this. But we were very clear from last summer on that this was where we were going to stand. We would say, 'We told you this.' And she's like, 'I know, but . . . ' And she tried divide and conquer. She'd talk to her father, then she'd talk to me. Talk to her father, talk to me. And it never worked. We had a united front. So she didn't have a leg to stand on. So she did give up after about three or four weeks.

"But there was this other issue of the debt she'd run up while she was still in school. She buys CDs, her collection is just unbelievable. She loves to eat out a lot, in nice places. She's getting interested in wine. . . . God only knows, she loves to live like that. And so she owed about two thousand on her Visa bill. So we decided we'd pay it off as a graduation present. I know we'd said we were never to give her another dime. But it seemed unfair for her to have that debt hanging over her head when she was just getting started."

We asked Scottie how Nina has been supporting herself since graduation. "She got herself a nice job in a travel agency, but it looks to me like she's still living beyond her means. And with the way they hand out credit cards it is very easy for her to do this. I keep saying, 'You can't.' And she's saying, 'I have to. I have to.' It just hasn't sunk in that you can't live like that constantly. As she fills up one credit card, she'll go into another one. And I talked to her a little bit about that when I was visiting her recently, and she says, 'I don't want to hear about this at the moment. I have it under control.' So I'm like, 'famous last words.' But I won't bring it up unless she asks me to pay for something again."

What would Scottie do if Nina came to her now for a loan? "If she wants me to pay off her back debt, I would have to put her on a budget, and make her send me an accounting every month. She also knows she could live at home and save on rent till she pays off her bills, but she doesn't want that. I hope it doesn't happen. I hope I never hear another word about this."

We asked financial counselor Meryl Siegel how she might help a woman like Scottie resolve the muddle she and her daughter have gotten into over the daughter's spending habits. "Very often in these mothers' minds not giving money equals separation," she said. "Frequently women who have not been able to separate from very controlling mothers don't have a good model for how the mother of an adult daughter can relinquish control and yet stay connected. They are afraid that if they give up control over a daughter's finances it means giving up their connection to her."

Siegel says, "I point out that every situation has both a financial and an emotional aspect. And you can't live your life based only on a balance sheet. In these cases, parents often have a lot of ambivalence about allowing an adult daughter to be independent. They think they're trying to make her independent at the same time they're overseeing her choices. It's not helpful to go through her bills and make a lot of judgments about how you would have spent money differently. Eating out, buying CDs, may be much more important to a young girl than they are to you."

But Siegel does not believe that it's useful for a parent to summarily drop all involvement with a daughter's finances. She advises, "Before you can step back altogether you may have to stay involved, but in a more constructive way than you did before. Instead of haggling over her inability to manage everything on her own, maybe you give her a subsidy up front and never ask to look at or hear about her monthly bills."

But what happens if she still overspends and comes back for more help? Siegel says she tells parents, "You have to acknowledge that she's put you in a situation where you're going to have to be more involved than you probably should be. As for how to proceed, you have two options. Either you say, 'You're going to have to pay this off,' and stick to it, or you say, 'I'll help you pay this off, but you have to tear up all your credit cards.' And you have a further choice of whether or not she has to pay you back for what you laid out. It will take a lot of backbone and clarity on the parent's part to ensure that this is your final word, and that you will not be drawn into a continuing round of negotiations. If that works, you've made a great breakthrough for both of you."

And if it doesn't? Should you let a daughter go broke or even declare bankruptcy if she has to? "Not the first time around, no," said Siegel. "But if this is a pattern, yes. Reluctantly. Because ultimately that's the only way she's ever going to grow up."

Chapter 7

Changes in *Your* Life

Anne Navasky is a fifty-five-year-old stockbroker in New York. She is in partnership with her eighty-four-year-old mother who still goes to work every day. Anne and her husband, Victor, have three children—Bruno, twenty-eight, Miri, twenty-seven, and Jenny, twenty, all living away from home. Anne imparts a sense of being able to ride out life's storms, the worst of which was undoubtedly Bruno's bout with cancer in his early teens. We asked how she feels about her life today. "I love my fifties," she said, "except for the fact that every time a friend gets sick, I think it's going to happen to me any minute. I'm constantly monitoring myself. But other than this unnatural—or natural—fear that something is about to go wrong physically, everything is great."

The big news in Anne's life is that she's taking guitar and singing lessons. She tried once before—when she turned forty—but couldn't practice when her kids were at home. She began studying guitar again after her fiftieth birthday. "Immediately it took and immediately I knew I would be doing this forever. I mean it's just joyous, and the feedback I got from the rest of the family was fabulous. I'm too shy to play for anybody, but I once gave a recital at an old age home, and the kids came and loved it. I just love the idea that I'm learning anything at this age. Now I've starting singing, it just feels very good. Then the singing has gone off in a direction all its own, and guitar went off into jazz. I practice in the morning, and Victor leaves the house singing, and there's music all day long.

"I've also started to travel by air, in a very limited way. I've always been afraid to fly. Recently I flew to Minneapolis, and I said to my mother, 'It's because the children are grown up, that I can do this. I have total confidence in them. I see that they are—they don't know what they want to do—but they are all going to be okay. And they can be okay without me, and I can now fly.'" Anne finds this time of life liberating in many ways. "The truth is I don't miss my kids when they're not around. I love it when they come home, but I'm not depressed when they go away. And yet while they're here I'm not thinking, Yech, I can hardly wait till they go."

Anne's happiness is marred by the fact that her exceptionally vital mother is beginning to show the effects of age. In recent years, she has suffered from cancer, a heart condition, and glaucoma. "It's very hard for me to watch this happening to her. And very hard, too, because everything bad that happens to her you see as your fate. This is where I am going, so it's a blow upon blow upon yourself."

Mindful that Anne and her mother have been closely connected as friends and business partners, we asked Anne if she plans to stop working when her mother retires. "I've thought a lot about that because I don't know how much my working now has to do with keeping her company, giving her something to do. Victor says, 'Well you can retire.' And I thought, No I can't. I like to have the security of a paycheck, and I work for a major corporation which is like a big mother—I've spent twenty years there—they take care of you, they give you your pension, they give you your medical insurance, and it's a very scary thing to leave."

Anne Navasky's thoughtful balance of the sweet and bittersweet concerns in her life seems typical for many women of our generation.

Not so long ago, women in their fifties and sixties were invisible, thought to be over-the-hill because they had completed their major life work—raising their children. The only task ahead was to take pleasure in their grandchildren and face death with grace. In the last few years, as life expectancy and disposable income have risen, a revisionist view has taken hold: Aging is a state of mind, so if women can will themselves into a positive attitude, and do enough yoga exercises, they can maintain their unabated vitality for decades to come.

What we have come away with after talking with dozens of women is that this cheery view is accurate, to a degree. Women of our generation *do* feel that this is a wonderful period in their lives, that they have the time and wisdom to do things they've always wanted to do and do them well. However, the good feeling is tempered by the awareness of mortality—our own and that of those we love. Our time is precious, because it is finite.

From Susan's journal, December 23, 1995

Tonight Sarah and I went to a party at the Barrons'—they are my friends but they are twenty years younger than I am, which makes them ten years older than Sarah—so, in fact, in many ways she has more in common with them and their guests than I do. As we stood around having drinks in their living room, several people came up, introduced themselves, and asked us if we were mother and daughter, because we look so much alike. For me it was one of those moments that you're both in and standing off to the side observing: I was pleased to be identified with Sarah and to have Sarah identified with me. But I knew that those people were looking at us as Youth and Age. One of those moments that brought home my mortality. The only saving grace was that I hoped they also thought, Well she does look pretty good—for her age.

Taking Stock

Within this framework, we women are assessing our lives—our commitment to our work and to our ideals; our deferred dreams and our new dreams; our relationship to our partners, and our capacity to live alone. Lorelle Phillips has just celebrated several rites of passage. "I've been coming to terms with my sixtieth birthday. And Roger and I recently moved. We always had a lot of ideas about where we wanted to wind up. My fantasy was to have a house on the water with lots of fireplaces. We had a big house in Westchester where we raised our children, and then we found a house right on the Hudson that was really incredible. And I said, 'I think I can move out of the house in Larchmont if we can move to this one.' It was an enormous upheaval. We had lived in that house for twenty-five years, and the accumulation of things that you have to throw out or go through is mind boggling and very stressful. So we did that, and now I'm faced with, what do you do when you get your dream? I have what I want. I have no dreams about anything else. So I can't deny that I'm entering into old age. I can't pretend I'm still in the house where we raised our family, and they're young, and I'm young. So the combination of turning sixty and moving to the house I'll grow old in is hard to swallow."

Letty Cottin Pogrebin believes that you must continue to create new dreams. In her book, *Getting Over Getting Older*, Letty writes about the importance of continuing to grow and change in midlife. Letty told us, "The problem for my husband and me—and it's really not a problem—is we're really happy with everything the way it is, and we tend to just keep doing what we find familiar and comfortable. But I feel it's essential at this age to keep pursuing the new. Since I'm not changing my marriage, and I'm not leaving this apartment, I want to effect change in some outward way." In addition to her longstanding involvement with the women's movement, Letty has over the last ten years become active in organizing American support for peace in the Middle East. "So that keeps the brain cells going," she says.

"I'm torn between two philosophies. On the one hand, life is good, and my philosophy is, if it's not broke, don't fix it. At the same time I'm very aware how easy it is to disengage at this age, and sameness is a form of disengagement to me. I don't want to lose what's good about my life, but at the same time I don't want to tame out. I think you need new dreams to aspire to. And they can be as simple as learning a new language or hiking. It's my dream now to be able to hike up to fifteen miles and eventually twenty miles a day. So I have new landmarks that I'd like to reach. They're not major, but they keep me reaching beyond my grasp."

For some the dream is to travel. For others it's a chance to paint full time. For many it's an opportunity to return to formal education. Paula S. was married at eighteen and had the first of her four children the following year. Now at age fifty-nine, Paula is back in school full time, earning her B.A. in religious studies as part of an adult program at a local college for women. "The whole experience is enormously touching," she says. "There's something about a group of women understanding each other's problems, comparing life experiences: Are you married? Do you have grandchildren? There's a sense of renewal which we all share with each other that is beautiful." One of Paula's daughters thinks it's wonderful that her mother is plunging into a new adventure; the other has asked her, "At this age, don't you just want peace and quiet?"

Most of the women we spoke with told us that, contrary to the popular cliché that parents are left grieving over an empty nest, they were energized by their freedom. Their lives were filled with new interests and activities. To their surprise, their children were often uncomfortable with the idea that they could change. Verdine Jones, whose two daughters are in their mid-twenties, has taken a challenging job with the California penal system, and she's begun investing in real estate. "I think Rhonda and Stacy like to see me basically as a mom because that's comfortable. But I say, 'I'm going to do my own thing now,' and they say, 'You should,' and they encourage that. Still and yet they want Mom! I don't cook the way I used to, I just used to cook constantly; and Stacy called me a few weeks ago and said, 'Mom, what did you cook today?' and I said, 'I told you I'm not doing that anymore.' "

Phyllis Wender, a New York literary agent, says that her business is better than ever and takes up more of her life, just when her husband, Ira, has more free time. Phyllis gets home later and cooks less. "Sometimes I think I need a wife," she told us. "Ira said to me the other day, 'Maybe I should learn how to cook.' And I said, 'What a nice idea.' Ira is proud of my success. He says, 'I did this all my life, now it's your turn.'"

Some of the things we women are dealing with are similar to experiences our daughters are facing: evaluating our careers, working on our relationships with our partners, finding new partners, thinking about the possibility of life without a partner, and so forth. We are also grappling with issues that are specific to our time of life: dealing with serious health issues, caring for aging parents, getting used to the fact that we ourselves are no longer young. Mindful of the conventional wisdom that a good mother does not burden her children with her own troubles, many women told us they are unclear how much of their concern about all these experiences they could or should reveal to their daughters.

Work and Self-definition

About a third of the women we interviewed mentioned that they had recently experienced or anticipated that they would soon face a significant change in their work life. Some felt they were reaching the pinnacle of their careers and were energized by taking on more responsibility. Some felt they were being slowly squeezed out of a position of authority by younger colleagues, closer in age to their daughters than to themselves. Some said that this was the moment to take a leap—start a bed and breakfast, become a free-lance computer consultant, go into private practice. Some mused about impending retirement with delight, some with ambivalence.

For about 20 percent of our interviewees, a work-related crisis was at the moment the central concern of their lives. An ancillary, but not incidental, concern was the possible impact of the crisis on their daughters.

How much can you burden her with your problems?

Erica R. has worked for a public relations firm that represents a number of furniture manufacturers. Recently the firm has lost several big clients, and Erica feels her job is in jeopardy. Her anxiety is compounded by the fact that her husband is currently out of work. "This is an issue for all of us at this age. Things are not what we expected them to be. We expected to struggle through our thirties and forties, but somehow at this age one expected to be established in a direction and not experiencing a lot of insecurity, a fear of no longer being on the cutting edge. Suddenly I feel I have to reinvent myself, but I don't quite know how. I could do my profession somewhere else. I could start on my own, which scares me to death. I could stay in the industry but do something else—have a fabric or antiques shop. But I've never quite felt confident enough to do it on my own. That's the difference between Katya and me. She always feels there's something she can do, she can overcome anything."

Erica's only child, Katya, twenty-six, works in television production. In three years she's risen from being a free-lance production assistant to her current job as a script coordinator on an animated cartoon series. She thinks she might like to shift into public relations or stay in television and look for work in front of the camera—all of which she talks over with her mother. "We discuss everything," Erica told us, "her personal life, her feelings, her trials and tribulations, her anxieties. And what we're discovering more and more is that we're so alike which, as she says, is good but also bad, because I'm a very hyper, worried, nervous sort of person." Nonetheless, Erica told us, Katya has a strong sense that she can depend on herself, whereas Erica's self-confidence is quite shaky.

Erica talks about her problems with friends and her husband. But not with Katya. She justifies her restraint by asking herself, "What could Katya do about it anyway? It would only make her anxious." However, because mother and daughter are so close, so attuned to each other, Katya has probably picked up the fact that her mother is worried about something. Perhaps Erica has even unconsciously given her quite explicit clues to her uneasiness.

It's understandable that a mother wants to protect her daughter from unpleasantness. It's been one of the ways we mothers have defined our role since our children were babies. But is it appropriate to conceal something central to your life from a twenty-five-year-old woman on the grounds of protecting her? Probably not. If Erica could let her daughter know her fears and hear, rather than speculate about, Katya's response, she might very well reduce both her daughter's anxiety and her own. She may discover that Katya has valuable insights to impart. Letting her daughter in on her most pressing concern is a way of saying, "I have confidence in your ability to handle this information about me and to help me through this crisis."

"I lost my job about two and a half months ago" were practically the first words out of the mouth of Carol Rusoff, as we sat down for lunch with her in a funky outdoor restaurant around the corner from her house in Venice, California. Carol, fifty-two, is the mother of Rebecca, twenty-five, a teacher who lives in northern California, and Annie, twenty-one, who's a student in Boston. Having been a single parent since the girls were young, Carol is used to telling them what's going on in her life. Her candor is consistent with her personality and style; she's amusing, loquacious, pleasantly outspoken, and enthusiastic. It was her enthusiasm that got her in trouble at her job. Carol was fired from her position as chairman of the arts department and theater teacher at a local private high school because of clashes with the administration. "They said, 'We don't want you to be an arts advocate to the administration. We want you to be part of the administration running your department.' I heard them, but I never went over to their side. I was always this rebellious antic arts person, which I think every institution should have, but they don't think so!"

Carol is both shaken by what happened and exhilarated by the possibility of change. "I was getting paid for something that I loved to do, so I miss that, and I also feel the loss of a paycheck. But I feel the possibility of growth within myself in a way that is exciting—if

I'm not afraid. And I *am* afraid: Who am I? I have no identity. I'm unemployed. Everyone is at work today, and I'm having lunch! I— who had a work ethic all my life—have the time to have lunch. When my kids were small, I stopped for six months but I always, always worked. It was something that interested me."

Because the school had to buy out her contract and her medical insurance is covered for the next eighteen months, Carol is not yet feeling financial pressure. However, she does have to plan ahead for a new job. She'd like to run a nonprofit theater, although the idea of fund-raising in this political climate is difficult and depressing. She's weighing an offer to teach theater in prisons.

Carol has told both of her daughters about all the possibilities. "Typically Rebecca has more trouble seeing me vulnerable. She wrote me pat but sweet and heartfelt letters about how I'm a wonderful woman, like I'm a goddess, a little bit larger than life. I don't think she likes to think about me flailing. Annie was here all summer. She was terrific, very straight arrow on her commentary about me, a little less romantic in how she views me. She can handle seeing me vulnerable.

"Annie is like me; she brings it down to the most practical common denominator: 'You've suffered for a week, Mom. Now, why don't you go do something?' When this first happened, she was very sweet. . . . We used to have a family ritual when the kids were small. When I put them to bed I'd say 'Thump when you are ready. Go upstairs, brush your teeth, get ready for bed and thump with your feet on the ceiling, and I'll hear that you're ready for me to come up.' So I was sad and miserable, and Annie said, 'Go upstairs and thump when you're ready,' and she came up and sat on my bed and talked. And it was a very big present."

Carol recognizes that the girls have different levels of tolerance for her openness. She understands that Rebecca needs to be more self-protective in her response to Carol's vulnerability. She considers it a bonus that Annie can reach out to comfort her. By now, they probably know, because she knows, that she isn't going to fall apart. In any case, she feels no need to protect them from the truth. In Carol's willingness to share her fears and frustrations, and in Annie's sensitive reaction, are the seeds of a new kind of relationship between a mother and an adult daughter—one that is based on honesty, interdependence, and the capacity to learn from each other.

This is the stage of life in which you and your daughter have a chance to redefine the guiding principles of your relationship. Because you are now both adults, it should be possible to benefit from each other's life experiences. The role of nurturer is no longer yours alone, but should pass freely back and forth between the two of you.

How much of a role model do you need to be?

Last year all the predictable rhythms of Nan Lyons's personal and professional life fell apart when Ivan, her husband and writing partner, died. In the months after his death, Nan faced the daunting task of building a career on her own. She began by attempting to honor the contract for a series of travel guides they had committed to together. When we talked to Nan she was elated that she had been able to deliver the first guide on schedule. "If you've worked with a partner, husband or not, you begin to doubt that you can work alone," said Nan. "I certainly doubted that I could. When Ivan died, I said 'I'm giving up this contract because I can't write without him.' Even before he died we had had this discussion. He said, 'You *can* write alone.' And I said, 'No,' and we went back and forth. And I guess that was on my mind a lot. It hasn't gotten to be wonderful yet, but it is comforting to know that I can do it. It will be wonderful, but it's too soon to use that word."

Knowing that her twenty-six-year-old daughter Samantha was concerned about her strengthened Nan's resolve. "It has always been important for me to show Sam that I am competent. It was important for me to have her see me as able to achieve what I wanted to achieve. Always. I made a conscious decision to present myself this way, because my mother presented herself to me as a victim. And I wanted for Sam not to have that and, in fact, to see me as someone who could achieve what I needed to achieve. It would drive me crazy for her to see me not able to handle what I needed to handle. And I wanted her to be able to call her own shots. And she does. She's not to be trifled with."

So exactly what did she say to Sam? "I was as honest as I knew how to be about the practical implications of the problem," she said. "That even though I wanted to do the work, and certainly needed the money, it was possible the publisher would pull the rug out from under me. And then I discussed with her my backup plans. How I was already looking into other projects in case this didn't work. I wanted her to know that a woman alone has to be able to think this way and deal with problems like this."

Does Nan think her forthrightfulness has had an effect on Sam? "Of course, you can never be sure. She used to be shyer. Now she's more flamboyant. You know, how you go into a room and work the room? I'm seeing more of that in Sam now. That could just be the self-confidence that comes with age, but I'm seeing it more. Just recently she did something remarkable. She had been accepted by a perfectly good graduate school, but the one she really wanted had turned her down. So a few days before the term began, she marched into the dean's office and told them that they had made a mistake in rejecting her and that they should really reconsider her application. I think they were stunned, but they took her seriously. In fact, she succeeded in changing their minds, and they accepted her on the spot. That's the kind of behavior I'm thrilled to see in her. Can I take any credit for it? I wouldn't go that far."

A year ago Diane Asselin remarried fifteen years after her first marriage ended in divorce. During the years she was single, Diane supported herself and her daughter, Michele, now twenty-three, by producing television programs, many of them aimed at children and adolescents. As head of her own production company, Diane became skilled at winning contracts and marketing her projects. In the months since her marriage, she and her husband have furnished a new apartment, traveled a great deal, arranged his daughter's wedding, entertained extensively, and gotten to know each other's friends. Diane says, "What's taken a back seat is my definition of myself as a worker, as someone who had to go out and make the work happen."

While Diane's change of direction has been wonderful for her, it has had a mixed effect on her daughter. "In terms of Michele, she didn't see it as 'Mom's worked hard, she can goof off for a year, she can travel a lot.' She thought, I wonder what she's going to do? She saw me for so many years as this independent person. She was always glad to hear when there was too much going on. So as I've worked less, that makes her nervous. She treated it with humor, but I'm sure she didn't want me turning into someone who shopped!"

Diane is slowly getting back into competitive gear. It's not made easier by the fact that the world in which she operates is changing. "It's a young people's business. I don't know who to go to anymore. All my old people whom I used to sell things to are leaving the business. And the luxurious days where you came in with a project, they gave you the money, and then you owned the material, don't exist." Recently she signed a contract to reedit some of her old programs in a new format. It's a big relief to Diane. And to her daughter. "Michele likes me to be successful. And even though Richard is very generous, I'm sure that psychologically I'm keeping my independence. I'm back doing what I've done for so long, thinking Oh God, what about this? What do I do about that? Juggling the books like I used to do at various times in my career—and it's familiar. There's something in me that likes all this activity. And this is the role model that Michele knows and likes, and it's the one I want to give her."

Nan and Diane have been successful at revitalizing their careers and preserving an image in their own and their daughters' eyes that is very important to them. But for some women linking professional success and competence as a mother may take too high a toll. They may not succeed professionally. They may no longer even want to. In any case, the notion that a woman's competence as a mother is being weighed in the balance needs to be challenged. Of course, there are many ways in which you continue to present your daughter with a model of how a mature woman faces defining moments in her life. But you are no longer responsible for shaping her character or her life. Now that you and your daughter are both adults, you no longer owe it to her to be a role model. What you continue to owe her— and what you would hope to receive from her in return—is respect and support. When it comes to making decisions about your life, your primary concern should be to find out what is best for you.

How You Relate to Men

How much of our young adult daughters' lives is consumed with choosing a partner or learning how to build a permanent relationship! Our daughters are examining, in the light of their own needs and decisions, how *we* relate to men. They want to know why we chose to marry their father, and why we are still together or not. They want to know *how* we've kept intact marriages going. The daughters of women who are not now married want to know how their mothers cope with the uncertainties of dating or the possibility of being alone.

In an unexpected—and pleasing—confluence of concerns, we are asking ourselves many of the same questions: Why this man? What investment must I make to keep a relationship vital? Is the effort worth it to me or would I rather live alone? Conversely, if I am alone, how much do I care about finding someone to share my life?

And finally, because this is the time when most of our girls are choosing partners, we find ourselves speculating about the impact of our choices on the romantic choices they make.

The ups and downs of marriage

We met Sally and Bruce McMillen when they came to New York so Sally could run in the Marathon. When we arrived at their hotel, Bruce was just leaving for his own five-mile jog through Central Park. They seemed to us to be a particularly attractive couple. We had arranged to interview Sally because, in addition to being the mother of an adult daughter, she is a well-known historian at Davidson College in North Carolina and specializes in the study of southern women. Sally began by talking about how nice it is to live and work in a community like Davidson. The interview moved on to a discussion of the social patterns that still characterize women in the South and then to a description of her relationship with twenty-two-year-old Carrie who manages a gourmet food shop in Washington, D.C. Suddenly Sally brought us up short. "I think that what has made Carrie and me become real close—and we've talked about this—is that I went through a divorce. Bruce is my first—and second—husband.

"We had a major family tragedy in 1982, when Bruce walked out of the family with very little notice. One day he said, 'I'm out of here. I need to find some space for myself.' Which, as you later learn, is a cover for 'I'm having an affair.' Within weeks he was gone, and it just tore the family apart. It was horrible. And Carrie still hasn't quite forgiven him."

When Bruce left, the McMillens' son, Blair, was twelve and Carrie was nine. Sally was finishing her Ph.D. in history at Duke. In 1985, when their divorce was final, Bruce remarried, and Sally landed her first teaching job at Middle Tennessee State University in Murfreesboro. Blair went off to boarding school, and Sally and Carrie moved to Tennessee. "We knew nobody, but I did have a job. We moved to this tiny little town, and she started in this tiny little school. And for two years—until she went off to boarding school—it was just we two women. And we dealt with life, and we dealt with each other. And she was very angry with me for moving her and making her go through this.

"One time in Murfreesboro, Carrie came home from school in a rage and wouldn't talk. I said, 'You're going to sit in that chair till you tell me what's the matter, and I'm going to sit here, too.' And we sat for maybe an hour and a half, silently, and then suddenly, Carrie started crying. She just broke down. And that's when I learned how angry she was with me for bringing her to this town she hated and this school she hated. She just sobbed. And we just talked and talked and talked. It kind of cleared a lot of stuff. Of course, nothing like that solves everything. But I hadn't realized that she had held in so much resentment."

Bruce and Sally were apart for seven years. After he left his second wife, they began seeing each other again. They remarried in 1991. "You'd think it would be easy to do this—I mean just put the family back together. But it doesn't work that way." Sally had come to understand the forces that had led Bruce to bolt. "We had moved to Charlotte for his new job. There was a lot riding on that, and he turned out to hate it. And I was all excited about what I was doing.

So my life was good and his was miserable. And his character really changed. He kind of flipped."

The children were much less forgiving of him. Sally said, "Even though I told them that this remarriage was what I wanted and that it was good for me, Carrie especially had her own issues with him, and still does. She was angry about the way he left. She hated the other woman. She was resentful of the pain he had caused me—and that was probably my fault, because I had told them way too much about what had happened and how I felt. She was still upset about some of the ways he dealt with her. She felt that he got too angry at her when she did something wrong. Some of this stuff got real picky, but it was important to her."

Two years ago, during Carrie's summer vacation, things came to a head. "I remember one night I went in to give her a kiss, and she was just quietly crying. And I asked what was the matter, and she said she knew she needed to talk to Bruce but she didn't know how. She was scared. And I said, 'Well I'll just sit here, and you'll make a list. And I'll write everything down. I'll be your secretary. Tell me all the things you're angry about.' So I sat there for about two hours, and I took notes for her. And she was crying. And I told her, 'This is what you need to talk to him about.'"

Sally was going to be out of town for a few days, and she suggested that Carrie and Bruce have their talk while she was gone. "And they went through the list of her complaints. And Bruce was gentle and loving. They talked about a lot of these things. It was an important step." We asked if Bruce and Carrie have resolved most of their problems. "It didn't resolve everything, but I try not to be in the middle. I try to ensure that if they have issues, they talk to each other about them."

We asked what impact all the turmoil in this family had on Carrie's relations with men. "I've liked the guys she's chosen so far. I think she has a pretty good attitude toward men. I think she's appropriately cautious." Sally laughed. "About the realities of life. Nineteen eighty-two made me realize that something can happen so fast, that something can slip away and all be gone. And that's life."

A child of an intact marriage does not normally have to distinguish between the man who is her father and the man who is her mother's husband. When a marriage breaks up, and a mother remarries, the daughter's relationship with her father and her stepfather are easily separated in her mind. But in this case Bruce is effectively both Carrie's father and her stepfather, and she has a history of grievance against the man with whom her mother is beginning a new life.

One of the most remarkable aspects of this story is how much Sally has done to alleviate the tension that this dynamic has caused. She didn't allow herself to become so self-absorbed in her own drama that she overlooked the impact of events on Carrie's emotions. She was able to differentiate her own needs from those of her daughter. When she saw that Carrie was on the verge of being swamped by rage, she helped her express her feelings, she listened attentively, and she wasn't threatened by Carrie's anger. After Sally and Bruce got back together, she did not require that her daughter explain the past in the same way she had. Finally, she helped Carrie talk to Bruce directly, smoothed the ground between them, but didn't get caught in the middle. She has never forgotten that she isn't the only player in this drama and can't solve everyone's problems.

Sandy Briggs, fifty-three, teaches English as a second language in a San Francisco high school and has developed a lucrative second career writing Spanish textbooks. She and her husband, Peter, have two daughters, Austen, twenty, and Samantha, twenty-five. Peter has been a senior executive of a small technology company for three years. At the time of our interview, he had just announced to Sandy that he was planning to quit. "He feels this job isn't going forward. He loves to get in and solve problems, but he doesn't have a sense of staying day to day because it might afford you some of the other things you might be able to do in your life. He doesn't want to do that. So I've known he's been working his way toward getting out of this one for about a year."

Sandy has tolerated Peter's volatile work history throughout their marriage. Once before, when Peter left a job, he was out of work for three years. Because Sandy's income was steady, they didn't have to move or pull the girls out of private school. Particularly during the times when he was unemployed, Peter was a very involved parent. "He's a wonderful father," Sandy says. "He's the primary chef. Sometimes when I get grumpy I say to him, 'Look, I'll do the cooking, you make some money.' "

But the impact on the Briggs family of Peter's latest career change could be different. "I think it's not so easy to bounce back when you're fifty-three years old. At the level and with the background of where he's been and what he's done, he can't just walk in and get a job like someone else would. And we're at the point at which I wish we were financially secure. So the big unknown in the next few years is, How *will* we plan for a time when neither of us will have a steady income? The answer is, I don't know. But I'm stubborn enough to say, 'I don't see why I should give up some of the ideas I have for a materially comfortable, not lavish, retirement just because you want to do your thing.' So that's the place where we have our rub."

Sandy seemed angry but not enraged. She is somewhat fatalistic. "Life hasn't been what I planned. I'll probably be teaching high school when I'm seventy-five years old. And I probably have missed out on some other job possibilities because I needed that security. But at the same time, some unexpected things, like the chance to write textbooks, have just fallen into my lap. I feel like there's lots of stuff still open to me. I'm willing to let life be an adventure and see where it goes."

In the past Sandy has explained to Austen and Samantha how Peter's restlessness has affected her. "I didn't want them to worry that the marriage would break up. I've said essentially, 'This is tough for all of us, but your dad and I are in it for the long haul.' He's still my best friend. So would I leave him because of this? No. It's frustrating. I'm not in control of this part of his life. But it'll work out." Sandy is not ignoring the truth, but she is clear-eyed about the tradeoffs, and that attitude is what she has tried to convey to her daughters.

Now that she's an adult, Samantha, not surprisingly, is very concerned about security. She worries because her boyfriend can't seem to settle on what he would like to do professionally. On the face of it, she appears to have chosen someone not unlike her father. Sandy wants Samantha to understand that, within the context of a good relationship, lack of security "need not be the end of the world. I tell her, 'Look, I've lived a good life. It doesn't mean I'm not worried about it. It doesn't mean I'm not pissed off. But it's okay, and I've got faith that we'll come through.' "

When there's a new man in your life

When divorced or widowed mothers date or settle down with a new man, a completely different dynamic comes into play. Several women told us they sensed that their daughters were happy to see them in a relationship, were probably relieved not to have to worry so much about their being alone, and yet didn't want the mother-daughter relationship to be threatened in any way. "I've just started seeing someone," said one recently divorced mother of two girls in their early twenties. "They're very excited he turned up, because they see their father dating lots of women, and they were afraid I was going to rot in Westchester. They commented to their cousins—not to me—that they were glad I had someone, but they hoped I never got married. At least it was an honest opinion!"

Diane Asselin, who remarried last year after being single for over a decade, told us, "I'd like to think this marriage has no effect on my relationship with my daughter, but I think if you interviewed her, she wouldn't say that. Because now there is another person to consider. Does she think I'm less available because there's someone else in my life? Probably. But I fight against it. I try to make it like 'everything is just the way it's always been, there's just an addition in my life.' "

Lyttleton Rich has been remarried less than a year to a man of whom she says, "My girls were more sure that I should be marrying him than I was for a long time." Lyttleton's two daughters, Mary, twenty-four, and Elizabeth, twenty-one, both live away from home, which Lyttleton thinks makes it easier for them to accept their mother's new circumstances. "Basically they're out of the nest. I think it would have been very difficult to raise teenagers with a stepfather all under the same roof."

Lyttleton's style is direct; from the time her daughters were little, she has made and enforced clear rules about things like summer jobs, curfews, and academic standards. Although the girls may not always have agreed with her, they knew exactly where they stood. Similarly, she and her new husband spent hours devising a prenuptial agreement to spell out their financial arrangements and guidelines governing their new role as stepparents. (In addition to Lyttleton's two daughters, her husband has four sons, ranging in age from sixteen to twenty-five. The youngest two visit their father on alternate weekends; the older boys come less frequently.)

"Even before Tom and I got married, we agreed that we wouldn't interfere with how the other raises his children—we've seen some other second marriages where that causes problems. And fortunately our kids are old enough for that not to be too much of an issue. But it does come up. Mary lives in Winston, and she comes home every weekend. Most of the time she stays over at a friend's, but she's in and out of our house. We have a three-story condo with a bedroom and bathroom upstairs that all our kids can use. And the master bedroom's on the second floor. So Mary would come home and use our bathroom—use our hair dryer, sit at my dressing table, use my makeup, and leave her towel on our bed. And Tom said, 'Does this always go on?' And I said, 'Tom, you can talk to her.' He said, 'I'm not going to talk to her, that's one of our agreements.' I said, 'Okay, I'll talk to her.' So I said, 'Mary, is there any reason you can't use the third-floor bathroom?' And she said, 'Mom, I've *always* shared the bathroom with you. It just doesn't feel right to be up on the third floor. It's just a bonding thing.' So I said, 'Well, I think you should try. This is an invasion of Tom's privacy. You and I have other ways to bond.'" On some level, a daughter sees her mother's new love as a rival for her mother's affection, a visible threat to her perception that she is the center of her mother's life. A mother needs to be conscious, as Lyttleton is, of what her daughter's actions mean. She may criticize her daughter's behavior, but she needs to address the anxiety it reveals. Lyttleton's shorthand—"You and I have other ways to bond"—is her way of letting Mary know that their connection is inviolable.

Taking your daughter's advice about men

A number of women described their fluctuating romantic circumstances. They're dating, they've just broken up, they're looking for someone new, they wonder if they'll ever find a partner. Their daughters are doing the same. What stood out for us were the sometimes humorous, sometimes touching, stories about a new reciprocity in their relationship—the daughters are the ones who offer practical, soothing, and clear-sighted advice to their moms.

Young women our daughters' age are more likely to insist upon equality in a relationship. "If you want to go out with him, call him," they are apt to say. And they take their mothers to task for being too needy, too dependent on men for their happiness. In September Gail Seiden's on-again, off-again boyfriend of sixteen years told her the relationship was over. "He did it abruptly, coldly. One of the things he said was 'I have to be surgical about this.' " Weeks later, Gail told her daughter, Dina, how hard it was not to pick up the phone and call him. " 'Surgical, Mom,' she says to me. 'Remember he said "surgical." Don't do this, Mom. Don't demean yourself.' And every time I think of calling, I hear her advice and I stop."

"When I go out with men, I become a sniveling, fourteen-year-old-virgin ruin of a woman," says Carol Rusoff, who's been divorced for eleven years. "He'll never call . . . he has called . . . he won't call again . . . I'm scared. The men I go out with who like me say, 'Why haven't you been married again? You're this. You're that.' So I have to ask myself why I haven't had a relationship. And the truth is I'm fiercely afraid. I think if you've been married for eighteen years, it's like you were in a vacuum. When I'm with men it's as though I'm with an extraterrestrial. I become shy, I become impossible. I haven't had that much experience with men. I'm deferential to them. I think we're a product of our times. So even though I came from this professional background where so much is expected of women, in many ways my female liberation has only been in terms of my career. With a man, who's interested in you as a woman, it's a whole different set of rules."

At the moment Carol is interested in two men. One of them lives in New York. "He answered an ad my sister placed in my name in *The New York Review of Books.* He's sixty-six and needy. He sends me fresh flowers every week." The other lives nearby in Los Angeles. "He is dallying with me. I'm practicing sex with him." Carol has discussed her love life with her daughters, Rebecca, twenty-five, and Annie, twenty-one. "I can't ask him for what I want. And although I don't think I should be talking about my sex life with my girls, it did come up with Annie, who's way sexually liberated compared to me. And she said to me very firmly, 'You have a right to pleasure. You have to tell him what you want. He'll never know if you don't tell him. And then if he's not nice about it, dump him.' "

But Carol is afraid to imperil this relationship. "And that's what my kids get really tired of hearing—'Oh, I wish I had a relationship, I wish somebody loved me.' That's what I whine about. I whine about being alone. And they don't want to hear me be vulnerable. 'Oh, Mom, you have so many friends and you're busy and you have a great life,' and I *whi-i-i-ine.* They say, 'Mom, if you have a good relationship, great. If you don't, so what?' They want me to be strong."

They may want you to be strong, but they also need to see you as human. Carol's willingness to let her daughters see that she is needy in this area of her life is a sign that she does not feel she must always hold herself up to them as a perfect role model. She is capable of putting herself in a dependent role in relationship to them, eliciting their empathy. When a mother can reveal herself this way from time to time, she gives her adult daughter the chance to offer the kind of reciprocal support that characterizes loving relationships between equals.

Barbara Weene, the forty-six-year-old mother of Rebekah, twenty-six, has been divorced since Rebekah was an infant. Recently Barbara broke up with a man she had been living with for three years. "I wanted the relationship to be more mutual, more committed. I wanted to discuss the future, he didn't want to discuss the future. He wants to go day to day. He's forty-four and never been married, so it was a little dangerous. And all along Rebekah was saying, 'I accept your decision to be with this person. You have every right to choose a person that you like. I can see a number of things in him that are attractive, I can see that you both have a lot of interests—in sports, et cetera, but I see you acquiescing too much, and that bothers me. You shouldn't have to do that.'" I think it bothers her as a woman and because of the implications for her own life.

"He was also extremely compulsive, and Rebekah didn't like that either. She'd say, 'He can't relax, he can't be flexible, he's extremely compulsive. You need someone you can relax with, who knows how to enjoy life. You've worked your tail off. I've watched you do it, and it's frustrating for me to see you at this point in your life still working so hard, even in a relationship.' And I think she was saying this for herself, too."

Some of the things Rebekah said hurt Barbara, despite the fact that she knew her daughter's perceptions were accurate. "I didn't want to think she was right even though the situation turned out to be exactly as she said." Finally Barbara decided that she could no longer tolerate her lover's indecision, and she asked him to move out. She misses him terribly, which she has told Rebekah. Nonetheless, she tries not to dwell on that when they talk. "She shouldn't be burdened with my misery. She has enough issues in her own life. I'll tell her that I'm having a good day or a bad day, but that basically I can manage this. Which I can."

We said that the measured, thoughtful way in which Rebekah stated her case sounded like the way a wise mother should talk to a daughter. And Barbara agreed. "We're very respectful of each other's feelings and opinions. I think when you're two women who have only each other to depend on, some of that happens. You take care of each other. And even though the daughter is significantly younger, it doesn't mean she has any less insights for her age."

Barbara has described loving and lovely ongoing conversations between two peers. She describes the special intimacy she and her daughter have achieved in the context of her being a single woman raising a daughter alone. We believe that the actual key is that she and Rebekah are, in Barbara's words, "very respectful of each other's feelings and opinions." Their kind of intimacy is, in fact, available to every mother and daughter who are willing to reveal themselves to each other, support each other, and be attentive to each other's needs.

Caring for an Aging Parent

For the first time in history, a significant number of middle-aged women are themselves still daughters. As recently as 1963, fewer than one out of four adults over the age of forty-five had a parent who was still alive. Today, about half the women of our generation have a living parent. And more than half of them are providing some kind of care for the older person. Not surprisingly, most of those elderly survivors are our mothers, since among people seventy-five and older, women outnumber men two to one. The primary responsibility for tending members of an extended family has always fallen to women. A study completed in the early 1980s reported that women in their fifties spent an average of fifteen hours a week taking care of their parents, and women in their sixties spent twenty-three. Women who were widowed, separated, or divorced provided three times more help than those who were married. Recent data suggest that about 20 percent of women in their fifties have a parent living with them, for whom they may or may not have some caretaking responsibility.

More than half of the women in our generation whose mothers are alive believe that they are their mother's primary confidante and her main emotional support. The women we interviewed whose mothers were living mentioned frequently that even if their mothers were currently quite self-sufficient, the day would come when they might have a diminished social life and fewer resources of their own to draw on. Most women fully expected that the responsibility for their mother's care would fall to them. Some had already begun organizing their mother's finances and paying the bills, mediating between her and her doctors, hiring practical nurses or finding companions, sometimes shopping and even cooking meals. And because, for the first time in history, so many women our age are in the work force, they sometimes found themselves stretched quite thin when they added parent care to all the other demands on their emotions and their time. Their daughters were also affected by the imminent loss of their grandmothers. Very often granddaughter and grandmother have had a close relationship. The mothers have found consolation in the fact that they and their daughters are grieving together.

Losing the mother you knew

Megan C.'s story is typical. Within the last two years, Megan has started her own small publishing business in New York; her older daughter, Amber, has lived with her periodically as she recovers from a serious illness; and on top of everything, Megan has taken charge of her sick mother back in Ohio. "My mother's in her nineties. She is tough. She's broken all kinds of bones, including a hip. She also has emphysema, congestive heart failure, there've been a few strokes, and now she's got liver cancer. Her doctors have thought she was dying for three years. They think she is a miracle woman. She goes back and forth between the nursing home and the hospital." Medicaid doesn't pay all the bills, so Megan covers the difference. Her finances are further eroded by the cost of racing to Ohio every few weeks with each emergency. And her emotions are battered as well by the fact that, at the moment, her mother won't speak to her. "She's very angry with me now, which I think may be a prelude to her dying. She's angry because she's dying, and because of the strokes, she can't verbalize it."

Both of Megan's daughters had more rapport with her mother than she did. They used to fly alone to visit her every summer. And particularly when their grandmother was becoming frail but still capable of expressing her feelings, Marjorie, the younger daughter, went to see her whenever she could. "I remember one visit," Megan said, "we flew out together to see her in the assisted living facility. It was a beautiful fall weekend. I still have this vision of my mother and my daughter sitting on the porch, holding hands. My mother was beaming; she didn't want to let her go. During this whole ordeal, both girls have been very concerned for me. Our grieving together has become part of the fabric of our lives."

Even before our mother dies, we often find ourselves mourning the loss of the mother we knew. Says Carol Rusoff, "I miss the woman who was my mother—the always curious and cultured and vivacious and fascinating woman. The wonderful grandmother who floated in the ocean with my daughter, Becky, and taught her to look at the sky and the clouds, and to dream. That woman is being replaced by a frantic old lady who either because of her personality or the symptoms of old age won't be accountable for any of her character defects. So my sister and I have a new job, which is taking care of her, and beginning to say to people who take care of her, 'My mother is very difficult.' She just lost her longtime companion and her brother—the last living relative of her generation. She won't take medication. She's in an agitated depression. But every so often she has a moment of incredible insight, sweetness, lucidity. That's one percent of the time. But when it's there, it's unique and irreplaceable."

Carol's daughter Rebecca, now twenty-five, was lucky enough to be with her grandmother for one of those moments. "She came down purposely to see her. There was a quiet urgency in her need," Carol told us. "We went over to my mother's house, and Becky got out the old family photo albums. She wanted to write captions for all of the pictures. Who was that man? What was my mother doing in that picture? How did she feel when it was taken?

"They were quite a sight together. Becky with her fabulous posture and shiny hair, and my mother bent over and crooked. She had to use this enormous magnifying glass. Sometimes my mother had trouble coming up with names and places. It was exhausting for her. Sometimes she fell asleep in mid-sentence, without dropping the glass. Her naps were like a comma, a pause, then she'd wake up and continue her sentence. I don't know which of the three of us the afternoon meant the most to."

Clarissa C. told us, "My mother's health is pretty good. She's not on any medicine. She eats well, sleeps a lot, and is stone deaf, which has isolated her. But it's more a question of my mother's personality. Some of it come and goes; some of it is gone. It's sort of like losing your best friend. And I think it's very painful to come and sit with her and see this. She's not suffering, but you know there are things you can't discuss with her anymore, partly because of the deafness, but also because her mind has changed quite a bit. And that's very painful. It isn't just like an elderly relative, it's your own mother!" Clarissa told us that her younger daughter, Edith, twenty-eight, whom she describes as very sensitive and very attuned to her family, is depressed and sad about her grandmother's decline. "She already knew intellectually what aging entails, but she sees firsthand now what it really means to grow old. I saw this with my grandmother. I was Edith's age, and it hit me very hard." Clarissa's older daughter, Donna, thirty-three, is married, is buying a house, is thinking about having a child, and lives further away. "She only sees her grandmother once or twice a year, so she doesn't have the same exposure to the reality of aging and dying that Edith has." Both daughters are very sympathetic to what Clarissa is going through. "They know that visiting my mother is an ordeal. You enter into your mother's world, a difficult one. You eat when she does, you nap when she does, for five or six days you are totally immersed in this. And because they've been there, they understand. They also understand why I need to be there.

"You have to get over your anger and your frustration that your mother could surmount her forgetfulness, her withdrawal into herself, if she really tried. You must accept her present condition to reach your peace with her. My mother came to an acceptance of her condition and a serenity in the face of her aging long before I did. She would say, 'What can you do? I'm old. This is the way it is.' And she wasn't depressed about it. So I no longer have this feeling of denial and anger, I'm happy to say.

"What I've learned from all of this is that you have to enter a difficult stage where you accept your mother as she is and don't try to bring back the person you once knew. And I want my daughters to understand that, and to understand that when I'm in my mother's condition, it's going to be easier for me than it will be for them."

"I don't want to be a burden to my kids"

Anne Navasky spoke about the irrational anger one feels at the signs of a mother's frailty. "I've always liked my mother and admired her. Compared to other mothers she was a model. We had the war, my father was off, so we were alone together. So that was probably very binding. There wasn't a significant time when I didn't think my mother was very good. And now that she's aging, it's very hard. Recently I yelled at her, and I feel so guilty. Part of it is that I feel angry. I don't want her to be decrepit; I don't want her falling apart. So it comes out in anger at the most vulnerable time for her, when she just needs someone to say, 'Oh, you're wonderful.' She's eighty-four, she's had three serious illnesses, and she still goes to work every day. Wouldn't you think I would be proud of that instead of yelling at her because she can't hear or she can't see or can't remember my friends' names—and I feel terrible about that, but I don't think she knows that. So you pick yourself up and try to be cheery about it but you just want to punch her for doing this to you. It's just so horrible and so selfish on my part!

"What I also feel bad about is that I rely on our working together as my time with her. I'm with her every day after all—what a good daughter I am, you know—and she's alone all the rest of the time, all the social time, and I feel guilty about that. But how much of this burden do we assume, bring on ourselves, thinking, Oh, my mother's sick and alone, I have to be there, when she's not calling for us to be there? How much of this burden do we bring on ourselves because we think it's our job, it's our duty? My mother is always saying, 'Go,' and I say, 'You're my mother. I can't leave you alone here.' Right now she is about to have a terrible operation to prevent her from going blind—it will take three months to recover—and my vacation is coming up. She says, 'Go. Go. There's nothing you can do.' And I think, How can I not be there?

"I talk to my kids about this. When my father was dying seven years ago, it was so painful. I told them I really did not want them to be around me when I was dying. It's so destructive. I said, 'I'll try to arrange it, and if I can't, you should.' And I've talked with Jenny about my anger now at my mother and how it makes me feel guilty. I told her partly to relieve my *own* guilt and partly to make her realize that this could happen to her, with us, and I hope that knowing how I was feeling would somehow protect her from going through it herself, or make her feel less guilty if she had to."

Anne got to the heart of what confounds so many of us at this stage in our lives. Our daughters are watching us cope with our mother's frailty, dependence, and ultimately, her demise, just as they are beginning to absorb the reality that we won't be around forever. What's so upsetting to us is the realization that even in the warmest of mother-daughter relationships, the dependent, aging parent ultimately becomes a burden. None of us wants to be the burden on our daughters that many of our aging mothers are to us, although we know full well that most of our mothers said exactly the same thing. Yet we don't know how to avoid it. As Cynthia G. says, "If your own mother is still alive, and she needs more and more of your care, how do you deal with the infantilizing of her? The diminishing of her. How does that affect what we think and who we are with our grown children? I see that being a burden is part of it. We indicate by joking, 'Oh, if I act like that, you should shoot me.' But that indicates only that we don't want to behave the way she does; it doesn't point to a solution."

Susannah Marks's mother died twenty-three years ago when Susannah's daughters were quite young. Susannah took care of her mother in her own home during her final years. "One thing I would like to tell my daughters is that one of the most satisfying experiences in my life was taking care of my mother at the end. In the last few months of her life. And it was terribly painful and terribly difficult. But it was one of the most rewarding things I've ever done. And I'd like to share that with them. But how can you say that to them without implying that you expect the same from them? It isn't a question that I *had* to do it—well I guess psychologically I had to do it. But it was a wonderful, enriching experience. But you can't say that. They saw it, but they saw also a lot of the unpleasant parts of the old age and dying process, and I don't know what all of it has meant to them."

There's no way to foresee how our own aging will play out, although the odds are better than ever that we will live long and eventually become dependent. There is no formula that can eliminate the concerns we have about what a burden we may become to our daughters. The only advice that seems valuable is not to hide from your daughters the complexity of emotions you feel as you tend the older generation; by doing so you are giving them permission to acknowledge whatever it is they feel if and when they must tend to you.

When You're Threatened with Serious Illness

Women of our generation have reached the stage of life when the news of serious illness among our peers feels more inevitable than shocking. Even though we want to believe it can't happen to *us*—we also know it will, and sooner than we'd like. The suspicious lump, the arthritic joint, the deteriorating organs, the recurrent hints of physical or mental illness are all intimations of our own mortality. This is the age when we know too much about chemotherapy regimens; when, as did our mothers before us, we prepare casseroles and cakes for our friends when they come home from the hospital or from the funeral; when our conversations turn more and more frequently to the search for meaning in the face of tragedy. We have moved into an unaccustomed place in the march of generations. Just as our daughters are taking off, making their own worlds and families, expanding their universe, we are made aware of our vulnerability, the diminished odds that we can avoid disaster.

Among the women we interviewed, approximately 15 percent told us about a serious illness in the past few years. Two thirds of those said they had been treated for cancer, most frequently of the breast. Some of the women took comfort from a daughter's active involvement in a nurturing role; others consoled themselves that their illness had not significantly disrupted their daughter's life. The biggest hurdle for most women came right at the start: Do you tell your daughter that you are facing a diagnosis of a serious illness? If so, when? And how?

The women we interviewed had widely different responses to these questions.

Letty Cottin Pogrebin, the mother of thirty-year-old twins Abigail and Robin, practices full disclosure. "A couple of years ago I had a breast cancer scare. Before the biopsy, I told the girls, because if it was going to be bad news and I hadn't prepared them somewhat in advance, they would have felt betrayed. In our family, if somebody forgets to tell someone something, it's taken very personally. Everybody tells everybody almost everything. It's our expression of intimacy."

Beth Curry's family, on the other hand, is more reticent. So it seemed natural for Beth to refrain from telling her daughter, Caroline, twenty-six, about a possible malignancy in her breast until the diagnosis was certain. "I didn't tell her until after the biopsy results because I didn't think there would be any problem, but when the doctor said the biopsy was positive, I told her. And she said, 'I can't believe that you didn't tell me sooner.' We asked Beth if she would do it differently the next time. 'No,' she said. 'A few months ago I had a scare in the other breast, and I thought, I'm not going to go through thirty years like this, telling everybody every time there's a problem. I said to Caroline, 'Okay this is it—I'll tell you when there's something wrong, but I'm not going to tell you every time there's something that *might* be.' "

Cynthia G. was also inclined not to upset her daughters, Leslie, thirty, and Nicole, twenty-eight, until her tentative diagnosis of breast cancer was confirmed. But Leslie overheard a conversation between Cynthia and her doctor on the telephone. "She did ask why didn't I tell her? I explained that I did not intend to lie to her, I just hadn't wanted to say anything until I knew what it was. And once she knew, I let her in on everything. I was still ambivalent about telling Nicole because she was so far from home, and I ultimately decided to wait until the very last minute before I had the operation. I wanted to save them the discomfort and anxiety—and to treat them like children. I admit it. And I certainly felt that way about my mother—and ended up not telling her until after the operation when I had something specific to tell her. So I certainly treated her like a child."

Alice Trillin was treated for lung cancer twenty years ago when her daughters Abigail and Sarah were seven and four. Since then she has had a public presence as an anti-smoking advocate; she has gone out of her way to share her information about the disease and up-to-date treatments with anyone who's newly diagnosed; and she spends a great deal of time offering care and support to victims of any kind of cancer. "I've thought a lot about how to tell your kids if you're really sick," says Alice. "You can help them if you can discuss it so that they don't get frightened. You may not need to tell them everything, but that's up to you. You need to tell them enough so that they're not frightened by what's going on or angry with you later for not having let them in on it.

"When I first got sick, they were so little. I didn't want to let them know that I had a life-threatening illness, and I didn't want them to hear the word *cancer*. The night before surgery, I sat them down and drew a picture of my lung. I explained that the doctor was going to take out some tissue that had been making me cough. I explained about the knife. I showed them a tiny biopsy scar that had stitches and was healing, and I told them that that was what I would have on my back. Later on I discovered that they believed I had a piece of Kleenex 'tissue' in my lung. But anyhow, no one ever mentioned the word *death*."

Four years ago while Abigail was working in California and Sarah was at college, Alice had some symptoms that indicated a possible recurrence of the disease. "I told them I needed to have back surgery, that a vertebra must have collapsed and needed repair. I did not mention the implications, and they didn't ask. In fact, it turned out to be a false alarm, and then I told them the whole story. In general, I think it's wrong to give them information they don't need and can't do anything about."

And that's the dilemma. When does protecting your daughter from unnecessary pain come across as failing to respect her need to be treated as an adult? As you face this problem in the years to come, you may come to learn that sharing the truth—and your fears about it—is very liberating. *When* you tell her has to be weighed separately. If she's in the midst of a crisis of her own, facing a deadline or an important exam, it's possible you'd like to defer your news temporarily until she's better equipped to deal with it. And once you've told her, you may discover that she can be a tremendous support to you.

Women told us over and over how moved they were to see their daughters take charge in a crisis. After Beth Curry told Caroline about her cancer, her daughter insisted on being involved in Beth's treatment. "For my first visit to the oncologist she came from Washington, and she said, 'Mom, I want to go with you.' It was the first time I had seen her playing the role of the person that needed to help me. She went with a pencil and paper and asked the doctor these questions, and I almost wanted to say, 'Wait a minute, this is *my* life!' And we've been able since then to talk a lot about my feelings during that period."

Cynthia G.'s daughter Leslie went with her mother for all her tests and doctor's appointments. She practically camped out in her mother's hospital room after the operation. "I'm still not able to look at all of this objectively, but all my friends say that she has grown enormously. There was an element of deep love—of being adult mother and adult daughter—that emerged during this period."

Four years ago, as a consequence of nearly twenty years of diabetes, Linda Censor suffered acute renal failure. She went on dialysis, and a search was begun for an eventual kidney transplant. Linda, the mother of Catherine, twenty-seven, and Rachel, twenty-four, says, "My kidney failure really brought us close together; we were always a close family, but this was like cement. I'm thinking particularly of Catherine who was out there doing her thing. When I needed her, she really came and focused in on me. She took me to the hospital to be fitted for my dialysis catheter. First we had manicures together around the corner from our house—I still remember crying the whole time.

"She was also the one who took me to my initial conference with the transplant surgeon. She was living at home. She would go with me, and she was the one who would talk to me and put what I was feeling into words. And the words were so right.

"And then it was Rachel's turn. She was the only one in the family who was a compatible donor. She took it upon herself to get all the testing, set up the date for the operation, give me a kidney. We were on separate floors in the hospital. My husband took Rachel, and Catherine took me. Catherine was working full time, but she was very concerned, she called me every day. She had developed the capability to come out of herself and respond to me and my problems."

When Rosemary T. was diagnosed with lymphoma she turned to her husband, her sister, and close friends who lived nearby in Chicago for support. Of her daughter Candace, twenty-six, Rosemary said, "I wasn't even going to tell her till after the operation. And my husband and my sister said you can't do that. So the night beforehand, we called her. And she, of course, fell apart. But she made a lot of jokes. And she flew home from Washington for the operation, and she was wonderful. She sat in the hospital room with me and made jokes and was very, very supportive.

"Once years ago, we were moving to the Upper Peninsula for the summer. And the day we were supposed to move, my back went out. She was about eleven. And she said, 'Now, Mommy, don't worry. We'll go to Burger King, and we'll bring in food and we'll take care of you.' She assumed that role then, but I don't think she ever did it again until this illness. And she didn't crumple. She would walk me up and down the halls with all my bags. I couldn't believe how weak I was and how it hurt. And she was walking beside me and making me laugh about having to go everywhere tethered to a post. And she tried to stay cheery about it, and it's hard for her to be cheery. She goes to the heart of the matter. She can be doom and despair, but she didn't do that."

Cynthia G. says, "I don't yet know what Leslie has carried away from this experience about her mortality or mine. She spent a lot of time at the hospital with my friends, and they were all talking about how *their* mothers were dying, and they didn't take into account that to her the word *mother* didn't automatically conjure up some wizened old lady on her last legs. She was hearing these details hour by hour, and the anxiety it provoked in her was more than I anticipated."

In fact, after Cynthia had been home from the hospital for a few days, Leslie showed up less and less frequently. "She had given up a certain amount of independence to immerse herself in what was happening to me, and she needed to regain some distance. To invest in her *own* life."

As Cynthia implies, welcoming your daughter's love and caring as an equal adult can tip easily into relying on her too much. Intimacy can turn into imposition. Another woman told us that during the first months after her mastectomy, "My daughter became my 'mommy.'" It's understandable that in moments of terror and pain you want to regress and be taken care of. And how wonderful that you can turn to your newly adult daughters for that loving care. But intense moments of intimacy need not, and probably cannot, be sustained. When your daughter needs to pull back rather than continue to devote so much of her energy to you, you must recognize that she has her own life to live, that this has been grueling for her, too, and that a mutually respectful autonomy can be good for both of you.

Facing Our Own Mortality

As she is well aware, Cynthia G.'s joke about her aging mother— "Shoot me when I get like that"—masks any real discussion of the implications of our inevitable aging. Few of us, and fewer of our daughters, are ready to face this fully. Only a handful of the mothers we spoke to said that they had even begun forthright discussion about preparations they'd made in anticipation of their own deaths. One woman told us, "I marched my three daughters over to the file cabinet where I keep my living will and health care proxy and all the rest of that stuff. And I showed them where it was, and they nodded and didn't say a word and changed the subject as fast as they could." Another said, "She doesn't want to hear about it, so I've written everything in a long letter and told her where it is, so she'll know how I feel when the time is right for her to know."

From Marilyn's journal, August 26, 1996

Kore, back from a weekend at a friend's beach house, reports that the friend's father played golf every day, and her mother and her "girl friends" and Kore and her friends all hung out together— shopped, gossiped, rented a movie. I said, "Gossiped? About who? Movie stars?" and she said, "No, we spent a lot of time talking about our boyfriends, about what's going on. You know."

But I didn't exactly. "Do you mean you talked about details of your sex lives?" "Yes." "Did you think the women were being nosy or just acting like pals?" "A little of both," she said, "but you've gotta remember most of my friend's moms are ten or fifteen years younger than you . . ." Then she caught herself, and said, "I don't mean you're old. You're in good shape. You and Dad are lively and interesting. You don't look or act like you're old." I heard the hint of anxiety in her voice that she usually gets when this topic comes up. Anytime I mention signs of decrepitude—shortness of breath, thickness of waist—she immediately reassures me, and maybe herself, that I'm holding my own.

This time I asked her directly what it means to her. She said, "I never think about you getting old or dying or anything, if that's what you mean." I said, "Well, I'm not exactly an antique, but I am certainly aging." Then we got into a brief and rather abstract discussion about the distinction.

We also talked about intimacy in general. About how a few friends' mothers can manage—better than I—to get into discussions about boyfriends, but most of the others cross over the line into being intrusive. I asked if she wished I opened up the discussion with her more than I do, if she missed it or thought I was too aloof. She said, "No." She felt more comfortable talking about such things with Kate anyway. I said that I would try to be more available if she ever wanted to talk that way, and might even try to start a conversation from time to time.

Then I returned to the subject of my aging. And she absolutely cut me off. I said, "I think this is something you *really* don't want to talk about." She laughed, agreed, and ended the conversation.

Anne S. and her only daughter Wendy, twenty-eight, have been more explicit with each other. Anne's mother died of pancreatic cancer in her late fifties, as did two of her uncles. Anne has already had one scare and suspects that she will get cancer sooner or later. "I'm not anxious about it. What happens, happens. I can't get myself all rattled about that. I just don't want to be sick." She has said to her sister, "Just make sure you have enough money to pay for the plane fare to fly east and toss me out the window. That's all I care about. I don't want to linger and suffer like Mom." In her living will and health care proxy, Anne has given that sister the responsibility for making medical decisions in her behalf if she's incapacitated. And she has explained all this to her daughter. "Wendy said she was a little hurt by that. I said, 'Wendy, you're the executor of my estate. Most kids your age couldn't take that on, and I would trust you to do it well. But I wouldn't trust you to pull the plug. You think about it.' And the next day, she said to me, 'I guess my feelings aren't hurt. I wouldn't want to do that.' " Anne told us, "When we both get older, maybe I'll change that. But for now I think it's best."

Joy W.'s family has had more than its fair share of medical traumas. Her bedridden mother lived with them for the five years preceding her death. Her husband has had several heart attacks. Her oldest daughter, Amanda, twenty-three, was in a serious auto accident when she was fifteen. Through it all Joy has been the stabilizing presence for everyone else. "But I did have cancer a year ago," she told us, "and I wanted to get a health proxy signed. I wanted Amanda to be my proxy holder because I thought she'd be more reasonable than my husband. Because I knew he would want to resurrect me to make dinner. And I did not want to come out with a stroke in a wheelchair and have to make dinner. So I said to them the night before the surgery, 'If I'm going to have a stroke, I don't want to come back, so don't resurrect me.' And they both fell apart. Amanda burst into tears and said, 'I want you to be my mother until I'm at least forty.' So I realized I had to do some magic. So I said, 'I'll be around until you're at least forty-two.' And let it go at that. I knew I wasn't going to fix it in two minutes. And I didn't want to spend the night before my operation comforting her. So I want to go back and revisit that at a calmer time. And I want to make it clear to her how I feel about this proxy. I really want to be let go. But the time to talk about this is not the night before your surgery. I need to face the fact that I haven't done it yet."

A moment of crisis is seldom the best time to discuss such potent material. Yet when the crisis is past, we all tend to put unpleasant subjects out of our minds. Every time we do that, however, we are actually passing up an opportunity to enrich our relationship with our loved ones.

We believe that it should be possible to share with your daughter the essence of whatever is happening to you at this stage of your life. If you can do this in a way that isn't intrusive—that's mutually acceptable to both of you—you are helping her to know who you are and to see you not just as *Mom* but as an independent adult with a multidimensional life of your own. You are providing her with a model that may be helpful when she in turn faces the vexing developmental tasks of midlife. You are developing the habit of discussing intimate subjects with her as an adult.

And something new is happening. Your daughter is a member of the coming generation, and she brings to your relationship a different perspective than the one you're accustomed to. You can learn from her and benefit from her experience. She can be a wonderful source of advice and information, as well as of solace and support.

Your Expectations and Her Life

Our daughters are the recipients of our dreams. Of our conscious and unconscious expectations for them. We have what Dr. Phoebe Kazdin Schnitzer calls "the expectation of similarity," the assumption that our daughters will share our values, our tastes, and our psychological makeup, as a matter of course. We expect that our daughters will do what we've been able to do, only better; do what we were never able to do and always wanted to.

When you and your daughter seem naturally attuned to each other, share values, or choose a similar lifestyle, it can add joy to your life. Carol Rusoff, an actress and drama teacher told us, "My younger daughter, Annie, in her last year of college did a major paper on myths and legends for children, which is my interest, and my other daughter is a teacher and took all my notes about theater for children and used them in her classroom, and I thought, These are little pieces of me, and it makes me really happy."

Conversely when you and your daughter are a bad fit temperamentally, or she seems to make choices just to spite you, her actions can feel like a betrayal. As one mother who was still smarting over a terrible rupture with her daughter said, "There's that invisible umbilical cord that you have with a daughter. You can understand her emotions, and you want so much to help her get through rough times. Also, having a daughter, it's your second chance to redo the mistakes you made when you were young. If she succeeds in life, it's like everything you did as a mother is justified, and if she doesn't follow the scenario you wanted, you've failed twice in your life."

In the course of our interviews, we heard stories of great expectations that were confirmed. And wrenching stories from women who felt that everything in their daughter's life was antithetical to the mother's dreams. Sometimes these women perceived that their expectations for their daughter and for their relationship with her were unrealistic, but they were powerless to relinquish their dreams and accept the reality.

It's not possible to raise children and not have wishes for them. It's also impossible not to communicate your ideas about a thousand things just by the way you act and speak, the kind of dog or car you own—to say nothing about the explicit statements you make to drive home your moral vision. Families transmit a series of expectations over generations—expectations about money and power, about the relative importance of sons versus daughters, or about the role assigned to children because they resemble a specific aunt or uncle or because of their birth order.

Women in our interviews told us that their expectations were often strongest for their firstborn child. Or their first girl. Shirley Strum Kenny had four sons before her daughter Sarah was born. "When the fourth boy got to be twelve years old, and he started acting up, you said, 'What is wrong with him?' and then you remember he's just going through that twelve-year-old stuff. But Sarah was a different experience. When she got to that stage, my feelings of bonds were so very close that I expected her to react to things the way I had reacted to them. And she didn't. She still doesn't. And it was difficult for me until I got comfortable with that fact."

Arlen M. and her husband had two daughters and then a son. Arlen now sees that Martha, the oldest daughter, was always expected to be the "good" girl—to fulfill every expectation her parents set for her. Harper, the second, was allowed to find her way more on her own. As Arlen said, "Harper is the kid who put pillows in her bed and skipped out at night to party. And we were always less tough on her than on Martha. Looking back I wish that we had not pushed Martha so hard. If I could do anything over with any of my children, she's the one. She is, I think, too intense, and I think part of that is our fault. She was the child who did what she was supposed to do in the first place. She's your typical first child. She was perfectly willing to do what we told her to do from day one.

"*Dallas*, the TV program, would come on on Friday night," said Arlen. "And Jerry was just insistent that the kids not watch it. And Martha went to a spend-the-night party, and the phone rang. She must have been in the fifth or sixth grade and she said, 'Mother, may I speak to Daddy?' And she said, 'Daddy, everybody is watching *Dallas*. Do I have to go in the other room?' I mean I just nearly died. I mean I just never would have considered going in the other room. I would have just sat there. I never would have told my father I was watching and neither would Harper. I think we just put too much expectation on Martha—like, not watching *Dallas*. I mean, so what? So what if you don't say, 'Yes, ma'am'? So what if you're not polite all the time? So what if you make a B instead of an A? So what if you choose sociology instead of chemistry? I think we wanted too much for her, and her nature was such that she was too willing to agree."

From Marilyn's journal, August 31, 1995

After interviews with Marianne Collins and Shelagh C. in Rockville Centre. Waiting for the train back, Susan and I talked again about how hypercritical we both are. She's probably more vocal about it than I am but not so dissimilar. Then we talked about how satisfied and comfortable these women seem to be with their daughters and their daughters seem to be with them. Susan wondered if it had any connection to a strong faith, in their case Catholicism. They don't seem to be very competitive for themselves or their children, they seem more accepting of whatever is. Whereas we maintain this absurdly high level of aspirations and achievement that we demand of ourselves and our children.

And which was demanded of us by our parents. We had to work for their approval. And they liked it best when something we did not only had value for its own sake but also reflected well on them. My need to be pleasing, socially seductive, with people I meet must come from some dynamic started by my mother when I was very young. It could have been worse, I could have been made to work at the piano, or, God help us, dance or something. Fortunately, I was allowed to do what I'm good at—being clever.

I think I wanted Kate to do that, too, and when she was very young she did—she was precocious verbally. But when she began to develop her shyness around age three, it drove me wild, because I wanted her to be forceful and fearless as well. And I guess there are times when I would like her to be more assertive today. Kore is that in spades. It seems to come naturally to her, and it has to have been reinforced by my approval all along.

We have already touched on moments when a mother's wishes for her daughter clashed with the daughter's choices for herself. What do quarrels over a young woman's personal style and habits, or her choice of partner reflect, if not a mismatch of expectations? In a few interviews, however, a mother's story about her expectations for the way her daughter would conduct her life, and how her daughter accepted or rejected that scenario, formed the very core of the narrative.

When She Fulfills Your Expectations for Her

We met Nancy Hernandez during her lunch break at Lincoln Hospital in the South Bronx, where she is the administrator of a group of sixteen outpatient clinics. Nancy was born in Puerto Rico forty-five years ago, but has lived in New York since she was an infant. Soon after she graduated from high school, she got married. She had the first of her three daughters when she was twenty-two, the same year she started working for the municipal hospital system. Nancy is finishing her B.A. in health administration at Lehman College in the Bronx. She and her husband live near the hospital in a neighborhood she describes as "drug infested, where the streets are filled with drinking, drugs, and killings."

From the time her daughters were young, Nancy did everything she could to make it easier for them to make their way in the world. She focused on their education. She arranged for the oldest girl to attend one of the city's elite private schools. She fought to get all three accepted into special programs. On weekends and after school, she took them to museums and enrolled them in music and dance programs, "anything to keep them away from the environment," she says. Nancy tells her daughters, "What I've been through I don't want you to go through—at the age of twenty getting married, two years later having a child, not being able to finish your education. Now, at my age, I'm trying to finish my college degree when I should have done it way back. You guys are young. I want you to finish your education while you're young. Not when you're in your late forties because your mind's not the same. I leave here, I go to school, by the time I get home . . . and homework . . . whew! In the morning I'll get up at five and do it. I want you guys to be comfortable, if you can finish your education without anyone interrupting you."

Nancy's husband approved of what she was doing, but he didn't take an active role in helping her. "He's from the old style, he's very *machismo*. 'I'm the man, you're the woman. You take care of the kids, you raise them, educate them. I'll be there if you need me, but other than that, that's it.' So I've basically been mother and father, though he's been there."

Nancy's mother was also very traditional in her ways of child rearing. She was loving, but her strict code of behavior made it impossible for Nancy to discuss with her mother some of the important things that were going on in her life. Nancy wanted to be more flexible and more connected. "I just kept on reading about how to be a good parent, or trying to be. And when I went back to school, we had even more in common." She actively solicits her daughters' points of view and respects their opinions. "When Yesenia and Veronica are home, we talk about issues that are happening nowadays, like politics, the environment that we live in, what's happening with the youth nowadays, drugs, alcoholism. Yesenia talks to me about my job, which she thinks I should be somewhere else, earning more.

"I also have a beautiful relationship with three other women at the hospital who do community outreach, so they're always moving around in the community. They tell me about their dealings with young people, and I pick up on what they're saying to them. And the message I picked up is—you have to be down to earth with your kids, you have to sit with them, speak to them. And my kids say, 'Mommy, you were always with us. You supported our decisions. When we wanted to go away to school, you didn't say no. You cried, but you didn't say no. You were there when we needed you, and this is only a little bit of how we can pay you back.' "

Nancy's daughters have exceeded her expectations for them. Yesenia, twenty-three, is completing a master's degree in international business. Last summer she was awarded a very competitive internship on Wall Street. Veronica is a junior at Brown. She plans to get a Ph.D. in American civilization and has already won a fellowship that will pay for her graduate education. The youngest, Omara, has followed Veronica to Choate, where she is a junior; Omara hopes to be a marine biologist. "When they were young," Nancy told us, "I thought, well, if they finish high school that's about it, with the environment I'm living in. But they've gone beyond that. I can imagine them being someone in the future you can look up to. And really making a difference, maybe only one percent of a difference, but making a difference. And that's what counts. I'm really very proud of them. I don't know if they even understand how proud I am. My heart glows when I see them. Even when they do something that's a little naughty, I think, well they have to do something a little naughty. They can't be perfect, they're not nuns."

"Quite frankly I believe that you must leave this world better than you found it, and I believe that you do that through your children. Your offspring. So I wanted my children to be the very best that they could be," says Geneva Leazer, a supervisor in a textile mill in North Carolina. Geneva and her nine siblings were raised by her grandparents. "I came from a dirt-poor background, and I wanted to be somebody. I worked after school for a family, washed the dishes and took care of the kids, and I thought, Hmm, why can't I have a life like that? I just plotted to get away as soon as I could. I wanted to be a doctor, but I realized that wasn't possible, because I didn't have anybody to send me to school. But there's no excuse—you can be somebody, you can do something, if only you try."

Geneva married young to the grandson of a prominent local farmer. They have two children, John Jr., now thirty-five, and Mary, twenty-five. When John Jr. was four, Geneva went to work in a local textile mill that was just beginning to hire blacks for other than custodial jobs. "I was one of the first blacks they hired for the manufacturing side. They put you through some things to even get hired! And I became an instructor, and then I became a supervisor. When I first became a supervisor—the first black one they had—the whole department quit. Then after being a supervisor for about three years, I was demoted unfairly and put back on the machine. And they left others in place that had less seniority than I did. The personnel manager knew—he told me discreetly, 'It's not right.' About three months later I was back as supervisor. Then I became a foreman, and then department manager. And the more they done to me, the more determined I was that I was going to stay. And I'm still there thirty-one years later."

Geneva vowed that her children would not have to repeat her experience. "No child of mine would ever have to work in a textile mill, and if they did, it's their fault, because I would see to it that they got their education. I believe that an education is probably the most important thing you can have, other than your self-esteem, and education sort of helps that, I would think.

"I believe in excelling. I look at it this way—of those to whom much is given, much is required." Her son, John Jr., was one of the first black students to attend Davidson College. He went on to get his Ph.D. in chemistry at the University of Pennsylvania and is now a research chemist with Merck near Philadelphia. "And Mary—God gave her a brain, too. And I wanted her to excel. If she only had the ability to make Cs or Bs, that was okay with me. But I knew where she was coming from, I knew she was well prepared, and I demanded As. She never had to wash dishes, she never had to help clean the house. 'I don't want anything to interfere with those As. Just get me As."

Mary earned a 4.0 GPA during her senior year at Davidson and graduated with distinction. After finishing law school at the University of North Carolina, she started working as an assistant district attorney in Mecklenburg County, where the family lives. Mary married her college boyfriend during her second year of law school. Soon after her wedding, she wrote Geneva a letter that her mother proudly showed us:

> Lately I have noticed as I grow older, you are in my thoughts more and more. I want to thank you for being the wonderful mother you have always been to me. When people go through important events in their lives, they tend to look back on their past. My marriage has had this effect on me. When I look back on my life, the strongest, warmest, most beautiful, most courageous thing I see is you, my mother.

Geneva does not deny that there have been times when her expectations and Mary's needs did not coincide. "I was very upset when she starting dating Mike. I didn't approve of him. I was afraid he was a distraction to her, because after she met him, her grades plummeted. Boy I ran right up to the school. I said to her, 'You can't do two things at once, you know, maintain this relationship and get good grades.' And I said, 'I don't want to see him around you anymore.' She asserted herself and said, 'Mamma, if Mike is not welcome, then I'm not welcome . . .' And I backed off. After that she wrote me a letter and promised me she was going to do better, and she brought those grades back on up there.

"He was there all the time. And he won me over, so he's been like my son, too. I think she probably selected him because she's the stronger of the two. But he loves her very much, and any time she's with him, I don't worry about it. I know Mike would do anything to protect Mary. So I feel very safe that she's protected and loved."

Mary and Mike talk about building a home on property behind her parents' house. "Oh my, we already have that planned out. If Mary has children, I'm gonna retire, I'll keep the grandkids. Mary's grandmother kept her when I was working. She's gonna pay me . . . maybe fifty dollars a week. That would be spending money for me." Geneva has already fixed her sights on helping the next generation. "I can take them fishing and boating. And then instead of going to Davidson, I want my grandkids to go to Harvard or maybe Oxford. Just reach for the stars, you know."

Geneva has managed to impose her dreams on her daughter without alienating her. Nancy Hernandez's daughters seem also to have interpreted their mother's expectations as a vote of confidence in their ability to succeed rather than as a burden to be borne. How have these women managed to stay connected to their daughters in a positive way without intruding beyond a point the daughters would find intolerable? How have they carried it off when so many other mothers with strong expectations for their daughters fail?

First of all, it needs to be acknowledged that for members of non-mainstream subcultures in the United States, getting a good education has provided a means of access into the dominant culture. For people of color, it has often meant the difference between barely surviving and getting ahead. Many African-American families have laid special stress on educating daughters so that they do not have to work as domestics; for young black women education offers the best route to achievement and independence. Mainstream society is often more receptive to upwardly mobile women of color than to men from black and Latino communities, because the men are seen as too threatening to the status quo. Thus, Latina mothers, as well as African-American ones, have learned that if their daughters can get themselves a good education, higher incomes and status will be their reward.

But beyond these ethnic considerations, the stories that Nancy and Geneva told us have implications for every mother. These two women do not seem to be living vicariously through their daughters. They have been successful in their own lives, they've won the respect of their peers, and they take pride in what they have achieved. Their daughters have had the benefit of observing their mothers' hard work and its rewards. When Nancy and Geneva talk of goals for their children, they are not speaking as women whose own ambitions have been consistently thwarted. "It's true that a mother's success helps her to have a sense of satisfaction. She's not somebody who is so empty that she needs somebody else to give her any gratification at all," says Raquel Limonic, a clinical psychologist at the Latino Mental Health Program of the Department of Psychiatry at Cambridge Hospital and Harvard Medical School.

We spoke to Limonic and her colleague, Dr. Margarita Alvarez, about the special problems that immigrant and minority women face when their daughters move into the mainstream culture. The risk for such mothers, said Alvarez and Limonic, is that, to the degree their daughters assimilate, they feel that they and their values are being rejected. And assimilating daughters often feel that their success is at the cost of continued connection with their mothers. But we all agreed that Nancy Hernandez and Geneva Leazer do not seem threatened by change. Nancy Hernandez, though rooted in her community, has herself moved into the mainstream professionally and shares mainstream cultural values. She sees her children's success and their cultural assimilation as a desirable continuation of her own. She doesn't fear being cast aside. And because her daughters have internalized her values, the girls probably don't feel that success will imperil their connection to her. In the case of Geneva and Mary Leazer, the literature suggests that because African-American daughters see so clearly how the predominantly white culture has treated their mothers and feel similar pressures themselves, their sense of connection in the face of oppression from the general society often outweighs the tensions within their relationship.

And finally, the overwhelming impression we carried away after talking with both Nancy and Geneva is that they have made their daughters feel loved and supported, even when the girls have made choices the mother was unhappy about. Geneva reversed her opinion of Mike when Mary told her how serious she was about him. Nancy spoke of her willingness to solicit her daughters' opinions and her sensitivity to issues that affect their generation. She revealed a tolerance for social behavior that differs from what she might actually prefer. However strong these mothers' expectations were and continue to be, they do not seem to have lost sight of their daughters' autonomy.

When a Mother's Expectations Are Dashed

What happens when a daughter does not live up to her mother's expectations for her? When a mother's "expectation of similarity" puts terrible burdens on their relationship? Two women we spoke to could talk of nothing but their frustration and bewilderment that daughters whom they had cared so much about had turned out so differently from their hopes for them.

Lois A. and her husband, Phil, live in St. Louis. Their only child, Karen, thirty-four, is a lawyer in Boston. They are a very tightly knit triangle. Karen was always a good student. After she graduated from Northwestern, her parents encouraged her to go to law school. Lois, an insurance broker, has been a working mother since her daughter was three. She and Phil fully expected that by now Karen would be married to a fellow professional, and juggling her career and motherhood. They planned to buy a condo in Vail so they could entertain their grandchildren.

Instead, Karen is unmarried, unsatisfied in her job, and unhappy in the knowledge that she has disappointed her parents. Lois sees parallels to Karen's disappointments in her own life, and she feels responsible for some of them. She also feels disappointed that their relationship isn't better. "We have a very tenuous relationship. We're very careful about what we say to each other. Much of the time I don't know how she really feels about anything." Despite moments of self-knowledge—often leavened with humor—Lois seems unable to shake off her feelings of failure as a mother.

Lois's biggest concern is that Karen is not currently in a relationship and seems to have chosen partners in the past whom Lois thinks were inappropriate. "The first time she told me about Karl she was very hesitant, and I kept trying to draw things out about him. And you know what? She knew I'd be upset about him because he wasn't educated, and that was the thing that bothered me most. Karl was an auto mechanic. I met him a few times. I know I sound like a snob, but he was from another world. He was from a small town in New Hampshire; his family seemed to me to be pretty dysfunctional; the parents had not had a very good relationship; his sister seemed to have a bad marriage. All of those things bothered me. And I didn't find him particularly charming. I tried to hold my tongue, but eventually it did come out. And even after they broke up, I think there was an awkwardness because she knew I had never been happy about it."

Karen's next serious romance was with a policeman. "I said to Karen, 'A mechanic, and a policeman. How do you find them?' and I thought, What's next? A fireman?" Lois never met the policeman, and she's not sure why the relationship ended. "I know the superficial reasons for it. He didn't get along with her friends, and he was something of a tightwad. Karen's not a snob, but he was always taking out coupons at a store, counting his pennies."

It's not clear why Karen's love life has come to naught. Perhaps she has just been unlucky. However, her choice of men who do not match her educational or professional level suggests either that she is not confident of her own strengths and her own worth, or that the issue is tied up with her parents' expectations for her. That is Lois's view. She believes that her daughter rejects professional men because her parents put a high priority on their suitability, yet when Karen chooses a man from a different background, she herself finds him wanting. Lois says, "I did things that made my parents happy. I married the kind of boy they wanted me to marry. My parents did interfere in a relationship with a boy I was in love with in college, and I always had that in the back of my mind with Karen. I wasn't going to say to her, 'This is what I expect you to do or not to do in terms of whom you bring home.' But she must have sensed it since she was hesitant to tell me about the policeman."

In any case, there is no one in Karen's life now, and she has told her mother, "I've met everybody there is to meet in Boston." Mother and daughter are beginning to face the likelihood that Karen may not marry. "It's not her age," says Lois, "it's how she positions herself in life." Lois told us that the night before she was to meet with us, "Karen asked me, 'What are you going to talk to them about? You can't talk about your son-in-law or your grandchildren,' which is what most people my age who have married daughters are talking about. It's just interesting for me to observe my friends who do have daughters— now they are on that best friend basis because they have much more in common."

Karen is not particularly happy in her current job. She has been thinking about changing firms for several years. Lois says, "She doesn't like the business of the law. She doesn't like to go out and market herself or the law firm." Is the law a good professional choice for her? "When Karen finished college, we asked her what she was going to do," Lois says. "You have to remember we're children of the fifties. When we got out of school you either knew you were going to be married or—if you were a boy—you went off to graduate school. My father-in-law was an attorney, so there was no question that Phil was going to be a lawyer. You knew your life was going to go into a certain pattern. When Karen said, 'Maybe I'd like to wait on tables for awhile,' Phil and I thought, After all this! and she said, 'Well . . . or maybe I'd like to go to graduate school, maybe history or political science.' And Phil said, 'What will you do with that?'

"Both of us agree this was the worst mistake we ever made. I think she went to law school because it was there. We had stressed that this was a profession that you could put your finger on and that at the end of law school you had a job. If I had it to do all over again I would have given her as many years as she needed. And I tell my friends who have younger children, 'Do not encourage them to go to graduate school right after college.' And she did not do particularly well in law school. I think she would have done much better in what-ever she had chosen if she had had that breathing time.

"There are things that I know I've done wrong. When Karen went off to college, she said, 'You know mother, I had to go to France for a month with you and Daddy when I was thirteen because you had never gone to France with your parents when you were thirteen. And I had to take a cross-country trip when I was fourteen because you had never taken a cross-country trip when you were fourteen. And I had to go to Europe with a high-school group when I was sixteen because you never got to go to Europe with a high-school group when you were sixteen. But fortunately,' she said, 'you worked your way through college so you've already gotten that out of your system, so I don't have to do that for you.' She had the humor to realize that in many ways I've lived through her, that I wanted her to have the things I had never had in life." By imposing on Karen the sense that she— Karen—should live Lois's life as Lois wished it to have been, Lois has unfortunately undermined Karen's ability to take pleasure in her own achievements.

"Karen worked hard. She always tried to get good marks because she knew that her father and I both thought that that was important. She would get a ninety-nine, and she'd say, 'So I bet you want to know who got one hundred.' The terrible thing is that that's how Phil and I were brought up. Our parents set expectations for us, they set goals. You knew what was expected of you. I thought we didn't pressure Karen as much as my mother and father had pressured me, but obviously we did."

Lois sees how powerfully the expectations that she and Phil had for Karen have colored their daughter's life. Now she must learn to see Karen for who she is and not measure her against a template of what she and Phil want her to be: She may not marry a man Lois approves of; she may not marry at all; she may never love her work. And Lois can try to narrow the emotional gap between herself and her daughter. According to psychologist Dr. Kathy Weingarten, "When a mother feels disappointed in her daughter, or distanced from her, the mother's task is to tolerate the disappointment of what cannot be and move forward into what can be. Mother and daughter must begin by finding one or two areas where they have something in common, even if it's very small . . . talking about books they've read or movies they've seen. Maybe they spend a weekend together exploring a city neither of them has been to. Intimacy develops through shared experience, moments of shared interaction. The critical task for the mother is to keep the disappointment at bay, so it doesn't seep into the moments of contact she and her daughter can have. You just build on what you can."

"A lot of this feels like it's anti-who-and-what I am"

Whereas Lois is reflective and remorseful about her sense of disconnection with her daughter, Mariella F. is just exasperated. During our meeting with Mariella, we were struck by the anger that permeated her description of her relationship with her daughter, Gabby, twenty-seven. Mariella is a fifty-one-year-old educational consultant in New York. She and her husband met and married in Greenwich Village in the sixties, and Mariella still thinks of herself as a politically aware, somewhat bohemian hippie. She is astonished and dismayed that every decision Gabby makes seems to be a repudiation of all that Mariella cares about in this world. There was a pattern to Mariella's narrative; whether she was commenting on Gabby's choice of college and graduate school, career, husband, wedding, or her lifestyle, Mariella began by describing the choice with disdain, and then segued into a complaint about how wounding the choice was to *her*.

About Gabby's choice of college, Mariella says, "She wanted to go to the University of Michigan, which I thought was the wrong school for her. She was an artsy kid who would have flourished at a small liberal arts school like Bard or Sarah Lawrence. She was never happy at Ann Arbor, but she went anyway, and she was extremely persistent about staying. I had been a high school teacher for twenty years—I had sent a huge number of kids off to college talking to them about what I thought would be appropriate and thinking of who they were and not what their parents wanted—I mean, I'm very kid-oriented and I always thought I was with her—and so when she decided to go to Michigan, it was like everything I knew in my heart and soul and in my guts was irrelevant to her."

About Gabby's husband, Mariella says, "He is nobody that I thought she would ever even talk to—I mean the guy's a nerd! But she is extremely happy, and I think that he is somebody who is very good for her." In this case at least, Mariella was able to see the positive aspects of Gabby's decision. But she soon returned to her negative assessment of him. "I think it's not within this young man's ability to connect and relate to us. I've only had one serious conversation with the guy, and I've known him since he's nineteen and now he's twenty-nine. I don't connect with this young man at all. Nor does my husband. So I would have been much happier if our only child would have partnered with somebody that we could feel could be part of who and what we are. And that hasn't happened. And that's disappointing for us."

Gabby has worked for four years at an international media firm, selling advertising space. Mariella says she is looking for a change, that she wants something more creative and challenging. "About a year and a half ago," says Mariella, "I was working on a project that was starting to deal with the Internet, and I said that I thought that whoever could create wonderful ads for the Internet would be in a wonderful position right now. And she's a very artistic, creative kid. And very interested in advertising, in creating ads. So it just seemed like a nonthreatening statement to make. And wow, did I get it! I thought I understood—it's creative, it's advertising, she's interested in technology, it's current, it's a future, but she said, 'I'm not interested in any of that. I'll find what I want.' So she's getting an MBA in marketing. I've always encouraged her to explore things, but then she gets angry that I'm intrusive. That I would be creating, in this case, a career path. I mean I didn't come up with this. I just looked at what she was doing and what she said she'd like, and what's happening out there. And I tried to put it together to give her some direction. I feel that there's a real rebellion whenever there's a direction, and a lot of this feels like it's anti-who-and-what I am."

No incident made Mariella feel so injured as her daughter's wedding. We were not surprised. Very often a wedding becomes a contest between a mother's expectations and a daughter's expression of who she is, and because the drama is played out in public, both women have a heavy emotional stake in the outcome. "Gabby wanted a *wedding* wedding," said Mariella incredulously. "I mean, I got married on the beach at Fire Island—a funky gathering that was a very personal expression of who and what my husband and I were. And she wanted something totally traditional, and of course I didn't know any of the traditions! I realized very early on that if this is what she wanted—I mean I had what I wanted—I just couldn't be very much a part of it because I didn't know anything about it. And I thought it was kind of silly, you know to have Martha Stewart and *Bride's Magazine* tell you what to do and how to do it. So I sort of stayed out of it.

"The first thing that she wanted was, she chose this stuffy colonial inn in Connecticut that meant nothing to us, that none of us had ever been to. So that was interesting. And then she had to go with me to select what I was going to wear. Well it didn't occur to me that somebody would have to approve what *I* was going to wear. She wanted me to wear one of these mother-of-the-bride, rose-colored, lacy numbers. It's like, 'What!' I couldn't do it. I said, 'I'm not going to do this. This is just a nightmare for me.' I had this wonderful gold-and-silver-beaded jacket over this wonderful pair of black silk pajamas that were just gorgeous and very comfortable—I mean you have it on all those hours—and I had to have it approved! And then my husband—that was the other thing that happened. Lou has never had a tuxedo on in his life. So we went to Barney's, and he got a gorgeous suit. I mean this was a big deal, he was giving the bride away. So Gabby and her fiancé came over, and I put on my outfit and Lou put on his suit, and they were unacceptable. It was like, 'What? These are unacceptable?' Lou was very good. He said, 'Okay, it's your day, I'll do whatever you want.' He went, he got a tuxedo. She made some changes to my outfit, but I wasn't about to go out and spend hundreds of dollars."

Mariella took little pleasure in the wedding. "Gabby said it was a perfect wedding. She couldn't imagine anything better. I didn't connect to any of it. It was alien to me." Nor does she feel comfortable in the household the newlyweds have created for themselves. "Walking into their apartment to a fully matched dining set with credenza, with dishes and silverware to match is just amazing to me! This is someone who I think would have had a wonderfully eclectic sense of exciting funky things, and it's not! It's the opposite! Where did she get this? How did she know what kind of dishes to buy? How did she know where to buy a dining room set? Why would she want that? I feel in many ways that I don't know her anymore. And it's sad for me."

Throughout the interview, Mariella's bewilderment and pain were palpable. She told us again and again how disappointed she was that she and Gabby shared so little. Yet she seemed unaware of why that was so—unaware of her impact on her daughter. It seemed to us that her constant criticism would make it very hard for Gabby to accept advice from her. The suggestion that Gabby look into advertising on the Internet, for example, may have been a good idea, but Gabby probably rejected it because anything her mother offers her feels like an attack on her identity.

Dr. Weingarten says, "Relationships between adult daughters and mothers derail if the mother has been too critical. If there's been too much blame, then innocent remarks the mother makes will be channeled by the daughter into that core criticism. Anything that comes from the mother is poison, it's toxic. And it's hard for such a mother to change because she doesn't truly value her daughter's choices. Nothing her daughter does is seen with curiosity or interest, let alone positively. The mother who can only be critical has probably suffered a narcissistic injury earlier in her life. And she feels wounded if her daughter doesn't accept any part of her. She thinks she's a person with wonderful values—where did this child come from?"

While Mariella was eloquent about the pain she felt at how Gabby's life was unfolding, she seemed to make no attempt to understand why her daughter made the choices she did. Mariella believes that her own left-liberal, antimaterialistic values—which were one possible reaction to the post-Depression era she grew up in—are the only values worth having. Her daughter grew up in a very different time with a different ideology and different peer pressures. Yet she did not present Gabby as a person with a context of her own, operating in a universe where there are many influences on her—not just her mother.

A clash of values becomes most difficult when a daughter asks her mother to do something that violates that mother's sense of who she is. Gabby's hope that Mariella would wear a traditional mother-of-the-bride outfit was that kind of violation. But Mariella's reaction could have been different. Instead of saying, defiantly, "I'm not going to do this," she might have found a way to compromise without feeling that she had compromised her own integrity. Gabby was not asking Mariella to wear something because she wanted her mother not to be herself. What she wanted was for her mother to blend with her vision of the wedding, which is a much bigger issue than getting her mother to look a certain way. Mariella might have said, "I understand that you want a certain look to your wedding, and it will require that I wear something I would not typically wear. And if I do it, I hope you understand that I'm doing it because it's what you want, and I love you. And I hope that you can acknowledge that." Dr. Weingarten says, "That kind of statement would produce a feeling that there's a transaction. That this is going to mean something to both mother and daughter. To me that puts everything on a level playing field, where each player acknowledges the other's needs, and any compromise does not involve a loss of integrity."

"I'm Living Proof That You Can Change"

In the last three years Ann Gottlieb has learned to accept that her daughter Mara, twenty-five, is different in fundamental ways from what Ann hoped for, and she has come to value the differences as integral parts of this person whom she loves. "I'm living proof that you can change," Ann says, "because my relationship with Mara has completely changed for the better." It took a tragic event to get the process of reconciliation started. "It is sad that something like the death of her father and my husband was the catalyst to change. But in my grief I needed her. And in needing her I had to become aware of what it meant to be her mother in a way that she wanted me to be her mother. And I think the reverse is true; she's also worked at it. In order to have a good relationship with her it was important that I see her differently and deal with her differently. I don't think that I was respectful enough of who she was as a person. For a long time I wanted her to be me, and she is the one who out of hand rejected that. She went into many areas that were different from me, and it took me some time to respect her for what she was and who she was, as someone completely separate."

Ann is a powerful executive in the cosmetics industry. She has a strong background in fashion. She dresses beautifully. She is a striking-looking woman for whom style is clearly important. Until last fall Mara worked in a police precinct office, helping women who were victims of domestic violence. She has just begun a graduate program in social work. Mara has no patience with high fashion. She thinks Ann's interests are superficial. "My sensibilities and my views of the world are very visual, and it was an issue for us because I always cared what she looked like, what she wore. I won't say Mara doesn't care what she looks like, but it was an issue between us always. I have finally learned to keep my mouth shut about what she's wearing. If I don't think it's flattering or if it doesn't go, I don't comment. It took me a long time to do that, and she has repaid me royally with much less anxiety as a result."

The pattern of behavior that Ann and Mara had formed over the years is all too familiar: a critical mother; an angry, sullen daughter; both of them frustrated by expectations for the other that neither could express. In their case, it took death and their need to support each other through the crisis to break the logjam. In addition to curbing her criticism of Mara, Ann had to learn to listen to Mara and accept her daughter's complaints about *her.*

"She has been very helpful in pointing out to me the things she needs from me that I haven't been giving her—respect for her friends, interest in her life—that's still a big issue for us. She's gay, and that is certainly something that I am accepting of, but there are issues that go along with that that have been difficult, and we talk about them." That Ann so casually refers to Mara's sexual preference indicates that she has already done more work learning to accept and respect her daughter's individuality than she was probably ready to give herself credit for. She is certainly respectful of Mara's needs as she confronts a current situation in Mara's life that she has reservations about. Mara's most recent lover is less educated and less sophisticated than Mara. And someone with whom Ann feels little rapport. Because Mara also has doubts about how committed she is to the relationship, Ann has not had to face the fact that Jan may be a permanent presence in her daughter's life. "But," she says, "if Mara loved her and thought it was right, it would not matter what I think, we would have a life separate from her and Jan. And in the same way, if I knew that this was Mara's life partner, I would be more accepting of the relationship because I want Mara in my life."

Because Ann is no longer so judgmental about Mara—because comments that come from her are no longer perceived by her daughter as "toxic or poisonous," in Dr. Weingarten's terms—Mara is able to take advantage of good advice from her mother. "Now that this incredible respect has grown between the two of us, I'm able to be very helpful to her in her work—how to deal with her superiors, how to handle situations, those kinds of things." Mara can also accept Ann's expertise about fashion. "She admires my style, and I try very hard not to make her into a little version of me. If I'm paying, she tends to take my advice, but I don't want her to buy something she won't wear. We keep going till we find something that satisfies both of us. But if she really likes something and I don't, I'm happy to get it for her."

Ann still has dreams and expectations for Mara, but they are shaped by a clear vision of Mara as an autonomous person. "I would like her to find a partner who has the same kind of curiosity and passion for what she's doing as Mara does. She definitely will be doing something with women—helping women in some way—and I hope she finds a life's work that she really enjoys because I know how important and wonderful it's been for me. Money won't be so important. She likes traveling well, but in general the symbols of money are not important to her."

Ann and Mara have talked a lot about the pain of the past and the transformation of their relationship. "I understand and I can be real sorry for what I did, but I did it, and it's over. The real issue for us has been that it's time to let go. It's the present and the future that we're putting our energy into."

"For a long time I wanted her to be me." Ann's words are a prescription for a mother's disappointment and a daughter's withdrawal. When you find yourself expecting too much of your daughter and getting too little, you need to redefine your expectations for the relationship. You must try to identify the ways the two of you are similar and build on your common interests. The harder task is to accept your differences—to acknowledge that she is her own person and that she has wishes for herself that you may never fully comprehend. You can bridge some of the gap by encouraging her to share more about what interests her and by letting her know why some things matter so much to you. In short, you must allow her to be who she really is rather than who you want her to be.

Part Three

Strengthening the Connection

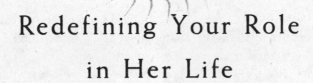

Chapter 9

Redefining Your Role
in Her Life

"The interesting thing is how much I've learned from my daughters. If you have a strict idea of how kids are supposed to be, and by God they're gonna be like that, well, you're going to have a lot of trouble. You can share more things with them as they become adults. You can see where they're going. I've learned with Austen to trust. And to tell her, okay, this isn't the way I'd do things, but if it's the way you want to do it, okay. And to know when to say, uh-uh. But by the time they're in their twenties, I don't say no anymore unless it involves our money, or involves hurting somebody in our family."—Sandy Briggs, mother of Austen, twenty, and Samantha, twenty-five

"I want to listen to Keri more. I'm working on this, because she says, 'Mom, when you say to me, "You really don't want to do that," you really mean that you—Lib—don't want to do it, and that's different from knowing what me—Keri—wants to do.' So now when I goof up on that, I'm able to hear it and say, 'I'm really sorry.' And she's even able to say, 'It's all right.' "—Lib O'Brien, mother of Keri, twenty-two

"Stepping back, that's the hardest thing. I used to be so close, and now my entire role consists of stepping back. I think Debbie is differentiating herself from me, and that means she can't be up under me. I think in some ways I don't have a clue how things are with her, and that's how it is. We do have our good moments. And what I have to remember is that I have to hold on to those moments for when she's gone off somewhere and not given me the phone number, and I'm miserable, and it feels like she's a million miles away."—Kaye T., mother of Debbie, thirty-two, and Janis, twenty-six

What is the role of the mother of an adult daughter? That question came up in almost every interview. In the middle of a story, women would pause to reflect on the nature of the mother–adult daughter relationship itself: How much can a mother intervene in her daughter's life? What is the value of my accumulated wisdom? How much of what I have to offer can she accept? What are the appropriate limits to my power?

In her book, *The Motherline: Every Woman's Journey to Find Her Female Roots*, psychotherapist Naomi Lowinsky describes the process through which mothers and adult daughters differentiate themselves from each other. In Dr. Lowinsky's image, "each woman stands on her own two feet, fully engaged in a struggle about identity, territory, and power. When the dialogue of development heats up in adolescence and young adulthood, it turns into a wrestling match for renegotiating an intimate relationship, but like a father teaching his son to box, the mother wrestling with her daughter knows she is the older, responsible one, and gives her daughter room to establish her own potency . . . Mothers and daughters wrestle with bodily, temperamental, stylistic, generational, and usually very emotional differences between them. It is a great gift to a daughter if a mother can at once be her own authentic self, and honor her daughter's struggle with her."

Some of the most compelling stories we heard centered around this struggle. Mothers talked movingly about trying to untangle themselves from too close an involvement in their daughters' lives; about recognizing, albeit with sadness, that they can't protect their daughters from pain; and about coming to see that much of what they might say to their daughters, even if well meant and well received, is of limited value to them.

How Much Advice Can You Give Her?

Giving and taking advice is an essential element in human discourse. We ask the saleslady if the beige blouse looks better than the white one. We trade tips about new products with someone we run into at the supermarket. We help a co-worker figure out the best way to deal with an arrogant new vice-president. Much of the time a mother can give, and an adult daughter can accept, advice in the same neutral mode: Yes, it's a good idea to invite her mother-in-law to brunch. No, she probably shouldn't try out the new recipe on a dinner party. Sometimes advice-giving becomes more problematic. Does your daughter call every day perplexed about something or other? Does she seem unable to make a decision *without* asking your opinion? Is there a pattern to the situations in which she seems unsure of herself? Does she seem to solicit your opinion and then get angry when you give it?

Most mothers told us they don't think it's appropriate to give advice any longer unless they're asked. Alice Van Tuyl, the mother of Sarah, thirty-two, and Elisabeth, twenty-nine, said, "I think the mother of young adult daughters should be a listener and a watcher. If you're too intrusive, you cut off the flow—you're not going to hear anything more. But you should keep all your antennae up. And once in a while you should be a speaker. I probably speak much too often. But I feel that as far as guiding, unless there's a real request for advice you probably can't do it anymore. And really it's a relief not to have to do it."

Alice brought up two major points that we heard mothers say time and again: the value of listening and the value of not giving advice if it hasn't been solicited. Nellie Lou Slagle said of her two daughters: "I want to be supportive and respectful of their lives and what they value, as I would of any adult. I don't want to be judgmental. Susie has this beautiful home, she's doing a wonderful job of decorating and landscaping. But there are things I wouldn't have done that way. I would have liked her to do the garden differently. But, hey, it's her house, it's her garden. I mean, that's the kind of thing my mother would have done! What purpose would it have served?"

If you and your newly adult daughter have not differentiated yourselves sufficiently, you risk falling into a loop of intrusiveness and resentment on your part, and dependency and resentment on hers. One mother said to us about her thirty-three-year-old daughter, "Carolyn asks my advice constantly. 'What do you think Amanda should wear to the birthday party?' 'I'm making a tomato sauce. Do you think I should add some fresh vegetables?' She asks advice on everything. She asks it enough and takes it enough that it's not difficult." But five minutes earlier, this mother had told us that she *did* feel put upon sometimes by her daughter's constant entreaties. "Carolyn has said that I think I'm always right and do everything right. And I know that my general reputation in the family is that I'm tough and competent. That I can do everything. But sometimes I can't help but be irritated when I do so much for her and she seems to take me for granted. Sometimes I think I should help her pull back. I'll ask, 'Well, what do you think?' And Carolyn will respond, 'That's what I'm asking *you*.' I think she's very dependent and needy. But then I remember how needy I was at a comparable age—needing more of my mother—so I can't say no. I think I can understand what it would mean to her to be turned down. I think it would be very hard on her."

The confusion this mother voiced found parallels in other women's stories. Many women sensed that even if a daughter seems to give them an opening, it's not really advice she's after. Half the women we spoke to told us a variant of the following: "If I get too involved, she'll say to me, 'I'm not asking you for advice, I just want you to listen.' " It's not that she wants you literally to keep silent; why would she bother to initiate a conversation if she wanted that? She wants you to hear her out; she wants you to be responsive, to validate *her* reasoning process. But she does not want you to jump in and solve her problem for her. Letty Cottin Pogrebin admits she still slips into the directive mode too often. "We'll be talking things over, and what I think just comes out. I don't think they ever say, 'What should I do about this?' It's more like, 'I'm having a problem,' or 'I'm thinking about this.' And we're chewing it over, and before you know it, my opinion comes out, because I'm generally too opinionated for my own good."

Why does Letty think she does that? She offers a very personal explanation. "I think it's because I lost my mother at such a young age, and my assumption is that I should just be welcomed in whatever I might have to say because I would so dearly welcome my mother. If I could pick up the phone and call her it would be a miracle to me. But to have not had that person in your life after age fifteen . . . my mother was always someone who thought the world of me and wanted the best for me; I felt unconditional love from her and when it was gone, I missed it. And because I feel that way about my daughters, I always assume that my interventions will be welcome. But I don't think they are. Looking at it from a little distance I don't think I should be so forthcoming. I should wait to be asked."

And what happens when she oversteps her bounds? "They tell me straight out. Kind of like, 'Mom, don't you think I know that?' or 'Do I really need to hear that?' or 'I don't need this, I don't need this kind of advice.' And after the fact I see that I probably wouldn't have liked that sort of advice myself. I think most kids don't like us to underestimate their capacity to solve their own problems. Even though for me, giving advice isn't a way of saying, 'You won't know what to do if I don't tell you.' It's a way of saying, 'I care. I want to talk about this. I like being part of your life.' "

"What if I'm wrong?"

Your daughter says she wants you to listen and not give advice. And, in principle, you agree. As Maureen E. said of her three grown daughters, "I can't live their lives for them. Suppose I'm wrong—look at the damage I would have done." Evelyn Tang also believes that giving advice can be destructive; but she does think you can offer information, as long as you're not trying to influence the result. Evelyn is a professor of neurology at the University of Southern California Medical School. Several years ago her daughter Frances was choosing between a Ph.D. program in biochemistry and medical school. "My husband and I tried not to influence her for a selfish reason—we didn't want to be blamed later on! We kept saying, 'It's your decision.' We felt the parent's job was to help children make informed decisions. To provide information. But what they choose to do is their own business. So my only comment to her was, 'You've worked in a lab, and you've seen what I do. To go on in biochemistry you have to absolutely love research, you have to be happy working on your own, collecting data, analyzing it, and maybe waiting years for a result. If you choose to be a doctor, it's still science, but it's more about working with people.' And that was the extent of my comments."

Frances chose medical school and is now an obstetrician-gynecologist at a major medical center in Los Angeles. Even in her conversation with us, Evelyn never said—although she implied—that she thought that Frances made the right decision.

Angela A. was similarly wary of offering advice too freely when her daughter Gretchen, who was twenty-two at the time, expressed fears about going through with her wedding two months before the event. "Gretchen was in Belgium on business, and she phoned us late at night to say that she wanted to call off the wedding," said Angela. "At the time my husband thought I should have immediately said, 'You're absolutely right,' but all I said was, 'It's apparent to me you've had a fight and you're very upset. I think you shouldn't make a decision when you're in the middle of Belgium while your fiancé is in Boston. You should come home and talk about this with him, or with us if that's what you want, but I want you to know that whatever you decide is fine with us.' Then when she went through a difficult time two years after she was married, my husband spent a lot of time telling me that I had missed an opportunity to save her. But I just had this feeling that you shouldn't save your children when they're adults. What are you saving them from? It's their lives."

We posed the question of advice—if, when, and how you can offer it to a daughter who is no longer a child—to four members of a long-standing women's book club in San Francisco. Their daughters ranged in age from twenty-seven to thirty-seven. Although the women were familiar with each other's opinions about literature, they were not particularly close friends. As the following transcript reveals, they were delighted to discover how similar their perceptions about advice-giving were.

Anita M. (age seventy-two, a graphic artist, mother of Ann, thirty-seven, and Maria, thirty-four): "When my daughters tell me they think I'm interfering, I tell them, 'I have no restraint where you're concerned!' I *have* intruded. When they have had some problems to deal with, sometimes I just can't resist saying, 'Let me advise you.' That kind of stuff. And I don't think I'm wrong. I make it obvious that they have a right to tell me to knock it off. I mean I'm not going in there and saying, 'Hey, why didn't you eat your broccoli?' or something like that. I'm not that intrusive. But if I sense something, I might ask about it. And I put it in such a way that they can say, 'No, thank you.' "

Mildred G. (age sixty, a university professor, mother of Jean, twenty-seven): "I agree. I would certainly express myself. I'd say, 'I find that my reaction is such-and-such, and you can react however you want.' And Jean has told me, 'That's enough,' on occasion. It gets easier every year as she grows up, because she has a clearer time realizing that she doesn't have to do what Mommy wants, but at the same time she's better able to absorb what I have to say and process it."

Meryl Siegel (age fifty-six, a financial consultant, mother of Jennifer, twenty-seven): "There are two principles at stake here: You have the right to tell them what you think, and they have the right to make their own decisions."

Anita: "I don't think it's a right. You tell kids—anybody—out of concern."

Joyce R. (age sixty-one, a psychiatrist, mother of Jane, thirty-one, and Judy, thirty-four): "My husband and I interfered directly when our fifteen-year-old was involved with a thirty-five-year-old man. We made it very clear that this had to stop. But that's appropriate with teenagers. When they're older, you have to do something different. I might still express my opinion, but they will do what they want."

Mildred: "My feeling is that success lies in picking your issues. You have to let the small things go. Then when you do say something, it has more weight."

Meryl: "It's very interesting in communication with anybody, how they interpret the message. As much as I'm asked, and I am asked a lot by Jennifer—and she knows clearly that she can take my advice or not—if she's struggling with something, like whether or not to go to law school, and I try to be supportive of going because that's what I think she wants, it gets turned into 'You really want me to go to law school.' And I had not pushed her, but that was her interpretation."

Joyce: "Oh, does that sound familiar. How did you resolve that?"

Meryl: "I said, 'That's what you think you heard, and I do think it's a good idea. But I'm not pushing it on you. If you want to choose law school or not is your business.' And we went on to talk at length about how one interprets messages."

Joyce: "Whatever I said it was usually wrong—well, it wasn't wrong exactly—but it wasn't what she wanted to hear. Actually she didn't want to hear anything. She just wanted me to listen."

Mildred: "Well, maybe that's not unique to daughters, maybe it's true of everybody."

Anita: "I can't tell you the frustration I've had responding to my daughter. Sometimes she will say, 'Mother, can't you just listen? I don't want any feedback.' And I will say, 'Well, I'm not a vegetable.'"

Joyce: "When my son was about thirty-five, he sent us a letter with an enclosed card that said 'When all else fails, try doing what your parents suggested.'"

Meryl: "I take it as a feather in my cap when either of my kids says, 'You were right.' And every so often it does happen. I think it's because I'm very, very judicious with what I say. I very seldom give direct advice. I'll say, 'I might do it this way, but you have to make your own choices.' Something like that."

From Marilyn's journal, July 23, 1995

Long touching conversation with Kate yesterday about Harriette. Kate is torn between thinking she should come home while H. is still alive—at least technically—and wanting to finish up everything she has to do in CA and hope that H. might even live for three weeks while she and Kelcey drive cross-country. The latter is unrealistic, I think. More probably, she'll have to fly in overnight for a funeral sometime this week, or from some point on the road. But if she comes home to see H. immediately, H. might conceivably still live another few days so that Kate would end up having to make two trips.

She asked for my advice. And I DIDN'T GIVE IT. I asked her what her issues were, and she said she was trying to figure out how to say good-bye. I said I thought that at this stage, the issue had nothing to do with H. and everything to do with what made each one of us comfortable. I said that different things matter to different people. Some people take great comfort in physical presence. They like to sit by a bedside, even if the dying person is unconscious. They like to go to the cemetery. Some people even like an open coffin. For me, none of these things matter. I believe that I'm saying good-bye in my mind. I prefer to summon up images of when Harriette was conscious and involved, and think about and mourn them rather than this unconscious shell of a body lying in the bed. But I stressed that it was Kate's call, and she had to ask herself what mattered to her.

I don't know how she'll decide, but I think she was looking for a framework that allowed her to make a decision. And I hope I gave her one.

July 30, 1995

Harriette died on the 25th. We had the funeral on the 27th, Kate came in on the redeye, spoke beautifully at the funeral—as did Kore—and then flew back to CA to start her cross-country trip.

Why must she make her own choices? Because you don't want to rob her of her own experiences, her own maturation process. Jane Morgan, whose two daughters, Leslie and Drew, are twenty-eight and twenty-three respectively, told us, 'I feel like this old woman who has lived this life and has all these answers. And when they give me a problem, I know what the result is going to be. And it makes me upset because I can see what is going to happen, and I can't tell them. I mean they've got to figure it out themselves. So my biggest problem is just in staying out of it and not letting them know that I know the answer. They say, ' Tell me what you think, Mom. You're always right.' Which I hate. I hate that. Because if I do know the answer, it's because of how old I am. And that's my biggest problem, trying to remember how it was in my twenties. So that I don't take that away from them, and they are able to learn the lessons naturally." As Jane knows, our advice is still potent for daughters at this age; they are often decisively influenced by it, in a positive *or* a negative way. Before we offer advice, we would do well to ask ourselves if what we have to say will reaffirm, rather than undermine, our daughters' independent judgment.

Jane also knows that, no matter how close she is to her daughters, no matter how open their communication is, she can't presume to know what's right for them. "Their lessons are maybe not what my lessons are anyway. I mean Drew and I are entirely different human beings. So for me to be saying, 'Oh, you ought to do this or you ought to do that,' is ridiculous. I may know the answer to what she's asking me, but that's not what she really needs to know. She'll say, 'Mom, why isn't so-and-so interested in me?' Well I know why. It's cause she's a real dynamo, because she's more self-directed than he is. She's stubborn, she has no patience—I can tell her all that, but what I don't know is what it all means to her. What's she working through with this guy? What does that kind of a person mean to her? That's for her to discover. Not me. It's not my life. Her life is different. And she's got to learn those lessons, and she has to go on with her life in her own way. And I've got to stay out of it at that point."

How Much Should You Try to Protect Her?

All our lives we've been trying to protect our daughters from danger, from making mistakes, from the unintended consequences of their behavior. But we've also always understood that we can't shield them from everything, and, in age-appropriate ways, we've helped them take on more responsibility for themselves. We remember the anxiety we felt when they crossed the street alone for the first time, or drove the car, or were allowed to change their weekend curfew to one o'clock so they could go with their friends to a club. As they have become adults our role in protecting them is necessarily diminished. At every stage, our role as mother has been, as Dr. Evelyn Bassoff writes, to "combine the right amount of maternal nurture with the right amount of maternal distance."

The right amount of maternal distance for the mother of an adult daughter is farther than we might have imagined and, in many cases, we are not the nurturers anymore. What we want to nurture is our daughter's sense that she can handle whatever life puts in her way without us.

When she has a chronic illness

Mothers of daughters who've suffered since childhood or adolescence with serious chronic illness have a history of helping their daughters monitor their symptoms, their medications, and their compliance with any restrictions the disease imposes on their lifestyle. Of necessity, the daughters have taken on the full responsibility for these matters as they have become adults and moved away from home. However, because the consequences can be so dire, their mothers often have a particularly hard time maintaining the right amount of maternal distance if they have reason to believe their daughters are not taking care of themselves properly. In the course of our project, we heard about four daughters who were living with chronic mental illness, five who had epilepsy, three who were diabetic, and two who had serious congenital conditions. Their mothers were able to overcome their impulse to interfere, even though their worries never completely go away.

Peggy R., sixty-two, who heads the development office of a private school in New York City, told us that her daughter, Leigh, twenty-eight, was diagnosed with epilepsy while she was in college. "She had trouble getting the seizures under control," Peggy said. "She couldn't stay out late and party. She hated taking her pills. So we would get the phone calls in the middle of the night from her roommates because she'd had another attack. And then she would resent us, because every time there was a seizure, we reproached her for not taking the medicine."

When Leigh was first diagnosed, Peggy felt guilty. She recalled several seizurelike instances in her childhood that may or may not have been related to epilepsy. Perhaps her daughter's disease was congenital. "You feel terrible thinking that your child is suffering from something that you may have caused but can't help," said Peggy. She now believes that Leigh's illness made them closer because "we suffered together. I saw several of the seizures, and Leigh finally came to realize that it's almost worse to see a grand mal seizure than to have one."

Leigh has been seizure-free for three years and doesn't talk about her illness much with her mother now. "It was a slow process of coming to terms with a chronic condition," says Peggy. Leigh worked in New York for several years after college and is now attending graduate school in Chicago. "She had roommates for several years and then lived alone, which was a huge confidence builder. And any fears I had about it, I tried not to express, because I wanted her to be able to be on her own."

One of her fears is that Leigh may be cutting down on her medication without consulting her doctor. Peggy's health plan pays for the medication, which she then forwards to Leigh, and lately she's had to remind Leigh that they need to reorder, rather than the other way around. "I don't think she's on top of it. And If I asked her, I couldn't be sure that she'd tell me the truth. I don't want to put her— or me—in that position. Ultimately this is her body and her life."

When she has an acute illness

Sometimes it takes a crisis for mothers to realize the limits of their ability to keep their daughters from physical peril or psychological pain. When Ellen A.'s daughter Jessica was stricken with lymphoma at age thirty, Ellen felt the same shocking revelation of powerlessness that any mother would feel no matter how old her child was. "You're totally helpless, you can't help your children. I've never felt so helpless in my life. After all, I'm a strong woman who raised four children alone, and I couldn't do anything for her. And that's when you know that no matter how much you love your children, no matter how much you're willing to do for them, you can't have the disease for them, you can't die for them. All you can do is tell them you love them and that you'll be there." Ellen flew to be with Jessica during the week that her diagnosis was confirmed, stayed for Jessica's first chemotherapy session, and then returned home.

Somewhat later in the course of her treatment, Jessica called in a panic. "She was depressed as all get out, even though by that time they had told her that she was totally disease-free. But it could still reappear. We know that. So she called me up one night, crying, and said, 'I'm so frightened, I don't want to die of cancer.' She is crying, and I cannot console her. There's nothing I can do, nothing. So I said, 'I'll get on the plane, and I'll be out there. It'll take a few hours, and I'll be there.' Finally she composed herself. And she's embarrassed—as if she should be embarrassed! And she said, 'I'll call my friend, Jack. If he's around, he'll come over and fix me supper, and I'll be better in a few hours.' So I said, 'I'll call you in three hours and see how you are.' And I'm sitting there thinking, I can't do anything for her. She's all the way across the country—what on earth am I going to do? So I called her back in three hours, and Jack indeed was there. And she said, 'I'm all right. I'm not fine, but I'm all right.' So I didn't go out.

"I didn't go out much during this whole thing. She just didn't seem to need to have me out there. Which of course made me feel terrible, like I wasn't needed. At the same time I knew she had all sorts of friends who were taking care of her, and she probably also wanted her privacy, so I just let it go. Even though I felt hopeless and helpless, I tried to see it from her perspective. I always try to see things from my children's perspective even though I probably fail most times. To see their viewpoint. I didn't like being treated like a baby, so I think I understand what they want."

When she is faced with a crisis

Laurie W.'s daughter Amanda was very explicit about her need to cope with a traumatic event on her own. Amanda was in her first year of law school in Philadelphia when she was attacked by an intruder early one morning in her apartment. "It was June, while she was studying for finals," Laurie, a fifty-year-old bank executive in Chicago, told us. "She called me during the day and said in a calm, but relatively upset voice that she was 'all right,' but that she had been raped. I was beside myself. After I had recovered from my own disbelief and shock—because it's hard to believe that such a thing can happen in your own family, even though you read that it does—my immediate thought was to clear my schedule so that I could get on a plane to be with her. Because of all the times a child would need a parent, this was it. And it would also be helping me to see her and be with her.

"So when we spoke again an hour or so later, I told her I was preparing to come, and she said very clearly that she would really prefer that I didn't. I was taken aback. It felt like a rejection. I tried to find out what it would mean to her for me to come or not come.

"She said she had a lot of friends and had already arranged to stay with a friend's mother so as not to be in the apartment, and although she wanted to see me, it was very important for her ability to hold herself together that I not be there. And that she could rely on her friends. The friends, the faculty adviser, the hospital, and the police had all been extremely supportive. If I arrived it would interfere with her ability to maintain her composure. She said she would make plans to come to Chicago soon. She felt she would just dissolve if I came.

"She convinced me that she had a point. That if I were there, I would become the person in charge. She would revert to being a child. Her ability to stay in charge depended on my *not* being there.

"So I thought about it," says Laurie, "and decided I had to do what she wanted. And we kept in very close touch, we spoke every day, sometimes two or three times a day. She got her finals rescheduled, she also dealt with the police, and the dean's office. I was in considerable distress that I wasn't there, but I felt that under the circumstances I should honor her need to manage this in a way that was most helpful to her, and I also realized that there was no specific task only I could attend to.

"We talked about it when she came home. And I admitted to her that from my own narrow perspective, I felt that I had been excluded. As we talked about it, I gradually began to feel more connected. She understood how hard it was for me not to be there, but she also understood it was a real vote of confidence for her. In retrospect, I feel it was the right thing to have done."

Ten years from now, Amanda might respond differently. Her fear of losing control, of regressing into a helplessness that she wants so much to resist, is typical of a young adult. After a few years, and with more experience taking charge of her life, a daughter may very well have the flexibility and the self-confidence to welcome her mother stepping in to help, rather than be threatened by it.

Dr. Stefan Stein, professor of clinical psychiatry at New York Hospital–Cornell Medical Center, New York, says, "It's very difficult for a parent to hold back when she feels that her child is in pain, and she's been there for her during every rough period in the past. But she must take her cues from her daughter. A crisis can be a critical event in a young woman's transformation from adolescence to adulthood, leading to growth and changes in self-perception. Accomplishments are one thing—graduating from college, getting a job, choosing a partner—but another way to measure the transformation is to consider the daughter's ability to manage adversity. And the ability of a parent to allow a child to do this is essential. It's a new challenge to be able to take a back seat. For a person accustomed to taking charge, this is particularly difficult. Restraint becomes one more measure of a parent's confidence in the child's ability to deal with the inevitable misfortunes of life."

It can be hard to acknowledge that you are no longer at the center of your daughter's life, that she will rely increasingly on her partner and friends for help. It's only human that you feel a twinge of sadness when she turns elsewhere for comfort, but you need to remind yourself that what feels like a rejection is really an expression of her increasing reliance on her own judgment and strength.

Acknowledging Her Autonomy

What does it really mean to say that our advice is often irrelevant or burdensome to our daughters, or that we cannot protect them from physical or psychological pain? It means that in the deepest sense we are learning to honor their autonomy. As mothers of adult daughters, that is our primary task. Since mothering is an area in which a woman's need to express power is traditionally sanctioned, it is often difficult for us to let go, especially if we have derived some of our self-esteem from our power to nurture.

From Susan's journal, September 4, 1996

A few days ago Phoebe came to visit from Boston. Upon arriving she was agitated because she had forgotten to bring her eye medicine. "What eye medicine?" I asked. Well, it seems that two weeks ago she got something in her eye that scratched her cornea, and she had to go to the emergency room to have them remove what turned out to be a sliver of metal. It was embedded so deep she had to go three times to see the doctor, who had put her on antibiotics to ward off ulceration. I was stunned that she had gone through all this without letting me know. I thought about it and thought about it and finally asked her why she hadn't told me. She said the following: She hadn't even considered telling me, it was something she could handle, and there was nothing I could do to help. If it had been more serious she would have told me, she was twenty-six years old, an adult fully capable of dealing with this particular problem. I said it felt to me like a lack of communication—that the channels of communication between us weren't open. She said, nonsense, we communicate about many things, more than many mothers and daughters. I told her that it reminded me of that terrible time in high school when she had an abortion and didn't tell me or her father until afterward. And I asked her if the same reasoning was in play—was she trying to protect me from being upset.

She said, "I knew you would bring up the abortion and think it was the same thing! But my behavior then has nothing to do with my behavior now. Now I am an adult. I am not protecting you from the truth, I just think it wasn't a big deal and I can handle it alone."

I must admit that it is difficult to accept that she doesn't need me in the way she used to, that she wouldn't call on me to at least ooh and ahh over the incident and talk it over with her. I guess there's still a time lag between her burgeoning adulthood and my acceptance of it.

"I wish she would let me participate more," Loretta G. says about her daughter Marie, who has just moved into a new apartment with her husband and young daughter. "She's so busy, with her residency and taking care of the baby and all, and I could help her, you know, with the fun things like decorating or helping her shop for clothes. But she's like, 'No, we're fine. We have one chair, and I have a dress. Things are fine.' " A few months ago Loretta, her husband, and their younger daughter, Diana, visited Marie when she was barely settled in. "At that time, there was nothing there. The TV was in the middle of the living room floor. And they even had a child's gate around the TV. And she had warned me before—'Don't do anything, I'll do it myself.' But I thought she wouldn't mind. So Diana and I went out and we bought a TV cabinet—it was no big deal—and we had to assemble it, it took two and a half hours screwing everything together. We finally had it all together and had the TV working, and Peter— that's Marie's husband—came in and he said, 'Oh, isn't this wonderful.' But when Marie came home, she burst out crying, 'I told you I didn't want you to do anything.' She was very angry. It was a terrible scene. Diana started crying. Peter withdrew to the other room. My husband threw his hands up and I apologized." Loretta laughed. "I'm not going to do that again."

But the incident still rankles. And Loretta has some sense that Marie sees her attempts to help as being intrusive. "She hasn't always been so prickly. But I see a lot of her friends are like that now—they want to do everything on their own. Maybe part of it is that she wants to show herself—and everyone else—that she can do it. So I have to roll with that, even though I don't love it." Loretta has not fully assimilated the fact that jumping in to "help" when Linda had explicitly told her not to was a slight to her daughter's sense of autonomy. Her task, as it is for the mother of any adult daughter, is to take pleasure in encouraging a daughter to manage her own life.

"I can't fix it"

It took several weeks of canceled and rescheduled appointments before Lucia C., the director of development for a large midwestern university, was able to find time to see us. But when we finally met, Lucia told us immediately that she was eager to talk about a recent contretemps she'd had with Hillary, twenty-nine, the oldest of her three children and the only girl. Hillary lives in northern California, where she works for a software company. She's living with a young man whom Lucia and her husband, Richard, like very much. Because Hillary is on the cusp of turning thirty, Lucia says, she is asking herself life-summary questions: "Do I want kids? Do I not want kids? Do I want to get married? Do I not want to get married? Do I want to do this kind of work for the rest of my life? Or try something completely different?" During our interview we barely said a word as Lucia tied together many issues that lie at the heart of the mother–adult daughter relationship: her strong sense of identification with Hillary, their mutual expectations of similarity, her desire to be a different—and better—mother than her mother had been to her, and her growing awareness that her role is no longer to be the "fix-it" lady in her daughter's life. Lucia described their relationship as "absolutely, totally open with each other." She said, "I absolutely adore her, but this crisis made me see we still have issues to work out.

"She called me a few weeks ago in this anxious tone of voice that I recognize so well. I'm anxious, my mother was a hysteric, they say my grandmother had anxiety attacks. And she was all roiled up about this wedding that we all had been invited to. Although she had already turned down the invitation, at the last minute her boss gave her an extra couple of days off, and she wanted to go. So she said she'd just called her cousin, the one who was getting married, and he had said, 'The guest list just went in and it's such a tight thing.' And she said, 'Oh, Mom, I feel so terrible. I wanna go. And I'm sick of my job, and I want to move to New York and go to work for MTV. But what would that mean for me and Arthur?' And this whole litany of problems. And I just snapped. I said, 'I can't fix this. I know how small the guest list is. Your dad is going, and I suppose you could take his place. But I'm not sure that would make them happy either. So I can't fix it.' And I thought, I can't deal with her right now, and I handed the phone to Richard. And she said, 'What's the matter with Mom?' And he said, 'Mom's had a tough week. You know she's working hard and she's up against a huge deadline. And she's tired.' And we didn't talk for a few days.

"I think that most mothers would do what I did. I mean maybe she should have called the mother of the bride. And maybe she could get to go and maybe she couldn't. But I couldn't fix it.

"And she called about a week later, and it's 'Hi, Mom, how are you?'

"I think it was a place where we were breaking apart. I think she's trying to break apart. Hillary and the boys and Richard and I all went to family therapy about six years ago. And the therapist said, ' The five of you are too close. You're too symbiotic. It's a good relationship, but you need to get away from each other a little bit.'

"So I think this was a step. I actually felt horrible later on. Maybe I could have dealt with it better. But I thought she's got a lot of good things going on in her life—she's got this great job, she's fabulous looking, she's got a wonderful guy in her life. So she can't go to a wedding! I think it was my better instinct to say you've got to do this on your own. You can't call me every time there's a crisis. And I think she really thought so, too. Although it was the most horrible non-communicative moment we've had in years. I mean we've had arguments. That's different. This was not talking enough.

"And she'd called at the wrong moment. I was stressed. It was after midnight, I'd had a grueling session with some of the trustees. It was a bad day. And I was just exhausted. I wanted someone to say, 'Let me take care of you,' as my husband was actually doing. But this was the straw that broke the camel's back, and I just went to pieces. I tried to reason with her first. You know, it's only a wedding and so on. You know, you have a wonderful boyfriend, and when you get to be a big power in the computer business you can move your whole company to Seattle or New York or wherever. And I reasoned and I reasoned, but she wouldn't say, 'Okay, I get your point.' And finally I just fell apart.

"The problem is that I know I've always overprotected her. And I don't think Richard was a part of this. I think I made things seem too easy for her, that Mother could fix things. That Mother would do it. So this must have been a jolt for her for me to say for the first time in my life, 'I can't fix it. There's nothing I can do.'

"When Hillary was looking at colleges, she chose the ones that were farthest from home. And she decided to go all the way to Berkeley. So I thought she wants to be away from us, and I didn't write so much, and I didn't call. And she got furious and said, 'All the other mothers call. How come you don't call?' And I said, 'I thought you wanted to break away. I thought you wanted to be away to be on your own.' And she said, 'You really hurt my feelings.' She was very hurt about it. I said, 'I was trying to let you go.' And she said, 'I didn't want you to let me go. I need my Mom to call me when I'm in college.'

"And she still brings it up. When there was that terrible fire in Oakland several years ago, we didn't call because she was living at the time in San Francisco and we heard the city itself was okay. And she said to somebody, 'You notice my mother hasn't called. My mother will think I'm just fine. Because my mother didn't call the entire time I was at college.' So you can't win.

"She's just beginning to know herself. And she's nearly thirty. Well, she's said it to me, 'I have friends who are further along than I am. Why did I make such a late start?' Actually it's probably not my fault, you know. They do just develop, and that's how she was going to develop. But I certainly did overprotect her. I tried to smooth the way, and when she was hurt by a friend, oh my God, it was like it was my friend who hurt me. I identified too strongly. I didn't have a sense of separation. And Richard kept telling me all those years, 'You're falling into her trap. She's upset, you're upset. She's disappointed, you're disappointed.

"My mother just died last year. She was a terrible mother. And not a very nice person either. My mother always told me that I was not a pretty girl. That I was not sweet. That I wasn't smart enough. So, of course, I decided that when I had children I would do the opposite. Always loving, always supportive. Always up. Never sick. My mother was always sick. I would never lie down in the afternoon with a cloth over my eyes.

"Hillary and I are funny together. We laugh a lot. We talk deep and long. We're very honest with each other. She'll tell me things about her sex life, up to a point. But she doesn't want to hear any of mine. She'll ask me advice. And I'll tell her what I think, or I'll say read this and tell me what happens.

"So I don't think there's much in her life she hasn't discussed with me. But I have noticed recently that the phone calls have been less frequent, especially since the phone call about the wedding. I think the call about the wedding was a kind of breaking point for us. I don't know for sure.

"She and Arthur are turning thirty around the same time. And she's arranged this big joint celebration. Which we've decided not to go to. We'll call, we'll send gifts, but she's done this on her own. It should be hers."

Lucia's refrain—"I can't fix it anymore"—reverberated through many of our interviews. What did mothers mean by it? They seem to be saying, in essence, "I don't have the answers, I don't have a magic wand, and even if I did, I don't think I should be using it in your behalf anymore. I believe that *you* have the tools to fix it yourself." In Naomi Lowinsky's words, they are granting a daughter "room to establish her own potency."

Lucia says she came to her realization as an epiphany. In a moment of stress. It's possible, in fact, that if she hadn't been so needy of support herself at the moment of Hillary's phone call she would not have reacted so dramatically. On the other hand, if she and her daughter had been farther along the developmental path toward a truly reciprocal relationship, she might even have mentioned all the things that had gone wrong in her day, and elicited Hillary's support and understanding for herself!

But this mother and daughter have only begun to redefine themselves more reciprocally. There will be inevitable back-sliding in the future, moments when they will both revert to wanting Lucia to intervene in some matter that should probably be Hillary's own. However, this crisis has helped both mother and daughter see the value of breaking their past pattern of overinvolvement with each other. Lucia's understanding that Hillary could celebrate a major milestone in her life without Richard and Lucia's participation is an important step. At this stage in our daughters' lives, we must confront the realization that as parents we are, and should be, less central to the life of a young woman on her own.

Tolerating the Differences

The mainstream American cultural predilection is for daughters to develop a strong sense of their own identity while staying connected to their mothers. But in other cultural traditions a daughter's autonomy is less highly prized. According to Dr. Margarita Alvarez, a staff psychologist at the Latino Mental Health Program of the department of psychiatry at the Cambridge Hospital and the Harvard Medical School—who is herself an immigrant to the United States—there is the potential for painful dislocation between the generations in communities of recent immigrants to this country. "What happens when what the mother has to offer was valuable in the old culture but seems irrelevant in the new? What if a daughter feels she cannot use what her mother has to teach? The idea of what makes a young woman 'competent' in America is different from the mother's traditional definition. Often the mother—who came here to provide a better life for her daughter—feels abandoned because the daughter takes more from the prevailing culture than from her mother. So the separation becomes very difficult for both." Dr. Alvarez believes that a resolution is possible. "The mother and daughter need to find some middle ground on which they can tolerate some of the differences. If the mother can tolerate her daughter's trying new things, then perhaps the daughter can also incorporate some of what her mother has to offer, and the daughter will ultimately be able to differentiate herself without severing their connection."

Los Angeles is the prototypical American city of the future. More than a third of the population are foreign born, more than half report that they speak a language other than English at home. In the San Fernando Valley, there are neighborhoods where English is almost completely supplanted by Khmer, Thai, Mandarin, Spanish, or Korean. As we drove to our appointment with Farouz P. we noticed that while most of the houses in her neighborhood were standard southern California low white stucco structures, with patios and swimming pools in the rear, the signs on the storefronts were mostly in Farsi. And the interior of Farouz's house—decorated with heavy silk upholstered furniture, ornate brass platters and candlesticks—along with a big bowl of pistachio nuts she put before us—spoke of her attachment to her Iranian heritage.

Farouz left Teheran eighteen years ago with her husband and two daughters, Isabelle, now twenty-five, and Clemence, twenty-three. A son, Edouard, sixteen, was born in Los Angeles. Farouz teaches math and accounting at a local college and her husband is also a professor. They settled in California because they knew their children could get a good education there. Providing a good education is very important to Farouz; she wants her children to prosper in this country. But what she believes is *really* important in raising children is the role of family. Everything that young people do should be done within the context of their family: Children should live with their parents until they marry; their social life should be with their families; young men are presentable suitors for her daughters if they come from "good families."

Farouz has sought to preserve in her home the values she grew up with in Teheran. She has tried to protect her daughters as young women are protected back home. "I never left my children by themselves. I never left them with a baby-sitter. We went out everywhere together. I was always with them. I always guided them. We are the people who have to take care of them. Until the girls finished college, I used to give them rides. I picked them up at school, took them to their work. I didn't want them to go into the parking lot at night." The girls lived at home through college and after. And in fact, Isabelle, who married last winter to "someone from a good family from Persia," has returned home for two months while her husband finds them a house in Seattle, where he has been transferred.

The cultural differences between the generations manifested themselves early on through language. "I speak Farsi all the time, they answer back in English. They cannot read Farsi." But Farouz reports that she had no serious rifts with her girls until they reached young adulthood. "Maybe two years ago the children went by themselves in the society. And I used to demand that they call me and say where they were. But their friends said, 'Oh you're a baby, you have to call your mother.' So I was not happy with their friends, the parties they went to. I thought that eleven o'clock is the time to come home. But they go out at eleven, because they explain the party starts then. And I hate that." When Farouz tried to enforce a curfew, the girls objected, and she didn't speak to them for several days. "I cried. I couldn't leave the house. I could not restrain them as much as I would like. Because my love is too much. We love our children, we are all in love with each other, even when we disagree. We are all there for each other. We try our best. These are things that bother me. Right now we are trying to compromise.

"Because when you are upset by your children, don't think if you don't talk to them that you solve anything. No, don't cut your friendship, don't cut your kindness to them. Be sure they always know you are in back of them, that you support them. Somehow when you don't talk to them you lose many things. Because this is my experience—we were very close, we were actually in love with each other, and then they did something wrong, and I started not talking to them. Then they come and hug me and kiss me. But then it's repeated, and the result is not good. It makes you separate, and this is not good. But I am that kind of person. I always think, what happened? Why is it like that? I have to do something. I have to solve the problem. I tried to show them if I say something to you, it's because I love you. I don't want to interfere in their lives. I tried to show them if the parents say something it comes out of love, not because you don't trust them."

Farouz still gets angry when her girls do something she disapproves of, but she tries not to lose her temper. "I am trying my best to talk to them even if I see something that I don't like, but sometimes I can't help myself." For example, she doesn't like their California manners and the casual way they dress. "I always say the girl has to be like a queen. They have to walk like a queen, they have to talk like a queen. I don't want bad stuff out of their mouths. I think Isabelle smokes, but not in front of me. Once I saw her with a cigarette, but she stamped it out right away. So sometimes I criticize them, but they don't accept it. Sometimes they try to hide what they do, so I think it is better if I don't say anything.

"You have to compromise. Right now I think I change a lot. We used to go out always all together. When we were invited somewhere, I wanted to go as a family. When my children declined, it was complicated for me, but now I accept it. And I started enjoying going alone with my husband, but before it was very difficult for me."

In Dr. Alvarez's terms, Farouz is learning to tolerate the new things that her daughters are introducing into their lives: their friends, their lifestyle, their independence. She understands that her ability to do so makes it more likely that her daughters will be able to incorporate some of the values that she wants to pass on to them—the importance of family, respect for education, and the value of their cultural antecedents. She is helping them to differentiate themselves from her without having to cut their ties. "I think you have to be very careful with your children or you will lose them. You never say, 'I hurt, and I don't want to talk to you.' This is what I found out. Maybe you hurt, but don't cut the relationship. Something small can happen, and it can break the relationship, so a parent must be careful. If something breaks, maybe you can glue it together, but you always see the crack. We have a poem in Farsi, it's very beautiful: A string, if you cut it or break it, you can tie it back together, but you always see where it was torn."

The dramatic cultural conflict in which Farouz is engaged is an exaggerated version of the struggle that every mother faces with her adult daughter. We all must learn not to give advice unless asked, we must recognize that we can't protect our daughter from the complexities of adult experience, and we must accept that she will turn to others to provide the support we once gave her. But this transformation in our relationship need not be a negative one; it should not leave us with a sense of loss. We should be able to capture what Naomi Lowinsky calls "the richness that is possible when mother and daughter have wrestled with their differences and found their own ground in life to stand on" because, as she writes, "far from creating separation, this kind of wrestling is the beginning of an authentic relationship."

Chapter 10

Getting Beyond Guilt

We mothers are forever ruminating about what we did wrong. If our daughter can't get through transitions without tremendous anxiety, if she always seems to pick partners who are not as supportive of her as she is of them, if she's unable to make a commitment to a man or a career path, we assume it's our fault. Mothers' stories are peppered with remorse: "I feel so bad about...," "If only I hadn't...," "If I had it to do over again, I would..." And even when mothers say, "I did the best I could," they are implying that someone else might have done better. We measure ourselves against a gold standard of mothering that is composed of the idealized mother we wish we had had, and the attentive, attuned mother postulated by all the child-rearing books we read when our children were young. In humility rather than in hubris, we have taken on the burden of being solely responsible for the shaping of our daughters' lives.

As Alice Trillin, mother of Abigail, twenty-seven, and Sarah, twenty-four, said to us, "You're always trying to figure out how not to screw it up. At each step. And it doesn't go away. The thing that's so difficult is how perfect we need to be as mothers, and how unbearable it is to think that we've made a mistake. We're all haunted by the possibility of making the mistake your mother made. We're constantly saying, let me not fall into this pattern. Although of course, we do sometimes. What astonishes me is how important it is not to screw up. And I think it's probably too important, and I'm much too vulnerable to the thought that I might have screwed up, when it's not so big a deal. Of course, I make mistakes all the time, and in general things work out all right. But for every little tiny error, I think, Oh if only I could take that back. It's more important than anything else in the world."

Taking the Blame

Why do mothers assume this burden of responsibility and blame? In large part, the sense of responsibility is ingrained in us by our culture. In her book, *The Reproduction of Mothering*, Nancy Chodorow describes why it is that "women have had primary responsibility for child care in families and outside of them; that women by and large want to mother, and get gratification from their mothering; and finally that, with all the conflicts and contradictions, women have succeeded at mothering." Dr. Chodorow argues that there is no aspect of child rearing other than birth and breast-feeding for which women are biologically more suited than men. It is for economic and psychological reasons, rather than biological ones, that our society has assigned the role of primacy in child rearing to women. As the development of capitalism led to the separation of home and the workplace, the world of production and commerce became the province of men, and the home became the woman's world. The proper outlet for a woman's energy "became centered on child care and taking care of men," and "women, as mothers, produced daughters with mothering capacities and the desire to mother. These capacities and needs are built into and grow out of the mother-daughter relationship itself. By contrast, women as mothers (and men as not-mothers) produce sons whose nurturant capacities and needs have been systematically curtailed and repressed." Although Chodorow and many other feminist scholars wish that these circumstances were different, they acknowledge that in the world we live in, men delegate child rearing and the responsibility for nurturing to women, and women happily accept the role.

It's a short step between accepting responsibility for raising children and being willing to accept blame for anything that goes awry. Before her death in 1988, sociologist Grace K. Baruch presented a preliminary paper entitled "Reflections on Guilt, Women, and Gender," in which she set out to examine if women are the guilty sex, and if so, why. Baruch noted some "risk factors" relative to guilt, which she culled from the current research. Her observations can be summarized in this way:

Women have been socialized to take responsibility for the well-being of others and they suffer stress from their involvement.

Because of the strong sense of identification between mothers and daughters and the closeness of their early relationship, a special empathy is likely to develop between them and to be passed on from generation to generation.

This sense of empathy is reinforced by the fact that women, who traditionally lack status and power in our society, have to be especially alert to cues from those around them.

Research on how people respond to negative events in the lives of others indicates that women are likely to believe they could have had an impact on the event and therefore feel guilty about it. If they could interpret the event as being something over which they had no control, they would be less likely to feel guilt and more likely to be angry—to blame someone or something other than themselves. Men's socialization, conversely, makes it easier for them to refuse to feel guilty and to blame others instead.

The notion that women have the primary responsibility for mothering—and are therefore to blame if any aspect of that mothering appears to go wrong—has been intensified by twentieth-century psychology and sociology. Freud and his followers emphasized the importance that experiences during infancy and childhood have in the formation of human personalities, and their theories have pervaded our culture. Women of our generation have internalized the explanations promulgated by Dr. Spock and many other neo-Freudian child-care experts that a failure to handle any episode or crisis in our child's life without a perfect understanding of the child's wishes and developmental needs could have lifelong implications for the child's mental health.

Adrienne Rich has railed against "the full weight and burden of maternal guilt, that daily, nightly, hourly, *Am I doing what is right? Am I doing enough? Am I doing too much?*" that oppressed mothers whose children were young in the 1950s and 1960s.

Little has changed today. In an essay entitled "The Fantasy of the Perfect Mother," Nancy Chodorow and Susan Contratto maintain that "the blame and idealization of mothers have become our cultural ideology."

Grace Baruch speculates that women are especially vulnerable to what she calls "false guilt." False guilt does not arise so much from a sense that we have acted against the dictates of our internal moral compass but rather "is triggered by others' distress or disapproval, by a fear of disconnection and separation rather than by pangs of conscience . . . Vulnerability to concern about disconnection may cause women to convert feelings of loneliness, fear, and especially anger into guilt or to say 'it is my fault.'" Mothers whose daughters make life choices that the mothers feel are contrary to the values they thought they had instilled, or mothers who feel left behind when their daughters want to spend more time with their friends and new families, often fail to acknowledge their own fear of rejection, and—even more frightening to admit—their anger at their daughters. They feel more comfortable blaming themselves for the situation. If only, they think, I had been a better mother, this never would have happened.

Judicious Responsibility

Most of the women we spoke to had trouble absolving themselves of guilt. Said Leah P., "I have this wonderful daughter, Joan. She's a social worker, which is not surprising because she's a caretaker. She's a very giving person, she likes to take care of children, pets, you name it. So she loves her job. She has a boyfriend at the moment, and I think it's a problematic relationship. And what the relationship has hammered home to me—I mean, I always knew it on some level—is how needy she is. He's needy too, so in some ways it's a perfect match. It makes me think, I can't believe that she needs love so badly that she has to find it with this troubled guy. And that makes me wonder, Didn't I give her the love she needed? She's so obsessed about this relationship. I see myself in that, too. I saw a movie recently, *The Brothers McMullen*, about three Irish brothers living on Long Island who all eventually find love. I left the theater very emotional and sad because it got me thinking about relationships, and how people can lose themselves in relationships. And I remember doing that when I was young—being so absorbed in another person that I lost my sense of myself. So when I see Joan as anxious and needy, I think, Oh, you could just substitute me. And then it's just one step to knowing that I did this to her. I imposed this on her when she was young. By being too demanding, too critical, imposing my fears on her. And worst of all, somehow making her not feel loved. Or that she had to worry that I was so demanding that she could never count on my love. Or whatever. Those thoughts swirl around and around in my head.

"Then I ask myself, 'When she shines, which she does a lot, do I take credit for that?' And I don't. I think that all good things about her are just who she is, and all the bad things are my fault."

Dr. Kathy Weingarten says, "My personal bias when I am trying to help a woman evaluate her relationship with a daughter is to avoid thinking in terms of personal failings and rather to look for as many contextual influences as possible: the genetic makeup of the child—

her temperament; the impact of the girl's father—was he a supportive husband? What personality traits did he bring to the relationship?; the other siblings, the schools, a child's peer group, her particular friends—what role did all of those influences have in making her who she is?" Elsewhere in our interview Leah told us that Joan had been an edgy, colicky baby, she had suffered from severe ear infections in childhood that required several hospitalizations, and her younger brother, born when Joan was three, was a gifted scholar and athlete throughout school and college. In addition, Leah described her husband, a musician, as very involved with the children—and also very anxious and hovering. But she didn't seem to connect these facts in any way to Joan's development; as she said, everything that went into influencing her daughter's vulnerability was her fault, and all the attendant guilt was hers as well.

If a mother were able to consider all the mitigating contextual factors, she would be more likely to take on what Dr. Weingarten calls "judicious responsibility" rather than "ultimate responsibility." In her book, *The Mother's Voice*, she writes, "Judicious responsibility does not exclude other adults or children from taking responsibility too. Nor does it obscure the responsibility that society has—but fatefully neglects—for meeting the needs of mothers, children, and their families."

Accepting judicious responsibility enables a mother to recognize that only a limited number of the many factors that went into shaping her daughter's life were under her control. "My daughter Emily once said to me, 'Do you blame yourself for my problems?' Martha R. told us. Martha, a fifty-seven-year-old homemaker, has suffered from recurrent bouts of depression for over thirty years. Her mother, sister, and several cousins are also depressives. Emily, a thirty-year-old emergency room nurse, developed signs of the disease in college; at one point her symptoms were so severe that she had to be hospitalized. A combination of psychotherapy and medication seems to keep Emily's disorder under control and, according to Martha, "she has made peace with her condition."

Martha has kept any sadness she feels about her impact on her daughter's development in perspective. She believes that the causes of Emily's illness were beyond her—Martha's—control. "I can't help the fact that she has the chemistry she does." And she has discussed with Emily the effect that her own episodes of deep depression undoubtedly had on her daughter's childhood. "I told her, 'I did the best I could.' My own illness played a part—just who I am played a big part—my own depressive illness. Who knows when I wasn't accessible when she needed me to be. I regret many things, but I don't feel guilty. I'm sorry that I wasn't more up to the job, but that's just the way it is. I think I'm a good mother. So when Emily asked me if I blamed myself, I think she expected me to be more defensive. But she thought about it, and she's very open to rethinking things. So I hope that she'd say I've been a good mother because that's what I put my energy into." Like Martha, we mothers must accept the fact that we did the best we could, while acknowledging that it may or may not have been what our daughters needed most.

Although we may understand that other people and situations have played an important role in the makeup of our daughters' lives, we mothers are still tormented by the belief that all of the ways in which we *did* influence them, every decision we made on their behalf, must be judged against a model of perfection. A Good Mother is always attentive to her children. A Bad Mother puts her own needs ahead of theirs. A Good Mother protects her children from harm. A Bad Mother exposes them to the vicissitudes of life. If we did not perfectly serve our daughters, then we must have failed them.

And yet we also know that there is no such thing as a perfect mother. In fact, as Naomi Lowinsky writes, we parents can't help but fail at times to protect and provide for our children; it is "an unavoidable condition of life, like death. The truth is that we are bound to fail our children by our own human limitations. We need to be people as well as mothers; we will always be balancing our own needs against those of others. We are certain to err on the side of too much or too little control, discipline, love, support, attention, money. We are doomed to fail the ones we love the most. . . . Disappointment and anger are givens in any parent-child relationship because what our children mean to us is very different from what we mean to them."

How Fathers Get off the Hook

If we women continue to think of ourselves as the nurturers and take upon ourselves the responsibility for having raised our daughters to be the women they are, then what role do husbands/fathers have? In many of our interviews, a mother told us that while her husband seemed to share her anxiety about some aspect of their daughter's life, he did not get so embroiled with the daughter about it. And even when parents together take a position that is not what the daughter wants to hear, the mother gets the lion's share of the blame. The following stories typify some of the situations that can arise as fathers and mothers play their socially preordained parts.

"We're usually in agreement on the issues with the girls. He can be as upset as I am, but he doesn't mix in. He'll say to me, 'Why don't they fix that place up? Buy some furniture. Get stuff on the walls,' and then when we visit Marie, he'll say, 'Doesn't this look nice? So airy and clean!' "—Loretta G., mother of Marie, thirty-two, and Diana, twenty-eight

"If Mandy has a grudge against us for something we've said or done, it's against me, it's not against my husband. And yet I've spent a good part of my time assuaging my husband's anger about her! I'm the one who's explaining her, and yet because he removes himself, he's the austere figure. I'm more vulnerable, the more prominent target."— Priscilla D., mother of Patsy, thirty, and Mandy, twenty-seven

"Her weight has been an issue. Not only between Karen and me, but my husband has felt strongly about it, too. And he's said to me— and I'm supposed to convey it to her—that she can be the nicest, the most charming person in the world, but unfortunately, you have to market yourself out there on the social scene, and he feels that perhaps the weight she almost uses as a defense."—Lois A., mother of Karen, thirty-four

While mothers were giving vent to their exasperation in stories like these, they usually undercut it by a shrug or a laugh, implying, "Oh, you know men." It seemed to us that they were also somewhat resigned to the fact that their daughters often do not apply the same standard of behavior to their father that they hold their mother to. These disparities of concern and conflict are expressions of the social assumptions that place the full responsibility for nurturing on mothers and the full onus on them when things go wrong. Dr. Kathy Weingarten explains: "I think that the discourse around mothers and daughters is significantly different than the cultural ideology or discourse around fathers and daughters. First of all there's the issue of how we're socialized in regard to emotional reactivity. The permeability of the boundary between mothers and daughters is greater.

"I work a lot with families of adolescents and people in their early twenties, and I don't see a mother taking on more or less distress based on what's happening in the life of a son versus a daughter, but I see a big difference between what the mother takes on—the mother's permeability—and the father's permeability. The mother seems to be much more porous, and the dad much more bounded. And when you're more porous, when your daughter's tension or distress can get inside you, there's much more of a need to do something about it. And my guess is that if a father is upset, there's a moment of permeability, and then like those amoebas that break apart and then re-form, his boundary re-forms and in fact he's intact. Much of the time he's not thinking about it, whereas moms really describe a semi-permeable state and that creates disequilibrium. And I think this creates great pain and consternation for moms."

From Marilyn's journal, July 30, 1995

Stimulated by the book by Mary Field Belenky et al, which builds on Carol Gilligan's work about how women stress context and connections. I've been reminded anew of the strength of female continuity and connection in the days since Harriette's death, particularly because we've had her sister, Mitzi, and the girls staying here all together. Hugh and a few members of his family are very close, but they don't work on maintaining the whole network like women do.

Hugh is the most connected man I know. He has close friends, male and female, whom he talks to for hours on the phone, or has dinner or lunch with. I think he gets a lot of his friends, particularly the men, to talk more intimately to him than they do with anyone else in their lives. And yet, in family matters, I do more of the work. I remember the birthdays and anniversaries of his relatives. That can't be just because I come from a family where that stuff mattered. I'm the one who reminds him before we go to a party, that so-and-so's first wife may be there, and therefore some things can and some can't be discussed. I'm the one who rescues him when he's been introduced to someone whom we had dinner with last year, and he's about to say how nice it is to meet them.

I'm more likely to look at relationships in terms of patterns, particularly when it comes to the girls. Hugh is more situational. I look at the continuity of our relationship with the girls as a series of developmental issues. When they were adolescent, I spent a fair amount of time explaining him to them and them to him. I brood about the mother/daughter process. Although he's always very receptive to any insight I might have, he's not likely to angst about patterns of connection per se.

What about the father who's as unhappy as the mother about something a daughter is doing, but doesn't bear the brunt of her wrath? Dr. Weingarten believes that the answer can be attributed to gendered differences in the style of discourse. Women in general have the habit of talking to each other. Men have a much greater tolerance for silence. "Clinically mothers and daughters have greater fluency in their dialogue, whether there is conflict or not. The conversational groove is greased between the mother and daughter in the way that it is usually less greased with the father-daughter. Often the mother is offering a sustained dialogue, even if that dialogue is a sustained series of arguments as opposed to sustained conversation. And this often is very different from what the dad is offering." It's not that the father is any less upset with the daughter than the mother is, or that the daughter is actually any less upset with him, it's just that they have less experience engaging each other than the mother and daughter do. Mothers don't want to relinquish their power to be engaged with their daughters, so they will tolerate being the occasional fall guy because the fathers and daughters aren't as connected, or are connected in a different way.

Clearing the Air

Even if a mother can come to understand that she is not responsible for all her daughter's unhappiness, even if she accepts the fact that the amount of anger and blame her daughter tosses at her may be disproportionate to what she actually did, she would still like to get beyond the weighing of relative culpability and try to make things better. What can she do?

Mollie M. breezed into our interview, started talking at once and never stopped. It was not that things welled up in a spontaneous way; Mollie was actually always in control. She told colorful anecdotes with a beginning, a middle, an end, and often a punch line. Frequently she was the butt of her own stories. Everything Mollie told us was lightened with humor, as if she were a stand-up comic, and we were the audience she was trying to win over. She presented herself as a cute suburban housewife with a conventional job. But actually she was a very successful real estate broker in La Jolla, California, and her life had had a lot of drama: Mollie had been married four times ("always a bride, never a bridesmaid!"), she admitted to considerable drug use in the 1970s, she was coping with a drugged-out stepson, and she had two angry daughters. Mollie described Tracy, her older daughter, as a "twenty-eight-year-old hippie dropout" just back home after five years in Bali. ("These spiritual people live only in the nicest places. They live in Santa Fe, they live in Malibu, they live in Mill Valley, they live in Kauai. My husband asks why are there no spiritual people in Detroit?") Her second daughter, twenty-two-year-old Marissa, Mollie described as "an uptight yuppie preprofessional."

Mollie began by saying that she was somehow chosen by fate to participate in our project. Her hippie daughter thought it "cosmic," because only the week before Mollie, Tracy, and Marissa had just had a major reconciliation after years of recrimination and blame on their parts and defensiveness and guilt on hers. "In a lot of ways I've achieved the dreams I set for myself," she said. She has a successful business, a good marriage—finally—good friends, a nice home. "But my relationship with my girls was the one area that didn't feel good. It was hanging out there and lurking. My whole life I have feared that I would have this terrible punishment. I thought I would get pregnant before I got married. It didn't happen. Then I was afraid I wouldn't be able to get pregnant. It didn't happen. Even all my husbands were nice. In the last couple of years, I've thought, well, my punishment is my girls. They're just gonna be angry, and we'll never get to feel better. I'll never be able to resolve this with them. But now I'm working on that, and I think it's better already. They do, too."

Tracy was the product of Mollie's very early, very brief marriage. She's had no contact with her biological father since she was an infant. Marissa was born during Mollie's equally short-term second marriage; her father adopted Tracy and is still very connected to the girls, although he lives in Milwaukee. Mollie was married to her third husband for nine years, and has been with her current husband for twelve. But the stability in her life now does not make up for the turmoil of her earlier years. "When the girls were young, I was young too and very crazy. My girls had to grow up with me, and it took its toll on them. They had a lot of anger, a lot of anger, and I would say to them, 'I kept you in the same town. The suburbs, which I hated. But fine, we'll be a nice family.' I made a decision—which in retrospect was the right one—to do whatever I had to do to stay in the same town. For friends and schools. So at least I did that. But they really suffered from the upheavals and the ups and downs."

Mollie thought she was doing a much better job than her own mother had done. Her mother stayed for a long time in an unhappy marriage and poured all her energy into her career as a costume designer in the film industry. Mollie always resented that her mother was seldom home and that she always seemed selfish and self-absorbed. "If anyone played her in a movie, it would have to be Rosalind Russell, with the cigarette and the suit. And I always wanted a mom who would bake for the class. And I did that. I went on the field trips, and I drove them to ballet. And we all had dinners together with only fresh food, and all of that. I thought that's what being a mom was about. So I couldn't understand where all this anger was coming from. And there's a tremendous amount of anger from both my girls."

The anger had been building for a long time. "One day Marissa said, 'You know how you feel about Nana? That's how I feel about you.' That took my breath away. And that's when I started to look at my relationship with them. But they were still too young for us to be able to talk it over calmly." When Tracy moved back from Bali, Mollie thought the timing was right. She asked the girls to set aside a day for the three of them to get together and talk things through. And that cosmic event happened the Saturday before our interview.

They spent five hours together at a quiet coffee shop, starting with breakfast, and ending, after many cups of coffee, with lunch. Mollie began by telling the girls, "I'm very upset about our relationship. I'm jealous of mothers and daughters who are close. We do things superficially, we go to lunch, Sunday suppers, but there isn't that deep connection. I'm envious of people who have that. And I think it's a good time to clear the air." Then she turned the discussion over to them. She had vowed to herself that she would not be defensive; she had promised herself she would let them say everything they wanted to without interrupting them with self-justification or rebuttal. Only when their anger was spent would she even comment on what they had to say. It wasn't that what they said was a revelation, but as Mollie reported, "For once in my life I really listened. I just let them unload."

They hit her with a barrage of complaints that centered on her selfishness. They told her how much they suffered from her capriciousness about marriage. "I would take out one man and put in another. It was hard for them. Tracy said the worst day of her life was the day my marriage with her father broke up. They said that I chose myself over them. Which is something I've always said about my mother. She chose her career, or her husbands, or whatever. They said, 'You didn't give us emotional support. You improved on Nana in the practical things, being there, picking us up on time, but you weren't any better in the emotional area.'

"They said, 'You were mean to us.' I said, 'How was I mean to you?' because I couldn't fathom . . . They said, 'You did verbal abuse.'

So I said, 'What did I say to you?' They said, 'You said we were spoiled and we were brats.' And it was like that. 'You said we were self-centered and selfish.' And I felt like saying, 'Well, you were.' But I didn't. I didn't.

"My husband had said, 'They're gonna do you in today.' But I thought, I trust my intuition. My intuition tells me that what they're saying is true, sincere, and honest. I owe it to them to listen. And after they were all finished, I apologized. I said I felt very bad that they had to grow up with me. I told them that during the seventies and eighties, many experts said it was better to break up a bad marriage than expose the kids to it. I said I was young and immature. And they had to grow up with me growing up. It was a crazy time. And I was very sorry that I had been so oblivious to how much they had suffered."

Mollie knew that it was not enough to make excuses or justify her behavior. A bona fide apology should include an acknowledgment that you did something wrong, that you know your behavior caused the other person pain; and that you want to modify the way you act in the future. Mollie did it all. She did not challenge her daughters' view of the past. She acknowledged that in her restless jumping from marriage to marriage, she was thinking more about herself than about the impact on her children. Although she was not selfish in the same ways that her mother had been, she appeared to her children to be just as selfish in others. By telling them she was sorry for how she had made them feel, she retrospectively validated their feelings. She let them know that she wanted to do things differently from now on.

We asked her how she thought the relationship between herself and her daughters would change. "I think we will build on it. They didn't gang up on me. I felt that it was a bonding thing for them. I realized how much they needed to say what they had to say, and for me to really hear them. And I've already made conscious adjustments. One thing . . . I've always signed my letters and notes 'Mother.' I call myself 'Mother.' They said, 'Mother is an institution. We want you to be a Mom.' So when I left Marissa a note the other day, I signed it 'Mom.' When I rang her doorbell today, I said, 'It's Mom.' Little things like that. Tracy said I don't hug and kiss her enough. So before I left for the airport on Sunday, I said, 'Come here, let me give you a hug.'

So I'm giving them what they told me they wanted and needed. And not just superficially."

These steps might seem insignificant to outsiders, but Mollie says, "You have to change things on a conscious level first, and then hopefully it becomes integrated on lower levels. I think human beings are always capable of change. I'm an improved version of my mom. So I'm hopeful. But you never know."

It's an incalculable benefit to your daughter if you can fully listen to her. Mollie's desire to improve her relationship with Tracy and Marissa was strong enough that she was able to listen, and also to let the girls suggest the first steps toward repair. It's hard to allow your daughter to express the hurts she thinks you have inflicted while resisting the impulse to counter with your version of the story. You have to be able to tolerate an onslaught of what might feel like mother-bashing and yet not feel like a victim. Another mother, equally unhappy about a recurring recriminatory tone in her daughter's dealings with her but less sure that she can maintain her composure throughout such a confrontation, might suggest that the two of them see a counselor together for a few sessions. Another possibility might be to initiate a correspondence on the subject. A mother might suggest that she and her daughter put their feelings about each other in a letter or a series of letters, thereby allowing each of them to read, absorb, and respond when the flush of anger has passed.

Blackmail for the Past

What *doesn't* work is when a mother makes what she thinks is a gesture of reconciliation in the form of a trip, a gift, or acts of seeming generosity. In a strained relationship such a gesture may be interpreted quite differently by her daughter in light of their long history.

"I was too involved with my career, I didn't think about her enough," said Natalie S., the sixty-two-year-old mother of thirty-two-year-old Elizabeth. "From the time she was old enough to talk, she'd say, 'Mom, when are you coming home? Why do you have to go to New York?' And I didn't really take it in. I was so involved with my own life. My husband, Patrick, was usually there; we had great live-in help. She seemed okay. And now that I see the results, I think about it all the time."

Natalie was one of a handful of women business majors in her college class and one of the first to become an account executive at the midwestern advertising agency where she is now the senior creative director. "Even when I was there, I wasn't there. On nights when I was home for dinner, I'd miss half the meal because I was on the phone. I remember once when the whole family went to a movie, I ran out during the opening credits to call a client. I thought it would take three minutes. An hour and a half later, the guy finally hung up, and I had missed the entire movie. Occasionally I'd take Liz along on a business trip. I thought it was a mother-daughter treat, and I'd always make sure to top it off with a nice dinner. But looking back now, I realize that she also had to spend hours hanging around the hotel suite, or swimming by herself in the hotel pool, while I was working. And all along I thought she seemed to be fine, and she wasn't. She didn't have a lot of friends, and she was maybe ten or fifteen pounds overweight. Our relationship wasn't really good, but it wasn't terrible either. In retrospect I don't think she trusted me, and I think she thinks I was not there for her, and I think she's right. And I have these terrible guilt feelings for having done this to this perfectly nice kid who deserved her mother's attention much more than she got it. I've had tremendous regrets about all this."

The current relationship between mother and daughter is tense. There are long periods when Elizabeth does not call, and even when they do talk, Natalie is very aware that she learns little about what is going on in her daughter's life or the lives of her two young grandsons. Natalie says, "Sometimes I get the feeling that if I didn't have money she'd never call." Often Elizabeth asks for money directly or tells her mother about something she wants in such a way that Natalie feels coerced into offering to buy it for her. "I'm pleased to be able to buy nice things for her, but often I'm incredibly resentful because I think her interest in me is only for what I can buy. And I'm just stunned that after all I've done, she still treats me like dirt."

Every ski season Natalie and Patrick rent a condo in Utah; they invite Elizabeth and her family to join them for one or two weekends and vacate it for a block of time so the children and grandchildren can have it to themselves. For the last several years Natalie has arranged for everyone to get together for a week at a spa in Baja California. Despite Natalie's attempts to bring the family together, to make up for the times they were separated emotionally or physically during Elizabeth's childhood, Elizabeth is as resentful as ever.

Elizabeth takes advantage of her mother's guilt by upping the ante. If Natalie offers to buy her a Jeep, Elizabeth has ten reasons why only a Range Rover will do. If Natalie offers to build a deck on Elizabeth's new house, Elizabeth wangles a built-in hot tub as well. Naturally these transactions feel to Natalie like blackmail for the past. Like most people who are being blackmailed, she is afraid not to pay up, because she fears that if she doesn't, she will have no contact with her daughter at all. And yet, since nothing Natalie is offering Elizabeth is a remedy for whatever Elizabeth thinks went wrong, it probably still feels like an attempt to buy her off. On balance, Natalie is willing to spend and yet angry that money is the metaphor for connection, and Elizabeth is willing to take and is equally angry that money is the currency of exchange.

When a relationship between mother and daughter is especially knotted, even the smallest, seemingly innocent spontaneous gesture may backfire. Martha B., a sixty-two-year-old Louisville socialite, and her daughter Kate, who lives in Vermont, have been fighting and making up and fighting and making up for years. Among the underlying issues that seem to surface every time they quarrel are Kate's anger at her mother's divorce and subsequent remarriage to a man with whom Kate never got on; her sense that her mother and the second husband were always away, leaving Kate and her younger brother with a succession of caretakers; her conviction that her mother forced her into a brief unhappy first marriage because Kate was pregnant and her mother was ashamed to have an unwed mother in the family; and so on. Martha says, "I'm as aware as anyone could be that in the past I did what I thought was best for *me*. However, in recent years I have apologized repeatedly for what I did and yet my daughter can't begin to let go of her rage."

When Kate explodes, she accuses her mother of being selfish. How does Martha feel about that? "Guilty. And miserable."

Martha says, "I do get some loving-type behavior from her. Calls and sweet talk and presents and caring kinds of things, but sometimes I think she does it only when she wants something in return. I'm not really sure that she loves me." Martha told us about an incident that took place two months ago after she had returned from a typically rancorous visit to her daughter's house. For years, as a hobby, Martha has made ceramics. She has given pots and bowls to many of her friends, and to Kate as well. "She loves my pots. She loves to eat from them and cook from them and serve from them and have them around, and hold them and touch them, so soon after I got home I found a box of them and I sent it to her. Two weeks later I get it back. 'I don't need any more pots.' So I said, 'Kate, why didn't you just break them or give them away? Why did you have to offend me by sending them back?' 'Well I thought you might have somebody else you wanted to give them to.' "

According to Dr. Kathy Weingarten, these sorts of transactions in troubled relationships are often examples of a mother giving what she thinks the daughter wants, not realizing that the daughter might see the gesture in a different context. In this case, the real communication is probably encoded in Kate's sending the pots back. It's as if she were saying, "Don't give me what I don't want. You didn't give me what I wanted and needed when I was younger. Why are you giving me all this stuff that I don't need now?" Says Dr. Weingarten, "Spontaneity is probably not a good idea in an estranged relationship. A spontaneous gesture on a mother's part—if there isn't a close connection—can just as easily be *mis*interpreted as interpreted in the way a mother would want. Even if the mother's impulse is to be generous, one probably needs to be more cautious in a relationship that is strained."

With all the goodwill in the world, many of us have been unable to get beyond the guilt we feel and our daughters play on. Unlike Mollie M., we may not have the self-confidence and forbearance that make it possible to sit down and take what a daughter has to dish out. Because it's one thing to acknowledge that she's right when she says, "You did A, you did B, you did C," but it's quite another to hear her say, "You did all those things, and you never really considered what it felt like to *me*."

When the mother wittingly or unwittingly manipulates a young child to pursue her own agenda, the result is an injury to the child's sense of self. It matters little whether the child protested at the time, acquiesced, or even seemed to feel positive about what was happening because that's what she thought the mother most wanted from her. Whatever the case, the child's authentic feelings were submerged or ignored. "The child has a primary need to be regarded as the person he is at any given time," writes Alice Miller in *Prisoners of Childhood*. Which means respecting the child's feelings, sensations, and his or her right to express them. Which means that even today, if you want to change your relationship with your daughter, it's not too late to begin listening carefully to her when she talks about what she thinks and feels.

Dr. Weingarten believes that people can create intimacy with each other "if they are open to sharing what they truly care about and open to trying to understand what the other finds meaningful. . . . In order to grasp what another person means, you have to really *listen* to that person. This, it turns out, is exceedingly difficult to do. We often think we understand someone else when we actually understand the sense *we* have made of what *that person has said*. . . . I have trained myself to no longer think that saying to someone, 'I know exactly what you mean,' is of benefit."

As a mother, you want your daughter to feel that when she tells you something powerful, you can listen without assuming that you know what she means because you've heard it before, or that you know the answers because you've gone through exactly the same thing yourself, or other similar preconceptions. You want her to feel comfortable taking whatever time she needs to discover for herself what she really feels. By listening in this way you create a context in which she has a chance to reveal that vision of herself that she most wants to share with you. The two of you are getting beyond the rhetoric of recrimination and approaching the realm of true mutual discourse.

Chapter 11

Expressing Your Voice

L ois A., and her husband, Phil, have an only daughter, Karen, thirty-four, who lives in Boston. Lois told us that she had mentioned to Karen that we were interviewing her for this book. "And she said to me that that reminded her of one thing—we were taking her to college her sophomore year and some discussion came up, and she remembers that I said, 'I'm not your best friend. I'm your mother.' And she said, 'That's always stayed with me.' That really took me aback. I was very surprised that this is what she remembered because I didn't remember it. She said, 'I felt that that always defined the parameters of our relationship.' And I said, 'Does it bother you?' And she said, 'No, but I'm just aware of it. I've talked to quite a few of my friends, and they say their mothers are their best friends, and I've always remembered what you said.'" Lois told us, "I guess I was a little hurt, but I didn't say anything. I thought probably it was true when she was eighteen or nineteen, and that's exactly what I would have said then, but I'm sorry that it's affected things so that at thirty-four we're still not close friends.

"Karen and I love each other," says Lois, "but we're really not comfortable with each other. We're guarded about what we share. It's very hard when you're communicating primarily long distance, and if you don't see somebody's face." Lois believes that Karen is not happy in her work and her love life, but she is acutely aware that she knows very little about her daughter's interior life. What became clear to us during our interview was how little of her *own* thoughts, feelings, beliefs, and experiences she has shared with her daughter. When Lois had a mastectomy ten years ago, she delayed telling Karen until after the fact to avoid upsetting her. A few years later, when Lois and Phil had a serious crisis in their marriage, they held back the news altogether. Last year while Lois's mother was wasting away from stomach cancer, Lois tended her almost every day. Yet when she talked to Karen during that period, she spoke mostly about inconsequential things because she didn't want to burden her daughter with her grief.

Lois wants intimacy with her daughter, but, as Dr. Kathy Weingarten writes, "For a mother to be intimate with her child she must be willing to let herself be known. For some mothers—mothers like me who grew up believing that we had to be 'selfless'; mothers who believe that maintaining a position of authority in every situation is fundamental to good parenting; mothers who fear burdening their children—letting themselves be known, sharing stories of who they really feel themselves to be, is challenging. In fact, it is the heart of the matter of intimacy."

Because Lois doesn't know how to reveal her intimate thoughts and feelings to Karen, Karen has no model for what an intimate relationship with her mother could be. Lois seems to believe that a "good" mother must say only cheery things to her daughter. A "good" mother must never let her daughter see her vulnerability. A "good" mother must never reveal her real feelings lest it be more than her daughter can bear.

Lois has not been able to communicate intimately with Karen because she has not found the voice with which to speak. She is out of touch with, and therefore unable to express, what she really thinks and feels about the defining issues in her life.

The subject of a woman's voice has been exhaustively examined and debated in the nearly twenty years since Carol Gilligan and others first began exploring the topic. Gilligan's book, *In a Different Voice*, details the difference between male and female psychological development, in which men become mature by establishing their separation from their mothers, and women mature while staying in connection. Separation implies a psychology based on the knowledge of rights and of justice—on a determination to create and maintain boundaries between people. Connection implies a psychology based on a sense of empathy, sharing, and taking responsibility for others. Because men dominate our society and models of male behavior have dominated psychological theory, Gilligan argues that women lose confidence in their own ways of knowing—their reliance on and belief in connection as a social value. Women's psychological development is often seen as a failure, partly because the male standard is used, and also because women are reluctant "to speak publicly in their own voice, given the constraints imposed on them by their lack of power and the politics of relations between the sexes."

According to Gilligan and her colleagues, young girls who can speak clearly and truthfully about their own feelings and experiences begin to equivocate as they become adolescent—they begin to lose their voice. They give up "what they know and what they have held fast to." By the time they are adult they have internalized self-doubt and accepted the notion that "womanhood will require a dissociative split between experience and what is generally taken to be reality." The true voice of women like Lois, Carol Gilligan would say, was drowned out by "an internal voice which was interfering with their ability to speak. That internal or internalized voice told a woman that it would be 'selfish' to bring her voice into relationships, that perhaps she did not know what she really wanted, or that her experience was not a reliable guide in thinking about what to do."

Lois is aware that she has been very diffident about asserting herself—expressing her voice—in any relationship. Lois was an only child. Her father died two years ago. While he was alive, his wife organized her life, and Lois's, around his needs. "When he died, I thought, This may finally give me a chance to do some things with my mother I couldn't do when he was alive—girl things. And then she got sick almost immediately, and it's very sad that we never got to do them."

Lois had married Phil, who was in his last year of law school, right after she finished college. Her parents agreed he was a terrific catch. He too was an only child, who remained close to his parents and supported them until their deaths a few years ago. "Phil became a lawyer because that's what his family expected. I don't know that he has ever loved it. He was a dutiful son." In their married life, Lois has usually deferred to Phil. And he tends to be the one who directs their daughter. "Although there are things I might have said differently if he weren't in charge," she says. But Phil definitely defines the terms of the relationship, and Lois accepts it. "You have to realize when we're together it's the three of us; there are no other people. I've thought about whether there's a way I could do things alone with Karen, but my husband doesn't have a lot of interests apart from the things we do together. He's not a golfer who goes off with his buddies somewhere. I think he would have a hard time understanding why I would want to go off with Karen to a spa, for example.

"Last night Karen called. I picked the telephone up downstairs and started to talk to her, and Phil walked in and I said, 'It's Karen.' And he said, 'Thanks for telling me!' and went upstairs and got on the line. Very rarely do I talk to Karen by myself. It's always Phil on one line and me on the other. I've never gone back East to visit her by myself, it's always the two of us going." Lois recognizes the parallels between the way she and Phil interact with Karen and the family dynamic she had with her own parents. "I thought about this in relation to when I used to visit my parents, because you have to realize that all my married life I was coming in from out of town, and I can never remember being alone just with my mother. It was always both my parents. I'd like things to be different, but I don't know how to do it without hurting my husband, and I really don't want to hurt him."

The way that Lois has framed the problem—how to be more intimate with Karen without hurting Phil—suggests some confusion about the true expression of care. As Carol Gilligan makes clear, women's sense of integrity appears to be entwined with an ethic of care. As we reach adulthood we need to have developed a firm definition of what caring for others really means. We should be able to distinguish between *helping* others and *pleasing* them. If we're still desperate to win approval, that indicates that our sense of personal integrity and strength is impaired. Like so many women, Lois spends too much of her energy trying to make other people happy. "I always feel that my whole life I've been trying to please everybody in my life. I really tried to please my parents, I tried to please my husband—I obviously did not do such a great job on that. I try to please strangers, selling them insurance. It's always emotional . . . A friend of mine said she eliminated the words 'I should' from her vocabulary years ago, and it was the most liberating thing—granted this person is one of the more selfish people—but that's not as bad as it might sound. I think I'm reaching this point. You wonder when it's your time."

It was significant that Lois used the word *selfish* to describe a woman who seems clearer about asserting herself than Lois is. Like so many of us, Lois reflexively denigrated a woman's taking her own feelings into account. We're so busy smoothing over the rough spots in a relationship, avoiding confrontations, making everything all right for others, that we often ignore our own needs in the process. As Carol Gilligan asks, "If it is good to be responsive to people, to act in connection with others and to be careful rather than careless about people's feelings and thoughts, empathic and attentive to their lives, then why is it 'selfish' to respond to yourself?" We must try to understand that our need to express our own beliefs and wishes is as important in connecting with those we care about as our responsiveness to their ideas and desires.

We find our "voice" within relationships. Although we tend to think of ourselves as having a coherent self and a set of core values that we try to express consistently in all of our relationships, in fact the way we express ourselves in nearly every transaction is modified by our relationship to the person who is listening to us. We speak one way to people who have power over us, and another way to people we perceive as equals, still differently to those we think are dependent on us. We vary our voices constantly when we choose to cajole, to bully, to dismiss, or otherwise to deal with the person we are engaged in a dialogue with. Even within the family, where we might think we are most free to speak in what we think of as our true inner voice, we modulate our voice all the time in response to those whose reactions we are exquisitely tuned to.

How can Lois begin to express her voice? She must start with small steps to undo the patterns of a lifetime in which she received, first from her father and then from her husband, the message that her voice was not valued. It might help her to understand her family dynamic in terms of a triangle—a common pattern that can often be untangled by applying some insights of family therapy that are usually credited to the late theorist Dr. Murray Bowen. Triangles allow two family members to deflect tensions between them onto a third member of the family. Issues that Lois and Phil should probably deal with between themselves are warping their relationship with Karen. In addition, both parents seem to blame each other for any faults they find in their relationship with their daughter.

Lois could begin to break up their triangle by initiating direct two-person conversations separately with her husband and her daughter. First of all, she might set aside time with Phil to talk over some of the things that are bothering her. In particular, she could tell him clearly that she'd like to spend time alone with Karen and have phone conversations with her daughter by herself. Perhaps he would like to do that as well. Three-way phone conversations tend to be difficult. When Phil has something he wants to talk to Karen about, Lois need not be part of the conversation. When Lois and Karen want to talk, Phil should bow out. When Lois and Phil talk to each other, it's important that they both take the "I" position. "I'd like . . ." "I want . . ." If these transactions are too difficult for Lois to carry off by herself, she might suggest that she and Phil—and at some point, she, Phil, and Karen—see a therapist together.

Lois must also find a way to tell Phil when she disagrees with something he says to their daughter. It's probably too much of a challenge to him to disagree in front of Karen, but she might tell him afterward that he was only speaking for himself, and that in the future they should talk things over ahead of time to see if they are in agreement. And if they can't agree, it won't hurt Karen to hear that they have separate opinions.

At some point, Lois might invite her daughter to spend some time together at a place that Karen chooses. If the pattern of their relationship has been of thwarted intimacy, Lois should not expect that they will suddenly open up to each other. But whatever they share— quiet time, going to a museum, shopping, having facials together, watching a movie on a VCR—is a stepping-stone toward greater emotional closeness.

A Mother's Voice

Most women of our generation believe that their mothers did not particularly want to reveal themselves to us. We believe they were willing to sacrifice intimacy with us in order to preserve their role as "mother." Society stressed respect for parents—a generational servitude that never ended—and for many women, respect in their maternal role was the one validation they got. To our mothers we were eternally children, and even as adults we were supposed to be excluded from knowing their adult secrets. We were seldom privy to their inner thoughts, their weaknesses, even some of their sweetest daydreams, because if we could see that kind of complexity in them we would be looking with a realistic rather than a reverential eye. And since they had, for the most part, accepted the general view that what they had to offer—as women—was not so important anyway, it followed that if we heard their voices clearly we would know that what they had to say was worth little—and so were they.

Some women did have mothers who were able to reveal themselves to their daughters in spite of the prevailing social constraints and who encouraged their daughters to be open and honest with them in return. Angela A. had such a mother. "I was raised with a great deal of sunshine in my life by a woman who was also one of the most independent people I've ever met. She had lots of opinions about things, and she was interested in mine. She was always accessible to talk to." Her mother's example influences Angela's relationship with Gretchen, twenty-eight, and Betsy, twenty-six. Angela has always stressed to her children the importance of interchange, sharing life experiences, finding a balance between work and family, between independence and connection. Before Angela took on her present job as chief executive of a computer software company, she studied psychology and worked for some years as a counseling psychologist. This background provided her with a vocabulary and a framework to express what she had probably instinctively understood about family dynamics.

Angela, who also has five sons, firmly believes that being connected to her children usually involves saying clearly what she thinks. She told us, "I feel comfortable saying anything to my daughters, including, 'I really don't think you should do that,' if they ask me a question directly. Even if they don't ask, if I feel strongly about it, I also feel I'm entitled to say it once. If they disagree or don't react to that in a way that breeds more discussion, then my gut reaction is to just go along, it's their life." Five years ago when Gretchen was planning her wedding, Angela was deeply involved. "And we never had one fight about the wedding. The tone of our friendship was, I was there to implement her plan. When her plan was taking a turn that I thought was not wise, I would present my viewpoint, and then it was her choice. And I think it's so fascinating that when you don't have an investment in the choice a child makes, the choice is usually the one that will be congruent with your own perception anyway. Because there isn't any power involved in that discussion—it was just about how should we do things."

When the subject is her own experience, Angela enjoys sharing what she's learned about the world of work, the relationship between men and women, the high spots and difficulties that any marriage encounters, and family life. But when the girls are weighing a decision that affects their own lives, she is much more measured in her response. She believes that listening is sometimes more valuable than expressing an opinion, *not* because she is afraid to voice an opinion but because her philosophical position is that the girls must figure things out for themselves. Moreover, she believes she really *can't* know what's best for them.

From Marilyn's journal, January 20, 1996

Susan asked me the other day if I think my girls know me. I said I thought they would describe me pretty accurately. I said that they probably underestimate my insecurities because I haven't chosen to share them with them. I don't feel that Phoebe Schnitzer's comment that many women have trouble explaining to their grown daughters that they have their own life and their own issues applies to me. I think my kids have always seen that.

One of the things that's revelatory to me from the interviews we've been doing, however, is that compared to a lot of women, I probably have fewer direct conversations with the girls. We *haven't* sat down and talked intimately about a lot of things. It's possible that I've internalized more of my mother's reticence about powerful subjects than I would have thought. I'm more likely to convey what I think in general conversation, in gossip about someone else, or other indirect ways.

Is that really true? I've talked pretty candidly about the fact that I expect them to be sexually active when they feel ready. That is, I've always talked to them as if that were my assumption. I've talked candidly about my own death and aging. Probably because it seems fairly remote to both them and me. But at least I've kept the subject from being taboo. I've talked about money, probably more than most.

What I have talked about less directly are feelings, hopes, dreams. I have talked about marriage, implying that I assume they will both marry and have kids, and I guess I've also implied that you marry for love, but expect it to be more of a negotiated relationship in the long run. I certainly haven't ever said that in a prescriptive way.

I've alluded to my sense of alienation from my parents, and given some details, but mostly tried to convey the notion that it's okay to criticize parents. To see them as people. And that it's sad for both generations if you can't be closer.

Gretchen has been married for five years, and although Betsy isn't in a serious relationship at the moment, she is beginning to think about what marriage would mean to her. Both girls want to know how Angela balanced child care and work when they were young, and how she keeps her marriage vital today. "My husband and I married when I was quite young, and we've been together for thirty-four years. They want to know how one negotiates the latter part of relationships. And I'm pretty comfortable having those conversations. My husband and I have never believed you should not fight in front of your children. And I've said to them 'Look, in marriage, you work some things out between you. But some conflicts will be discussed and never resolved—there are some areas where there will always be conflict.' So that's intriguing to them. I think that's a little bit of what helped Gretchen when she was working out some problems with her husband—she thought it was worth continuing the struggle. She had seen her dad and me have moments in which we could not believe we were really married to this person, and yet we could never have thought of not being married to this person. So she has learned that relationships have ups, downs, and plateaus. The other thing that both girls have articulated is that they value the relationship separate from the two people; there's something about weaving that cloth together that's important."

Betsy's close friends are beginning to pair off, and, says Angela, "She's asked me how you know when you're ready to make a commitment, how can you be sure you've chosen the right person. And we've had long talks about how you don't meet the right person to marry until you're ready to marry. You wouldn't recognize that person, you wouldn't have the appropriate things to offer the relationship. I've told her this is the time to work on yourself, learn to be at ease with yourself. So that whether you meet someone or not, because you've reached that stage, you can be all things to yourself. And both of my daughters and I have talked about the fact that being an independent woman doesn't mean simply that you have a good job and you know how to handle money. It also means that you can take care of yourself emotionally. That if you're feeling bad about something, you know what you need to do to feel better. You can do that for yourself. Until you can do that, you can't take 'care' of anybody else."

Because Angela doesn't operate in the realm of "I ought to do this" or "as a mother, I should do that," she's able to take a position that she feels is important to her own sense of well-being even if it may not please her daughter. "I created an expectation that I would always be there for them, and now I want to live my own life more," she says. She told us that Gretchen would be coming home with her baby in a few months. "I think she was slightly annoyed when I announced that I would continue going to my office three full days a week," says Angela. "Gretchen's implication is, why wouldn't I want to spend all my time with this treasure she's bringing home to show me? But I've put in my time doing child care, plus I didn't think it was the right thing to do. I have adult responsibilities to my colleagues and our clients. Also I have a great need for solitude, so sometimes I'll just want to be by myself. Even when the children were little, there would be a couple of hours in the afternoon when I would be in my room, when I would read or I would sew or I would write. And they were welcome to come in and do something quiet. They didn't mind it then because they had each other, but when they were more adult sometimes they saw my need for solitude as being somewhat selfish." From the way Angela tossed off that loaded word—selfish—we saw that she understood the difference between what it meant to them and to her. To her children, selfish is a pejorative word, meaning "Mom is not paying attention to us" and to her it's a positive word, meaning "I'm paying attention to myself."

Angela's self-confidence brims over in her conversation about her work and family. She herself attributes her ease in self-expression to the example her mother has set. Erica R., on the other hand, told us of a life marred by an unhappy childhood and permanent alienation from her mother. She was candid about her diffidence in relationships with men and at work. But with the help of a psychotherapist, Erica has focused much of her energy on making sure that she not reproduce between herself and her only child, Katya, now twenty-six, the feelings of isolation she grew up with. Erica has developed intimacy with Katya in a way that is consistent with her own reserved, judicious personality.

"We're very good at sensing when the other is in some sort of turmoil," says Erica. "We try to figure out what the turmoil is, but if one person is not ready to discuss it—and that's a rule really—we don't push. If I sense there's this barrier there, and her answers become halting and staggered, I realize this is no time to talk about it. Neither one of us has trouble discussing a problem when we're finally ready to do it. I think it's normal that, knowing each other's personalities, we don't want to burden the other one with something that they're not ready to hear." Erica's approach illustrates one of the intrinsic aspects of intimacy: When the other person is not ready to receive the thoughts and feelings that you have to offer, your attempt, rather than being intimate, is actually intrusive.

When You Think Your Voice Is Also Hers

In our attempts to be intimate we sometimes assume that our feelings and thoughts are the same as our daughter's feelings and thoughts. It's the "I understand exactly what you mean" syndrome, which we described at the end of the last chapter. As a mother you may have the best intentions in the world, but if you have neglected to hear a daughter out, then any opinions or feelings you express have the potential to do harm. According to a well-reported study by Mary Belenky and colleagues of how women develop or suppress their own voices, mothers who don't listen well perpetuate "the inherent inequality built into the parent-child relationship as a permanent condition." They are missing the chance to foster a relationship in which "equality, collegiality and intimacy between daughters and parents—especially mothers—becomes valued as a central achievement."

Of all the women we spoke to, Ginny P. was easily the most sensitive—we thought actually oversensitive—to the impact of anything she might have to say to her daughters, Barbara, thirty-four, and Sandra, twenty-nine. In an effort to avoid being intrusive in any way, she is extremely self-censorious. "I believe that almost anything you have to say can be so powerful that it debilitates them," says Ginny. She has come to this position in the light of what she now understands about her relationship with her own mother. She told us an illustrative story:

"Just before I got married, I was very depressed. For very good reasons. And my mother came to my room, and she said, 'Are you worried about the wedding?' And I said, 'Yeah. I mean I think I'm worried about that.' She wanted me to be worried about that. So that became what I was worried about. And she told me that when she was my age just before her wedding, her mother saw that she was depressed and sent her to Atlantic City. What she was telling me was that this happens to other people, and she went ahead and married my father anyway. And this kind of conventional wisdom was supposed to help me. And it did! It comforted me. Not because of the information—I was right, I should never have married Tom. And the things I was feeling were very rational thoughts about him. But she was giving me something of herself—which she had never done before. The event was not the communication of information about marriage or that she was like that too, but it was *my mother was talking to me*. My mother was sympathizing. My mother was showing me that she was connected to me, she wasn't off in la-la-land, that's what she was communicating. That's what made me feel better.

"Had somebody said to me, 'Maybe you should think about it. Or, do you want to postpone it? What is it exactly that you're thinking about here—are you worried about him, or are you just nervous?' But to so strongly identify my feelings with her feelings is taking something away from me. It was taking an experience, it was taking my own sense of judgment. Who's going to sort that out?"

By making the common enough assumption that she knew what her daughter was feeling because she had been through a similar situation herself, Ginny's mother allowed her own voice to silence Ginny's.

Dr. Belenky identifies a group of parents who characteristically say what is on their minds, but do not strive to understand their daughters' points of view. These relationships are based on what Belenky describes as "one-way talk:" "[The parents do] all the active thinking and talking about the ins and outs and the rights and wrongs of the situation. [They expect] their daughters to absorb their ideas, but they seldom encourage their daughters to think things through for themselves." On the other hand, in what we would call "two-way talk," parents offer equality and collegiality as the framework of a conversation. Only two-way talk promotes intimacy and helps the daughter develop her own voice.

Promoting Two-Way Talk

It takes enormous strength to keep up a dialogue with a daughter when the two of you profoundly disagree about something basic to your innermost sense of who you are. Maureen E. has lived through such a clash of values with two of her three daughters. She has managed to express herself on the subject that divides them while encouraging them to believe that everything they have to say is important for her to hear.

The issue is religion. Maureen and her husband are devout Catholics and raised their five children in the church. Her two younger daughters, Margaret, thirty-three, and Patricia, twenty-nine, have organized their lives around their membership in an evangelical Protestant church. Although Maureen argues forcefully that their choice of faith is wrong for this life and the world to come, she doesn't denigrate the seriousness of their commitment or their right to make their own decisions. Since they were raised with a strong involvement in religion, perhaps it's not surprising that the girls chose to make church membership a focal point of their lives. However it was somewhat by accident that they found their particular sect. "I was involved years ago in a group at our parish called 'charismatics,'" says Maureen. "Once Margaret came along with me, although at the time she was more into boys and cheerleading than religion. Anyhow, about four years ago, she was living in Manhattan, and not going to any church there, and met someone who told her about a group like that. So she went, and that's how she got involved with her church. Then when Patricia moved into the city, she called Margaret out of the blue and asked to go to church with her. And a few weeks later she went back again, and now Patricia is more into it than, I think, Margaret."

In an increasing involvement that made their mother nervous, both girls gave up their jobs to work full time for the church. Patricia is preparing to be a foreign missionary and Margaret is an administrator at the headquarters in New York. Margaret's husband is also active in the church.

"I can't find any fault with their lifestyle," says Maureen, "with how they're living and how they plan to live their lives, but I am disappointed that they didn't find this in the Catholic church."

How much does Maureen tell them her feelings? "Well, the belief systems are different. Things I believe in they don't believe in and vice versa, so we do discuss it and sometimes we have screaming matches. My husband is even more upset than I am." How far does she pursue it? "They're grown women. This is their life. I can only tell them how I think. They don't have to listen to me. And a lot of times we say we'd better not discuss this for awhile, because we really do get upset."

What is the force of Maureen's argument? "Fundamentalists think the Bible is it—if it says it happened in the Bible, it's so, it happened and that's it. And I don't believe that way. I believe the essence of it, but I think a lot of it is stories or parables to just help you through things. But they believe there was an Adam and an Eve, and it happened just the way it said, and there was a Jonah who got swallowed up by a whale. And I say, 'Just think about what you're saying! Use your head!' They believe if you're not born again, you're not saved, and that really bothers me. I keep saying, 'Do you think that your father and I won't be saved?' I know they're very confused because they don't want to believe that. Then they'll turn around and say things to me that will make me stop and think. It's hard to argue with them because they know their Bible, they can quote chapter and verse. Sometimes I'll look something up, and I'll say, 'This is it! I think I finally have them now.' And then the minute I say it, they have an answer for me. But there are certain things you know are right in your gut regardless of what it says anyplace, and this is one of those things where I know I'm right, even though I can't prove it like they can."

Maureen is also upset because the girls have turned their backs on religious ceremonies that have brought their parents great comfort. "If something were to happen to them and they were to die, there's no ritual in their church, and Catholics have a lot of ritual. I said to them, 'What would happen, where would be the closure? In the Catholic church you bring the body into the church, they have a funeral mass, the priest goes with you to the cemetery. You don't have any of that.' They said, 'We don't need any of that.' And I said, 'Well, I would need that for you.' And the fact that my grandchildren won't make a first communion, won't make a confirmation. Things like that are very troubling to me."

Maureen does not avoid confrontation, but she engages with her daughter in a style that promotes two-way talk. Her tone is not reproachful. She does not tell the girls what they should do. She is not trying to inculcate guilt—the subtext of her argument is never 'how could you do this to me?' Instead, she tries to learn from what they have to offer; she listens to their explanations and recognizes that their choice has great value for them. At one point, in a further attempt to understand the girls' point of view, Maureen invited herself along to their church services. "I said to myself, I have to go in and see firsthand what this is. My husband won't set foot in that church and that bothers them, I think. And I found out it's not a cult. This pastor has written a number of books that I'd read. On the way they said, 'Now, Mom, at some point they might say, is there anyone here for the first time? and when you stand up, they just applaud.' And I said, 'Forget it. I'm not getting up.' And there I was, and the pastor said, 'Is there anyone here . . .' and before he finished I was on my feet and all these people were hugging me! I'm very glad I went because I got to see what kind of people were there. I came out feeling really good about this community because I was the oldest person there—I saw young people, families, every color, every race, every age.

"They're very fine people. So I can appreciate what this means in the girls' life, because it certainly has done good things for them. And I couldn't ask for better lives—they don't drink, they don't smoke, they don't gossip, they don't do anything wrong, they lead very good lives. But something tells me they should be more involved in other things."

Despite their disagreements, Maureen and her daughters are not estranged. "I feel we're very close. I really do. At this point I feel closest to Margaret, I don't know why. Maybe because she just got married and there were a great deal of arrangements to be made, and she really let me have my way!" What do they come to you for advice about? "Everything. Everything from recipes to how to furnish an apartment to their relationships. Strangely enough they keep telling my husband and myself that they came to their church because we gave them such wonderful examples, because we were so involved in our religion."

And so the debate rages on, but with a mutual respect that enables everyone to know when enough's enough. "A lot of time my husband and I bring it up," says Maureen. "Fortunately we can do that and then say, 'Do you want to go for a soda?' " Patricia has been in Russia on church business. She is about to come home for a month and Maureen says, "I know we're probably going to have words. I know we'll be discussing religion, and I'll be trying to change her thoughts."

"Will Patricia try to change yours?" we asked. "Sure. But I'm sixty-two, and I'm not going to change. I think I'm right. I guess that's why I keep at it," she said with a laugh. "Maybe someday they'll see that we're right."

From Susan's journal, February 28, 1996

Neither of my daughters and I have had a moment of tension together in quite awhile. I attribute this to the fact that I am showing more restraint when they do or say something I may not agree with. On the other hand, I am trying to be clear and direct when I am bothered by something. Case in point: I was in Boston last weekend and spent time with Phoebe. After lunch on Saturday, just as we were getting ready to leave the restaurant, she asked me my opinion about whether or not she should buy a duplicate pair of boots—she loves the ones she owns and she is afraid they will stop making that particular style. I had the distinct feeling she was setting me up to buy them for her. I said, "Look, I'll buy them for you, but I don't want to feel manipulated. So if you want me to buy something for you just be honest and say so, and I'll decide whether I want to do it." She said, "I wasn't going to mention this because I knew you'd feel like I wanted you to buy them, but . . ." And then she laughed. She understood what I was saying, and I think in the future she will not be manipulative in this way. And, of course, I bought her the boots.

"I've Tried to Encourage Her to Have a Voice"

Barbara Weene knows that she was trained to be voiceless. Says Barbara, "I got married when I was very young because my family wanted me to become a nun, and I didn't want that for myself. My mother's sister was a nun, and there was lots of pressure put on me. My parents didn't think women should be educated, so there were no other options. And then when I got a divorce my mother was very upset. She said, 'What did I do to deserve this?' She would say all the time that she was disappointed with me for lots of things. She said that a lot more than she said anything else. She never talked back to my father when he acted horribly, even when he insulted her publicly, because women of that generation didn't do that. And she expected me to be passive too, because basically you teach your daughter to do that, to not have a voice. I feel my weakness has been typically one that women face—I try to fix things for other people and make them healthy. But what it ends up doing is making me not healthy."

Barbara has tried to break the cycle with her own daughter, Rebekah, twenty-six. "I've encouraged her to have a voice. I've made a conscious effort to let her know what I feel about things, to share with her as much of myself as I think she can handle. I talk about how messed up I get with men, about how lonely I feel sometimes, about my worries for the future. I also let her know when I take pleasure in something and why. And I see it paying off. For instance, my father would tell my mother in public to shut up, and my mother would just look embarrassed and kind of smile and be quiet. It always bothered me that she didn't say, 'Excuse me, but you're not going to say this in front of other people.' I encourage my daughter to stick up for herself so she says, 'Gramp, when you do this, I want to leave the room. It's disrespectful, and I don't care what Grandma did, it's not appropriate.' So she said this and left the room. And he says to me, 'You trained your daughter to dislike her grandfather.' And I said, 'You have your own relationship with her, and I'm not going to be responsible for what it is. And the other thing I want to say to you is that all my life I've wanted to say to you exactly what she did!' So

I'm really proud of her because she has the courage to do what I couldn't.

"She still has a ways to go, but she's working on it. She knows that she picks relationships with guys where she does all the work. She was seeing one guy, whom I didn't like very much, but I didn't say anything to her. And she told me she woke up at six one morning and began to cry and said, 'What am I doing here? This guy is totally involved with himself, he's not offering anything to me. I realized he wasn't going to fix me, and he wasn't going to fix anything in my life. So I got up and got my stuff and walked down the hill. I said to myself, This is your life. You've just got to do it. I decided I have to take care of myself for awhile.' "

It's thrilling to see your young adult daughter speak for herself in a voice that is uniquely her own. The spread of feminist ideas among young women, and even young men, in your daughter's generation gives her a cultural support that most of us lacked. But you can help her by speaking authentically to her—by being expressive about your thoughts and feelings, by sharing your experiences, by engaging in a candid dialogue that invites her to truly know you. And you are giving her a model to share more of herself with you. Being able to listen to each other and draw forth an authentic voice from each other confirms that yours is finally a relationship of true friends.

Part Four

Looking Ahead

Chapter 12

Friends for Life

Marianne Collins, sixty-three, is a coordinator of Catholic youth activities in Merrick, Long Island. Her three daughters, aged twenty-nine to thirty-eight, live within a fifteen-minute drive of Marianne's house and spend every summer weekend with Marianne and her husband at the beach. Marianne is one of a group of twelve women who became friends when their children were young, and who are now seeing their bonds of affection carried into the next generation. "We have this wonderful group in the sense that it's not unusual for all the mothers and daughters to get together—go out to dinner or something—it's a great, great feeling. It's so special when you do things like this. I just recently said to the girls, 'We're really due to have another mother-daughter gathering.' And all the girls get along with each other, too. And not just within the family. It's the clique, the group, whatever you want to call them.

"You have to understand—these kids all grew up together. When we all got together it was a great thing to see. It had a lot of impact because there was a huge support system out there. It was like, you didn't have just one mother, you had twelve mothers. It got to be like a joke, but in fact it was very powerful. It reinforced everything. And then they got to that point of life when you have to decide what direction you want to go in. We'd say to them, 'Go speak to Mary Jane, she's a social worker.' Or 'Go speak to Eileen, she's a librarian.' All these people could guide them.

"I moved into Merrick in 1961. Between 1961 and 1965 was when everyone joined the parish. So it was through the church and through the schools. It was a very common tight bond. All the kids were in classes together. At one point we had thirty-two kids involved. You know from the oldest one to the youngest. And the youngest of the women was convinced that we would never be around when her kids grew up. But we were. And we're as close now as ever."

The women we interviewed spoke repeatedly of the pleasure they received from being connected generation to generation. They saw themselves as links in what Naomi Lowinsky calls the "Motherline": Each of us is the daughter of a mother who was a daughter, and so on back through time, just as each of us is the mother of a daughter who may be a mother in the future. "Our daughters were in our bodies as we were in our mothers'," writes Lowinsky. "A son is different. The identification is at a slight remove, a responsibility for his otherness informs a mother's fantasies of who her son will be."

Are We More Intimate with Daughters Than with Sons?

We asked women who had both daughters and sons if indeed they did experience different levels of intimacy in their relationships with their children that were attributable to gender. Tina S., the mother of Todd, thirty-one, and Christy, twenty-seven, said, "I loved my son from the moment I saw him. I love him dearly to this day. I feel intensely connected to him. He is much more like me in lots of ways than is my daughter. Yet the bond from the moment I held this girl child was extraordinary. I knew that something *else* had happened to me. It wasn't just another child to love. This was a *girl*—this was a daughter. I felt the same connection to my mother, even though we were not close in the ways that I'm close to my daughter. We were close in the sense that we talked all the time, and in the sense that *I was her daughter.* That bond was there. And it's so strong, I think, the strongest thing in the world. It's made of iron—that bond between mother and daughter. And however the relationships work themselves out, and whatever happens around it, my God, it's incredible."

Arlen M., mother of Martha, twenty-six, Harper, twenty-three, and Jeremy, sixteen, told us, "I am much freer to just love Jeremy. I've tried to figure this out. My husband is much more uptight with what things Jeremy does and doesn't do. It's because I don't look at him as an extension of me. I don't feel that I gave him these things or didn't give him these things, or it's my responsibility for him to be a certain way. I just don't have as much of me somehow in my mind caught up in that relationship. I feel much more responsible for the girls as to who they are and what they will become. With the girls I used to think, Why doesn't Jerry understand them? And it's because he doesn't have a female perspective—something I think is real important. Like the girls' relationship with their girl friends—he didn't have a clue about what was going on there when they were embroiled in some fight or other, because guy friends don't relate the way girl friends do. And so he wouldn't know to be concerned about things that I would know, and it's the same for me with Jeremy.

"I watch my mother with my sister-in-law and my brother. She absolutely adores my brother, he can do no wrong, she puts up with things from him that she wouldn't even consider from us. She will fuss at me and fuss at my sister—she doesn't fuss with my brother. But part of it is she doesn't feel the closeness with him that she does with us."

Mildred G., mother of Walter, thirty, and Jean, twenty-seven, said, "Some of the closeness between mothers and daughters is based on biology. You can talk to your daughter about basic things—about menstruation, about sex, about contraception, about pregnancy, about the childbirth experience, and about nursing and raising a child. And you don't share those things with your son."

Shirley Strum Kenny, mother of four sons and Sarah, twenty-five, said, "After four boys, I felt I was gifted with this child. I don't have a sister and she does not have a sister, and I think we fill that need in each other. If she's feeling bad about something, she tells me, and we can comfort each other, and I can tell her if I'm feeling bad about something. We have that kind of relationship, a very special closeness, and I think there are things we feel that the males in our family don't feel."

Letty Cottin Pogrebin, mother of Abigail and Robin, thirty-year-old twins, and David, twenty-eight, told us, "The mother-daughter relationship is different because of how enmeshed it is in your life. It's much more there, it's much more of a presence. I know if a day has gone by, and I haven't spoken to one of my daughters, it feels like a hole in my life. Whereas with David I can go up to three days and I'll notice that we haven't spoken, but the conversation can be a two-minute thing—how's everything? what have you been doing? what are you up to?—just to hear his voice. And he'll say the same to me, and then it's good-bye. Whereas with the girls it would be ten minutes, fifteen minutes of schmoozing. The difference is quantitative, not qualitative."

Adrian P., mother of Camilla, twenty-five, and Michael, twenty-two, said, "I love both my kids, but in different ways. Very equally, and very passionately. Still I think my relationship with Camilla is special. Maybe it's because there are certain physical things about her life as a woman, or certain challenges, or the fact that you can be more physical with girls—I certainly feel more comfortable hugging her—or touching her in general than I do with him. I worry about her more. I guess I ache more for her than I do for him. Because he's a man. I think I can imagine what it's like in her circumstance more than I can in his."

Angela A. has five sons and two daughters, Gretchen, twenty-eight, and Betsy, twenty-six. Angela's training as a clinical psychologist and her close reading of feminist developmental theory made her comments seem especially thought provoking to us. "My experience as a mother is that from birth my girls were different from my boys," Angela told us. "The girls are also different from each other, but there has always been a greater opportunity with my daughters to be honest about who I was. And my sons seem to need not so much less honesty from me but less intimacy from me. They grew stronger by the distance I permitted them to have, whereas the girls grew stronger by knowing that they never needed to separate by disconnecting completely. The difference I saw—my husband and I saw this played out so distinctly—when the boys went off to college, they didn't call home for three weeks. And the girls went off and called three minutes later. And over the school year the boys would call maybe once every two weeks, and the girls would call whenever they wanted to talk— which was frequently. Now, either men and women use the phone differently—which I think is also true—or something else was going on. I believe the girls got stronger because they knew they could always come back to that primary connection and take a little more from it and then go off and face whatever challenge was in front of them. And the boys seemed to express their strength to themselves by not going back to that connection.

"I think if you asked my sons and my daughters to define the word intimacy, the girls would define it in terms of connection and contact and would use emotional language. I think my boys would not describe it that way. They would talk about doing things together. I also think this womanness, this way of being . . . We've taken three trips now with three generations, with my mom, myself, and the girls. The third time I noticed my girls had a series of questions they needed to ask my mother which were not unlike some of the questions they had asked me: How do you handle the pressures of marriage? How do you raise kids with good values? How do you keep a family together? How do you find time for yourself? They needed to hear those answers. I had felt those pressures in my generation, my mom had felt them in hers. It was really okay that they felt them in theirs."

Angela's boys don't seek that kind of conversation with her, and they don't seek it with their father. Says Angela, "Every conversation I've observed between my husband and my sons starts with 'So how's business?' or 'What are you doing?' or 'Did you read this article?' And the girls and I always start out with 'How are you feeling?' We're much more concerned with how things are than what's happening. It's the quality of what's going on that interests us."

Recently Gretchen, who lives in London, had a baby. Physical distance imposed an artificial separation on their relationship. "I think there were a thousand times in any given week when she would have liked just to pick up the phone and ask me about the changes in her body, her expectations about maternity. I arranged my schedule so that I could be there as soon after she had the baby as possible. My own mother had done that for me after each pregnancy. It enabled me to enjoy being a mother, but it also let me watch my mother bond with her grandchild. The women in our family really value that generational thing that women can do for each other. And Gretchen and I had the most wonderful two and a half weeks together with this new baby who came into my daughter's life at approximately the same time Gretchen was born into mine."

We asked Angela if she believes that the strong connection she feels with her daughters, as compared to her sons, is biological and innate. Or it is culturally imposed? "Probably a little bit of both," she said. "I think it's there to begin with, and then we probably reinforce it by the different ways we treat sons and daughters as they're growing up. What fascinates me is whether the differences are reactions to how sons and daughters act *toward* you as the mom, or does the mom behave differently to begin with?"

During the past few decades, questions have been raised among feminist psychologists about why mothers and daughters so often feel a special intimacy with each other, and whether it must of necessity always be reproduced. Elsewhere we have touched on the argument made by Nancy Chodorow and others that a special intimacy between women is the outgrowth of cultural assumptions about gender rather than the result of biological forces. In her book, *The Mother's Voice*, Dr. Kathy Weingarten takes this argument a step forward and challenges Chodorow, based on her own experience as a parent and clinician. Chodorow says that mothers perceive their sons as more different— more "other"—than their daughters. But Dr. Weingarten writes that the differences between herself and her firstborn son had no bearing on the degree of connection she felt toward him—that difference per se need not interfere with intimacy. In fact, she felt more closely connected to him from the moment of his birth onward than to anyone else in her life, including her second child, a daughter. As he grew, the fact of his gender, and the cultural demands that he—and she—dealt with it in certain prescribed ways, began to intrude. Her subsequent history with him has been an effort not to lose that early sense of connection. On the basis of her experience, Dr. Weingarten believes the cultural assumption that males lack the capacity to remain in connection can be negated if a mother works hard at understanding, and making herself understood by, her son.

This line of argument is provocative. It challenges mothers not to confuse sameness with closeness. It challenges them to try to stay in connection with sons. It challenges them to question the notion that they and their daughters will, a priori, be strongly connected, to focus instead on examining their relationship for what it is, and to search for ways in which they might make it better.

Can We Be Friends?

When we asked Angela A. how she would describe her relationship with Gretchen and Betsy, she said "warm" and "wonderful." These words recurred, along with "intense," "honest," "intimate," "empathetic," and the like, when we asked every woman we interviewed the same question. But the word that subsumed all these expressions of feeling, the word that was repeated most often was "friend."

Nellie Jenkins, mother of Natalie, twenty-one: "I think we're moving toward being friends. Before it was more a mother-daughter thing. Before I was more in charge. Now nobody needs to be."

Constance J., mother of Abby, thirty-two: "I think now we would consider ourselves more friends than mother and daughter. Now when she calls and asks my advice about something, she could just as well call a friend and ask the same question. I don't think she's calling me as an authority figure in her life, or that I know more than she does; it's more a sharing of the answer kind of thing. And it's the same for me. I ask her advice—but I could have asked another friend. I ask her because I respect Abby's opinion better than a friend's in some respects. I just don't think of her anymore as a daughter in the sense that I have any say in her life or any control over her life. And I don't want that. I think she's blossomed into her own woman, and maybe I can just be there to help her in some of her decisions through life."

Vivian Hedges, mother of Tina, thirty-one: "Absolutely it's a friendship. But I don't call her to unload on her. It's 'Hello, sweetie, what are you doing?' Or 'Let's go shopping, we haven't gone to Loehmann's in a long time.' Not a heavy, analyzed kind of friendship."

Lorelle Phillips, mother of Sarah, thirty-three: "I think Sarah and I have a wonderful relationship. Nurturing. Close. Positive. And complex. The fact that we can have conflicts, and then resolve them, and go on from there—the fact that we're involved in each other's lives, that we can have a good time with one another—I can't imagine it being better."

Evelyn Tang, mother of Frances, thirty: "To me the high points are she and I sitting together just chatting, visiting, no big discussion, just sharing mutual things."

Helen Rucker, mother of Bridget Mary, thirty: "When she was in high school, I never liked it when people said, 'Oh, you're such good friends.' No. I was her mother. I could sit down and say, 'What are you doing about your college applications, or about the jobs you're supposed to do around the house?' Which is the mother role. But it evolved into a friendship as she got older. Or certainly as she became sexually active. Or when she moved away from home."

"I think my daughters are the most important women in my life," says Letty Cottin Pogrebin. "I have friends, but if someone asked me, 'Who's the first person you would call to tell something important, or good, or bad,' it would be my husband, then my daughters, and my son. I must say I value the girls' opinions more than, or as much as, those of my female friends. I think they're very honest about why they're saying what they're saying. And they know me very well, they know my flaws a lot better than my friends do."

Honesty, acceptance, generosity, loyalty, and trust—these are all attributes of true friendship that Letty writes about in her book, *Among*

Friends, in which she analyzed friendships among men, women, men and women, family members, co-workers, within racial and ethnic groups, and across cultural divides. We asked her why she didn't include mothers and their adult daughters in her pool. Equality is essential for friendship, Letty believes, and when she wrote the book her daughters were just eighteen—more her children than her equals. If she were writing today she would address the subject from firsthand experience. "How to be a friend and still be a parent is the issue with grown-up children," Letty feels. "If you're still in the control mode—if there's a power imbalance—then you're not friends."

"Friendship Is Not What I Want"

A small group of the mothers we interviewed firmly believe that, as one of them put it, "a parent should remain parental." They may wish to perpetuate a subtle imbalance of power; they may want to retain the role of nurturer as exclusively their own. While they feel close to their daughters, they do *not* want an intimate, mutually reciprocal relationship. Says Paula S., mother of Maud, thirty-four, and Jessie, twenty-eight, "I don't think friendship is what I want. I think friendship involves a kind of intimacy, a sharing. I want serious boundaries that are respected. I like the generation gap. I want the generation gap. I think it's healthier for everybody. I always want to be the mother. I don't want to be a pal to my kids."

Sylvia Karchmar says of Lara, twenty-eight, and Dorian, twenty-five, "I've always wanted them to know that I am someone they can come to with whatever is on their minds, but I don't want them to think that I'm their girl friend. I want to keep my credibility as their mother because you only have one mother. You can have lots and lots of friends, but a mother is a different level of relationship."

Martha R., mother of Emily, thirty, is also leery of mutuality. "I don't really embrace the notion of mothers and daughters being swell pals, that sort of thing. I mean, Emily and I are close—we depend on each other—but I'm still very much the mother. I guess I still believe there are certain things you don't need to share with your children. I want to protect her. I don't want her to feel alarmed. I don't want her to feel burdened. I don't want her to feel she has a mother she has to worry about."

Nancy Washington, mother of Linda, thirty-two, and Laura, twenty-eight, said, "I would not call us friends. I never wanted people to look at the three of us and say, 'Are you sisters?' I don't think that's a compliment. I say firmly, 'I am their mother.' I always felt that I want to be someone like my Aunt Jean, someone who is very comforting."

Comforting, protecting, nurturing are words that don't seem incompatible with friendship. We all value friends to whom we have turned for consolation and care when we have been in need, and whom we have in turn nurtured during stressful episodes in their lives. Friends understand and accept imbalances of need and control if they are temporary, but the long-term survival of a friendship depends upon an overriding equality in which need and nurture flow in both directions. The mothers who don't want to be friends want to preserve the role of caregiver or authority figure for themselves. They put less value on the reciprocal intimacy that makes true friendship possible.

And, as we have said, they were in a minority.

Friends—in a Category of Their Own

Most of the women we spoke to were pleased by the growing equality between themselves and their daughters. They were relieved to have moved beyond the caretaking mode. And yet—a mother's long history as the comforter, the nurturer, the caregiver cannot easily be ignored or abandoned. The reciprocity of need and nurture that characterizes other friendships can probably never exist between parent and adult child because the mother retains vestiges of her maternal role. Lucy Rose Fischer has studied the relationships between adult daughters and their mothers from the daughters' perspective. In her book, *Linked Lives*, Fischer states that "most mothers and daughters are both close and distant, and most are both peerlike and parental at the same time." Because of patterns inherent in the family structure, she believes, genuine peerlike friendships are somewhat uncommon and often somewhat cool in their nature, while relationships in which "mutual mothering" prevails are more common and more intimate. By mutual mothering, she means that each woman responds to the needs of the other, alternately nurturing and allowing herself to be cared for as the situation demands. Because mothers have the long history of being the nurturer, they probably continue in that role more than the daughter does, but there is enough give and take to make both women comfortable.

Mothers who are happy to call their relationship a friendship recognize this as a conundrum they are willing to live with. As Alice Van Tuyl, mother of Sarah, thirty-two, and Elizabeth, twenty-nine, says, "Friends is only one aspect of our relationship—we are also more than friends. You can never just be a friend to your daughter unless you have had nothing to do with her growing up and have just arrived when she's twenty-one. I don't think you can ever be just a friend. It's an inadequate word to describe the relationship. Behind the friend is always the parent. And you don't entirely abandon or abdicate that. Your worry level is always there. You don't have that for a friend no matter how close. You don't think, Gosh, I hope they're driving carefully tonight. I know they went to Boston for the weekend. And you're glad when the phone rings and they're home. Even your best friend doesn't call you when she gets home."

There's another way in which our friendship with daughters differs from other friendships. A frequent precondition of friendship is a similarity of life experience. Like Alice Van Tuyl, Jane Morgan uses the word *friend* when she describes her relationship with Leslie, twenty-eight, and Drew, twenty-three, but she knows that their dissimilar generational experience makes the friendship very different from those she shares with her contemporaries. "I surely do enjoy them," says Jane. "They are intellectually stimulating. They make me laugh. There's not anybody I'd rather be with. I can always count on them. So they're friends, but they're not people I share my innermost feelings with. For that I want maturity, an intellectual development, a wisdom that doesn't come to someone in her twenties. A life of living and understanding. My kids certainly are wonderful, and I love doing things with them, but I wouldn't consider them my best friends. I know they consider me one of their best friends, and I consider my mother one of my best friends, but I know I wasn't one of hers.

"I'm certainly not like my mother, and that's the nicest thing she ever did for me, she never criticized me, not one time. She accepted me for who I was. 'You look terrible' or 'You don't study enough'—I never remember any criticisms like that. She just allowed me to be who I was. And she just enjoyed me, even though she and I actually had very little in common. But we are real good friends in the way that mothers and daughters are friends."

The mother-daughter friendship is a very special friendship indeed. In some respects it will fall short of other friendships because it can never be truly mutual. In her book, *When You and Your Mother Can't Be Friends*, Victoria Secunda notes that your daughter probably has a key to your house, but you don't have a key to hers. On the other hand, as one mother told us, "It's more than friendship because you're bound for life." A mother-daughter friendship can surpass other relationships because it incorporates all the years you have spent intimately studying each other and learning to interpret each other's behavior, because of your shared memories, because you nurtured her and she grew under your care, because of your mutual experience as women.

Varieties of Friendship

Cathy Ravella is a fifty-four-year-old nurse and therapist in Pittsburgh. She spent three and a half years working for a Catholic relief agency in Kenya, where her daughter, Erica, and her son, Damien, were born. Erica, thirty, works for the Library of Congress in Washington, and, until recently, moonlighted as a dancer with a rock and roll band. Cathy told us that although her mother was "a formidable figure," they were very close. "We spent hours together on the phone. I felt I could have heart-to-heart talks with her. Even toward the end when she was really ill, I would drive up to Buffalo and sit with her and we would talk. We had a very easy relationship."

Cathy assumed that she and Erica would be similarly close, but it hasn't worked out that way. "Erica will tell me things, but she's some-one who just doesn't want to talk about her feelings much. I used to think she was keeping me away, but I think now that's just the way she is. Erica also doesn't like to talk on the phone. I said to her recently, 'I miss grandma. She and I used to sit and talk on the phone for hours.' And Erica said to me, 'Yeah, I don't know how I could be related to you and Grandma.' So she recognizes her own style.

"I have a friend whose daughter is like a chip off the old block. They're very close, they talk every day. At one point I thought, Gee, I wish I had that. I would ask myself, 'What's wrong with our relationship?' and then I thought, Well I'm not my mother, and Erica's not me. And there's nothing wrong with our relationship. I have to accept it more on her terms. And it took me a long time to get to that appreciation—to recognize that she's her own person, and not just part of me."

We all know that we are more intimate with some friends than others and yet we appreciate them all. Even though her friendship with Erica is less intimate than Cathy wishes it were, she has learned to value it for what it is. " 'Friend' has a lot of different meanings," says Cathy. "I have friends I can pick up the phone and talk with about anything. Erica and I don't have that kind of relationship, so we're not 'friends' in that way. But we're 'friends' in that we like to spend time together. She enjoys my company and I enjoy hers. There's a growing mutual respect between us—for our differences rather than where we're the same."

Because we mothers believe that the mother-daughter relationship has the potential to be uniquely intimate and fulfilling, we are troubled when our own connection to our daughter turns out to be something different. When that does happen, for whatever reason, it's important to sustain whatever connection we have. And hope that we may build on it. As Cathy Ravella says, "I'd like to think Erica and I will continue to be as close as we are now and maybe even become closer. We'll probably never live in the same city again, and since she doesn't like to talk on the phone, it makes it hard. I'll probably have to make more of the effort, but I don't mind that. I don't think the effort has to be equal."

If you're the mother of more than one daughter, you know that you find different things of value and different kinds of intimacy in your friendship with each one. Variations in intimacy may be influenced by your daughters' sibling order, their differing relationships with their father, the fact that you share more interests with one than with another. Your relationships with your daughters may vary because one is married and another not, one is more like you physically, one reminds you of a beloved parent or sibling, one seems more emotionally in tune with you, and one—being quite unlike you— brings a new perspective to your life. It's not that you love one more than the other, it's that your friendship with each is precious in its own way. Of her daughters, Rhonda, twenty-eight, and Stacy, twenty-five, Verdine Jones says, "Rhonda is short dresses, high heels, lipstick, makeup, prissy type; Stacy is tennis shoes, shorts, and the music-in-the-ear type. My relationship with Rhonda is more like a friend, in which we can discuss practically everything except what goes on with me and my husband sexually. I don't think there's anything else that I have not discussed. Stacy is a fun person. She is a joy to be with, she keeps you laughing, she has a real good sense of humor. She's my fun friend, not as intimate as Rhonda. If you want to have a good time, go with Stacy; if you want to discuss stuff, go with Rhonda."

Says Nancy Hernandez, mother of Yesenia, twenty-three, Veronica, twenty, and Omara, sixteen. "I would say with my oldest it's like a stamp to a letter, we're just glued together. With Veronica, it's perfect communication. I call her my calm—whenever I'm upset she's able to calm me down, she sits with me, she looks for all the solutions as to why this or that happened. I would say she's my problem-solver. And Omara is my hurricane. Though this year she's been quiet."

Maureen E. told us that her relationship with her oldest daughter, Cathleen, thirty-eight, is somewhat circumscribed because Cathleen is married, has a child, and has lived for some years in a city three hundred miles away from Maureen. Cathleen has always been "my most independent child," says Maureen. Patricia, the youngest, used to be the daughter with whom Maureen was most intimate, but in the past year Patricia has been living far away from home and, Maureen feels, is in the midst of making some major decisions about where her life is headed. "So for this reason, I'm just a little more cautious with her. I'd like her to lighten up."

At the moment Maureen feels closest to her middle daughter, Margaret. "We had words on the phone not long ago, and she called back later, and I remember saying to her, 'I'm sorry it got to that point, but I've got to tell you something. You're the only one of the three of you I would have gone this far with. I feel it's a compliment to you because I can let all this out to you, where I would not to the other two.' So I must feel closer to her and can open up more to her just now. We have the same sense of humor. I think our relationship is one of mutual admiration. I admire a lot of the traits that she has that I don't have. She has a lot of my mother's traits. I just feel it's a good warm relationship in that I can say things to Margaret that I wouldn't say to the other two girls."

In any friendship there are periods when the relationship is intense and periods when it is cooler. Maureen implies that there may be fluctuations in the relative closeness of mothers and individual daughters as well. Just now, for a variety of practical and emotional reasons she and Margaret are particularly close. In the future, circumstances may lead to a greater intimacy with one of the other girls.

The Years Ahead

What does it really mean to be your daughter's friend? It means you can cook and savor a Thanksgiving dinner together one year, yet go in different directions the next. It means that when you have lunch together, sometimes you pick up the tab, sometimes she does, and sometimes you go Dutch. It means that you can trade advice about finances and office politics, yet accept the fact that you have different taste in clothes.

Mother-daughter friendship is often enhanced with the passing of time. In one landmark study, based on interviews with daughters aged thirty-five to fifty-five, most of the daughters reported that, in general, their relationship with their mothers was rewarding and that it had improved as they had moved toward their thirties. What the daughters prized in their relationships was their mother's companionship; they reported a link between their sense of well-being and their bonds of affection to the mother.

Our interviews frequently substantiated these feelings of well-being from the *mothers'* point of view. Women whose daughters had successfully passed through the typical turbulence of early adulthood—who had established themselves in careers and settled down with permanent partners, for example—told us of passing into a period of particular intimacy with their daughters. Mothers attributed this to the increase of shared experience, which, as we know, fosters friendship. Says Constance J., "Abby and I always got along well. But when she was going from being a single woman living with a guy to a married woman, that somehow put us on a different level. It took away the mother-daughter hierarchy and made us more friends. She was never outspoken about her life in general; I mean if I asked her a question she'd tell me the answer, but she wouldn't come to me and say, 'Oh mom, I had the greatest date last night.' I'd have to pull it out of her. She has a shy side to her, but getting married eliminated all that. It was like we were both the same, woman to woman."

Those women whose daughters had themselves become mothers often said that that was the most bonding tie of all. However, the daughters who were subjects of the mother-daughter study reported that when they became mothers themselves they were *less* emotionally tied to their own mothers. A bit of reflection leads to the conclusion that this is neither a paradox nor a threat to their mothers—that is to say, us. It's been our life's goal for our daughters to need us less, to be able to take care of themselves, and, ultimately, to draw their richest emotional sustenance from their partners and children—their new nuclear family.

Therefore, even if it's been a somewhat rocky road with your daughter, time is on your side. By the time she's in her mid-thirties, she will probably have come around to a more forgiving sense of why the two of you have the relationship you do.

But why settle for that? There's a much richer goal than mere acceptance on her part. We believe that mothers and their adult daughters can achieve a rich friendship, and many of the women whose stories we've presented point the way to just that.

We believe it can't be said often enough: The key to a better relationship is to treat your daughter like an adult, with the respect that you have for your dearest friends. She may make choices that are very different from the ones you would have chosen for her; and—

because she is her own person—you must especially respect the ways in which she is different.

Sondra L. a very elegant, very social woman talked to us at length about her relationship with her two daughters—one, a corporate executive who is gay, and the other a Generation X would-be artist who lives with a man whom her mother dislikes. After a difficult decade or so, Sondra has learned to value both young women for their strengths and has stopped trying to mold them into her image of what they should be. "If you continue to infantilize your daughters they might be around a lot," says Sondra, "but I don't think you really have a good relationship unless you can stop that and become two adult women friends. I mean you're always going to be mother and daughter, but you have to give them room to be who they are, and I think that letting go is a hard thing that all mothers have to go through."

In our interview with photographer-writer Gay Block, she told us how her unhappy relationship with her mother had impaired her ability to mother her daughter, Alison. Following our conversation, Gay wrote down some thoughts—which she sent us—about how, after years of therapy and hard work, she has reached the point where she and Alison can be friends:

When Alison was very young, she was already headstrong and independent. Her oft-repeated motto, "I'll do it myself," was a family joke. My son Barry was easier in many ways. Alison was much less malleable and it was always obvious she'd be an adult I wanted to spend time with.

A bedtime ritual began when she was about nine: I'd say, "Let's see how soft we can kiss goodnight." We'd brush lips and I'd say, "softer," and we'd do it over and over again. We both loved it. She told me after she began living with Stéphane [her husband since '93] that this was a formative lesson in sensuality for her.

Alison and I were very close, I felt. When my lover Debbie left me in June 1984, we were together much of that summer before she went off to college. A lot *too* much, but she was a comfort, a friend. I took her to college, helped with her dorm room, and we talked often. She told me about her first sexual experience, her first year, and about all her friends, male and female. So it came as a shock in her senior year when she told me she was seeing a psychologist, and he had suggested she read a book about dysfunctional families. I was really dismayed, tried to argue a bit with her, and then left it alone.

That revelation was the beginning of the difficulty between us which just now—eight years later—seems to be ending. Sometimes during those years I could hear her dead tone of voice on the phone, and it reminded me of how I had felt talking to my mother all my young married life. I really didn't want to live that way and knew I might eventually have to tell her what I had come to wish my own mother had said to me: "It's very painful to hear you talk to me this way, and I know you can't possibly enjoy our relationship. Sometimes you say things to me which hurt me— they're cruel and ugly—and I know you can't enjoy doing this. I'll always love you, always be here for you as your mother, but I'd prefer us not to talk very much until you *want* to talk to me, until you're not angry with me."

I never had to say this. We rocked along, good and bad. I helped her plan her wedding, and I spent a lot of time and energy doing it. I did this intentionally, knowing the resentment she carried about my neglecting her in high school. We became very close during this time. After the wedding I was shocked again to hear her say I hadn't come to her room—she was staying with her best friend at the hotel while Stéphane stayed in their apartment the week of the wedding—just to hang out with her and Caryn. I said I didn't think she wanted me to, but if she had invited me I would have been there in a second. Perhaps my own insecurity often got in my way with Alison.

During the next two years she saw a psychiatrist, and she felt he helped her a lot. I agree. And this past year of distance, with them living in Paris, has been a year of growth and independence, I must assume, because our relationship is better than it has ever been.

Recently we all got together for my son's wedding. And I told her on the spur of the moment, "I just love Stéphane, in his own right for who he is, but I love him even more because I see how happy you are and how beautiful you are, and your beauty doesn't come just from the outside, you're beautiful on the inside because you are happy, because you love life, and you trust life, and that's a lot to be able to see in your daughter." And three days later as we were saying good-bye at the wedding, she said, "I know you've said before that you love me and value me, and I know you've meant it before, but this is the first time that I've ever understood that you meant it." So that's a really big thing and it makes me feel, not that we won't have problems again, but that she's heard it.

"I Couldn't Choose Better Friends"

Shelagh C., sixty-two, is a librarian in a suburban community on Long Island. She and her husband have six daughters ranging in age from twenty-five to thirty-eight, and a twenty-year-old son living at home. Five of the six daughters live within an hour or so of their parents' home, and the family remains very close. One daughter is a lawyer; one is studying law; one is a trained nurse working in pharmaceutical sales; the other three are building successful careers in business. Five of the daughters have married—one in circumstances that made Shelagh unhappy—and the youngest is engaged; two are separating from their husbands, which Shelagh, a devout Catholic, finds particularly traumatic. Several of the girls are stressed by the need to balance work and child care in ways that Shelagh didn't have to. In the last ten years Shelagh has also coped with the effects of her husband's heart attack, his subsequent stroke, and the deaths of her parents and her beloved only sister.

Throughout her life, the sources of Shelagh's strength have been an abiding faith in God, an ability to see the humor, or at least the humanity, in the problems that beset her, and a sense of self-worth that her mother instilled in her. "I had a wonderful relationship with my mother," she says. "My mother was a dreamer. She had wonderful dreams for her two daughters. My father was not a well man and it was a struggle. He spent a lot of time in hospitals and was on disability in his forties. So it was a struggle. But she put those dreams in my head and I could carry them through. My sister and I more than filled my mom's dreams. She said, 'I sent two little girls out into the world, and I got back nine grandchildren.' But it was rough. When I was ready for college, my sister still had to finish high school. We went to this wonderful French school, French nuns. But it wasn't free. So I went to Fordham at night and worked to help pay for her.

"My mother was a feisty sixty-two-year-old woman when she died. I miss her. And then I lost my sister four years ago. She was only fifty-three. And that makes a void in my life. That's why I'm so happy that my girls will have one another. There's something about sisters that no one else can replace."

The close connection Shelagh felt with her mother and her sister has carried over into her relationship with her daughters. Shelagh sees her relationship with her girls as a process; as she watches them go through the defining experiences of adulthood, she's been willing to reconsider convictions she's held dear all her life. Although she holds strong opinions and has no trouble voicing them, she is also respectful of what they have to say. She's come to trust their ability to make the right choices for themselves. When she faces stress in her own life, she counts on her daughters for *their* support and guidance. Shelagh and her girls have become, in her own words, "loving friends."

At the heart of Shelagh's ability to stay connected is her readiness to know her daughters in all their complexities and to accept the ways in which they are different from her or from her expectations for them. "I remember when the oldest ones were teenagers," says Shelagh. "That was probably the worst time, with the cars, the parties, the staying out past their curfew. My husband was sure that they were up to no good. He would say that to me. His favorite saying was 'Nothing good is going on at three in the morning.' And I have always taken any class that would help me grow and help me get on better with my children. At church they had this course where they talked about sharing—having an open meeting with your family. I thought this is really a good idea because I'd been going through a whole summer without getting a good night's sleep.

"So we had open family meetings. I advised everyone of the time. I would throw out a question, and everyone would discuss it. And it was a disaster, because everyone would end up yelling and screaming and crying. And my husband would walk out because he felt he was the one getting all the blame. Mary Anne, the pet of the family, always wanted everybody to be happy, and she ended up in tears. And I don't know if it helped them or not, but it helped me and my husband to understand them better. Once at one of these meetings one of my girls said, 'Well you dressed us up in white starched dresses and white shoes, and thought we were going to be just perfect little girls all our lives, and that's just not true.' And I thought this kid gave me something that I should have realized. I'm not a perfect parent. I'm not gonna have perfect children. And for that alone it was good.

"So I had to learn to trust their judgment. I certainly do now. That's been an ongoing process. And that's one thing I wish I could have learned earlier on. To trust them. If I had drawn back a little bit earlier . . . I think it got better with each one. The first one, you know it's like the first pancake that you throw out. That poor kid. I think I dumped everything on Colleen, the oldest one. Because I wanted her to be the perfect one, or else everybody else was going to be rotten."

The greatest anguish for Shelagh has been caused by the crises surrounding several of her daughters' marriages—when decisions they've made have challenged some of Shelagh's most deeply felt values. The revelation that her daughters might make life choices radically different from ones she would have expected began when her third daughter Dolores, now thirty-three, eloped at age nineteen. "Dolores has always been someone who marched to her own drum. She's just not as open as the rest of us, I'd have to say. She does things differently than the rest of my daughters, and I've come to see that that's just her way to be.

"She married a guy out of the blue that nobody ever thought she'd marry," says Shelagh. "He's a very solid guy. I like him now. But at the time I thought she wasn't ready to marry anyone!" A year and a half earlier Dolores was in a very serious car accident. She was in a coma for two weeks, and the family doubted at first that she would survive. It took months of physical therapy before she was able to go back to work. "I think that because physically she was doing so well, I think that there was turmoil inside that I was missing. It was at a time that I had four or five other teenagers at home, I wasn't zeroing in on one kid. And then suddenly she announced that she and Oscar were going to get married. I thought she hadn't given herself enough time to get back on her feet to make such a major decision. And my husband and I didn't really know him. And his background was totally different—his people were from Latin America and we're Irish. So I was opposed to it, and they decided they didn't want to go through the hassle of a big wedding. And because they eloped they didn't get married in the Church."

Although Shelagh had trouble giving the young couple her blessing, she did not cut off her ties to them. "For awhile they lived in a little apartment in Brooklyn. And I said that they were welcome in my home, but I was not going to visit them because this to me was open approval, and I could not give that yet because I didn't consider them really married. And they came to visit us, and I began to realize that this was not a silly whim. That she really was in love with this man. He really probably was a gem that I would discover.

"I can't say that it was a happy time. But we kept seeing them. And a year later they came to us and said they wanted to be married in the Church. And I put them in touch with this young priest I know, and so they had a small wedding, and afterward we gave a dinner for forty or fifty friends, and it was very nice." The religious ceremony eliminated one source of Shelagh's unhappiness. As for her daughter's husband, Shelagh eventually had to admit that she had misjudged him and that Dolores had made the right choice for herself.

More recently, the breakup of two other daughters' marriages is testing Shelagh in even more profound ways. Colleen, the oldest, has left her husband and moved with her two children into a house near her parents; Eileen, the thirty-two-year-old, is on the verge of splitting up. Although Shelagh understands what attracted her daughters to marry the men they did, she believes that both these relationships will, and should, end in divorce. "Divorce is a tough worry. I think I'm different than when Dolores got married. I'm not so black and white now. I see more gray areas. If they have to make a difficult decision I'll support them.

"With Colleen, it's just a bad situation that went on for too long. I can't completely dislike him—he's a personable man, and a good father—but they had terrible fights over money, over how much he was drinking. And I think he thought she would just take it. He just kept chipping away at her self-esteem. And it was affecting the children. I could see that the oldest one, in particular, was getting to be a nervous wreck. So when she told us she was leaving, I couldn't in my heart say she was wrong.

"As for Eileen—her husband walked out on her. It wasn't out of nowhere. I knew things weren't the way they should be. Eileen is a little bit in denial and has been for a long time. She didn't confide in us about a lot that was going on, but because they live so close I could tell he wasn't around enough. She tried so hard to cover things up and make things right. But I think they're headed for a divorce." Believing the marriage to be over, Shelagh is concentrating her energy on her daughter's state of mind. "She said to me that she hoped he would get some help. And I said to her, 'What about you? Don't you think you should get some help?' She became very upset with me. 'There's nothing wrong with me!' And I said, 'That's not what I'm saying. I'm not saying there's anything wrong with you. I'm just saying you need to work out how you feel about all this, and where you're going with your life. I'm here to talk to you, but I have limits. There are limits; there are things you're not going to want to tell me that you should speak to someone else about.' She's not ready for that yet, but I think she will be.

"This has been a terrible cross. And I am so sad for my daughters. I know it happens, sure it does. I just never thought it would happen to my kids. I would like to be in denial about it, but I can't be. And if they do get divorced, and if they would meet somebody, I'd think differently than I would have before. About marriage being indissoluble. It's different when it's people you care about. I never thought I would say this, but I hope they meet other men and have a full life. I don't want them to be alone."

Shelagh shares her concerns about Colleen and Eileen with her other daughters. "And I know the minute I call one of them and say I'm worried about something, she'll call her sister and say 'Mom says . . . ' And that's fine by me. We don't hide much from one another. There are also times when I know they've got things in their lives that they're not going to confide in me, so if they can talk to one another about things, that's okay with me. I don't have to know every single thing!"

Shelagh reserves some of her deepest feelings for her dialogue with God. "Some things only God and I can think about. My emotional health or what's going on in my soul. I go to Eileen's house and I think, Oh God, how can this happen to this girl? And I deeply feel so saddened by it, yet I can't express that to anybody. But I'll say it to God. I'll say, this is really a terrible piece of work. And even though I think my girls know I'm feeling and caring, I don't have to express it on that level to them. I don't feel that I need to do that. When I have some frustrations about things that I think they can help me with, then I turn to them."

One of the things that's of concern to Shelagh these days is her husband's health. Following his stroke a year ago, he has retired from his work as a claims manager for an insurance company, but Shelagh believes that he's still not properly taking care of himself. "I find that I do talk more to my daughters about their father now. I'll say, 'You know your father is driving me crazy, he's not exercising enough,' and I feel I can talk to them now that way because I'm not talking in a bitter way. I talk to them more as a wife than as a mother. And they understand more what I feel, now that they're wives. And they help me to look at things a little bit better. They'll say, 'Well, you know he was never going to do that, so why did you think he would?'

"When he got sick, they were my support system. Holly, since she was trained as a nurse, was really wonderful. She did most of the discussion with the doctors and guided me through the process. In general I go to her with my health concerns about my husband, or about myself, because I feel that she, more than the others, can handle that. She'll give me feedback without being frightened by what I'm telling her. It's more professional advice I'm going to get, not just emotional. Deirdre is my emotional solace. I can confide my fears to her. And it's not that she won't be emotional too, but she won't go to pieces. In general they're good about giving me advice, or telling me when I'm off track about something."

Such as? "Well, soon after my sister died, one of her daughters got married. And I had assumed that I would just step in and help her plan the whole affair. But it didn't work out that way, and I was hurt. And my children helped me see that it couldn't have been any other way. Her children needed some distance from me. My daughters helped me vent my feelings, and they also helped me get through a very difficult transition."

This is a time of many transitions in Shelagh's life. She's begun to pass on to her daughters some of the responsibility for keeping the family connected. "I've reached the point where I don't have to do everything. I like to cook and I enjoy it. And I'm very proud of how they cook. And they do nice things, too. In March, we always have a traditional corned beef and cabbage St. Patrick's Day dinner. And in Irish families we do jigs and everyone's supposed to perform. It's wonderful to see. The grandchildren will sing and dance and recite. So anyway, last Easter I threw it out—I said, 'What are we doing for Easter?' And everybody just sat and looked at me, like, what does she mean? Then Holly jumped in and said, 'I'll do Easter brunch.' Then she had a conflict with her in-laws, so Deirdre said, 'No, I'll do Easter brunch.' So I had two of them fighting over it. I said, 'I think it's great that you're jumping in to take over the holidays. I'm not averse to that at all.' It worked out great. And it was wonderful for me to go and be a guest."

In the past few weeks, Shelagh has decided to accept an attractive retirement plan at the library, although she's not quite ready to stop working. "I don't want to think of it as retirement, I want to think of it as a change in my life. I love my job and I like what I do, but I've worked there for twenty years, and I don't have any qualms about trying something new. I've made enough contacts in the library world and in this community that I know I can find part-time work. And it will be nice to have something I can do at home."

Shelagh's daughters realize she is ready for a change. "They also realize that their father is going to be sixty-five and he's not in good health, and that's really one of my concerns, for us to spend more time together. I want to do this. I don't want to look back in two years and think that he wanted me to be around and I wasn't." For the first time in his life, Shelagh's husband is available to help out with his grandchildren. "He's perfectly happy to be at everybody's beck and call. He'll pick kids up at school and take them to a soccer game. He says, 'Well, I don't mind.' But I'm not going to do that, and I want to make sure they understand it. I said, 'When I retire, it does not mean I'm available for unlimited baby-sitting.' I think it's going to be much easier for them to ask me, but I don't want to change the way I've been dealing with it. We have a good agreement. If it's something special, I'll do it. I mean don't call me if you're having your hair done. I never felt imposed upon, I have to say. If I did, they would know about it. But the temptation is going to be greater for them now."

It seemed to us that Shelagh can be as forthright as she is with her daughters because they have established such a high level of mutual trust. She agrees. "Sure, you have friends too, but there are some things I wouldn't confide in them. I feel with my daughters it's different, I trust them totally. We can be honest with one another and not get hurt. They like to call me and tell me things that are going on in their lives—if it happens to be a wonderful moment or if it's a dread. They invite me to their homes. They love to drop in on me.

"We also look to one another for that wonderful support. It's like soulmates. Because you know one another so well. And from me, not just support, but that I'm their fan. I really am. When they come in, if they have a new hairdo, I love to tell them how great they look. I always feel good to see them. And they feel that way about coming. It's not a drag to be together. I couldn't choose better friends right now."

Several weeks after we interviewed Cathy Ravella, whose relationship with her daughter, Erica, we described earlier, we received the following letter:

Dear Susan and Marilyn,

Thinking about my interview, I have this to add. I'm continuing to ponder the implications of the word friend *as it applies to me and my daughter.*

I feel a tremendous sense of continuity in the women's line of my family. My grandmother Kate (for whom I'm named) I never knew. She died the week I was born.

My mom described her as a "powerful" woman. Erica fancied a photo of Gran as a young girl astride a white horse carrying a shotgun. Perhaps as a teen she identified with her. I certainly identified with my mom. I'm not sure if Erica identifies with me, but she does with my mother. So is the line complete?

In my treasures from Africa is a doll that Erica received at age two at her "naming" ceremony. Actually it is the "spirit of her firstborn daughter," named Lotian.

It was a wonderful ceremony with the Pokot people of northern Kenya. I know that there is a very primitive part of me that waits for Lotian to make her entrance into the world.

As all grandmothers look to the future in that generation, for the continuity of their line, I connect with her yet-to-be. Hopefully you know what I'm trying to say.

Best,
Cathy Ravella

Chapter 13

Our Personal Journey

W hen we were the age our daughters are now, we kept our mothers at arm's length because they couldn't see us as anything other than reflections of themselves. They interpreted our decisions to lead lives that were not what they had expected as an insult to them rather than as a statement of our individuality. Their continued disapproval was very threatening to our fledgling sense of adulthood. Although our mothers were quite different in style and temperament from each other, neither of them could hear us when we tried to say, "See me for who I am." Nor were they willing to reveal much about their inner lives to us. Every conversation we had with them was shadowed by things unsaid or said badly. They were probably as hurt and baffled as we were. During the final decades of our mothers' lives, we became more forgiving of their limitations but no more intimate with them.

Even though we had worked hard to establish closer relationships with our daughters than we had had with our mothers, we feared that intermittent tension with them, if unheeded, could become chronic, leading to their thinking of us in the same dismal way we had thought about our mothers.

In the course of this project we have both begun to examine our relationships with our daughters with new insight. We are teaching ourselves to consider what our behavior looks like from their point of view and to question whether we are treating them as the adults they have become rather than as the children they used to be.

Although we differ in our style of interaction with our daughters, we both tend to offer our opinions too readily, whether or not our daughters solicit them. We have come to see that this kind of behavior is based on the vestiges of a model of mother that is no longer appropriate for women with adult daughters.

At first we thought that the best way to respond to our daughters' transformation into adulthood was to back off, to stop giving advice, to stifle our impulses to tell them our points of view. But we soon became convinced that silence is not the answer. While we wanted to be less free with advice, opinions, and judgments, we also wanted to be able to state our deepest feelings and concerns in a way that was consistent with our daughters' new status. That desire has forced us to focus more on how our words are perceived. We've discovered that when our aim is not to affect our daughters' behavior but simply to say what we think is true, we tend to frame things differently and they are more likely to hear us out.

We have been moved by women who are at ease with the knowledge that their stint as "mother" is over, that they have done the best job they could of preparing a daughter for adult life, and that whatever happens henceforth is up to her. If the daughter makes a decision that her mother thinks may not be "good" for her, the mother can accept it as "right" for her because it fills a need that the mother may or may not ever fully comprehend. If it turns out to be a mistake, it's a mistake the daughter has some need to make. These mothers can be supportive, they can be consoling, but they feel little impulse to step in and direct their daughters.

This attitude has come to mean more and more to us as we try to redefine our proper role in our daughters' lives. We have come a long way from where we started. We now believe that our advice is frequently useless, even when our daughters seek it; that they are learning to be adults by solving their own problems, even making their own mistakes, if necessary, and learning from them; that because we differ from our girls in temperament, generational attitudes, and life experience, we can't really know what's best for them in any case.

The paradox—the revelation—has been that by giving up the outmoded wish to control our daughters on some level, we're not losing a connection but actually gaining a stronger one. Achieving an adult friendship with them is much more of an enriching experience than we would have imagined. Our inclination as mothers had often been to concentrate on what was going on in our daughters' lives, because we thought that was the parental way of staying connected. But now we've come to value a greater reciprocity in our relationship with them. We've learned to share more of what is going on in our lives— the good news and the bad; the daily details as well as our more profound thoughts about our work, our friendships, or whatever else is causing us concern. We've revisited stories about our past and memories from their childhood that we can be more expressive about and our daughters can assimilate better now than before. We've learned to ask for their advice and their opinions. Because they know us so well, they often have penetrating insights to offer. Sometimes, their youth and generational experience give them the perspective to make cogent suggestions that never would have occurred to us.

Despite all our best intentions, there are still moments that don't go smoothly—when we've done or said something, or one of our daughters has, that has been wounding or been misinterpreted. Rather than let these events go by unchallenged, we've tried to turn them into opportunities to increase our communication, to let our daughters know what their behavior has meant to us and try to find out what ours has meant to them.

Neither of us has been shaken by the kind of health crisis, or the loss of a partner, that women of our generation frequently face. Given that, and given the age and life experience of our daughters, it's probably understandable that we still do more of the caretaking than they do. All four of our girls are establishing independent lives, surrounded by close and supportive friends. The three oldest have taken the first solid steps toward establishing their careers. But none has married, none has had children. Until they form their own families, their parents and siblings are the only family they have. They turn to us more than we turn to them for comfort and reassurance. Even that is changing as they take more and more emotional responsibility for their own lives.

Although we know that in our hearts we will never relinquish our deeply ingrained expectations that we will be the ones to whom our daughters turn when something important happens to them, we know in our minds that they will rely increasingly on their partners and other loved ones—perhaps on their sisters—for the support that was once a parent's prerogative to give. And we believe that this is the way it should be. In the years to come, we hope to approach true equality, true intimacy, and a capacity for taking care of each other in a truly reciprocal way. We look forward to loving friendships with our daughters for the rest of our shared adult lives.

Notes

Chapter 1 The Developmental Paths of Mothers and Daughters

Page 7 "Questions crept in . . . Terri Apter, *Secret Paths* (New York, W. W. Norton, 1995), 20.

Page 8 Family therapist Marianne Walters . . . Marianne Walters, "Mothers and Daughters" in *The Invisible Web*, Marianne Walters, Betty Carter, Peggy Papp, Olga Silverstein (New York: Guilford Press, 1988), 49.

Page 9 In fact, as psychologist Carol Gilligan has written . . . Carol Gilligan, *In a Different Voice* (Cambridge, MA: Harvard University Press, 1993), xxiii.

Page 9 Women's development properly reflects . . . *Ibid.*, 23.

Page 9 In her book . . . Kathy Weingarten, *The Mother's Voice* (New York: Harcourt Brace, 1994), 194–206.

Page 10 Our daughters are making . . . Calvin A. Colarusso and Robert

A. Nemiroff, *Adult Development* (New York: Plenum Press, 1981), 35–42, 48–49.

Page 12 Clinical psychologist Dr. Evelyn Bassoff . . . Evelyn Bassoff, *Mothers and Daughters* (New York: NAL, 1988), 222.

Page 12 Over thirty years ago . . . The original research was conducted in Kansas City from 1952 to 1962, and the results were published in Bernice L. Neugarten with Howard Berkowitz, *Personality in Middle and Late Life* (New York: Atherton Press, 1964). The findings are summarized in Bernice L. Neugarten, "Toward a Psychology of the Life Cycle," in *The Human Life Cycle*, ed. W. C. Sze (New York: Jason Aronson, 1975), 379–394.

Page 12 Terri Apter takes Dr. Neugarten's work . . . Apter, 23–24.

Page 21 In her book about the continuing development . . . *Ibid.*, 32.

Chapter 2 The Burden of the Past: How Your Mother Mothered You

Page 30 One definition of a good mother . . . James Garbarino, Edna Guttmann, and Janis Wilson Seeley, *The Psychologically Battered Child* (San Francisco: Jossey-Bass, 1986), 231.

Page 32 In her book . . . Hope Edelman, *Motherless Daughters* (New York: Delta, 1994), 235–258.

Page 39 In her influential book . . . Alice Miller, "The Drama of the Gifted Child and the Psychoanalyst's Narcissistic Disturbance," *Prisoners of Childhood*, tr. Ruth Ward (New York: Basic Books, 1981), 3–29.

Page 39 Psychiatrist Ivan Boszormenyi-Nagy . . . Ivan Boszormenyi-Nagy and Geraldine Spark, *Invisible Loyalties* (New York: Harper & Row, 1973), 165.

Page 40 But, in Boszormenyi-Nagy's view . . . Ivan Boszormenyi-Nagy and Barbara Krasner, *Between Give and Take* (New York: Brunner/Mazel, 1986), 189.

Page 40 If parentification is couched . . . *Invisible Loyalties,* 151–152.

Page 52 As Dr. Evelyn Bassoff writes . . . Bassoff, 241–242.

Page 53 As he explains . . . *Invisible Loyalties,* 87.

Page 62 Another explanation for the propensity . . . Bassoff, 224–225.

Page 63 Psychologist Terri Apter . . . Apter, 276.

Chapter 3 Your Daughter's Personal Style and Habits

Page 86 Women in our culture . . . For further discussion of this argument, see Naomi Wolf, *The Beauty Myth* (London: Chatto & Windus, 1990).

Chapter 4 Your Daughter's Love Life

Page 96 In her book . . . Weingarten, 107.
Page 113 Many of us remember . . . Susan Faludi, *Backlash* (New York: Crown, 1991), 3–19.
Page 126 From the time daughters . . . Walters et al., 43–44.
Page 127 And our culture does nothing . . . *Ibid.*, 43.

Chapter 5 When Your Daughter Lives at Home

Page 133 It is a time when . . . Monica McGoldrick, "Women Through the Family Life Cycle," in *Women in Families*, eds. Monica McGoldrick, Carol Anderson, and Froma Walsh (New York: W. W. Norton, 1991), 218.
Page 141 A generation or so ago . . . For more on this, see Monica McGoldrick, John K. Pearce, and Joseph Giordano, *Ethnicity in Family Therapy* (New York: Guilford Press, 1982).
Page 150 It is not uncommon . . . Beverly Greene, "African-American Women," in *Women of Color*, eds. Lillian Comas-Diaz and Beverly Greene (New York: Guilford Press, 1994), 14.

Chapter 6 Can She Fend for Herself?

Page 161 Most African-American women . . . Lillian Comas-Diaz and Beverly Greene, "Women of Color with Professional Status," in Comas-Diaz and Greene, 348.
Page 161 Today about 70 percent . . . March 1995 figures, U.S. Bureau of Labor Statistics.
Page 161 Recent studies estimate . . . Betty A. Rubin, "Tapping into the Fast-Growing Women's Market," *Private Asset Management*, July 2, 1995, 9.

Page 162 The largest private sector employer...*The New York Times,* March 3, 1996, I, 28.

Page 180 In March 1996, Dr. Kenny... *Newsday,* March 5, 1996, B, 18.

Chapter 7 Changes in *Your* Life

Page 192 Letty Cottin Pogrebin believes... *Getting Over Getting Older* (Boston: Little, Brown, 1996).

Page 211 For the first time in history... Monica McGoldrick, "Women Through the Family Life Cycle" in McGoldrick et al., 200–226; Rosalind C. Barnett and Martha Carroll Sherman, "Relationships Between Older Parents and Their Adult Daughters and Their Influence on Parents' Health," Wellesley College Center for Research on Women, Working Papers Series, No. 238, 1991; Abigail M. Lang and Elaine Brody, "Characteristics of Middle-Aged Daughters and Help to Their Elderly Mothers," *Journal of Marriage and the Family,* February 1983, 193–202.

Page 211 A study completed... Lang and Brody, 193–202.

Page 211 Recent data suggest... Andrew Scharlach, professor of social welfare, University of California at Berkeley, interview with authors, August 5, 1996.

Page 211 More than half of the women... Lang and Brody, 196.

Chapter 8 Your Expectations and Her Life

Page 227 Families transmit.... See, for example, Monica McGoldrick, *You Can Go Home Again* (New York: W. W. Norton, 1995), 21–33, 85–125.

Page 234 First of all, it needs... Comas-Diaz and Greene, "Women of Color with Professional Status" in Comas-Diaz and Greene, 347–367.

Page 235 In the case of... See, for example, Monica McGoldrick, Nydia Garcia-Preto, Paulette Moore Hines, Evelyn Lee, "Ethnicity and Women," in Monica McGoldrick et al., 169–199. Also, Alice Walker, *In Search of Our Mothers' Gardens* (New York: Harcourt Brace, 1983).

Chapter 9 Redefining Your Role in Her Life

Page 250 In Dr. Lowinsky's image . . . Naomi Lowinsky, *The Motherline* (Los Angeles: Jeremy P. Tarcher/Perigree, 1992), 55.

Page 259 At every stage . . . Bassoff, 221.

Page 273 We should be able to . . . Lowinsky, 56.

Chapter 10 Getting Beyond Guilt

Page 275 In her book . . . Nancy Chodorow, *The Reproduction of Mothering* (Berkeley: U. of California Press, 1978), 7.

Page 275 The proper outlet . . . *Ibid.*, 5, 7.

Page 276 Before her death . . . Grace K. Baruch, "Reflections on Guilt, Women, and Gender," Wellesley College Center for Research on Women, Working Papers Series, No. 176, 1988.

Page 277 Adrienne Rich has railed . . . Adrienne Rich, *Of Women Born* (New York: W. W. Norton, 1976), 223.

Page 277 In an essay entitled . . . Nancy Chodorow and Susan Contratto, "The Fantasy of the Perfect Mother" in *Rethinking the Family*, ed. Barrie Thorne (Boston: Northeastern University Press, 1992), 191–211.

Page 277 Grace Baruch speculates . . . Baruch, 7.

Page 279 If a mother were able . . . Weingarten, 52.

Page 280 In fact, as Naomi Lowinsky writes . . . Lowinsky, 58–60.

Page 292 "The child has . . . Miller, 7.

Page 292 Dr. Weingarten believes . . . Weingarten, 178–179.

Chapter 11 Expressing Your Voice

Page 294 Lois wants intimacy . . . Weingarten, 180.

Page 295 Women's psychological development . . . Gilligan, 8–9, 70.

Page 295 They give up . . . *Ibid.*, xxi.

Page 295 The true voice . . . *Ibid.*, ix.

Page 296 As Carol Gilligan makes clear . . . *Ibid.*,171.

Page 297 As Carol Gilligan asks . . . *Ibid.*, xiii.

Page 304 Erica's approach illustrates . . . For a fuller discussion of nonintimate interaction, see Weingarten, 178–186.

Page 304 According to a well-reported study . . . Mary Field Belenky, Blythe McVicker Clinchy, Nancy Rule Goldberger, Jill Mattuck Tarule, *Women's Ways of Knowing* (New York: Basic Books, 1986), 165.

Page 305 Dr. Belenky identifies . . . *Ibid.,* 164–167, 176–189.

Chapter 12 Friends For Life

Page 316 "Our daughters were in our bodies . . . Lowinsky, 54.

Page 320 In her book . . . Weingarten, 167–171.

Page 322 Honesty, acceptance, generosity . . . Letty Cottin Pogrebin, *Among Friends* (New York: McGraw-Hill, 1987).

Page 324 In her book . . . Lucy Rose Fischer, *Linked Lives* (New York: Harper & Row, 1986), 11, 58–60.

Page 326 In her book . . . Victoria Secunda, *When You and Your Mother Can't Be Friends* (New York: Dell Publishing, 1990), 314.

Page 329 In one landmark study . . . Grace Baruch and Rosalind Barnett, "Adult Daughters' Relationship with Their Mothers," *Journal of Marriage and the Family,* August 1983, 601–606. Baruch and Barnett also report an important caveat: When the mother becomes old and frail, the distress associated with the relationship may overshadow the rewards.

Page 330 However, the daughters who were . . . *Ibid.*

Bibliography

Apter, Terri. *Secret Paths: Women in the New Midlife.* New York, W. W. Norton, 1995.

Barnett, Rosalind C. "Adult Daughters and Their Mothers: Harmony or Hostility?" Wellesley College Center for Research on Women, Working Paper Series, No. 209, 1990.

Barnett, Rosalind C., and Martha Carroll Sherman. "Relationships Between Older Parents and Their Adult Daughters and Their Influence on Parents' Health." Wellesley College Center for Research on Women, Working Papers Series, No. 238, 1991.

Baruch, Grace K. "Reflections on Guilt, Women, and Gender." Wellesley College Center for Research on Women, Working Papers Series, No. 176, 1988.

Baruch, Grace, and Rosalind Barnett. "Adult Daughters' Relationship with Their Mothers." *Journal of Marriage and the Family*, August 1983, pp. 601–606.

Bassoff, Evelyn. *Mothers and Daughters: Loving and Letting Go.* New York: NAL, 1988.

Bateson, Mary Catherine. *Composing a Life.* New York: Plume, 1990.

Belenky, Mary Field; Clinchy, Blythe McVicker; Goldberger, Nancy Rule; and Tarule, Jill Mattuck. *Women's Ways of Knowing: The Development of Self, Voice, and Mind.* New York: Basic Books, 1986.

Boszormenyi-Nagy, Ivan, and Geraldine Spark. *Invisible Loyalties: Reciprocity in Intergenerational Family Therapy.* New York: Harper & Row, 1973.

Boszormenyi-Nagy, Ivan, and Barbara Krasner. *Between Give and Take: A Clinical Guide to Contextual Therapy.* New York: Brunner/Mazel, 1986.

Chodorow, Nancy. *The Reproduction of Mothering: Psychoanalysis and the Sociology of Gender.* Berkeley: University of California Press, 1978.

Chodorow, Nancy, and Susan Contratto. "The Fantasy of the Perfect Mother" in *Rethinking the Family: Some Feminist Questions.* Edited by Barrie Thorne. Boston: Northeastern University Press, 1992.

Colarusso, Calvin A., and Robert A. Nemiroff. *Adult Development.* New York: Plenum Press, 1981.

Comas-Diaz, Lillian, and Beverly Greene. "Women of Color with Professional Status" in *Women of Color: Integrating Ethnic and Gender Identities in Psychotherapy.* Edited by Comas-Diaz and Greene. New York: Guilford Press, 1994.

Edelman, Hope. *Motherless Daughters: The Legacy of Loss.* New York: Delta, 1994.

Faludi, Susan. *Backlash: The Undeclared War Against American Women.* New York: Crown, 1991.

Fischer, Lucy Rose. *Linked Lives: Adult Daughters and Their Mothers.* New York: Harper & Row, 1986.

Garbarino, James; Guttmann, Edna; and Seeley, Janis Wilson. *The Psychologically Battered Child: Strategies for Identification, Assessment, and Intervention.* San Francisco: Jossey-Bass, 1986.

Gilligan, Carol. *In a Different Voice.* Cambridge, MA: Harvard University Press, 1993.

Greene, Beverly. "African-American Women" in *Women of Color: Integrating Ethnic and Gender Identities in Psychotherapy.* Edited by Lillian Comas-Diaz and Beverly Greene. New York: Guilford Press, 1994.

Jordan, Judith V. "Empathy and Self Boundaries," The Stone Center, Wellesley College, Works in Progress Series, No. 16, 1984.

Lang, Abigail M., and Elaine Brody. "Characteristics of Middle Aged Daughters and Help to Their Elderly Mothers." *Journal of Marriage and the Family,* February 1983, pp. 193–202.

Lerner, Harriet. *The Dance of Intimacy: A Woman's Guide to Courageous Acts of Change in Key Relationships.* New York: Harper & Row, 1989.

Lowinsky, Naomi. *The Motherline: Every Woman's Journey to Find Her Female Roots.* Los Angeles: Jeremy P. Tarcher/Perigree, 1992.

McGoldrick, Monica. *You Can Go Home Again: Reconnecting with Your Family.* New York: W. W. Norton, 1995.

McGoldrick, Monica; Anderson, Carol M; and Walsh, Froma, eds. *Women in Families.* New York: W. W. Norton, 1991.

McGoldrick, Monica; Pearce, John K.; and Giordano, Joseph. *Ethnicity in Family Therapy.* New York: Guilford Press, 1982.

Miller, Alice. *Prisoners of Childhood,* tr. Ruth Ward. New York: Basic Books, 1981.

Miller, Jean Baker. *Toward a New Psychology of Women.* Boston: Beacon Press, 1986.

Neugarten, Bernice L. "Toward a Psychology of the Life Cycle" in *The Human Life Cycle.* Edited by W. C. Sze. New York: Jason Aronson, 1975, pp. 379–394.

Neugarten, Bernice L., with Howard Berkowitz. *Personality in Middle and Late Life: Empirical Studies.* New York: Atherton Press, 1964.

Pogrebin, Letty Cottin. *Among Friends: Who We Like, Why We Like Them, and What We Do About It.* New York: McGraw-Hill, 1987.

————. *Getting Over Getting Older: An Intimate Journey.* Boston: Little, Brown, 1996.

Rich, Adrienne. *Of Women Born: Motherhood as Experience and Institution.* New York: W. W. Norton, 1976.

Scarf, Maggie. *Intimate Worlds: Life Inside the Family.* New York: Random House, 1995.

Secunda, Victoria. *When You and Your Mother Can't Be Friends: Resolving the Most Complicated Relationship of Your Life.* New York: Dell Publishing, 1990.

Walker, Alice. *In Search of Our Mothers' Gardens.* New York: Harcourt Brace, 1983.

Walters, Marianne; Carter, Betty; Papp, Peggy; and Silverstein, Olga. *The Invisible Web: Gender Patterns in Family Relationships.* New York: Guilford Press, 1988.

Weingarten, Kathy. *The Mother's Voice: Strengthening Intimacy in Families.* New York: Harcourt Brace, 1994.

Wolf, Naomi. *The Beauty Myth.* London: Chatto & Windus, 1990.